Vectors of the Counter-Initiation

The Course and Destiny of Inverted Spirituality

BY THE SAME AUTHOR

Doorkeeper of the Heart: Versions of Rabi'a

Hammering Hot Iron:
A Spiritual Critique of Robert Bly's Iron John

The System of Antichrist:
Truth and Falsehood in Postmodernism and the New Age

Cracks in the Great Wall:
UFOs and Traditional Metaphysics

Legends of the End:
Prophecies of the End Times, Antichrist,
Apocalypse, and Messiah from Eight Religious Traditions

The Virtues of the Prophet:
A Young Muslim's Guide to the Greater Jihad,
The War Against the Passions

Knowings: In the Arts
of Metaphysics, Cosmology, and the Spiritual Path

Who is the Earth?
How To See God in the Natural World

Reflections of Tasawwuf:
Essays, Poems, and Narrative on Sufi Themes

Shadow of the Rose:
The Esoterism of the Romantic Tradition
(with Jennifer Doane Upton)

Findings in the Arts of Metaphysics, Cosmology
and the Spiritual Path

The Science of the Greater Jihad:
Essays in Principial Psychology

The Wars of Love, and Other Poems

CHARLES UPTON

VECTORS *of the* COUNTER-INITIATION

The Course and Destiny of INVERTED SPIRITUALITY

SOPHIA PERENNIS

SAN RAFAEL, CA

First published in the USA
by Sophia Perennis

Series editor: James R. Wetmore

For information, address:
Sophia Perennis, P.O. Box 151011
San Rafael, CA 94915
sophiaperennis.com

Library of Congress Cataloging-in-Publication Data

Upton, Charles, 1948–
Vectors of the counter-initiation:
the course and destiny of inverted spirituality /
Charles Upton.—1st ed.

p. cm.
ISBN 978 1 59731 132 8 (pbk: alk. paper)
1. Religion and international relations.
2. Conspiracy theories.
BL65.155U68 2012
204—dc23 2012019837

Cover Image: *The Tower of Babel*
Gustave Doré (1832–1883)
Cover Design: Cristy Deming

CONTENTS

Introduction

OVER THE PAST, say, 40 years, the belief that we are being routinely lied to by our leaders has spread beyond its earlier counterculture boundaries and entered the population as a whole; it might be said that we now live in the "age of paranoia", a development that has obviously been greatly aided and expanded by the world-wide web.

The genre and worldview known as "conspiracy theory" is based on the assumption that groups of powerful men and women have been developing and imposing largely clandestine agendas that are not in the best interests of the majority of the population of the nation or the world. And this is simple realism: according to this definition, every government and major corporation on earth is in some sense a "conspiracy". *Paranoia* enters the picture when accounts and explanations of such agendas are put forward that go beyond what we can actually prove based on the facts available to us. We know we are often lied to; we know that plans are being made for us that constitute an attack on our vital interests, if not our essential humanity; and certainly much of this is common knowledge, or knowledge easily accessed with a minimum of research. But it is equally certain that not all the plans being made for us *are* common knowledge, nor are their specifics obtainable by even the most dedicated and painstaking investigations. And the anxiety produced by the certainty that we are under attack, coupled with the inevitable uncertainty as to many of the names and strategies of our attackers, tempts us to grasp for any data, no matter how poorly established, to adopt any paradigm, no matter how implausible, so as to the reach the "closure" we imagine will put our anxiety to rest.

This state of affairs is in many ways the product of—as well as a heroic if sometimes misguided response to—the destruction of our intellectual tradition. Academia, in its decadence, has increasingly become a purveyor of political correctness, the promotion of radical technocracy, and a vector of other elements of social engineering imposed by the elites. In response to this narrowing of focus, the "conspiracy theory industry" has grown up to challenge the official version of reality by asserting alternate views. But when thesis and antithesis are reduced to naked propaganda vs. the reaction against such propaganda, a synthesis with any degree of real objectivity is hard to come by. Unofficial investigators have provided valuable insights into neglected, if not deliberately suppressed, causal factors behind historical developments and political events, including the clandestine activities of governments, financial interests and intelligence agencies, and the influence of secret societies. But this in itself has not succeeded in re-establishing those dimensions of breadth, intellectual freedom and scholarly objectivity that were more in evidence in the days before the universities fell under the sort of control by government and corporate interests that they must contend with today. In response to the increasingly obvious inadequacy and dishonesty of the established explanations, the conspiracists have tended to search for this or that "magic bullet", in many cases attributing too much causative power to certain factors simply because their opponents have unfairly minimized their influence or even denied their existence. The general "dumbing down of America", whether the product of deliberate social engineering or simply general cultural decay, has given birth to a class of passionate, obsessive investigators, a "freelance intelligentia" marginalized in terms of the intellectual mainstream (if such a thing still exists), but one that is increasingly able to call the worldview of that mainstream into question—without, however, overcoming the general fragmentation of our collective sense of reality that is inseparable from the post-modern ethos. This is largely due to the fact that the dominant "over-arching paradigms" of secular humanism—those of Freud, Marx and Darwin, for example—have either been discredited in many ways or else have become increasingly painful to live with, or live *in*. There is a pervasive suspicion of the *comprehensive explanation*—even in its last stronghold, the realm of the physical sciences. We have been too often and too bitterly disappointed by perhaps three centuries of provisional, ephemeral, failed worldviews, and deeply unnerved by the terrors they have sometimes unleashed. The agents of official reality have dealt with this disappointment by establishing a deconstructionist and nihilistic "hermeneutics of suspicion", beneath which very definite views of reality, and very definite *commands*, often lie hidden; the conspiracists have responded by heroically resurrecting *certainty* as a virtue, but placing it—weakened and disoriented by the blows of their enemies—on foundations that are often too unreliable and too narrow. "Established" sociology and historiography tend to say: "Social trends emerge from a confluence of impersonal forces, bringing some classes and individuals to prominence and submerging others; people may analyze these trends or seize upon them as opportunities, but they certainly do not consciously create them". "Alternate" sociology, on the other hand, says: "Social trends are manufactured by powerful individuals and groups". Did Nazism spontaneously "arise" from the impersonal forces operating in post-WWI Germany, or was it created by Hitler, his predecessors and colleagues, and the people who funded them? Both views obviously have an element of truth; both need to be taken into consideration. There is a danger that those who see Hitler as a pawn of history will forget to ask where his money came from, while those who see him as a pawn of financiers will ignore the objective conditions that made him possible and in the absence of which he would never have appeared. Suffice it to say that both the abstract analysis of impersonal trends and a factual investigation of the actions of specific individuals and groups are insufficient when taken in isolation. As René Guénon expressed it, the growth of Anti-Tradition and Counter-Tradition are made possible by the impersonal degeneration of the cosmic environment due to cyclical conditions; nonetheless neither can be actualized without the conscious and deliberate actions of human beings.

My own response to the present inability (or unwillingness) of our society to articulate explanatory views adequate to the conditions we face—and remembering that the university system of Europe was founded not by technocrats or sociologists but by *monks*—has been to return to the perennial principles of universal metaphysics. Change cannot be correctly evaluated if the yardsticks we use to measure it are changing too. But eternal principles—not simply conservative nostalgias, which are no more fundamentally reliable than the meaningless worship of innovation they are reacting against—have the power to correctly evaluate and hierarchicalize the forms and events of the contingent world, and put everything in its place. In this book I have attempted, among other things, to place certain assertions of the conspiracists in a wider context, one that is ultimately metaphysical, or at least informed by certain metaphysical principles; in so doing this I have hoped to compensate for various deficiencies in the conspiratorial worldview and bring out its wider implications. Because metaphysics is a "Kingdom Not of This World", it can provide us with a vantage point from which we can gaze deeply into This World without being imprisoned and blinded by its assumptions. Only if we are certain that our destiny is not limited to the relative and contingent realm can we witness that realm without fear.

Informed speculation in areas of uncertainty is entirely justified; certainty attempting to assert itself in a vacuum, based on little more than an emotional need for closure, is not. Without certainty, however—especially in the absence of an immediate, serious and unavoidable challenge that invokes the "fight or flight" response—we cannot function; we are paralyzed. But certainty on the factual level, though highly important to pursue, can never be complete, because the truth of facts cannot always be firmly established, and more and more of them keep coming every day, no matter what we do. This is why I have founded my sense of certainty on the unanimous testimony of the great wisdom traditions—a certainty that has allowed me to survey this world of ambiguities, contradictions and perpetual lack-of-closure that we call time and history, make sense of it, and act accordingly. And since my criteria are essentially religious, I have necessarily been led to ask, and try to answer, the following questions: How have the dark agendas of the powers that be, the "Rulers of the Darkness of This World", both human and superhuman, affected the world of traditional religion, metaphysics, and the spiritual Path? What plans for religion and spirituality might they be likely to hatch in the future, perhaps the very near future? And though I certainly cannot name all the names of our common enemies, I can, following French metaphysician René Guénon, most certainly name these Principalities and Powers in their aggregate: they are the "saints of Satan", the *awliya al-Shaytan*—the forces of the Counter-Initiation.

The Counter-Initiation is the regime of the Rulers of the Darkness of his World. This World, *al-Dunya*, is not nature, or society, or history, or our fellow human beings. It tries to convince us that if we have turned away from these things we have turned away from it—but that is not the case. This World is nothing but a web of identifications, a way of arranging experience into a pattern by the power of memory and then identifying with it, after which we become blind to anything beyond it. It defines itself as the only game in town, and if it can't eradicate the intuition of God in us it simply presents God to us as a Stranger, an Alien. "Go ahead, renounce the World," it mocks, "what will you be left with then? Nothing but a blank wall called 'God'; try to worship *that* and see how far you get." But in the true renunciation of the World, not one real, living thing is renounced, only a collective dream sucks the life out of everything it touches. Every real, living thing is a sign of God—but only if, by His power, we know how to see His Presence in it. The Counter-Initiation is This World's idea of God, an empty screen upon which—to shield ourselves from that terrible emptiness, which is nothing but the emptiness of our own ego—we rush to paint the lurid shapes of our collective idols and obsessions.

Those who are ignorant of the World are no more free of that World than those who are obsessed by it. And as for those who believe they have risen above *al-Dunya* into the realm of eternal principles simply because they have a mental understanding of them, under their false spiritual complacency there often lies a concrete physical fear. Our attachment to This World cannot simply be dismissed; it must be renounced—and you can't renounce something unless you know what you're renouncing, and why. Certainly *al-Dunya* is a projection of the passions, but one of the most common ways that worldliness fools us is to offer those passions back to us with a different name and a different face, so that they no longer appear as vices but as necessary compromises, legitimate goals, even spiritual ideals. I hope that this book will be helpful in exposing some of these false ideals. This World is made up of nothing but idols, which are both masks of the ego and masks of God; until the ego is unmasked and dispelled we will always mistakenly worship this or that creature in the place of the Creator. Furthermore, the act of overthrowing collective idols can also let us glimpse the ego in action, and aid in its deconstruction. When the Power to sense the presence of God, a Power that we have projected on the idols of our passions and attachments, finds no lodging-place there and comes rolling back on us, demanding to know why we have sent it into exile, that's when we begin to wonder how we could have been so completely deceived, what were the forces that deceived us, and by what Power that deception has finally come to an end.

But to really receive this Power after its long exile is not easy, because if we sincerely desire to live consciously in the Presence of God, then This World will be unmasked—and *al-Dunya* without its collective mask of officially sanctioned fear and desire is not a pretty sight. If even half the findings of the conspiracy theorists are accurate, then our clandestine human controllers have vastly more power to determine our beliefs, engineer our perceptions and compel our deeds than we ever imagined; and if they do, we had better discover and acknowledge this fact as quickly as possible, and take the appropriate steps to counter it. But one temptation must be resisted at all cost—the tendency, most often unconscious, to put the social engineers and mind-controllers in the place of God. This is exactly what our would-be masters would like us to do, which is why—as Michael Hoffman points out—they will sometimes openly reveal their methods, hoping to awe us into submission. If we start to see them as all-powerful, or at least as the only game in town—something we will have to make accommodations with whether we like it or not—then they have won. Only if we understand that God, not any human power, is *Lord of the worlds* and *owner of the Day of Judgment*, that He totally transcends This World while remaining immanent within it, active to save us and guide us in all the events of our lives, can we face the human and trans-human evil of these latter days with courage, equanimity, and hope.

A book such as this one, where an attempt is made to apply metaphysical principles to human history, must cross and recross the "intermediary world" between history and metaphysics: the world of *myth*, a word that is used here to refer not to fallacies that have been exposed, but to "stories that are always true", whether or not the legends that recount them can be proved to refer to actual historical events. Plato called time "the moving image of Eternity"; and history, to anyone with a metaphysical view of things, appears precisely as a dramatization of eternal principles. Both legends and contemporary speculations as to what might have taken place in the past can be vehicles for an allegorical understanding of history; as long as myths and speculations are not presented as established facts, and insofar as they retain their connection with eternal principles, both of them can illuminate, if not actual historical happenings, at least the deeper meaning of contemporary events as they unfold before our eyes. To apply myth and scripture *literally* to history in attempt to make specific predictions or find out what "really happened" according to our usual sense of historical time is to fall into many traps; but to totally divorce them from history is to deny that the will of God can operate in collective human life. The correct method here, in my opinion, is first to follow myth, scripture and legend to the level of Principle, and then take a look at history from that vantage point. Did God really command Abraham to sacrifice his only son, and then withdraw his command at the last minute? Maybe He did and maybe He didn't; on the literal historical level, there's no way we can know. But we can certainly understand this story as illustrating the principle that God is the only Father, that life and death are in His hands, and that to believe that we literally own either our creative productions or our actual sons is to bind them to our egos, and consequently murder them, while to recognize that all of our creative acts belong to God and are sent by God is to release them into life. And once we know this, we can speculate on the story of Abraham as possibly indicating a cultural turn against child sacrifice in the ancient Near East; and we can also see ways in which contemporary society sacrifices its own children, as for example by sending young men and women to war. Likewise, to take the biblical legend of the Tower of Babel as the story of a titanic attempt to *reach* heaven instead of receiving from it in gratitude, whether or not the Tower was ever actually built (though it would certainly seem to suggest a Mesopotamian ziggurat), we can ask how such a "tower" might be rising in our own time, what shape it might assume in the future, and what the ultimate destiny of such a development might be. As long as we don't take myth and scripture literally, we can use them to throw a penetrating light on the meaning of *literal* events, whether past, present or future. In any case, I hope the reader will bear with me in my attempt to bring myth, legend and history together (especially in chapters Five, Six and Ten), not always to make concrete predictions or claim reliable knowledge of historical events, but rather to demonstrate how history can be understood more holistically in the light of eternal principles. The Counter-Initiation may or may not be definable in terms of one or more secret societies or secret histories (personally, I believe it can, up to a point), but it most certainly is a clandestine *spirit* that has dogged man's tracks in his earthly pilgrimage ever since the Fall.

I am a student of comparative religion and traditional metaphysics who has been deeply influenced by the so-called "Traditionalist" or "Perennialist" school—not only by the "founders" of the School, René Guénon and Ananda K. Coomaraswamy, but also by their colleagues and successors, including Frithjof Schuon, Titus Burckhardt, Martin Lings, Seyyed Hossein Nasr, Leo Schaya and Whitall Perry. But the dominant social "demonology" of our time, the worldview of those who see the New World Order as a developing empire of global oppression, a regime which shows signs of seeking to create a One-World Religion for purposes of pacification and control, have also been an important influence. I have therefore asked myself both what common ground there may be between these two schools of thought, between the metaphysicians and the conspiracy theorists, and in what specific ways the ideas and insights of one might be able to legitimately criticize, supplement and expand those of the other. In this I have done my best to build on the insights of René Guénon, who almost alone among the Perennialists was not only a metaphysician but an investigative researcher. I would not have done this, I would have left This World alone according to the *hadith* "Say *Allah* and leave them to their empty talk", were it not for the fact that the powers that be are trespassing on the field of religion, including esoteric religion, making plans for it and working to pervert it; in order to protect ourselves from these attacks, not all of which are easily discerned, we need to investigate them and understand them. The critics of the New World Order and the coming One-World Religion have many reasons for seeing "Perennialism", insofar as they are aware of it, as a potential tributary to that regime, either because they mistake it for syncretism or because Perennialism itself is tempted to syncretism; yet René Guénon, for one, provided sound criteria based on a synthesis of metaphysics, eschatology and social analysis that have much to contribute to New World Order studies by placing them in a wider context adequate to the collective darkness we face. Perennialism can throw a penetrating light on the various deviant forms of religion that the New World Order is attracting and developing, while avoiding the pitfall of seeing the enemies of the spiritual life from the standpoint of only one religious tradition, in view of the fact that these forces menace, seek to control, and hope to ultimately liquidate all true religions; nonetheless they do not seem sufficiently aware at this point in time of the dangers of globalist co-optation, and of the doctrinal, spiritual, and investigative work necessary to head it off. And the investigators of the New World Order can certainly highlight a number of areas where Perennialism is in danger of being infiltrated and co-opted by that Order.

This book was conceived of as a sequel to *The System of Antichrist: Truth and Falsehood in Postmodernism and the New Age* [Sophia Perennis, 2001], which makes it my second published work in the genre of "metaphysics and social criticism". It ranges from religion and metaphysics to history and social criticism, and as such also deals with the realm of the paranormal, which is impinging more and more upon our collective experience and worldview, especially in light of the fact that the world of psychic powers and entities is of great interest to certain sectors of the globalist elites in our time, both as a set of beliefs they can manipulate for purposes of social engineering and as a possible source of power they might be able to tap directly. *The System of Antichrist* was basically a critique of various New Age belief-systems—of what René Guénon called "Pseudo-Initiation"—along with a comparative presentation of the lore of the End Times from eight religious traditions. The present work, while it updates certain themes dealt with in the earlier book, such as the UFO phenomenon, is more directly centered on the truly *inverted* spirituality of the Counter-Initiation, though *Antichrist* certainly touched on this theme. (NOTE: Pseudo-initiates seek spiritual enlightenment in a foolish, illegitimate and self-contradictory manner, outside the grace of God. Counter-initiates seek it for purposes of power and dominance, in conscious rebellion against God. The first group are often the pawns of the second—unwitting vectors for their influence.)

But, some will ask, is the line between true and false spiritualities really so hard and fast? Aren't those who defend the revealed religions against Neo-Paganism and the New Age simply self-interested hierophants defending their own turf? And didn't William Blake himself say, in his Proverbs of Hell, "if the fool would persist in his folly he would become wise" and "the road of excess leads to the palace of wisdom" and "everything possible to be believed is an image of truth"? In this time when all forms, even the most ancient sacred forms, appear to be dissolving, isn't it possible that sincerity could simply encounter Infinity face to face, with no forms either to bring them together or keep them apart? Perhaps it is. Yet sincerity is in no way a given, and unmediated contact with the Infinite is simply another name for death. So form is a necessity in the spiritual life, and only those forms that have the Absolute at one end and the exact human shape at the other, by which I mean the forms of true religion, can liberate us from both the petrification of self-enclosed form and the chaos of formlessness, which are inseparable from each other, given that petrification longs for chaos, and chaos petrifies. The forms of false Religion, on the other hand, can't even imagine what Liberation might be. They worship This World and call it Heaven, they plunge into the petrifying chaos of This World and call it Paradise—all the time secretly fearing that it might be Hell. *If the fool would persist in his folly*—but he never does. It kills him first, or tempts him to feel, like the Pharisees, that he "has his reward", or petrifies him to the point where "persistence" no longer has any positive meaning. Before Liberation, we pray toward the *Qibla* only, not toward the point of Passion or the point of Dissipation or the point of Stony Death. After Liberation, *wherever you turn, there is the face of God*—and everything possible to be believed *is* an image of Truth. Admittedly, the duality between true and false religion is not absolute; eventually we will have to give even the Devil his due—but only the one who takes the true and leaves the false will ever understand this. The purpose of separating true and false religion, of distinguishing between true Initiation and the Counter-Initiation, of choosing the Real over the illusory, is not to begin pogroms or institute tribunals or even allow ourselves a moment of complacency or thankfulness that we are not like the rest of men; it is to turn false religion and Counter-Initiation from deceivers into teachers: "I lay before you Death and Life—therefore choose Life".

1

What is the Counter-Initiation?

AS MANY HAVE pointed out, including Lee Penn, John Coleman, Henry Makow and the late Fr. Malachi Martin, the New World Order is a one-world financial system which is in the process of giving rise to a one-world government, and which is slated to be crowned and completed by a one-world religion. The "religion" of the today's globalists, insofar as they may be said to have one, appears to be based not only on a synthesis of every pseudo-spirituality under the sun, but also on a syncretistic perversion of the sacred forms the world's faiths, on what might be called "the spirit of Assisi"—by which I certainly do not mean the spirit of St. Francis! The Traditionalist/Perennialist School also speak in terms of a unity of religions, but unlike the globalists they view it as intrinsic and transcendent, not as the hoped-for future result of any form of syncretism or political unification in this world.

Frithjof Schuon (1907–1998), following René Guénon and Ananda K. Coomaraswamy, enunciated a doctrine he called "the Transcendent Unity of Religions", which states that every true and God-given religion provides a valid view of, as well as an effective means of access to, the one Divine Reality. All the paths up the mountainside meet at the same Summit—a Summit that, since it is truly transcendent, lies beyond the realm of form, in a "kingdom not of this world". The Transcendent Unity of Religions is a highly dangerous doctrine to announce; it is nonetheless necessary. Without it, now that almost everyone on earth is daily confronted with a plurality of religions, the certainty that God and the metaphysical order are objective and universal realities is compromised. Differing conceptions of God lose their objective Referent, and are reduced to mere "belief systems", to nothing more than various notions held by this or that human group; God becomes "our deity", not *the* Deity. But as soon as the Transcendent Unity of Religions *is* announced, it unavoidably gives rise to the false and pernicious notion that to syncretize the religions is to approach a higher truth than any single religion can provide on its own. This deviation is inescapable, and is precisely what will open the door to the coming regime of Antichrist.

Anyone who bases his critique of the Darkness of This World on the orthodox doctrines of a single God-given revelation, if he has sufficient courage and insight, will see far; the solid fulcrum of that orthodoxy will allow him to lift a great weight of error into the light. But this perspective will *not* allow him to see how the other religions are menaced by the same Counter-Initiatory forces that threaten his own. Nor will it do any of us any good, really, to renounce whatever cosmopolitanism we may have attained in the field of "comparative religion", simply because we see the destructive uses to which it is sometimes put. An understanding of the differing perspectives of the world's faiths, as well as what is common to all of them, is of great value in today's "pluralistic" world. And once we have proved to ourselves that faiths other than the religion of our birth are capable of producing saints, to deny this knowledge out of the shock we feel when confronted with the evils of syncretism—including the temptation to "mutual apostasy"—is to turn against recognized truth, and thus against God. To deny what we know out of fear is to plunge the mind into darkness.

To syncretize the religions, however—beginning with the exaltation of tolerance over truth—is also to court darkness; it is to predefine their fundamental revealed doctrines, established by God and existing as living paths back to Him, as "dogmatisms" or "excesses" that are seen only as *divisive*, and that consequently should be moderated, de-emphasized, or thrown out. Such misplaced tolerance opens the door to syncretism, and syncretism is the mutual suicide of the world's religions. And comparative religion itself, if its dangers are not recognized and compensated for, may unwittingly serve such syncretism. Doctrines proper to one religion that are scandalous to another may be "soft-pedaled", swept under the rug, or covertly altered so as to moderate potential disagreement.

My own way of avoiding the twin pitfalls of exclusivism and syncretism has been to criticize the counterfeit "religion" of the Counter-Initiation from a plurality of orthodox perspectives, not only one—to pose, following my own understanding of Schuon, a truly *transcendent* unity of religions within the mind of God as against the artificial, worldly unification of religions that syncretism presupposes, but to do so with the uncompromising rigor that is usually associated only with those who defend their own exclusivist religious ramparts against everything that lies beyond the walls. The Traditionalists/Perennialists at their best have always supported these exclusivists against the common enemy, even if those they support sometimes see them as part of that enemy. Yet no one can deny that the temptation to an accommodating worldly ecumenism, designed and patronized by secularist authorities, has also made its appearance in the Perennialist world.[1]

René Guénon, in *The Reign of Quantity and the Signs of the Times*, laid out the phases of the destruction of sacred tradition at the end of the Latter Days, the Kali-yuga: First Anti-Tradition, which is more or less synonymous with secularism or materialism; then (or concurrently) the spread of Pseudo-Initiation, which appears most clearly in our time as the New Age movement; and finally Counter-Tradition and Counter-Initiation. Anti-Tradition is the province of

1. Evidence is mounting that certain secularist and/or Counter-Initiatory forces have "recognized" Perennialism and begun to factor it into their plans. In a 2010 episode of the *Inspector Lewis* television detective series entitled "The Allegory of Love" (produced in Britain and aired on PBS), Traditionalism/Perennialism is "showcased" in a way that has nothing whatever to do with the plot. At one point the detective sidekick of Inspector Lewis, a cynical, nihilistic ex-Catholic-seminary student, spies a book by Titus Burckhardt in the library of a Muslim professor at Oxford they are interrogating, and treats us to a fairly cogent capsule definition of "Perennialism"—but with absolutely no reference to the fact that the Perennialists are also by-and-large *Traditionalists* who require adherence to one of the revealed faiths, as Burckhardt certainly did. We then see a quick unexplained shot of the "Traditionalist spiderweb" diagram of concentric circles with radii, apparently to implant it in the consciousness of the audience as a waking suggestion for future use. Perennialism is presented not in a Traditionalist context but in one of fantasy literature—of Harry Potter and the mythopoesis of C. S. Lewis, which are put on the

skeptics; Pseudo-Initiation, of the imbalanced or deluded; Counter-Initiation, of the conscious enemies of true spirituality, particularly initiatory or esoteric spirituality—those whom Guénon calls "Satan's contemplatives", the *Awliya al-Shaytan*.

The Counter-Initiation bears six fundamental marks:

(1) "Exoterically" it espouses a horizontal, worldly, quasi-political unity of religions rather than a vertical, transcendent, spiritual one;
(2) "Esoterically" it holds to a form of predatory "spiritual Darwinism" based upon a Luciferian counterfeit of the Hierarchy of Being, where higher levels represent not more subtle, capacious, luminous and concrete *realities* as discerned by the Intellect, but greater degrees of *power and authority* as achieved (or supposedly achievable) by the will;
(3) It grows in large part out of legitimate esoteric organizations which have deviated and consequently inverted, most likely because they have abandoned the various religious revelations to which they own their existence;
(4) It gives the horizontal antiquity of its supposed origins precedence over the sense of vertical derivation from Divine Revelation, which it either de-emphasizes or denies [see p. 265]; consequently it deifies matter and replaces Eternity with endless time;

same level, Lewis' books being emptied of all Christian content. But it is made quite clear that Perennialism is not some Neo-Pagan religion for the hippies and the peasants, but a *universalism for the intellectual elite*. The episode in question also mentions a group called "The New Inklings". When I accessed their website in January of 2012, I found something called "Project Conversion" where one Andrew Bowen tried the experiment of "immersing" himself in a different religion each month over the period of a year—something as inimical to the spirit of the original Inklings (C.S. Lewis, J.R.R. Tolkien, Owen Barfield, and Charles Williams, all committed Christians) as anything I can imagine: a "serial syncretism" that could only destroy any possibility of true religious commitment, and may have been designed to do just that. Perennialism has always opposed syncretism, but the association of Perennialism with the New Inklings in "The Allegory of Love" could only identify it with syncretism in people's minds. Who is setting up this identification, and why? (Tavistock? Hello?)

(5) It defines religion as a man-made affair in which the human relationship with "spiritual" powers is not reverential but utilitarian, thus reducing esoterism to a purely technical knowledge that is free to express itself in terms of psychic or technological magic, thus deifying matter by a different route;
(6) It the mis-applies the norms of the individual spiritual Path to the supposed spiritual evolution of macrocosm or the human collective.

Or, to put it more simply: *syncretism; inverted hierarchy; deviated esoterism; dominance of history over Revelation; Promethean magic;* and *spiritual evolutionism*—the six-fold falsification of the Transcendent Unity of Religions and the Primordial Tradition. Syncretism is Unity when separated from Transcendence, the vision of Immanence of God now fallen to the level of a glamorized materialism. Inverted hierarchy is the Transcendence when separated from Unity, a system in which levels believed to be ontologically higher are actually lower because more deeply sunk in egotism and self-will. Deviated esoterism is the Inner aspect of religion which, in denying the Outer, ends by becoming Outer itself—not by virtue of an orthodox Outwardness, but rather a heterodox one, an Outwardness only pretending to Inwardness, and one to which no true Inwardness corresponds. The exaltation of history over Revelation, antiquity over Eternity replaces the certainty of immediate Divinely-inspired Intellection with the uncertainties of human memory. Magic is the false belief that man, not God, is the ultimate performer of all action; Promethean magic is the disastrous mis-application of this belief to the spiritual Path. And spiritual evolutionism is the replacement of Providence with natural law and Grace with arcane subtle-material forces. Not every instance of the Counter-Initiation fully manifests all of these marks, but all will be involved in any Counter-Initiatory conception, either actually or potentially.

Syncretism is espoused innocently by the deluded Pseudo-Initiates, who see it as the expression of a kind of universal, or potentially universal, esoterism or mysticism; it is also often promoted—in a more cynical, though still sometimes idealistic, manner—by the Anti-Traditional secularists, who hope to "guide" religious believers toward a "brotherhood of man" by manipulating religious dogmas they themselves do not believe in. As soon as the understanding is lost that the Reality common to all true religions must transcend form, syncretism is born; a worldly unification of religions, impossible to achieve in any stable form and destructive to attempt, is envisioned in place of their intrinsic, transcendent unity, which is inseparable from the necessary and providential nature of their differences. This perverse exteriorization of the Transcendent Unity of Religions, its descent from the level of an esoteric (though relatively elementary) understanding to that of an exoteric doctrine, is one of the primary driving forces behind the false spirituality of the Counter-Initiation.

Inverted hierarchy is based on a Prometheanism that hopes to "take heaven by storm"; in its most extreme form it manifests as a Luciferian belief that God Himself is not *intrinsically* Absolute, but only accidentally so. He is in no way the personal name and face of the Real Nature of things, but merely a divine tyrant. He is totally devoid of love, and whatever wisdom he may possess is no more than a superhuman cunning in service to the power-motive. He occupies the Divine Throne only because he has been successful in taking it and maintaining his possession of it; consequently he might well be deposed by a Promethean rebellion led by a new, up-and coming God, more powerful, more ruthless, more cunning, more predatory than he is. This characterization of inverted hierarchy might seem to many like an extreme conception of things that is rarely met with. And yet any conception of the spiritual life that defines spirituality as a personal achievement rather than as a willing response to Grace has already taken the first step on the Luciferian road. It has falsely defined spirituality, which in its true form requires the transcendence and annihilation of the ego, as an enhancement and empowerment of that ego; consequently it has sabotaged itself from the outset.

As for deviated esoterism, we must start with the understanding that each revealed or primal religion has an "esoteric" center: for the Hindus, the Vedanta and the Yoga traditions; for Judaism, the Kabbalah; for Christianity, the sacraments and the Hesychasm of the Eastern Orthodox; for Islam, Sufism; for Buddhism, the Vajrayana. All these are ways of drawing closer to Absolute Reality in this very life. But when they deviate from this goal in the direction of magic and occultism, they become the seed of the worst spiritual evil the human race is capable of, according to the principle of *corruptio optima pessima*, "the corruption of the best is the worst".

To grant precedence to the horizontal transmission of spirituality over its vertical descent from the Divine is to pervert the notion of the *sanatana dharma*, the Primordial Tradition. It is to espouse a heretical Deism according to which God intervened in the universe only at its creation, or at the creation of man, but in no way continues to guide us through Revelation or Providence. True spirituality has indeed been transmitted horizontally "from the Stone Age till now", but only by virtue of its periodic renewal through vertical Divine Revelation, as well as through an inner intellective understanding of this Revelation's meaning and application. To de-emphasize Revelation in the name of the venerable antiquity of spiritual legend and lore, precious as these are, is to degrade *deva-yana*, the path of the gods, to the level of *pitri-yana*, the path of the ancestors, and thus risk exposure to the dangerous psychic residues that, according to Guénon, haunt the precincts of dead religions. And it is also to allow any group claiming, sincerely or otherwise, to have inherited the "wisdom of the ages" to undermine and supersede the revealed faiths.

To define religion as man-made is not only to implicitly deny the existence of God, as well as defining God as passive and man as active; it is also to absolutize human intent while providing no objective criteria according to which that intent could be evaluated as wise or foolish, kind or cruel, sound or corrupt. A man-made religion cannot serve Divine purposes, only human ones; and human purposes alienated from the Divine, if not actively opposed to it, will necessarily be based on blind human passion.

Finally, to mis-apply the norms of individual spiritual development to the supposed spiritual evolution of the universe or the human collective, as Teilhard de Chardin did, is to pervert the theological virtue of Hope. If the world is inevitably evolving toward God, then we need do nothing but wait; unfortunately, the outcome we are waiting for will not appear in our lifetimes. We may work for what we believe to be the welfare of our grandchildren and great-grandchildren, but we ourselves are spiritually doomed; we may be compost for the field of collective God-realization, but we cannot hope to realize Him ourselves, or even hear His voice. We could have turned to Him, prayed to Him for the Mercy we desperately need, and met Him in the midst of that need—but once our hope has been diverted in the direction of a collective good only to be realized by future evolution, the door of that Mercy is closed to us. And—viewed objectively—is a collective "hope" that is to be realized only at the price of generations of spiritual despair really a very likely outcome? Communist playwright Berthold Brecht, in one of his poems, once lamented: "Ah we, who desired to prepare the soil for kindness/ Could not ourselves be kind"; however, anyone who believes that universal benevolence might somehow miraculously arise out of generations of cruelty can only be characterized as morally insane.

The Counter-Initiation is the ego's idea of spirituality. It first appears in the Old Testament in the person of the Serpent, who represents the temptation to hide *Intellectus/Nous* behind the veil of *ratio/dianoia*, to replace unitary cardiac consciousness with discursive cerebral consciousness. Mental, rational consciousness is valid on its own level, but only when illumined by the spiritual Intellect, which properly rules it.

The next phase of the Counter-Initiation is represented by the murder of Abel, the herder, by his brother Cain, the farmer, who went on to found the first city. Urban life sprang from organized agriculture, which was inseparable from astronomy/astrology and the priestly mysteries of calendar lore, the dark side of which was the belief that it might be possible to predict, and thus potentially control, the actions of God. Later on in Genesis it appears as those "sons of God who looked upon the daughters of men and found them fair", who mated with them and spawned a race of giants, the *nephilim*. These "sons of God" are dealt with at greater length in the books of Enoch, where they are called the "Watchers". The Watchers symbolize principles of the Intellect who are tempted to turn their gaze upon something lower than God, or rather upon God's manifestations as if these existed or could exist apart from Him, thus precipitating a fall from the level of consciousness centered in the Intellect to one centered in the a will. The *nephilim* are the Titans, who represent an imbalanced hypertrophy of the will based on an infusion of energy illegitimately stolen from the Intellect. The will is only truly itself in submission to the Intellect; when it usurps the place of the Intellect rather than submitting to it, it is transformed into self-will, and wreaks havoc in the psyche, the social dimension, and the natural world.

The final solidification and breakup of the dark side of the agricultural/astronomical "esoterism" represented by Cain is symbolized in Genesis by the Tower of Babel. René Guénon and Frithjof Schuon teach that in the Golden Age all of humanity spoke a single spiritual "language" (for which read "held a common spiritual worldview") known as the Primordial Tradition. Later on in the present cycle of manifestation (of which all we know of as "history" forms only a very small part), this common vision of God and the metaphysical order was lost—perhaps due to the event which appears in Genesis as the Flood. The Tower of Babel would then represent an attempt by a later society and regime to reconstitute this original vision *by power alone*, to found an oppressive political empire based on an *enforced syncretism* of all religions. Such syncretism earned God's wrath, however, and the Tower fell, because it was and is His Will that there be a plurality of religions in our times rather than a One World Religion, precisely to prevent the resurrection of the kind of evil world empire that Babylon represents. Guénon, in *Symbols of the Sacred Science*, sees the Tower of Babel as representing a revolt of the *kshatriya* or noble/warrior caste against the *brahmin* or priestly caste, a revolt that can be considered as the outer reflection of the revolt of the will, now become self-will, against the Intellect, this being is the essence of the Fall. The Serpent in Genesis tempted Adam to abandon the Tree of Life—the Intellect—and falsely seek Divine Knowledge, by the power of rebellious self-will alone, in the tree of the knowledge of good and evil: the principle of discursive reason, a faculty that is commanded to serve such Knowledge, but which, operating on its own, can never understand or establish it.[2] (*see facing page*)

When the two angel-travelers visited Lot in Sodom to inform him that the city would be destroyed, and the mob demanded that he turn them over so the Sodomites could rape them, this too was a manifestation of the Counter-Initiation: to rape the angels of God, to "have knowledge" of them by force, is a symbol of the ego's desire to possess Divine knowledge on the ego's own terms—not to receive it, but to steal it, like the Titan Prometheus stole fire from Zeus. This

2. Perhaps the best literary image we have of the Counter-Initiation as enforced syncretism in service to the power motive appears in Herman Melville's *Moby Dick*, where Captain Ahab commands his crew, made up of many races and religions—Christian, Pagan, Parsee—to swear a Satanic oath to hunt the White Whale. Moby Dick is a telling symbol, not of God, but of God's reflection in nature, and ultimately of the powers of nature falsely considered as independent of God. In Jewish esoterism, Leviathan the sea-monster corresponds to the *kundalini* or "serpent-power" of Hindu yoga; both words mean "coiled". *Kundalini* is *potentia*, the psychophysical power stored in both nature and the "natural man". If awakened and guided by the Spirit, it will provide the energy necessary to travel the spiritual Path—but if awakened artificially, by a Promethean self-will rather than the Grace of God, it will wreak havoc on the soul. Melville shows how the powers of nature in exile from God can be tapped only in hatred of nature (and of God too), thus exposing the secret affinity between nature-worship and technological destruction.

The harpoon that figures prominently in Ahab's Counter-Initiatory rites can be fruitfully compared to the "Spear of Destiny" dealt with by occult conspiracy writer Trevor Ravenscroft. The spear, possibly at one time a Lombard royal ensign but later identified as the spear that pierced the side of Christ, is part of the regalia of the Holy Roman emperors. Bound to it is an iron nail which, according to legend, is one of the nails of the Crucifixion, discovered by St. Helena on Mount Calvary. Originally the fastening of the nail to the spear would have represented the Christianizing of the Teutonic tribes. But if it is true, as Ravenscroft claims, that the Nazis considered the spear to be a sort of magical talisman, this would indicate its degeneration into a symbol of the inverted syncretism of the Counter-Initiation. The nail also reminds us of that other nail by which Ahab fixed a gold doubloon to the Pequod's mast, thus (as it were) crucifying the Sun. And certainly Ahab's harpoon, quenched at its forging in Pagan blood and baptized in the Devil's name, stands as an eloquent symbol of the will to murder Christ, given that the whole voyage of the Pequod is presented as the antithesis to Father Mapple's Christian sermon near the beginning of the book, where he takes the prophet Jonah to task for his rebellion against God; any contemporary conspiracy theorist who suspects that transnational capitalism is captained by Luciferians will find it all there in *Moby Dick*. Ahab mysteriously claims that he bears on his head the weight of the Iron Crown of Lombardy, which according to legend was forged partly out of another of the Crucifixion nails St. Helena found, and has supposedly been the crown of several Holy Roman Emperors. All this reminds us of the prophecy of René Guénon in *The Reign of Quantity and the Signs of the Times* that the kingdom of Antichrist will be like a Satanic inversion of a Holy Empire. (A more complete version of Melville's vision of America as Counter-Initiatory Empire appears in his poem *Clarel*.)

Promethean lust after the secrets of God has re-appeared in our own time in the form of psychedelic drugs. When Jesus said "And from the days of John the Baptist until now, the kingdom of heaven suffereth violence, and the violent bear it away" [Matt. 11:12], He was referring to the attempt to access the mysteries through ascetic rigor, and contrasting it with His own ministry, in which the mysteries are given, by God's generosity, to all who are willing to receive them, in humility and faith. John the Baptist was in no way an agent of the Counter-Initiation, but when Truth is *given*, only to be rejected by those who will not humble themselves to receive it, but would rather "take heaven by storm", this is the Counter-Initiation precisely.

When the magicians of Pharaoh, in Exodus, threw down their staffs before Moses, turning them into serpents, and Moses threw down his, which also became a serpent and ate up the serpents of magic, this represents a triumph of the true Divine Initiation over the Counter-Initiation. The serpent symbolizes wisdom. The many serpents of the magicians indicate psychic knowledge, which is always ambiguous and multiple, while the serpent of Moses symbolizes Spiritual Wisdom, which is always One.

According to the Noble Qur'an [20:96], the Golden Calf was made by one al-Samiri, who brought it to life by "throwing in"—presumably into the molten metal or into the fire beneath it—a handful of earth taken from a footprint of the Prophet Moses (though some say of Gabriel). This is a picture of how Counter-Initiatory magic is always based on power stolen from the Spirit, power which consequently can only express itself on a lower level—and not legitimately so, as with valid forms of theurgy, but purely through counterfeit and inversion.

The Roman Empire, like Babel, also practiced religious syncretism as a method of social control; even Yah-weh was worshipped in Rome at one time. The gods of Rome's conquered peoples found "refuge" in the Pantheon. But whereas each, within its original context, had represented its nation's conception of the highest Reality, or one aspect of it, now all the gods were relativized; none could any more represent or give access to the Absolute, since the "absolute" common to them and of which they were particularized expressions was now the Roman Empire. Christ himself was in danger of being reduced to a tribal god functioning under imperial patronage, a fate that early Christianity avoided only by the blood of the martyrs. Roman syncretism was finally suppressed by the triumph of Christianity under Constantine.

In the Gospels, the Counter-Initiation appears most clearly in the person of Judas Iscariot. Judas was certainly an "initiate" of Jesus Christ, a member of His inner circle who was privy to his explicit teachings, one to whom He spoke "openly" rather than "in parables". And if, as some speculate, his betrayal was an attempt to exteriorize Jesus' ministry, to transform His "kingdom not of this world" into a worldly regime, possibly by forcing Jesus to manifest the fullness of His theurgic power in order to save himself from martyrdom, this would certainly fit the definition of "deviated esoterism". And the fact that Judas was the Apostles' treasurer, who betrayed Jesus for thirty pieces of silver, makes him the archetype of those international banking interests whom some believe are involved with a deviated Luciferian esoterism in our own time.

Before the advent of the Prophet Muhammad, peace and blessings be upon him, the Kaaba in Mecca—which Islamic tradition teaches had been constructed by Abraham, and according to some accounts by Adam himself—had degenerated into just such a pantheon of pagan gods, representing in this case not an empire but the mercantile hegemony of the tribe of the Quraysh, who were enriched by the trade attracted by Mecca's role as a pilgrimage destination; Muhammad cast the pagan idols out of the Kaaba and reinstituted the original Abrahamic worship of the One God.

After the fall of the Roman Empire, the next attempt to establish an international power bloc based upon, or at least covertly related to, a form of religious syncretism, was initiated by the Knights Templar in their degeneracy, and later expressed in terms of the Freemasonic tradition to which the Templars were somehow related. The spurious "Templar" organizations that grew up within Freemasonry in modern times, often making the claim that the Masons are the true successors of the Knights Templar, have hidden by their obviously fantastic nature the fact that there could have been an actual relationship between the Order of the Temple and one or more groups of "proto-Freemasons" whom they encountered in the Holy

Land. This relationship might well have begun as a true echo of the Transcendent Unity of Religions, or rather of the Primordial Tradition, but if any of the negative assertions regarding "Templar rites" are actually valid—the veneration of Baphomet, the trampling on the cross, etc.—this might indicate that the Order later degenerated into a clandestine religious syncretism, perhaps incorporating elements of deviated Sufism, which would have turned it over to the Counter-Initiation [see Chapter Ten], and constituted the "inner" aspect of its transformation from a spiritual elect into a globalist elite, an ancestor of today's international banking system.

In most or all of the above cases, we can discern a loss of or turning away from principial Unity toward cosmic multiplicity, followed by an attempt to re-unify through force what had once been recognized as intrinsically one in essence. The Tree of Life is abandoned for the Tree of the Knowledge of Good and Evil, according to the false suggestion of the Serpent that the absolutization of the *dvandvas*, the pairs-of-opposites, is what constitutes Divine knowledge (this being the archetypal origin of the Manichaean dualism). The split between Abel the herder, whose relationship to the world is unitary, immediate and thus relatively eternal, and Cain the farmer, whose relationship is relatively fragmented since it is more involved with memory and anticipation, leads to the triumph of an established system of calendar-time under city-centered agriculture. The agricultural city-state, through the centralization of the market, exerts control not only over the farmers, but over the herding tribes as well. The sons of God turn their gaze away from the One God and toward the many daughters of men. Nimrod, the great hunter, attempts to impose his vision of syncretism through religious imperialism at the Tower of Babel, hunting and taking as trophies the various local or tribal religions he conquers—a process we can see operating in Egypt as well. The Greco-Roman world, having lost the vision of principial Unity and descended into a literalistic polytheism, ends in the attempt of the Roman Empire to forcibly syncretize the religions of its conquered nations for purposes of power and hegemony. Judas—if the above speculation is accurate—attempts to tap Jesus' spiritual power to ensure the triumph of the Jewish missionary effort, whose ultimate goal was to take over the Roman

Empire by conversion rather than conquest. Among the Arabic sons of Ishmael the original Abrahamic monotheism degenerates into Pagan polytheism; the many pagan gods are then "unified" into a single system by the tribe of the Quraysh at the Kaaba in Mecca, in order to reap the profits of the pilgrimage trade. The Templars begin as Christian warrior-monks, encounter an esoteric version of the Transcendent Unity of Religions in Jerusalem, and then externalize and pervert this *intrinsic* universalism by transforming it into the "universalism" of international finance.

Many researchers in the genre termed "conspiracy theory", such as Henry Makow and Alan Watt, see esoteric or occult forces lying behind the destructive agendas and actions of the power elites; in this I believe that they are definitely on the right track. What most of them do not understand, however, is that there is a true esoterism as well as a deviated one, and that the greatest evil in this world derives from originally legitimate esoteric organizations who have turned against God and gone over to the "dark side".

"Esoteric" does not equal "occult". To say that all esoteric spirituality is evil, as some conspiracy theorists do, is like the saying that the Catholic Mass is evil because there is such a thing as the Black Mass. I have written this book both to clarify the distinction between sacred esoterism and satanic occultism, and to provide a new perspective on the influence of such occultism on world affairs. Readers wishing to explore these ideas further should read five books. One, *The System of Antichrist: Truth and Falsehood in Postmodernism and the New Age*, is by me. Another is by a friend of mine, Lee Penn; it's all about the co-optation of religion by the Globalists and is entitled *False Dawn: The United Religions Initiative, Globalism and the Quest for a One-World Religion.* The last three are by René Guénon—his prophetic masterpiece *The Reign of Quantity and the Signs of the Times*, and his two books of esoteric investigative reporting, *The Spiritist Error*, and *Theosophy: The History of a Pseudo-Religion*; these three books will give the reader a good idea of what Guénon means by the Counter-Initiation. But the reader should also be on the lookout for Guénon's major error—his belief that Freemasonry could be "purified" so as to function as a kind of "esoteric Christianity", somewhat on the order of Sufism within Islam, a belief he apparently never abandoned until the last year or so of his life. Ironically, he never seemed to have understood that Freemasonry perfectly fits his own definition of the Counter-Initiation. In Guénon's time, or from his perspective, the Counter-Initiation appeared in terms of this or that secret society operating in the shadowy underworld of European occultism; but as Lee Penn has demonstrated, it has now come up into the open, and moved inexorably toward the centers of global power. In the words of American Eastern Orthodox priest Seraphim Rose (who was influenced by Guénon), "in our time Satan has walked naked into human history."

This brings up the question of the true nature of esoteric "initiatory" spirituality, whether or not it appears in the guise of this or that secret society. I believe that esoterism—the discipline and Grace by which spiritual realities are seen not "in a glass, darkly" but "face to face"—is the inner essence of all true religion, though it is only clearly distinguished from the "exoteric" domain in the Abrahamic religions, most particularly in Islam, where Sufism or *tasawwuf* represents a separate "estate" within that religion, the domain of the "organized mystics". (Guénon ultimately became a Muslim and a Sufi, and spent his later years in Egypt.) Kabbalah holds a somewhat similar position within Judaism, but today we are seeing the growth of both pseudo-Sufism and pseudo-Kabbalah. One of the strategies of the powers that be is to separate the esoteric aspects of religions from their outer or "exoteric" expressions, thereby ultimately destroying both; thus they will support and patronize "non-Islamic Sufism" and "non-Jewish Kabbalah"—which of course will often result in persecution of true Sufis by the short-sighted exoteric religious authorities of Islam; it's the old strategy of divide and conquer. (Sufism and Kabbalah have sometimes been subject to various deviations even within the context of their parent religions, but that's another matter.) Esoterism begins as a spiritual "mystery" which *cannot* be divulged, only realized. Under the pressure of misunderstanding and persecution on the part of the exoteric religious authorities it may have to go underground, after which the original spiritual *mystery* it incarnates begins to be falsely associated with the kind of *secrecy* that has now become necessary for self-defense. And various esoteric networks, since they possess established lines of clandestine communication and are often international in scope, sometimes become infiltrated later on by subversive political and/or spiritual forces, by spies and agents of various descriptions, who will use them for their own ends, either to forward certain political agendas or, in the case of actual Luciferian or Satanic infiltration, directly in service to the Powers of Darkness. Consequently, corrupt and deviated esoteric organizations may become laboratories where political evil and spiritual evil cross-pollinate and unite.

Freemasonry is a case in point. It shows signs of having been influenced at its inception by something like an Islamic Sufi order, possibly a craft guild that was charged with maintaining the sacred buildings on the Temple Mount, the al-Aqsa Masjid and the Dome of the Rock; since the Knights were headquartered on the Mount during the Crusades, they could have come into contact with such a guild of sacred craftsmen, who would likely have been legitimately Islamic. But if it is true as some claim that members of this guild later accompanied the Templars to Europe, they would have become separated from Islam, their parent religion, and so could only have become a subversive force in the Christian world. And one of the things the globalists continue to do in our time is separate esoteric spiritual practices and doctrines from the religions that gave birth to them, thus turning both of them over to the Devil [see Chapter Ten].

Kabbalah also became separated from its parent religion, Judaism, during the Renaissance, which is why has it acted as the seed of so much subversive occultism in the west. Within Judaism, Kabbalah (unless it becomes deviated) is a divine mystery given by God by which saints and sages can come closer to Him. But there is always the temptation in esoteric spiritualities like this to pervert the mysteries, to use them for purposes of magic and social subversion. This may have begun with the Kabbalist Isaac Luria, one of the greatest exemplars of the tradition, but also someone who taught certain doctrines that were highly susceptible to perversion. The central doctrine of the Kabbalah is the Tree of Life composed of the Ten Sefiroth, which are powers or principles within the Divine Nature by which God manifests spiritual, psychic and material universes. According to Luria, of the Ten Sefiroth, the seven lower "vessels" were shattered because they could not contain the creative light of God, leaving only the highest three intact (these being similar in many ways to the Christian Trinity). The operative aspect of Lurianic Kabbalah was based on the work of restoring these shattered vessels. But somewhere along the line, perhaps not with Luria himself, this restoration or *tikkun* became interpreted in an outer, socio-political way, thus generating a spiritually perverted stream of ideas that resulted in the false Messiah Shabbetai Zevi (1626–1676, a sincere lunatic, apparently a bi-polar psychotic), and his "successor" Jacob Frank (1726–1791, a cynical and corrupt mountebank), who together perverted much of Judaism, ideas which contributed to the progressivism of the 18th century European "Enlightenment", to the French Revolution, and ultimately to Marxism [see *To Eliminate the Opiate* by Rabbi Marvin S. Antelman]. And as Henry Makow asserts, this deviated Kabbalah may form part of the ideology of those globalist elites he calls the Illuminati [see his *Illuminati* and *Illuminati 2*], who, he claims, have many Masonic affiliations.[3] Makow believes that Shabbetean/Frankist Jews infiltrated Freemasonry in the 18th Century, influencing the development of the Bavarian Illuminati and setting up Masonry as a vector for the secret influence of international banking interests; and it is true that Gershom Scholem presents Frank as quite lavish with bribes and often flush with ready cash from unknown sources.

The term *Illuminati* is used by conspiracy theorists to denote a partly clandestine network within the globalist elite, a cadre who wield power largely through financial manipulation and social engineering, and who also seem to hold in common certain Counter-Traditional "religious" beliefs. If we were to search for evidence of such Illuminati according to the description rather than the name,

3. Writers like Coleman and Makow present many startling facts and/or assertions that they then proceed to weave together into a seemingly coherent pattern, though whether this pattern represents established reality or conjecture is hard to determine. The best way to begin reading such material, in my opinion, is to select certain things asserted as factual which, if true, would have wide-ranging implications, and research these independently. For example, Jim Garrison's scenario relating to the conspiracy behind the assassination of JFK may or may not be accurate, in whole or in part—but if his single assertion that Lee Harvey Oswald received a high-level U.S. security clearance *after* he agitated for Castro on the streets of New Orleans and "defected" to Russia is true, then the entire official version of the assassination represented by the Warren Commission Report collapses like a house of cards.

we would not come up empty-handed, as Lee Penn has amply demonstrated in his *False Dawn*, drawing only upon entirely public statements by those who act, or aspire to act, as a global ruling class. These "Illuminati" appear to have no direct historical connection to the Bavarian secret society of the same name, founded by Adam Weishaupt in 1776, where occultism and revolutionary politics met and mingled, and I doubt that they are as unified a force as Makow presents them—there is always in-fighting among the elites, just as there is factionalism among revolutionaries and turf wars between drug gangs and intelligence agencies. Nonetheless, revolutionary conspiracies on the part of the disenfranchised and/or social engineering projects sponsored by the elites (which, rather counter-intuitively, sometimes blend into one), operating in tandem with various occult beliefs and practices, have a long history which certainly predates the Bavarian Illuminati; they are clearly in evidence today.

In the process of drawing closer to God by an esoteric path such as Kabbalah or Sufism, the worshipper rises consciously, by God's Grace, through all the planes of Being that form the "Jacob's Ladder" stretching from this world to the Throne of God. But if he stops short of his ultimate goal, if he is seduced by the powers that reside on the "middle rungs" of the Ladder, then he has failed in his spiritual path and may end as a magician, if not the kind of wizard who uses these powers (or is used *by* them) to control people and institutions for his own ends. It is these wizards who will ultimately be hired, or rather "harvested", by the Antichrist. And one of the best ways the powers of such people can be blocked or defended against is for sincere worshippers traveling this or that esoteric way to remain faithful to God, to put His commandments and His good pleasure first, and to renounce all temptations to magic, even the magic of foolishly believing that we can "command" God to appear, or apply His power to good works according to our own conception, not His.

My own path is Islamic Sufism, or *tasawwuf*. In essence it is a path of the "practice of the presence of God", of cultivating the realization that we are always in His presence, and of putting God's wishes before our own desires, even our desire to see His face—though without that desire, no one would ever embark upon the Sufi path in the first place, the ultimate goal of Sufism being *ma'rifa*, direct knowledge or experience of God in this life. Sufism, however, has also been perverted in some cases. For example, some deviated Sufis practice *ruhaniyyat*, a kind of sacred magic, usually only for "good" purposes, forgetting that the road to Hell is paved with good intentions [see Chapter Four]. The major Sufi popularizer in the west at the end of the 20th century, Idries Shah, was reputed to be a Freemason, wrote books on magic, was a colleague of Gerald Gardner, the main influence behind modern Wicca, and was himself a founding member of the Club of Rome. He, along with Hazrat Inayat Khan—who was sponsored in the West by the Theosophical Society—was one of the major driving forces behind today's tendency, among western "Sufis", to separate Sufism from Islam and thereby turn it into a universalist pseudo-religion; here we can clearly see the inroads made into the Sufi world by the globalists in their campaign to co-opt the world's religions, including their esoteric dimensions. We may thank God that a true, Islamic Sufism still exists—a real alternative to the Wahhabis and other Islamic extremists, but one that has retained its independence and consequently owes nothing, in terms of either ideology or patronage, to the globalists or the Western powers.

This campaign, once mostly clandestine, to co-opt Sufism has recently begun to come out into the open. According to an article by Ali Eteraz available on the website of the Council of Foreign Relations (accessed 7/28/2010), "*Why are U.S. think tanks pushing for state-sponsored Islam in Pakistan?*"..."Well, now, according to commentators from the BBC to the *Economist* to the *Boston Globe*, Sufism, being defined as Islam's moderate or mystical side, is apparently just the thing we need to deal with violent Muslim extremists. Sufis are the best allies to the West, these authors say; support them, and countries as diverse as Pakistan and Somalia could turn around." But Sufis cannot in all cases be strictly distinguished from Islamic militants, as the above passage implies, through they are certainly opposed to the Wahhabis. Elements of the Naqshbandi Sufi Order have formed an important part of the armed Chechen resistance to Russian imperialism, which might be seen as making them allies of the west in another sense, and there was apparently also a Naqshbandi brigade who fought the American occupation in Iraq. (Idries Shah claimed to be a Naqshbandi, but he in no way represented normative Naqshbandi Sufism, which has a tradition of being solidly Islamic, while Shah was at pains to "streamline" Sufism and separate it from Islam.) The fact is that Sufism is not a unified movement capable of being co-opted as a whole, and it embraces a spiritual core that resists being politicized in any way. Nonetheless, it may be that the western powers are playing both sides of the "good Muslim/bad Muslim" dichotomy, supporting both tolerant Sufis and Islamic terrorists, as long as they are sometimes willing to do its dirty work. We know, for example, that Osama bin Laden emerged from the CIA-supported Islamic insurgency against the Russian occupation of Afghanistan, and the various insurgencies the U.S. and the western powers supported in the "Arab Spring" appear to include elements of al-Qaeda, or at least groups going by that name.

Sufism is certainly not the only esoteric spirituality that has been subject to interference by the powers that be; Henry Makow cites the case of the Kabbalah, which he sees as forming an important aspect of the deviated esoterism practiced by some among the global financial elites. Unfortunately Makow, in line with many other conspiracy theorists, does not grasp the distinction between deviated esoterism and esoterism per se; once again, to characterize Sufism, Kabbalah, Hindu Yoga etc. as evil because perverted forms of them have been practiced by elements within the global elites is like saying that the Catholic Mass is evil because Black Masses exist; this is part and parcel of the wider tendency, common among Evangelical Christians and Islamic fundamentalists, to see the moral dimension of religion as good and orthodox and the mystical dimension as heterodox and evil; if this were the case, some of the greatest saints and theologians of Christianity, Judaism and Islam would have to be classed as Satanists. To adopt this belief is to give aid and comfort to the Counter-Initiation, as well as to any forces, either pervertedly "spiritual" or simply secular and materialist, who want to deconstruct the world's religions. This is an area where the conspiracy theorists definitely need to develop a degree of sophistication in religious matters, and one where the Perennialists/Traditionalists, starting with René Guénon (though he is certainly not beyond criticism, as we will see), could be of the immense help to them.

Nor are strictly esoteric spiritualities the only ones of interest to the globalist elites. Lee Penn, in "The Religious Face of the New World Order: Benedict XVI Calls for a 'true World Political Authority'" [*http://www.leepenn.org/LP-Index.html*], analyzes Pope Benedict XVI's 2009 encyclical *Caritas in Veritate* as an essentially anti-Catholic globalist manifesto. There is little doubt in my mind that the present "Novus Ordo" Catholic Church, perhaps partly under the Masonic influence which some traditional Catholics discerned at the Second Vatican Council, ultimately aims to act as "melting pot" for many different faiths. (If the Church can officially prohibit homosexuality while shielding homosexual pedophile priests, what's to prevent it from forbidding the Catholic faithful from becoming Freemasons while reserving this "privilege" for the Vatican elite?) Soon after Tony Blair—whose Faith Foundation has full Vatican support—converted to Novus Ordo Catholicism, he traveled to the Yucatan to participate in a Mayan ritual, thereby demonstrating just how "Catholic" he hopes his constituency will be. And Pope John Paul II invited practitioners of Voudoo and various primitive religions to the annual interfaith summit and prayer-meeting at Assisi. Not every primitive religion is spiritually subversive, but since these traditions have had a long time to degenerate, the job of separating the sacred from the corrupt in them is complex and uncertain. As for Voudoo, it embraces certain subtle cosmological conceptions, which might class it as a form of deviated esoterism; and though the Yoruba influence is central to it, it shows signs of having sprung from an ancient African syncretism, perhaps further elaborated during the period of Black slavery in the New World. Voudoo is not all black magic, but it obviously includes elements of such magic, such as the laying of curses. And certain branches of Voudoo—the Pethro rites, for example—are entirely Satanic. Furthermore, the practice at Assisi of praying with the believers of this or that non-Christian religion—false or not, degenerate or not, Satanic or not—is immensely destructive, even (or especially!) in the case of a mixture of Christian forms with those of another valid and God-given religion. Such a practice constitutes a sacrilegious violation of both traditions; since it falls into the darkness between two distinct rays of Divine light, it acts as a sort of demonic invocation. (Pope Benedict has apparently reversed his predecessor's policy by coming out against Voudoo and witchcraft; instead, he invited prominent atheist philosopher A.C. Grayling to the 2011 Assisi Summit; the atheist declined.)

The Church's call for a One-World Government, for *unity* at any cost, becomes even more explicit in "Towards Reforming the International Financial and Monetary Systems in the Context of Global Public Authority", a paper produced by the Pontifical Council for Justice and Peace, October of 2011. Here are some excerpts:

> [One] can see an emerging requirement for a body that will carry out the functions of a kind of "central world bank" that regulates the flow and system of monetary exchanges similar to the national central banks . . . [the stages in the creation of this bank] ought to be conceived of as some of the first steps in view of a *public Authority with universal jurisdiction*. . . . In a world on its way to rapid globalization, the reference to a world Authority becomes the only horizon compatible with the new realities of our time and the needs of humankind. However, it should not be forgotten that this development, given wounded human nature, *will not come about without anguish and suffering*.Through the account of the Tower of Babel (Gen. 11:1–9), the Bible warns us how the "diversity" of peoples can turn into a vehicle for selfishness and an instrument of division. . . . The image of the Tower of Babel also warns us that we must avoid a "unity" that is only apparent, where selfishness and divisions endure. . . .

A universal world authority brought about through anguish and suffering, where diversity is in effect outlawed—a true *imposed* unification—is what the Novus Ordo Catholic Church is openly calling for. Here the Tower of Babel is used as an image of the evils of diversity, symbolized by "the confusion of tongues". What these so-called Catholics conveniently forget is that the confusion of tongues was ordained by God Himself. He prevented the completion of the Tower not to end a true, organic unity but to terminate a false, Promethean unification. So the Novus Ordo Church reveals where it stands: with Nimrod the great architect, not with God. And this is what God, in the eleventh chapter of Genesis, says about "global unification":

> And the Lord said, "Behold, the people is *one*, and they have all one language, and *this* is what they do? [i.e., build a city and a

> tower whose top would reach to heaven] And now nothing will be restrained from them, which they have imagined to do. Go to, let us go down, and there confound their language, that they may not understand one another's speech." So the Lord scattered them abroad from thence upon the face of all the earth.

Here we can see how the Pontifical Council has produced a complete inversion of the clear meaning of scripture; when rebellion against God reaches a certain point it has to declare itself openly. And the Novus Ordo Church is certainly not alone in this rebellion. Suffice it to say that the powers that be are now moving to subvert and control *every* religion or spiritual organization that they feel has significant influence in the world, or might be useful to them in other ways.[4]

Some investigators claim that the financial/political elites who constitute today's globalists have been a subversive force for aeons. John Coleman, in *The Conspirator's Hierarchy: The Committee of 300*—based partly on his researches at the British Museum, to which he claims to have had special access as a member of British Intelligence—traces the ancestry and ideology of the Venetian Black Nobility back to the heretical Cathars and Bogomils, and ultimately to Babylonian Manichaeism. (Likewise Henry Makow quotes a supposed "Illuminati defector" as maintaining that the Illuminati began at the Tower of Babel, which is at least mythically correct.) The Black Nobility were descended from the Black Guelphs of Dante's time, an oligarchic merchant class who expanded the international banking system founded by the Templars and Hospitalers and supported the Pope as a temporal ruler against the Holy Roman Empire backed by the Ghibellines; this Nobility contributed to many of the royal bloodlines of Europe, including the House of Windsor. Langue d'Oc, the Cathar stronghold in Southern France, was the site of an early "Renaissance before the Renaissance" where the rising mercantile bourgeoisie rivaled the feudal system; many merchants from this

4. The transformation of the Catholic Church into a Counter-Initiatory world power is predicted by Dostoevsky in his famous chapter "The Grand Inquisitor" from *The Brothers Karamazov*.

region fled to Italy during the Albigensian Crusade (1209-1229), becoming connected to the Black Guelphs. (As for the Templar connection to Langue d'Oc, according to Piers Paul Read in his book *The Templars*, Eleanor of Aquitaine exempted the Knights Templar from paying harbor dues at the port of La Rochelle, which suggests that they shared certain financial interests.) In any case, whether or not John Coleman's and Henry Makow's "conspiracy theories" can in all cases be independently corroborated, I believe that Coleman, Makow, Alan Watt and others are definitely on to something when they claim that a globalist "shadow government" composed of dynastic oligarchs wielding clandestine financial power does in fact exist, a hidden "aristocracy" who sometimes espouse an essentially Luciferian ideology and are involved in massive acts of propaganda and social engineering to further their aims; certainly the notion that the world is controlled more by financial interests than by national governments has gone "mainstream" in Europe and the United States in the 21st century, particularly in view of the global debt crisis. Ferdinand Lundberg in *The Rich and the Super-Rich*—minus the "paranoid" style—named and analyzed this oligarchy in 1968, at least on the national level (thus more-or-less updating *The Power Elite* by C. Wright Mills, 1956), and since then researchers like Peter Levenda have done much to document the involvement of the elites and intelligence services in various aspects of the "occult". Furthermore, in tracing the "Counter-Initiatory" lineage back to Manichaeism, Coleman is essentially in line with the Bible and the Qur'an, in both of which Babylon (as well as Egypt) appears as a heartland of false spirituality and oppressive imperial power. (Both civilizations arose from profound spiritual conceptions amounting to revelations, but by the time Abraham migrated from Ur and Moses and his people fled Egypt, the spiritual peaks of these civilizations had passed, which is why God had begun to prepare the new dispensations that were destined to supersede them.) As the Old Testament speaks of the Babylonian Tower whose construction was terminated by God, so the Book of Revelations pictures a future global society based on spiritual evil named "Babylon the Great", which is also destined to be destroyed by Divine action; Revelations 18 in particular can be taken as a mythopoetic portrayal of a global mercantile empire that maintains its position partly through propaganda and social engineering, since one of the types of merchandise it trades in is *souls of men*. In addition, the Qur'an mentions the fallen angels Harut and Marut (as testers by God's will, not deceivers in their own right) who taught magic to the human race in Babylon; these figures might well symbolize the Manichaean dualism, the false absolutization of the *dvandvas*, the pairs-of-opposites, which was the essential content of the Serpent's lie in Genesis: that to know "good and evil", not the Sovereign Good into which no evil can come, is to "be like God". (Though Manichaeanism grew out of Zoroastrianism, the earliest Zoroastrianism we know of, based on the *Gathas*, was unitarian rather than dualistic; the Zoroastrian tradition became dualistic only in its later degeneration.)

In conclusion, I offer this book not as an exhaustively-researched analysis of the Counter-Initiation and its relationship to globalism, but only as a catalogue of symptoms, marks or signposts by which its presence and action can be discerned. We may never be able to neutralize or even seriously limit the Counter-Initiation as a clandestine movement of inverted spiritual imperialism, but at least we can avoid it as a *temptation*, and—with God's help—purify ourselves of whatever influences emanating from it might have touched our lives, poisoned our souls, and darkened our minds.[5]

5. I need to make it clear at this point that when I characterize a spiritual group as "Counter-Initiatory" I don't mean that they are criminals and should be treated as such by that fact alone; I mean that their activities and worldview are destructive to true religion and valid initiatory spirituality—but in a democratic society they have, and should have, the legal "right" to be destructive in that sense. The religions must protect themselves from false spiritualities by theological and theurgic means, not legal ones, unless directly attacked; if civil society did not guarantee freedom of religion, then *all* religion, orthodox and heterodox alike, would suffer. The level on which we must preserve religious freedom is very different from the level where we must distinguish between orthodox and heterodox doctrine. Orthodox religions have a right to preserve their doctrines and traditions and point out deviations, but in a democratic society they should have no legal right to enforce adherence to orthodoxy or the rejection of heresy, any more than society should have the right to curtail their activities unless they violate the kind of criminal law that is applicable to society as a whole.

2

Vigilance in the Interfaith Arena

I: The Interfaith Movement as a Social Control System

IN THIS CHAPTER I will do my best to demonstrate that the Interfaith Movement, while capable of doing real good in bringing greater peace and understanding between the religions, is also fraught with dangers, especially for those committed to one of the traditional wisdom paths or world religions. When traditional believers enter the Interfaith arena, they may find themselves required, at least by default, to except the legitimacy of the New Age, Theosophy, occultism, witchcraft and/or Neo-Paganism, many of whose members make no secret of their hatred of Christianity and/or Islam. Neo-Pagans certainly have no love for the Prophet Muhammad, peace and blessings be upon him, who destroyed Pagan worship in Arabia, and they often represent Paganism as the secret or esoteric core of Christianity, thus denying the validity of the Christian revelation. And Annie Besant of the Theosophical Society (a Fabian Socialist) openly declared that it was the goal of her organization to "chase God from the skies". A live-and-let-live attitude toward such "spiritualities" is usually the best course in our pluralistic society; mutual recrimination serves no useful purpose, though the traditional religions certainly have both the right and the duty to defend themselves when attacked. But if traditional believers allow themselves to be drawn into making common cause with groups that, all surface courtesies aside, are inherently inimical to them, then they will end either by compromising themselves, or by being forced to come into conflict with those groups simply to restore their own integrity—a conflict that would never have been necessary if both sides had simply maintained proper discretion and kept to their own sides of the fence.

But there is a greater danger which those entering the Interfaith arena may be exposed to—the danger of social control. In an e-mail to me, Prof. Rodney Blackhirst of LaTrobe University in Bendigo, Australia, [author of *Primordial Alchemy*, Sophia Perennis, 2008], put his finger on the problem of the use of the Interfaith Movement to extend control over the world's religions by placing them under secular authority:

> I am... concerned about secularizing "inter-faith" movements. I might have told you that here in Bendigo I was invited onto an inter-faith council, supported by the local government. But then I found they wanted to start a series of "inter-faith services"—prayer services that cater to everyone at once. I objected to this but was told that government funding had such strings attached. The government, that is, has a policy of discouraging the various religions from conducting "exclusive" religious services. I can foresee a time when it will be illegal (under anti-discrimination laws) for Muslims to conduct a prayer service that doesn't cater to Christians or Buddhists. That is where we are heading.

And of course exclusive services for Christians or Buddhists or anyone else would be prohibited as well under such rules, or at least serious curtailed. Lee Penn, for one, has documented, in *False Dawn: The United Religions Initiative, Globalism and the Quest for a One-World Religion* [Sophia Perennis, 2005], the stated desire of certain figures in the Interfaith Movement to prohibit religious proselytization as representing a kind of religions "imperialism" in the doctrinal sphere [see below]. In any case, Prof. Blackhirst's experience is evidence of an intent on the part of some governments and globalist power elites to homogenize the religions so as to destroy their autonomy. [NOTE: I refer anyone wishing to further research the globalist agenda to co-opt and control the traditional faiths both to *False Dawn*, available at on the web at *www.falsedawn.us*, and to "The Religious Face of the New World Order: From the Vatican to the White House to the United Religions Initiative", Lee Penn's detailed analysis of Benedict XVI's *Caritas in Veritate*, where the pope openly calls for a One World Government: *http://www.usasurvival.org/docs/Global_Religion.pdf*].

My own personal experience with the Interfaith Movement as sponsored by the rich and powerful involves the Rumi Forum based in Washington, D.C., on whose website statements by and "photo op" images of ambassadors and State Department heads routinely appear. The Rumi Forum is a branch of the movement headed by Turkish Muslim Fethullah Gülen. [For a fuller account of my encounter with this organization, see Chapter Seven, "The Real Rumi".]

The co-optation of the Interfaith Movement by the globalist elites is in effect both an anti-Islamic insurgency that is hard to see, and a temptation to self-betrayal that is hard to resist. Sufis who have been marginalized vis-à-vis Islam as a whole, and who live in fear of the Islamicist militants—consciously in the Middle East, often unconsciously in the West—and who also worry about being put in the same class as those militants by Western governments, and consequently subjected at least to surveillance and at worse to persecution in the West as they have been in the East—are easily influenced by the blandishments of powerful national or globalist patrons, whose line often goes something like this: "We have been watching you closely and we fully support your message of tolerance, spirituality and high ideals; that's why we want to do all we can to help you in your work. We are pleased to invite you to our interfaith conferences, to introduce you to wealthy and influential patrons willing help you in your efforts, to put you in touch with groups eager to ally with you, to put in a good word for you with funding sources happy to support your wonderful mission in the most substantive terms. Neither you nor we want to see the power of the Islamicists, our common enemy, expand any further— right? That's why we are sure that you will be as happy to accept our support as we are happy to provide it. (And if we see that you are *not* in fact willing to accept that support, what can we conclude? Perhaps you are not as opposed to the Islamicists as we first assumed; if this turns out to be the case, we will have to revise our understanding of you and take the appropriate steps.)" What Sufi leader, no matter how solid his spiritual integrity, could count himself totally immune from the influence this kind of explicit-carrot-implicit-stick approach, or completely aware of all the hidden agendas that might lie behind it?

II: The Structure of Interfaith: Some Fundamental Theses

In order to exercise the necessary vigilance when approaching the Interfaith arena, especially when involving oneself with initiatives which are extra-national or global in scope, three basic theses should be taken into account:

(1) *The global elites are committed to moving the world toward one or another form or degree of "global governance".* This thesis is easy to accept since it more-or-less goes without saying. In the face of the general trend toward globalization, firstly I would caution those approaching the Interfaith world against an uncritical acceptance of the idea of *unity,* a word that is often employed as a rallying-cry, if not a kind of fetish, but is not always clearly defined. When encountering this concept in the Interfaith realm, one should ask two basic questions: 1) "Exactly what does the word 'unity' mean in the present context? Mutual respect and discretion? Mutual action toward common goals? Doctrinal unity? Political unity? All or none of the above?", and 2) "Would the achievement of this or that particular sort of unity really be a good thing? If so, why? If not, why not?" Global unity is often unthinkingly presented as if synonymous with global peace and justice. Global imperialism and hegemony, however, represent a very different form of "unity" from that envisioned by the interfaith idealists, just as "pacification" is poles apart from real peace. Secondly, we must also avoid, like the plague, the often half-conscious idea that "if it is inevitable then it must be accepted; we may or may not like globalization, but this is essentially irrelevant; given that it is already here, we must make the best of it and do what we can to mitigate its evils". And although some may actually be called (not simply *tempted*) to this kind of effort, we too often use a similar argument when it comes to dealing with our own passions:

"I may not like sin, but since it is inevitable I guess I'll have to make the best of it". A pointed quote from Frithjof Schuon is relevant at this point: "There is no possible alliance between the principle of good and organized sin; what we mean is that the powers of the world, which are necessarily sinful powers, organize sin with a view to abolishing the effects of sin". [*Esoterism as Principle and as Way*, Perennial Books edition, p.161]

2) *The Interfaith Movement represents an important element in the push for global governance as envisioned by the elites, or at least by many influential individuals and institutions among them.* This thesis can be demonstrated by examining the *curriculum vitae* of one Eboo Patel, chosen almost at random out of many possible examples; the following passage is taken from Lee Penn's "The Religious Face of the New World Order: From the Vatican to the White House to the United Religions Initiative", p.69: "Eboo Patel was one of 25 people selected in March 2009 for one-year terms on the President's Advisory Council on Faith-Based and Neighborhood Partnerships. Patel is founder and executive director of the Interfaith Youth Core (IFYC), which is an ally of the United Religions Initiative. Patel holds a doctorate in the sociology of religion from Oxford University, where he studied as a Rhodes Scholar. He serves on the Religious Advisory Committee of the Council on Foreign Relations, and was recently selected to join the Young Global Leaders network of the World Economic Forum. In April 2009, Patel's IFYC worked jointly with Tony Blair's Faith Foundation to select 12 young adults to lead interfaith efforts to achieve the UN's Millennium Development Goals. It would be difficult for anyone to improve upon this ... convergence of globalist, elite credentials and connections...." This sort of networking of organizations highly influential on a global scale provides much of the context in which today's Interfaith Movement must operate.

3) *Through the Interfaith Movement and other venues, the global elites support ever-increasing secular control of the world religions; some elements at least loosely associated with these elites are concurrently doing "research and development" with a view to establishing a single, unified One World Religion.* In order to evidence the truth of the first part of this thesis, one need only ask: Are the majority of

those dedicated to "global governance" people of deep religious faith? Are they essentially traditional in their outlook? Some, certainly, are people of faith, but many are essentially secularists—and if this is the case, then why are they so interested in religion? Why do they so vigorously patronize and fund the Interfaith Movement? The obvious answer is: to further their own ends. And what are these ends? Have they anything to do with the salvation of souls, or with the deepening of metaphysical understanding on the part of those open to it, for the purpose of gaining final Liberation from the world of becoming? Obviously not. By and large the global elites see religion not as a doorway to the Transcendent, a path to God established by God, on His own initiative, by which we may return to Him, but as a socio-political control system or ensemble of such systems. They hope to influence the world religions as a way of extending their own influence over the various "sectors" these religions represent. In order to further this agenda they most often appeal—for obvious reasons—to religious "idealism" rather than to the separatist "tribal" identities that the religions also foster; they seek the "universalist" common denominator among the religions as a way of preventing interreligious violence and stabilizing the emerging global order. And this apparently benign agenda has put the minds of many religious leaders, even highly traditional if not "Traditionalist" ones, at ease regarding the Interfaith Movement as a whole. But what price "stability"? Patronage is inseparable from control, and to the degree that the religions accept patronage from essentially secular forces, and dialogue on ground provided and defined by these forces—on their "premises" in both the spacial and the logical senses of that word—they are abdicating their own jurisdictional, and in some cases even doctrinal, independence. For example, any Islamic nation that wishes to enter the European Union must accept homosexuality as a socially legitimate lifestyle, thus abrogating those parts of the *shari'ah* based on Q. 29:28–29.[1]

1. There is a great difference between gay-baiting, which is cruel and socially destructive—and under which I include job and health insurance discrimination—and opposition to gay "marriage", which is itself a violation of the natural rights of heterosexuals. Marriage is an image of God's spiritual union with the human soul

As for the second part of the thesis, that some elements within or allied to the global elites are consciously trying to develop a One World Religion, such proposals mostly emanate, at least in the public sphere, from New Age organizations either patronized by or seeking patronage from these elites. Other groups, less radically syncretistic but probably even more influential, seek not so much to blend the world's religions into one as to federate them under a single secular authority. The United Religions Initiative, for one, was launched in order to found a United Religions Organization somewhat on the model of the U.N., though at this writing it appears to be more of a global network, though of extremely wide scope, than a centralized organization. But the line between this kind of networking and an actual move toward religious amalgamation not always clear. In 2000, when an interviewer asked New Age guru Neale Donald Walsch to "name a few enterprises in the world you believe are working toward goals", which are similar to yours he replied: "Well, there is the United Religions Initiative out of San Francisco, undertaken by Bishop William Swing, the Episcopal Archbishop of California. He has had a vision of a one-world religion—not a single religion, but a united religions organization to which delegates from

or with His creation, which renews the life of that soul or that creation, just as heterosexual reproduction renews the life of the race; as such, heterosexual unions have always been considered to have a sacred dimension, in every society we know of. When gay relationships are defined as marriages, the sacred dimension of heterosexuality is called into question, with devastating results for any society which attempts it. In traditional Christianity, marriage is a sacrament; the Prophet Muhammad, peace and blessings be upon him, said "marriage is half the religion". And if homosexuals begin to call for equal "reproductive rights" with heterosexuals, this will only further the degradation of the human being to the level of an industrial product. Furthermore, the fact that homosexuality is prohibited in the Abrahamic religions—as it is among the higher castes in Hinduism—makes the more excessive demands of gay "rights" advocates of great use to the secular globalists in their campaign to undermine the authority of religious institutions and traditions. "Don't ask don't tell" is actually a rather civilized approach to the issue; it emphasizes the virtue of discretion and reminds us that morality has much more to do with the examination of our own consciences before God than with judging others. The alternative to "don't ask don't tell" is for society to be *required* to ask and homosexuals *required* to tell; can this really be called "liberation"? A society without privacy is a society without freedom.

all the world's religions would come, much as they do to the United Nations" [*False Dawn*, p.135]. Walsch's spirit guide, who claims to be Jesus, commented further: "The discussions at these important gatherings will not focus on eliminating the differences between religions, for it will be recognized that diversity of spiritual expression is a *blessing*, not a problem. Rather, the focus will be on finding ways to honor those differences, seeing what they can further reveal to humanity about the Totality of God, and looking to see whether the *combination of all these different views* might produce a Whole that is Greater than the Sum of Its Parts" [ibid., p.136]. How respect for "diversity of spiritual expression", which must also respect the boundaries between the faiths, is compatible with "the combination, and Sum, of all these views" is not immediately apparent. (Walsch also spoke highly of Hitler as someone who did the Jews a favor by killing them; see *False Dawn*, p.330.)

Furthermore, as Lee Penn has shown, the United Religions Initiative harbors certain attitudes inimical to autonomy on the part of the world religions. "Many leaders of the URI, including Bishop Swing himself, habitually equate evangelism—preaching the Gospel—with conquest and manipulative proselytism. If these leaders have their way, the open proclamation of traditional Christian belief will be increasingly stigmatized as 'hate speech'; legal repression could follow" [ibid., p.176]. "At a public April 1997 URI forum at Grace Cathedral, Sri Ravi Peruman (who was on the URI board from 1997 through 2002) said that religions have 'invaded and crusaded', 'subverted and converted'. *Pacific Church News* reported: 'Calling statements about "authentic religious freedom" for everyone "the freedom to proselytize", Peruman said that there should be a universal *Declaration of Rights* not to be converted to another religion'" [ibid., p.180]. (In response to this statement, which Lee Penn alerted me to, I wrote a short manifesto declaring the right of every religion to proselytize as long as manipulative and coercive methods were not used. Prof. Huston Smith signed it, but withdrew his signature after a phone conversation with Bishop Swing.) Nor is the United Religions Initiative the only forum where "proselytization" is a bad word. At the World Millennium Peace Summit in the year 2000, sponsored by Ted Turner and the Ford Foundation among others, a Buddhist teacher who condemned all attempts at religious conversion received a standing ovation [see *False Dawn*, p. 52]—as if the Dalai Lama, for example, never does anything to propagate Buddhism!

However, we need not always characterize the agendas of the secularist sponsors of the Interfaith Movement as "cynical" or "conspiratorial" in order to understand the inherent drawbacks of their approach. Secularists, in sincerely pursuing their own ideal of the common good, will inevitably come into opposition at one point with the idea of the good held by the traditional religions, since the secularist sees his good only in terms of this world, while the religious believer sees his in terms of both this world and the next, with the next world taking precedence—as well as in terms of a Divine Reality that pervades, and transcends, both worlds. Such faith-based perspectives leave the highest secular idealism far behind—even if it clothes itself in "spiritual" garb, as New Age idealism always has insofar as it hopes to "tap spiritual energy" to further its *own* agenda (not God's) for global unity and/or environmental regeneration. The perspectives of the traditional religions can only be damaged or obscured by any attempt to place them within a worldly context that is simply too narrow to contain them.

But we must also entertain the possibility that the dangers of the Interfaith Movement go beyond those created by well-meaning but narrow-minded idealists. In *The Reign of Quantity and the Signs of the Times*, René Guénon spoke of the various stages of "anti-Traditional action". The first is "Anti-Tradition" per se, the general materialist or secular tendency to debunk religion. The second is "Pseudo-Initiation", the development of various illegitimate groups and doctrines invented by well-meaning but deluded pseudo-esoterics. The third is "Counter-Tradition" or "Counter-Initiation", the conscious and deliberate perversion of esoterism, and consequently of all true religion, by subversive groups and individuals in direct contact with the Powers of Darkness. Let us see what the Interfaith Movement might look like according to these three categories.

Anti-Tradition, in terms of the patronage of the Interfaith Movement by secularist individuals or institutions, has already been dealt with above. But what about Pseudo-Initiation? There is no question that pseudo-initiatic organizations play a large role in the world of the elites. I will never forget the day in the early 1990's when I was invited to a hillside palace in Hillsboro, California, where the CEOs of the big Silicon Valley computer corporations, Hewlett-Packard and others, were pow-wowing with their psychics, mediums and New Age gurus, in the belief that they were forging the new Universal Paradigm. That experience taught me just how "counterculture" certain elements of the ruling elite can actually be. (And lest it be thought that such antics are limited to places like California, a Sufi of my acquaintance who lives in Austria tells me that things look quite similar today from his perspective.) Such figures as Barbara Marx Hubbard and Robert Muller, firm supporters of the United Religions Initiative, are equally at home in the world of alternative "spiritualities" and that of the global elites, and both are deeply influenced by the Theosophical movement founded in 1875 by Mme. Blavatsky, which René Guénon exposed as "pseudo-initiatory" in his book *Theosophy, the History of a Pseudo Religion* [Sophia Perennis, 2003]. The Theosophists, many of whom support the United Religions Initiative, have been associated with the Interfaith Movement at least since 1893, when they were prominently represented at the famous World's Parliament of Religions in Chicago. According to Marcus Braybrooke, historian of the Interfaith Movement, "Theosophists can claim to have been amongst the first to suggest a unity of religions."

Barbara Marx Hubbard, a New Age teacher and futurist who channels "the Christ voice", was "one of the directors of the World Future Society along with Robert McNamara (formerly the U.S. Secretary of Defense and president of the World Bank), Maurice Strong (who was secretary general of the UN Conference on Environment and Development), and scholars from Georgetown University, George Washington University, and the University of Maryland" [*False Dawn*, p.326]; she remains a member of their advisory board. Robert Muller, who passed away in 2010, was a former Assistant Secretary-General of the UN, whose World Core Curriculum earned a UNESCO prize in 1989. He later served as Chancellor of the UN University for Peace in Costa Rica. Muller was associated with two different branches of the Theosophical movement. The first is SHARE International, founded by Theosophical spin-off Benjamin Creme, a group that believes that "Maitreya" the "World Teacher" is about to return—and has in fact recently announced that return in the person of Raj Patel, an academic who has been a visiting professor at Yale and the University of California at Berkeley, late of the World Monetary Fund and the World Bank, though he now describes himself as an "anarchist". Muller's other Theosophical connection was the Lucis Trust (which grew out of the Lucifer Publishing Company), founded on the teachings of Alice Bailey—the same Alice Bailey who once spoke highly of Adolph Hitler as a person "who lifted a distressed people upon his shoulders" [ibid., pp. 275 and 300].

As for the true Counter-Initiation—esoteric spirituality consciously counterfeited (insofar as those conversant with psychic realities but ignorant of spiritual ones may be termed "conscious") by those dedicated to destroying true esoterism (and true religion along with it, esoterism being religion's spiritual heart)—its existence and activities are very hard to document, since if the Counter-Initiation did indeed exist (and I believe it does) it would be effectively Satanic, and real Satanists (not "stage Satanists" like Anton LaVey) are necessarily quite secretive about their activities. René Guénon—who characterized even the Pseudo-Initiation as "unconscious Satanism"—accepted the existence of what he called the Counter-Initiation, based in part on his extensive personal experience with the world of the occult in the first half of the 20th century. In *The Reign of Quantity*, p. 262, he says:

> [The] "counter-initiation"... cannot be regarded as a purely human invention, such as would in no way be distinguishable... from plain "pseudo-initiation"; in fact it is much more than that, and, in order that it may really be so, it must in a certain sense, so far as its actual origin is concerned, proceed from the unique source to which all initiation is attached, the very source from which... everything in our world that manifests a "non-human" element proceeds; but the "counter-initiation" proceeds from that source by a degeneration carried to its extreme limit, and that limit is represented by the "inversion" that constitutes "satanism" properly so called.

The Counter-Initiation would likely constitute a small but possibly very influential spectrum of cabals within the global elites—perhaps related to or identifiable with those that some call the "Illuminati"—and unless we axiomatically disallow that true Satanism could exist, despite the many groups who identify themselves as Satanists, then a moment's reflection will immediately inform us that a conscious Satanist would like nothing better than to place him- or herself in a position of global influence. Whether we think it likely that actual Satanists could rise to such positions of worldly power (leaving aside the quite suggestive example of Adolf Hitler), or see such a possibility as unlikely in the extreme, will depend largely upon whether we view Satanists exclusively as mentally disordered individuals occupying the world of "heavy metal bands" and fringe cults, or as also including within their number persons who are highly competent and motivated in worldly terms. Fr. Malachi Martin, for one, claimed that the "Luciferians" he encountered as an exorcist in New York City were almost always members of the professional, financial or political elites. Anyone who sees This World as an organized expression of the Good, who believes that the social, political and financial powers that be exist primarily for altruistic purpose, and that ruthless individual and corporate ambition is not a dominant factor in national and global dynamics, will find it hard to take seriously the existence of something like a Counter-Initiation. Any *realist*, however, who knows that no power elite is eager to make the general public privy to its goals and activities, and who is also cognizant of the role that religious forces, legitimate or otherwise, have played in human history, will be compelled to accept at least the possibility that Counter-Initiatory organizations and agendas might actually exist. And if this realist also believes in God and the supernatural order, as any *true* realist must, then the idea that Shaytan has his agents operating in this world, just as God has, will in no way be foreign to him; rather, it will be a foregone conclusion. Someone would not need to be an avowed Satanist or Luciferian to fill such a role; publicly visible or self-identified Luciferians are likely to be much less dangerous than members of the power elite who see power as the highest value and define all reality in terms of it, thus turning this valuation into something like

an inverted metaphysical principle. The following words are attributed to Henry Kissinger, speaking at the Bilderberger Conference in Evians, France in 1991; they were allegedly transcribed from a tape recording made by one of the Swiss delegates:

> Today, America would be outraged if U.N. troops entered Los Angeles to restore order. Tomorrow they will be grateful! This is especially true if they were told that there were an outside threat from beyond, whether real or promulgated, that threatened our very existence. It is then that all peoples of the world will plead to deliver them from this evil. The one thing every man fears is the unknown. When presented with this scenario, individual rights will be willingly relinquished for the guarantee of their well-being granted to them by the World Government.

This statement, assuming it is accurately attributed, is certainly sinister enough. General Douglas MacArthur, however, was closer to a true Luciferian worldview when, in his VJ Day broadcast from the U.S.S. Missouri, Tokyo Bay, September 2, 1945, he declaimed, "If we cannot devise some more equitable system, our Armageddon will be at our door. The problem basically is theological and involves a spiritual recrudescence, an improvement of human character that will synchronize with our most matchless advances in science, art, literature and all the material and cultural developments of the past two thousand years"—and when, 17 years later, in his farewell address at West Point, on May 12, 1962, he said, "the primary target in war [is] no longer limited to the armed forces of an enemy, but [is] instead *to include his civil populations*," and alluded to "the ultimate conflict between a *united human race* and *the sinister forces of some other planetary galaxy*. . . ."

The notion of a "spiritual recrudescence" that will produce "a united human race" is opposed to the fundamental doctrines and eschatologies of all the major religions, including Christianity, Islam, Judaism, Hinduism and Buddhism; and the idea that the imposition of a One World Government so as to solve global problems will require a religious revolution—and that the next war will be, in effect, a "war in heaven" [cf. Rev. 12:17]—is Luciferian precisely. Nor is MacArthur alone in seeing some form of religion as the necessary basis and justification for global solutions to global problems, even if these solutions are draconian in nature. In the words of depopulationist Paul Ehrlich, "We must have population control at home, hopefully through a system of incentives and penalties, but *by compulsion* if voluntary methods fail.... We can no longer afford to treat the symptoms of the cancer of population growth; the cancer itself must be cut out.... The operation will demand many apparently brutal and heartless decisions.... Since the roots of our trouble are so largely religious, the remedy must also be essentially religious" [*The Population Bomb*, 1968, pp. xi, 166–167, 171–172].

It is my belief that the global elites embrace elements that are not simply secular or Anti-Traditional, but truly Counter-Traditional and Counter-Initiatory, elements seeking employ "the truths of the ages", along with any false spiritual innovations that may also suit their purpose, to further their essentially worldly aims. Some within the global elites, for example, have adopted various New Age doctrines and practices since these are "easily transportable" and not tied to the "backward" traditional cultures they often see as a break on progress and an impediment to full globalization. As the New Age loses force as a popular movement, certain of its ideas are being taken up by various elements within the elites as fodder for a "meta-paradigm" which they hope will be of help to them in creating their One World Religion. (William Quinn's *The Only Tradition* throws some light on these plans from the inside, just as Lee Penn's *False Dawn* does from the outside; it is one of Penn's great virtues as a researcher that he almost never attributes agendas to the groups and movements he investigates that they themselves do not openly assert.)

New Age ideas, however, being more Pseudo-Initiatory than Counter-Initiatory, are most likely held by the lower eschelons of the elites, or rather by those professional classes who like to believe that they are part of the elites because they identify with them and accept flattery from them; the higher eschelons, who are either secularist or overtly Luciferian and Counter-Initiatory, are probably interested in New Age ideas only as a way of controlling their pawns and/or screening their activities. An inverted "esoterism" for the elites, a popular New Ageism and/or Neo-Paganism for the masses, with the world religions neutralized and put firmly in their place partly with the often unwitting aid of an increasingly powerful and well-funded Interfaith Movement falsely presented as "the only alternative" to tribalist religious terrorism—this, as I see it, is a dominant strand in the religious agenda of the globalists.

I hasten to add that just as all well-meaning secularist/idealists are not really secret members of Pseudo-initiatic organizations, so we should be careful not to identify all sincere but deluded Pseudo-initiates, such as the members of the Theosophical or Anthroposophical Societies or the Freemasons, as conscious agents of the Counter-Initiation; they are not necessarily agents, but they might in some cases be pawns. If Counter-initiatory agents do in fact operate through such organizations, it is likely that they make up only a small percentage of those organizations' membership, and that their actual role is unknown to the rank and file. This, at least, was Guénon's belief.

A contemporary example of the dangers of the Interfaith Movement is reflected in the "A Common Word between Us and You" initiative, whose stated goals I heartily support. This initiative, headed by His Highness Prince Ghazi bin Muhammad al-Talal of Jordan—based on a document drawn up in response to certain problematic statements made by Pope Benedict XVI at the Regensburg Conference in 2006 and signed by prominent Muslim authorities from around the world—is the best imaginable presentation of an Islam, based on orthodox Qur'anic norms, that is both entirely traditional and entirely open to and accepting of the other revealed faiths. However, this admirable effort is compromised from the outset by a naive and/or fully conscious and deliberate alliance with secularist/globalist forces. The Common Word website is copyrighted under the name of Prince Ghazi; another Jordanian prince, His Royal Highness Prince El Hassan Bin Talal, the uncle of King Abdullah, is a co-chair of Mikhail Gorbachev's State of the World Forum, a major player among elite globalist organizations and a firm supporter of the United Religions Initiative. (Gorbachev is an avowed atheist who claims to worship the earth.) He was also president of the Club of Rome between 1999 and 2007, and is associated (as is Ghazi Bin

Talal) with the World Future Council, Gold Mercury International (a think-tank dedicated to "global governance"), and the International Board of the Council on Foreign Relations. These Arab princes do not necessarily harbor any evil intent, nor is it strictly impossible, given their status and connections, that they might be able to do some good. However—also in light of that status and those connections—we certainly cannot assume that A Common Word is an entirely independent effort initiated by traditional Muslims who simply want to live in peace with the Christian world.

As of this writing, the latest development in the widespread trend of interfaith dialogue sponsored by the powers that be is The King Abdullah Center for Interreligious and Intercultural Dialogue. Funded mostly by Saudi Arabia, it grew in part out of a meeting between Saudi King Abdullah and Pope Benedict XVI. It will be based in Vienna, consist of a council of Christians, Muslims, Jews, Hindus and Buddhists, and be dedicated to "bringing the religions together". (Weirdly enough, the meeting where the plans for the Center were finalized took place in Vienna at the Hofburg, the former Imperial residence, where the Spear of Destiny is kept.) The glaring discrepancy between this ambitious goal and the total lack of religious freedom in Saudi Arabia itself points up one of the perennial limitations of various conclaves of high-level religious leaders, politicians and academics: they have next to no influence upon actual conditions "on the ground".[2] Religious dignitaries may meet and smile at each other; religious populations, once they have come into conflict—often as a result of inflammatory pressures applied by essentially secular forces for their own ends, as in Serbia, Northern Ireland and elsewhere—will not automatically regain trust and a feeling of "brotherhood" simply because their representatives are in dialogue; the Interfaith Movement is thus under constant, unavoidable pressure to become an elitist affair, either by design or simply

2. King Abdullah of Saudi Arabia—not to be confused with the King of Jordan—may nonetheless see the Center named after him as a way of slowly introducing religious freedom into his kingdom "from the outside". Before he took the throne, he was reputed to have said that he wanted to get rid of both the Wahhabis and the Americans.

by default. Such dialogues may even have the negative effect of convincing those religious populations that their leaders are selling out their faiths by relativizing them—and this is not always an excessive or imbalanced conclusion. As Frithjof Schuon says:

> Every religion by definition wants to be the best, and "must want" to be the best, as a whole and also as regards its constitutive elements; this is only natural, so to speak, or rather "supernaturally natural"... religious oppositions cannot but be, not only because forms exclude one another ... but because, in the case of religions, each form vehicles an element of absoluteness that constitutes the justification for its existence; now the absolute does not tolerate otherness nor, with all the more reason, plurality.... To say form is to say exclusion of possibilities, whence the necessity for those excluded to become realized in other forms.... [*Christianity/Islam: Essays in Esoteric Ecumenism*, p.151]

I don't mean to imply that sincere interfaith initiatives never arise from the "grassroots"; the Christian/Muslim Dialogue in my home town is a good example of this. Local leaders rarely speak at these dialogues, however, which have largely become a venue for a constant parade of speakers from think tanks, large academic institutions, and the State Department.

Seyyed Hossein Nasr has succinctly summed up the dangers and essential barrenness of any essentially worldly interfaith activity, as follows:

> [P]eople search in these ecumenical movements for a common denominator which, in certain instances, sacrifices divinely ordained qualitative differences for the sake of a purely human and often quantitative egalitarianism. In such cases the so-called "ecumenical" forces in question are no more than a concealed form of the secularism and humanism which gripped the West at the time of the Renaissance and which in their own turn caused religious divisions within Christianity. This type of ecumenism, whose hidden motive is much more worldly than religious, goes hand in hand with the kind of charity that is

> willing to forego the love of God for the love of the neighbor and in fact insists upon the love of the neighbor in spite of a total lack of love for God and the Transcendent. The mentality which advocates this kind of "charity" affords one more example of the loss of the transcendent dimension and the reduction of all things to the purely worldly. It is yet another manifestation of the secular character of modernism which in this case has penetrated into the supreme Christian virtue of charity and, to the extent that it has been successful, has deprived this virtue of any spiritual significance.... It would be less harmful to oppose other religions, as has been done by so many religious authorities throughout history, than to be willing to destroy essential aspects of one's own religion in order to reach a common denominator with another group of men who are asked to undergo the same losses. To say the least, a league of religions could not guarantee religious peace, any more than the League of Nations guaranteed political peace [preface to *Shi'ite Islam* by 'Allamah Sayyid Muhammad Husayn Tabataba'i: SUNY, 1977; pp. 5–6].

The only reliable way to defuse interreligious conflict is for the faithful to feel that their spiritual lives are successful, that they are drawing closer to God; and this is something that cannot be produced by political action or social engineering. When a believer begins to sense, often unconsciously, that his or her religion is not delivering what it promised, one common reaction is to project this dissatisfaction on another group; they, not we, are the sinners, the infidels. And in the process religion is reduced from a relationship with the Absolute to a way of asserting "cultural identity". But anyone who truly feels God's presence and mercy will have little interest in such comparisons; the inflated currency of the world has no attraction for him; he has found the Pearl of Great Price.

III: The Specific Danger Posed by the Interfaith Movement to the Traditionalist/Perennialist School

It is an unfortunate fact that the Traditionalist/Perennialist world, despite its long history of quite perceptively criticizing worldly ecumenism, is not immune to the dangers and temptations of today's highly secularized and politicized Interfaith Movement; this temptation particularly involves the suggestion that the "plenary" or "quintessential esoterism" the Perennialists espouse not only transcends, but in some sense supersedes, what Frithjof Schuon has named the "confessional" faiths. In Islamic history it was Imam al-Ghazzali who did more than anyone else to reconcile the exoteric and esoteric poles of his faith; his job was to demonstrate to the exoteric legalists how esoteric Islam—Sufism—is intrinsically orthodox. In our own time, however, we face a different and perhaps even more serious dilemma: today, at least in certain cases, we must work to convince certain "esoterics" themselves that their understanding is actually orthodox, that it forms the inner core of their chosen revelation and that, in terms of this world, it cannot viably exist outside it.

Frithjof Schuon made a fruitful distinction between confessional esoterism, which is limited to the inner understanding and exegesis of a single religious revelation, and plenary esoterism, which pertains to the Truth per se. What is sometimes forgotten, however, is that this distinction has to do with the *expression* of spiritual truth—either before the eyes of the world or in terms of one's own merely mental understanding—rather than its full and concrete realization in dimensions beyond thought. The ultimate goal of esoterism is the direct realization of the Absolute, not the expression of metaphysical principles in this or that philosophical or mythopoetic language, whether such expression pertains to a single revelation, to several revelations simultaneously, or to the Truth itself without immediate reference to any particular revelation. If the concept of the Transcendent Unity of Religions is valid, then all true and revealed religions necessarily meet in the Transcendent, in the Absolute; consequently the esoterism of any true "confessional" faith must provide access to this Absolute—and in the realm of the

Absolute, the distinction between the realization attainable by confessional esoterism and that expressed by plenary esoterism necessarily disappears; this distinction resides not in the transcendent Truth itself but in the reverberations of that Truth on the conceptual plane. The highest realization of a fully-realized Sufi, for example, who thinks and speaks only in terms of Qur'an and hadith, and that of a "plenary esoterist" who has command of many religious languages and conceptual perspectives, are identical—necessarily so, since God is One. If each of the revealed traditions did not in itself give access to Absolute Truth, we would be justified, if not duty-bound, either to syncretize them as representing various *fragments* of the Truth, or else reject them all.

However, the identity of confessional and plenary esoterism, as we have pointed out, ceases to apply as soon as the *expression* of this realization comes into play. Realization of the Absolute makes the universal expression of metaphysical truth possible, but does not guarantee it. We cannot confidently assert, for example, that the spiritual degree of Meister Eckhart, or Dante, or Dionysius the Areopagite, or Ibn al-'Arabi, or Jalalluddin Rumi, or Nagarjuna, or Shankara was necessarily inferior to that of René Guénon or Frithjof Schuon because Eckhart, Dante and Dionysius limited themselves to the language of Christianity, Ibn al-'Arabi and Rumi to that of Islam, Nagarjuna to that of Buddhism, and Shankara to that of Hinduism. Vertical depth of realization does not guarantee horizontal plenitude of expression, nor is such horizontal plenitude always a sign of vertical depth; if we can't accept this idea we will forced to the absurd conclusion that Ibn al-'Arabi or Meister Eckhart could not have attained the highest degree of *jñana* because both were largely ignorant of Buddhism, for example, or Hinduism. If this were true we would have to admit that Intellection can be fundamentally limited by accidental factors related to politics and history, and that the widespread religious pluralism intrinsic to the modern world represents a true *evolution* in the spiritual possibilities of the human collective—a notion that is directly at odds with the traditional and Perennialist doctrine that the spiritual receptivity of that collective necessarily degenerates as the cycle-of-manifestation proceeds. The lack of horizontal plenitude *may* indicate that, in terms of the soul in question, what is known and realized in the Inner has not entirely penetrated the Outer and thereby fully alchemized the thought, the feeling, and the will of its recipient; it may also simply reflect a difference in social milieu, and consequently in the *swadharma* or particular spiritual duty and destiny of the one inhabiting and speaking to that milieu. And certainly many of those who reached the highest realization never taught openly or wrote a single word.

As Martin Lings pointed out in *The Eleventh Hour*, one of the graces of the latter days is "encyclopedic knowledge"; it is much easier now that it was even at the beginning of the 20th century to *express* (*not* realize) spiritual and/or esoteric truth in a universal manner. Unfortunately, this very facility can fool the one capable of it into believing that he or she is the equal, or even the superior, of many earlier sages; a comparison of the *texts* appears to give clear evidence that this is the case. The actual text in question here, however, is not the one written by you or me, but the one written by God, in relation to which we are neither the pen or the word, but the blank page. "To know is to be" is only true if, God willing, we have paid the price to make it true. If not, then this dictum is no more intrinsically valid than "to think is to do" or "to fantasize is to create". God, when He intends to speak, is capable of speaking through whatever mouth is available to Him, whether or not His instrument has concretely actualized the truth he or she expresses. God may pick us up, speak the very Truth through our mouths, then lay us down again untransformed and unrepentant. *As for the poets, the erring follow them. Hast thou not seen how they stray in every valley, and say that which they do not? Save those who believe, and do good works, and remember Allah much, and vindicate themselves after they have been wronged?* [Q. 26:224–227] The "knowledge" that is intrinsically one with "being" is *total* and *stable* realization, not simply the intermittent intuition of spiritual realities, even if such intuition derives from levels of knowing that transcend the rational mind.

The realm of spiritual expression, however, must not be left to the Devil; the clear and accurate expression of metaphysical truth is a sacred duty, and when it comes to such expression plenary esoterism excels, since it is able to see the doctrines of all confessional esoterisms in their metaphysical transparency, and thus as legitimate modes of the expression of esoterism per se—of a concrete Intellective realization that is totally independent of any expression of metaphysical ideas, or any lack of it; and this plenary vision is something that the intrinsically confessional esoterics, not to mention the exoterics, will *not* see. The lesser cannot beget the greater; exoterism cannot in and of itself beget confessional esoterism, nor can it give rise to plenary esoterism, either in terms of universal expression or of concrete realization. Esoterism is necessarily based on direct Intellection, though such Intellection can rarely develop outside of a traditional milieu based on a Divine revelation. But if, as Schuon said, "revelation is the intellection of the macrocosm, as intellection is the revelation of the microcosm", then plenary esoterism, confessional esoterism and exoteric religion, from one perspective, form a single whole; they cannot viably exist without each other in this world. A plenary expression of esoteric truth that contradicts the principles of the confessional esoterisms—or a confessional esoterism that contradicts the doctrines of the exoterism of the religion proper to it—cannot exist without generating and spreading error. It is crucial that we clearly understand this, in view of the fact that This World is presently doing all it can to drive esoterism and exoterism apart so as to destroy both of them (in earthly manifestation, that is, not in Principle); this is one of the central methods and agendas of the Counter-Initiation. And one of the ways in which the Prince of This World is working to widen the split between the Inner and the Outer is by tempting us to identify exoterism and confessional esoterism with orthodox Tradition, while falsely seeing plenary esoterism as situated outside Tradition and superseding it, since it is necessarily based upon direct Intellection of a Reality that cannot be limited to this or that particular tradition (which confessional esoterism also is, though the confessional esoterists can't see this). Frithjof Schuon, however, though he might have flirted with this error from time to time, also taught that "To be orthodox means to participate by way of a doctrine that can properly be called 'traditional' in the immutability of the principles which govern the universe and *fashion our intelligence*" [*Logic and*

Transcendence, World Wisdom Books, p.1]; In other words, Intellection is intrinsic not just to plenary esoterism but to confessional esoterism as well because it is intrinsic to Revelation itself. The concrete metaphysical realization of which both plenary esoterism and confessional esoterism are the outward expressions is *formless*; it can neither possess a form of its own nor exist without form in this world; the only forms entirely proper to it, which alone allow it to take its place on earth in its concrete and operative fullness, are those of the orthodox faiths.

It is inevitable, however, that some who a espouse plenary esoterism they understand as transcending the formal limits of the confessional faiths will not retain a firm grasp on this truth—for how can one truly "grasp" the formless? Even the most rudimentary approach to this esoterism—the concept of the Transcendent Unity of Religions—is a difficult for many to comprehend since the unity in question is precisely transcendent, beyond human conception. Yet the very act of announcing it necessarily challenges us to understand it, at which point the human mind must swing into action, generating images and concepts which, while they may approach the truth of the Transcendent, can never equal it or exhaust it. This inescapable attempt to understand plenary esoterism with the thinking mind will inevitably generate certain errors that only a fuller and deeper *jñanic* realization has the power to dispel. One is the tendency to see plenary esoterism as superseding orthodoxy and tradition instead of subsisting as the quintessence of their confessional esoterisms (an idea that will not always be entirely conscious or explicit); the other is to consider it to be only "natural" that the doctrine of the Transcendent Unity of Religions should outwardly express itself and "take its place" in the context of the Interfaith Movement. The first error is based on a false idea of transcendence, the second on a false idea of unity.[3]

3. One way of preventing the growth of such errors is to understand *every* mental conception of Transcendent Truth as an error in the absolute or apophatic sense, though often quasi-absolutely necessary on the doctrinal level. The Sufi method of contemplating the inconceivable Divine, known as *fikr*, recognizes this limitation, but also puts it to use. In the course of this practice we negate every human conception of the Divine as it arises, until a shift takes place in which our human attempt

The first error must ultimately lead those deluded by it to seek or develop forms through which plenary esoterism may ritually express itself, forms which will necessarily be heterodox in nature. As for the second error, it is much more likely that the Interfaith Movement will falsify and pervert the Transcendent Unity of Religions than that the TUR will influence the Interfaith Movement in any positive way, given that this movement is often horizontal, anti-traditional, and suspicious of the very concept of transcendence, which it tends to see as the origin of all dangerously exclusivist religious claims—and of environmental destruction as well, since the "Green" element within the Interfaith Movement commonly misinterprets the traditional doctrine of God's transcendence as "hatred of the Earth". Unfortunately, Perennialism is now being presented to the Interfaith Movement—or perhaps it would be better to say that it is being viewed by that movement—simply as a more sophisticated sort of worldly ecumenism.[4]

If the true nature of esoterism is not rigorously understood—which includes the understanding that in essence it is a realization, not a doctrine—then it will be used as an excuse to play fast and loose with orthodox dogmatic formulations, thus undermining the traditional faiths and generating an alternate heterodox dogmatism of its own. Historically, this has been the fate of every form of eso-

---

to understand God is replaced by God's self-revelation to us; we come to realize that knowledge of God not is a product of our effort, inevitably compromised by our limitations, but of His generosity, mercifully provided to us in view of those limitations.

4. In a separate but related error, certain Muslims (Muhammed Hajji Legenhausen, for example, as well as contributors to the *Sunni Forum* blog) are beginning to see Perennialism as a philosophical or theological school within Islam, a school they consider heretical. This is due in part to the fact that most of the Christian Perennialists among Schuon's followers, particularly Rama Coomaraswamy and Alvin Moore Jr., have passed on, after which it has fallen primarily to the Muslim Perennialists to define Perennialism and speak for it to the world. And to the degree that they denature it by a sometimes unconscious tendency to claim it for Islam alone, they actually are transforming it into something like a heresy that can only provoke a legitimate, if short-sighted, reaction on the part of those who wish to preserve the Islamic tradition. The Qur'an certainly admits the validity of "Torah and Gospel", but not as aspects of the specific revelation given to the Prophet Muhammad, peace and blessings be upon him.

terism that has departed from its parent religion. The difference with Perennialism is that it is, as it were, an esoterism of *all* the religions, which means that it will either be the quintessential exegesis of these religions, allowing those who understand it to live them in their esoteric depths—on a level which, in terms of realization though not in terms of doctrine, necessarily transcends those religions *vertically*, in the same sense that Allah is not limited by Islam because He is not limited by anything—or else the seed of a highly sophisticated "generic metaphysics" that will exercise a dissolving influence on the religions, and thus be of great and destructive use to the New World Order. Schuon never had a universal *appeal*, nor is he likely to attain one now that he has passed on; the valid and profound aspects of his writings are of universal *significance*, not appeal. But God help us if his ideas are ever adopted by the global elites! If so he might suffer the dark fate of being adopted, as my wife Jennifer Doane Upton puts it, as "the Thomas Aquinas of the One-World Religion", now that he is no longer around to prevent it. As we pointed out above, a spurious universal "esoterism" for the globalist intellectuals, a shapeless Neo-Paganism for the masses, with the world's religions neutralized by national and international laws defining certain of their fundamental doctrines as "hate speech", and proselytization as tantamount to the invasion by one nation of the sovereign territory of another—this, as I see it, is a major element in the globalist agenda. The ultimate goal of this agenda in the religious sphere appears to be the federation of the traditional religions under a non-religious authority, if not an actual syncretistic One-World Religion, presented as the only alternative to the claims of these religions, now increasingly defined as actual or incipient "tribalist religious extremisms". This trend must be resisted at all cost if the religions are to retain their sacred traditions and their legitimate independence, without which their God-given authority in spiritual if not social matters will quickly become a thing of the past.

The Interfaith Movement, whatever real ability it may have to serve tolerance and understanding between the religions, is inseparably wedded to activism—and activism, in our time, is a fundamentally secular pursuit; to paraphrase T. S. Eliot, "Where is the God lost in religion? Where is the religion lost in 'faith-based initiatives'?" When a religion or a spiritual path begins to lose force, the sense among its followers that they have found a true way to self-transcendence, to union with Absolute Reality, or at least that they enjoy God's protection and favor, begins to wane. It is at this point that the desire to "make a difference in the world" often becomes inflamed; if you fear that if you've lost your soul, at least you can hope that the world will not be lost as well. The irony here is that this weakening of spiritual hope inevitably coincides with the loss of any ability to make a *real* difference in the world; the limited but authentic power to raise the world to the Spirit through vision, and then act accordingly, is replaced by the fundamentally illusory impulse to harness the Spirit to action itself, in order to better fulfill certain idealistic but nonetheless worldly agendas. And to the degree that the Interfaith Movement occupies the shapeless "interzone" *between* the religions, rather than acting to deepen each believer's faith in his or her own revelation—and how could it be expected to do that?—it must partake of this sort of faithlessness. If one feels isolated in one's own religion, one will begin to define faith more in terms of human fellowship than of intimacy with God; the next step is to try and expand this "fellowship" to include members of other faiths. But this feeling of isolation has little to do with lack of human fellowship; much like our sense of "alienation from nature", it is nothing, really, but the feeling of separation from God. We project this separation on nature and society because, now that the separation has taken place, they are all we can see. But to seek union with nature and society in order to overcome alienation is to move precisely in the wrong direction; only intimacy with God can draw us together in Spirit with our fellow human beings, and let us feel at home in the universe. Until we confront our real loneliness, the "flight of the alone to the Alone" can never take place.

IV: Is Perennialism a Spiritual Path?

Perennialism, for those who are open to it, is a fruitful way of establishing a basically spiritual and traditional worldview in our time, a powerful reminder that God and the metaphysical order are real and a strong defense against secularism, materialism and the myth of progress. But in terms of any traditional spiritual Path, it does not represent even the first step. It is not in itself a viable rendition of the Path, but only, so to speak, the path to the Path. That humanity has always had some form of the true Path available to it—that the Primordial Tradition is a reality—is true; that the religions really do meet in a Transcendent Unity—that all God-given religions do indeed provide differing but equally valid perspectives on, and ways of spiritually relating to, the same Absolute Reality—is also true.

But then what? These truths, even though many will not accept them (nor is it always spiritually necessary that they should), amount to mere truisms; neither the knowledge that a Primordial Tradition exists, nor that the Transcendent Unity of Religions is true, is the "one thing needful" for the salvation of the soul and/or liberation from the bonds of contingent existence. To know that ships exist is necessary if we are ever to embark on one, but that knowledge in itself is not the embarkation, nor the purchase of the ticket, nor even the mapping of the voyage. Those who loiter in the neighborhood of the ticket booth, either failing to choose a traditional Path or treating it as secondary to the Perennialist doctrines themselves, and meanwhile thinking that they have found something "quintessential" that will raise them to a higher spiritual level or be an unfailing source of strength and guidance that will steady them when confronted by the rigors of life, have founded their house on sand. And if they loiter there too long, they risk being harvested by the Counter-Initiation, which knows all too well how to present secondary matters as essential, make them glamorous and fascinating to those who are beginning to fear (and are eager to repress the fact) that they may have wasted their spiritual potential on increasingly barren preliminary investigations and failed to take even the first real step. Frithjof Schuon always emphasized that he had not brought a new revelation; the notions of Perennialism, the Primordial Tradition, the Transcendent Unity of Religions in and of themselves can provide neither salvation nor *gnosis*, though they certainly may support these aims; only spiritual ways sent by God can do that, and the reliable ways to God are precisely the "confessional" faiths, understood and lived in their esoteric depths. And, although the *opus* of the great Traditionalist/Perennialist authors may (or may not) allow us to see more deeply into these faiths, it can never replace them; this is what the Traditionalist/Perennialists, or at least the "classical" Traditionalist/Perennialists, have always taught. Perhaps it is time for some (as I know it is time for *me*) who have absorbed the Perennialist worldview to return—or rather *advance*—to exclusive commitment to a single religion, abandoning the desire to *preach* Perennialism to their co-religionists, while considering this allegiance to one religious form not as an abandonment of Perennialist principles but as the fullest expression of them. After absorbing and learning from a number of spiritual perspectives it can be difficult to choose only one; it can seem like a painful narrowing of vision. But just as it is no real loss to give up the horizontal breadth of promiscuity for the vertical depth of a marriage blessed by God, so the adoption of a single religious language and practice can open the soul to concrete depths of realization that spiritual dissipation, no matter how apparently "intelligent" it may be, has never dreamt of. The Sufis call it *jam'*; the Christians, *recollection*. In Schuon's phrase, this is part of what it means "to have a Center".

According to Titus Burckhardt in "A Letter on Spiritual Method" from *Mirror of the Intellect*, "There is no spiritual path outside the following traditions or religions: Judaism, Christianity, Islam, Buddhism, Hinduism and Taoism; but Hinduism is closed for those who have not been born into a Hindu caste, and Taoism is inaccessible". And in the succinct and quintessential words of Frithjof Schuon in *From the Divine to the Human*, "A given religion in reality sums up all religions . . . all religion is to be found in a given religion, because Truth is one." The major *spiritual* (not social) use of "comparative religion" is to allow faiths other than one's own to illuminate elements that are really and legitimately there in one's own faith, but which have for one reason or another become obscured. But if a believer is not sufficiently integrated into his or her own religion—a difficult thing to achieve in today's world due to a virtually infinite choice of distractions as well as the progressive degeneration of the religious collectives—that believer will feel the need to "supplement" his or her religious life with heterogeneous elements. If a given religion sums up all religions, however, then such syncretism is unnecessary, and in fact destructive. The deepening of one's commitment to and understanding of one's chosen path will not inevitably lead to exclusivism, or to the kind of idolatrous identification with one's religion that would tend to set it up as a substitute for God, nor will initiation (formal or otherwise) into the esoteric dimension of one's faith necessarily block access to "plenary" or "quintessential" esoterism, to "esoterism as such"; a Traditional initiation, barring the rare exception, is in fact the only reliable path to esoterism as such. To live one's religion in its esoteric depths with little or no support from one's co-religionists, a fate which some will find unavoidable, is a heavy burden to bear; as Rabi'a al-Adawiyya said in one of her poems, "I am a stranger in Your country/ And lonely among Your worshippers: /This is the substance of my complaint". Such isolation may in fact be the precise *asceticism* demanded of esoterics, especially in the modern world. Rabi'a's poem is not just a lament, however, but a cry to God, Who is well known for rewarding those who have sacrificed human fellowship in order to draw closer to Him with His very presence. To "understand" esoterism from the outside, through an intellective insight into the doctrines of many faiths, but not to take the further step of coming into an *existential* and *operative* relationship to the esoterism of *one* faith, is to miss the boat. Perennialism, for those of an intellectual bent who believe in God, is the best possible preparation for a spiritual life lived in its esoteric depths—but if it sets itself up as an esoteric spiritual Path in its own right, then God help us.

3

Traditional vs. Counter-Traditional Perspectives on The Divine Feminine & The Sacredness of Nature

Where Man is not, Nature is barren.
—William Blake

WARS INEVITABLY PRODUCE three things: profiteering, deception, and a curtailment of human rights—and the war to save the Earth from environmental catastrophe is no exception. Those involved in this war are seeking not only to deal with concrete problems but to change the basic worldview they believe is behind the crisis, replacing it one that allows for "sustainability". And if there is a single dominant theme in this struggle which pertains directly to the realm of religion and spirituality, it is the resurgence of the "Great Goddess", the mass reawakening to an awareness of the Divine Feminine. But this reawakening has not produced unanimity as to how to regard the transpersonal feminine principle, or even complete agreement on the necessity of seeing this principle as central to the renewed vision of the natural world as sacred. Furthermore, as with any "new" or resurrected myth, either spontaneously arisen or deliberately constructed, the powers that be will inevitably try their best to co-opt it so as to support and justify their own agendas.

I: The Divine Feminine according to the Traditionalists/Perennialists

The Divine Feminine was central to the doctrine of Frithjof Schuon, but he was in no way a Pagan or a materialist. He conceived of her, whom he identified with the Blessed Virgin Mary, not as a goddess in her own right but as the principle of Divine manifestation, identifiable with the Hindu doctrine of *Maya*, if not the *Shakti* of the tantrics. In terms of the macrocosm, she is virgin nature; in terms of the human microcosm, she is "pure prayer", pure receptivity to God; in terms of the Divine she is "*maya-in-divinis*", the eternal prefiguration of cosmic manifestation within the Deity, identifiable in some ways with the *ayan al-thabita* or "permanent archetypes" of Ibn al-'Arabi. *In divinis*, as well as in cosmic manifestation, the masculine pole is an expression of the Absolute, the feminine pole of the Infinite. And on the highest level, in the depths of the Divine Nature, the Absolute and the Infinite—*Shiva* and *Shakti*—are One.

René Guénon wrote little of the Divine Feminine, though he considered the feminine mysteries, proper to the *kshatriya* caste, as subordinate to the masculine mysteries which were the province of the *brahmins*. His notion of the transpersonal feminine principle appears most clearly in *The Reign of Quantity and the Signs of the Times*, where he conceives of the four ages of the *manvantara* or *maha-yuga*, the Hindu cycle-of-manifestation, in more or less Aristotelian terms as descending from the pole of Essence, which is masculine (in Islamic terms, the "Pen"), to the pole of Substance, which is feminine (in Islamic terms, the "Guarded Tablet"). In the original *Satya-yuga* or Golden Age (also known as *Krita-yuga*), manifestation remains in close proximity to the Essential Pole, and is thus relatively eternal; space and form take precedence over time and matter. But in the ultimate Kali-yuga or Iron Age, time and matter become progressively absolutized, while eternal form is obscured. This is the age of secularism, materialism and historical consciousness, which ends in dissolution—a dissolution that is foreshadowed in physics by the worldview of Heisenberg, where matter loses its former claims to solidity and is reduced to a swarm of "non-localized" sub-atomic particles. The same impending dissolution is reflected in the findings of certain other sciences, where advances in historical research, archaeology, paleontology and materialistic cosmogony have finally exercised a dissolving effect even on our sense of linear time, transforming it—in the consciousness of humanity, and with the help of the electronic media—into a collection of many different time-periods more or less conceived of as "alternative realities" inhabiting a chaotic "simultaneity". This is precisely the materialistic counterfeit of Eternity, the Essential Pole veiled and imperfectly imitated by the Substantial Pole.

Carl Jung—though I hesitate to mention him in the same context as Schuon and Guénon—saw the raising of the Assumption of the Virgin Mary to full dogmatic status by the Catholic Church in 1950 as an expression of the same zeitgeist that produced the dialectical materialism of the Marxists; Mary, the maternal principle, the Christian rendition of the Divine Feminine, represents by her Assumption the quasi-deification of matter—a development that, in Guénonian terms, was to be expected as the *manvantara* drew near to its end and came into the gravitational attraction of the Substantial Pole. There is an element of truth in this insight, but in another and more important sense the Assumption of the Virgin represents a return of matter, of the Substantial Pole, to its original Edenic union with the Essential Pole, as in the case of the glorified body assumed by Christ after His Resurrection: not the deification of matter per se, but the perfect receptivity of matter to the Spirit. (Anyone who has seen a photograph of the incorrupt corpse of St. Bernadette Soubirous has gazed upon the very icon of this receptivity.) The quasi-deification of matter is the Promethean hubris of the Substantial Pole, not its real spiritual function, which is to mirror the Essential Pole both cosmically and *in divinis*. This perfect receptivity is precisely the quality that matter as a whole has lost in the Kali-yuga; thus the Assumption of the Virgin Mary into heaven signifies that the original receptive virginity of the Substantial Pole can only be restored in another world. What neither Schuon nor Jung seemed to have realized, or at least never directly expressed (both of them inherited the Germanic sensitivity to the Divine Feminine) was that the theophany of the Substantial Pole represented by the doctrine of the Assumption and the many apparitions of the Virgin in the 20th century is precisely a sign of the dissolution of matter, its return to its non-material, transcendent Principle, Schuon's *maya-in-divinis*. The Substantial Pole can only be purified by her re-marriage to the Essential Pole, a state that Mary as "bride of the Holy Spirit" symbolizes and embodies. But when the Substantial Pole, at the end of the *manvantara*, assumes in its materialistic hubris the prerogatives of the Essential Pole, but cannot support them [see *I Ching*, Richard Wilhelm's translation, Hexagram 2 (*Kun*, "the Receptive), top line], this is a sign of apocalypse. Eternal stability of form is a manifestation of the Absolute via the Essential Pole, which is embodied through its reflection within the mirror of the Substantial Pole. The quality proper to the Substantial Pole is not Absoluteness, however, but Infinity; by the unveiling of the Substantial Pole at the end of the *yuga*, manifest form is not established, but dissolved. As the creative function of Substantial Pole is to receive and embody the forms emanating from God via the Essential Pole, so its eschatological function is to return those forms to God by dissolving them in the Infinite; and the hubris of matter falsely adopting the prerogatives of the Spirit is the lawful agent of this dissolution. To attempt to hold to form in opposition to the Spirit, not as an expression of It, is—in the words of Chuang Tzu—to be "destroyed on the lathe of Heaven".

II: The Divine Feminine according to the Greens and the Neo-Pagans

The "Green" or neo-Pagan worldview, however, does not conceive of the Divine Feminine in these terms; quite the contrary. Matter and the Earth are seen as Divine *without* understanding this as an eschatological sign, or seeing them as a manifestation of anything hierarchically superior to them on the Great Chain of Being; the tendency is rather to deify matter itself in order, as it were, to *magically render it immortal*. The earth is worshipped as the presumably immortal goddess Gaia, in denial of the obvious fact that all forms that are limited in space are also limited in time; no planet, no star, no galaxy can last forever. Furthermore, the feminine principle has no metaphysical significance (in the traditional sense) in the Neo-Pagan ethos; unlike the Virgin Mary[1] or the Hindu Kali, it has no

1. Mary perhaps most resembles Kali by virtues of her apparitions in the 20th century where she informed us that the cup of Divine Wrath is now full and about to overflow.

relationship to transcendence or eternity, nor is it considered to be either a spiritual disposition of the human soul or the essence of that soul. It is little more than matter "deified" because matter, energy, space and time are seen as all there is.

This deification of matter, coupled with the divorce of the sense of immortality from Eternity and the Celestial Order, and its re-interpretation as endless, or nearly endless time—a prospect which suggests to the Hindus and the Buddhists only ongoing suffering and incompletion, a perpetual wandering in the wilderness of *samsara*—is a fundamental aspect of Counter-initiatory "spirituality". If religion is to be rendered worldly and thus defined as something that can be created and maintained by human effort—by the power of the Counter-initiatory elites, that is—it must be divorced from Eternity, and consequently separated from God. And to project immortality upon ever-changing material forms is essentially to deny the immortality of the human soul, to render it volatile, ephemeral. Such a spiritually-inverted conception is of great use to those elites who wish to grant the natural world the same if not greater "rights" than those allowed to humanity—at least to *sub-elite* humanity. To assert as an element of human dignity the right to "conquer" nature at whatever cost is to corrupt that dignity, replacing it with blind arrogance, but to exalt "environmental rights" above human rights not only violates the dignity of the human form but is destructive to nature as well, since it defines the human race and the natural world as intrinsic adversaries every bit as much as the myth of the "triumph over nature" does.

III: The Shadow-Side of Environmentalism

Insofar as environmentalism becomes a religion, it must replace the idea of a Transcendent God with the notion of the natural world or the Earth as sacred; and as soon as it does this, it is required to subordinate humanity to this sacred Earth, defining us not as stewards of creation in the name of God, but as servants of a creation now seen as replacing God. And the only "morality" dictated by and intrinsic to a "sacred Earth" is instinct and natural law. But if simply following the dictates of instinct works to preserve the "balance of nature" on the animal level, why is the same not true on the human one, in view of the fact that the destruction of the natural world occurs when the human instinct to seek security, pleasure and power transgresses its proper limits? Because humanity occupies a higher ontological plane, and so must be held to a higher standard. Animals do not fall below themselves by following instinct; human beings do.

The most extreme way of serving a natural world worshipped without reference to God will necessarily be *human sacrifice*, especially in these times when overpopulation is seen as threatening the integrity of the environment. It is true that martyrdom is considered to be a pre-eminent way of worshipping the Transcendent God in the Abrahamic faiths, but if such martyrdom is to be legitimate it must be *voluntary*; the enforced sacrifice of others in service to a deity or deities is specifically disallowed in Judaism, Christianity and Islam, as evidenced by the fact that God, after commanding Abraham to sacrifice his only son, sent an angel to stay his hand; this is the precise point in Genesis where the child sacrifice practiced in the ancient Near East was prohibited by divine decree in terms of what was to become the Abrahamic tradition. Nor can *suicide* in any way be identified with martyrdom, a principle graphically illustrated in the Gospels by the clear distinction drawn between the self-offering of Jesus, the Savior, and the suicide of Judas, the betrayer. To remain faithful to life, even to the point of incurring the wrath of the Darkness of This World, whose principle is death, is one thing; to take one's own life in despairing service to the Darkness of This World is another. To destroy yourself at the behest of This World is to increase its power; to hold to the values of life, even if This World kills you for it, is to deal it a mortal blow. Nor can Islam be accused of mistaking suicide for martyrdom, the anti-Islamic crimes of the Wahhabi terrorists notwithstanding: according to the *hadith*, "It is reported—but Allah knows best—that the Prophet Muhammad—may peace be upon him—said, 'He who commits suicide by throttling himself shall keep on throttling himself in the Hell Fire forever and he who commits suicide by stabbing himself shall keep on stabbing himself in the Hell-Fire forever....[and] whoever commits suicide with a piece of iron will be punished with the same piece of iron in the Hell Fire.'" The Prophet

Muhammad also ended the pre-Islamic Arab practice of female infanticide, which may well have been committed in either implicit or overt worship of the Triple Goddess of the Pagan Arabs: al-Uzza, al-Lat and Manat.

There are a number of indications that the ethos of human sacrifice may be returning, consciously or otherwise, via the renewal of nature-worship in our time, though I hasten to emphasize that to simply equate a love of the environment and the desire to preserve it with an acceptance of human sacrifice is both destructive and absurd. Nonetheless, given that every spiritual worldview is subject to its own sorts of perversions, we must be on the lookout for the reappearance of such atavistic tendencies, especially in view of the fact that our Pagan ancestors practiced human sacrifice for countless generations, making it an inescapable part of our unconscious racial memory. (Who is to say, for example, that the Mexican drug gangs, some of whom appear to be actual Satanists, and who in a certain sense are "plant worshippers"—Coca and Cannabis being, so to speak, "the maize of the Kali-yuga"—do not represent an unconscious return to a quasi-Aztec ethos, due to the weakening of Christianity in Latin America? Nonetheless—needless to say—there's no way the cartels can be described as environmentalists! For a telling commentary on such atavism, see the fable *Ragnarök* by Jorge Luis Borges, from his book *Labyrinths*.)

Perhaps the most well-accepted approach to human sacrifice in our times is the practice of abortion-on-demand, which is certainly related to the environmental ethos, given that over-population is seen as a major threat to the environment. Certainly a newly-fertilized human egg can be seen as "merely a few cells, not a human person"—but those few human cells are nonetheless destined to become a human person, and who can say exactly when the transition from "mere biological material" to "someone" actually takes place? For some primitive tribes it was thought to happen not before birth or even at birth, but after it, at the moment the child was named, before which time he or she could be legally killed. To prohibit abortion under any circumstances is one extreme, but to see it not even as the taking or preventing of a human life is certainly another. In any case, an embryo cannot be legitimately defined simply as "part of the mother's body"; it represents a new and distinct principle of life.

Closely related to abortion is euthanasia, which is becoming more and more acceptable in this society, beginning with the legalization of physician-assisted suicide. If an embryo is "not a human being" because it does not represent a fully-developed and viable human body, how much of a jump is it to define the old and decrepit as "non-humans" according to similar standards, especially those who require extraordinary means to keep them alive? An embryo cannot protest being aborted; by the same token, a human being in a coma whom we have chosen to terminate is also incapable of protest or resistance. Such a person may know or suspect that their relatives and/or physicians intend to end their lives—recent studies have proven that a significant percentage of patients who were believed to be in a "vegetative" state are actually fully conscious, simply unable to communicate, and cases of recovery of consciousness after presumed "brain-death" have also been reported. But if the victim cannot protest or hire a lawyer, then his or her murderers have little to worry about, at least in worldly terms. And in the context of "conserving resources" and setting "limits to growth" in order to save the Earth, both abortion and euthanasia can legitimately be seen as forms of human sacrifice in the cult of Gaia.

Voluntary suicide can also be viewed, under certain circumstances, as a human sacrifice offered to Gaia. Bron Taylor, in *Dark Green Religion*, cites two telling examples of an attraction to death as a way of worshipping nature. In the first, an Australian ecofeminist, attacked by a crocodile and seriously injured, expresses her feelings about the event and the lessons she learned from it as follows:

> "The crocodile rushed up alongside the canoe, and its beautiful, gold-flecked eyes looked straight into mine" [during her long convalescence she] reported feeling "a golden glow over my life" [and said] "[I am] unsure who I should thank"... "Crocodiles and other creatures that can take human life ... present a test of our acceptance of our ecological identity

> [allowing us] to recognize ourselves in mutual, ecological terms, as part of the food chain, eater as well as eaten."

I'm sure that this woman's encounter with the crocodile taught her many real things, including the contingency and fragility of our human lives on earth. But am I alone in sensing something profoundly *unnatural* in this attitude to the rigors of the natural world? That someone could be so cut off from life that she would almost welcome being nearly killed by a crocodile, as if it were a rare experience of *intimacy*, speaks volumes about the impulses behind nature-worship in our time (as well as about the type of woman who can often form better relationships with animals than she can with men). These impulses are routinely expressed in terms of a hatred of the Transcendent God, Who is seen as cold, tyrannical, "patriarchal", life-denying, almost *mechanical*. Something is terribly wrong here. That the vision of the interconnectedness and sacredness of all life should lead us to deny the Creator, and that faith in the Creator should cause some of us to look upon the natural world as exploitable because essentially dead, are two sides of the same tragedy—so unnecessary, yet apparently so inevitable—which in metaphysical terms is the denial of the traditional doctrine of the Transcendence and Immanence of God. Gary Snyder once said to me—ironically revealing another face of this tragedy, which is the central blindness of the post-Renaissance western mind—"Face it, Charles; Buddhism is *atheism*". But Lakota holy man Black Elk was no atheist, any more than the Celtic Christian monks, or the Eastern Orthodox hermits of the great northern forests were; like them, he knew Wakan Tanka as both beyond all things and manifest in and through all things. And although he was a Catholic catechist among the Lakota for longer than he was a traditional medicine man, it was his traditional Lakota spirituality that allowed him to recognize in the Catholic faith—despite the depredations of the missionaries—one more manifestation of the unanimous Primordial Tradition.

The second example is a more complete portrait of the impulse to self-immolation in the service of Gaia. Convicted of environmental terrorism and sentenced to life imprisonment, Earth Liberation Front member William C. Rogers left the following suicide note:

> Certain human creatures have been waging war against the Earth for millennia. I chose to fight on the side of the bears, mountain lions, skunks, bats, saguaro, cliff rose and all things wild. I am just the most recent casualty in that war. But tonight I have made a jail break—I am returning home, to the Earth, to the place of my origins.

To fight to preserve nature in service to both nature and humanity is one thing; to take the side of nature *against* humanity—as was advocated in that strange, unnatural motion picture *Avatar*—is inherently suicidal: the one who embraces self-betrayal cannot remain faithful to nature, to man, or to anything else. And if, in line with the canons of nature-worship, the "absolute" is considered to be essentially material, then "union" with this absolute must be accomplished in material terms, by feeding one's body to a predator or leaving it to decompose in the earth; as we have seen, the concept of a *spiritual* death, a death of the ego, as the door to union with God, becomes unintelligible and meaningless under the Gaian ethos.[2]

IV: The Plans of the Depopulationists

As we have already pointed out contemporary environmentalism is inseparable from the push to reduce the human population. And

2. *Sophia, the Journal of Traditional Studies*, vol. 13. no. 1 (2007) carried a letter-to-the-editor with a chilling argument in support of suicide—something like a manifesto by Jack Kevorkian with a metaphysical twist—written as an ill-conceived "defense" of Frithjof Schuon's "private revelation" in *The Transformation of Man*, his last prose work, that Judas—who took his own life—was ultimately saved. Suicide might have a place in the Bushido ethic, for example, but in Christian terms it is a crime, and when Judas became a follower of Jesus he renounced his allegiance to any other moral standard. The writer cast about for any tradition anywhere where suicide is allowed, including the Gainj tribe of New Zealand, demonstrating by this mix-and-match syncretism precisely how comparative religion can be misused to undermine the integrity of an orthodox tradition based on a unique Divine revelation.

when it seems as if the manipulation of human attitudes—through radical feminism, gay "marriage", the widespread availability of pornography, etc.—might be insufficient to produce the necessary result, various proposals to reduce the population by force begin to make themselves heard, with China's "one child per couple" policy as the example often cited.

In order to give the reader an overview of the depopulationist agenda, I can think of no better way than to present a synopsis of Lee Penn's articles "Depopulation: Making the World Safe for the Elite" [*SPC Journal*, vol. 33:2–33:3, 2009] and "Depopulation: Making the Abolition of Man a Reality" [*SPC Journal*, vol. 33:4–34:1, 2010]. The first of these articles details various proposals by a number of elitist-depopulationists:

> Paul R. Ehrlich:
>
> [H]e suggested levying tax penalties for each child born, "luxury taxes" on "layettes, cribs, diapers, diaper services, expensive toys," financial rewards for waiting until age 25 to marry, rewards for "each five years of a childless marriage," and rewards for men who have vasectomies before begetting more than two children." Ehrlich favored the U.S. government "insisting on population control as the price of food aid" to Third World countries, adding that our country "must be relentless in pushing for population control around the world."...All this, and more, would be carried out by..."A Federal Department of Population and Environment (DPE) ...with the power to take whatever steps are necessary to establish a reasonable population size in the United States [and] promote intensive investigation of new techniques of birth control, possibly leading to *the development of mass sterilization agents*"... implementing a gradual population decrease and moving toward a sustainable economy "would require... giving up many things that we now consider essential freedoms"... Ehrlich imagined that "the government's propaganda efforts" [his own words!] could be "adjusted to produce whatever birth rate was deemed desirable." [T]he US "must... clamp severe controls on the media, especially on advertising in

> the media".... Ehrlich's proposals assume the addition of world government to his new, more powerful national government..."procedures must be set up for monitoring and regulating the world system...." In 1991, Ehrlich proposed a *stealthy* expansion of global governance.... "Successful international regulation has historically been achieved by bringing it in through the back door...."

[*Comment:* It is possible to draw parallels between the "mitigated castration" represented by vasectomy and the worshipful self-castration of the Pagan devotees of the Great Mother Goddess Cybele. The fact is that one reason for the declining human fertility rate is the physiological (not only psychological) feminization of the human male, as well as of many male animals. It has been conjectured that this is the effect of environmental pollution, especially with agents that are chemically similar to estrogen. But in light of some of Ehrlich's proposals, can we blame various "conspiracy theorists" for suggesting that human fertility is being interfered with by the deliberate introduction of "mass sterilization agents" into our air and water? In any case, this feminization process is right in line with René Guénon's doctrine that at the end of the *manvantara* the Substantial Pole, the *yin* principle, gains ascendancy over the Essential Pole or *yang* principle.]

John Holdren:

> [Holdren] is a former professor at the University of California/Berkeley and Harvard University whom President Obama chose in 2009 as director of the Office of Science and Technology.... Holdren has co-authored academic journal articles and other publications with Ehrlich from 1970 through 1995. In 1970, Holdren and Ehrlich began their testimony before the President's Commission on Population Growth and the American Future thus: "In an agricultural or technological society, each human individual has a negative impact on his or her environment."

Garrett Hardin (1915–2003):

> "The community, which guarantees the survival of children, must have the power to decide how many children shall be born.". . . The first phase [in achieving this power] would be voluntary, with the goal of "no unwanted children." Birth control would be offered to all, with abortion as "a backup method.". . . Then would come the second phase, education to "change people's attitudes" "in the elementary grades we must keep the option of childlessness alive in the child's mind. At the secondary level we need to display a wide spectrum of enticing vocations available to non-parents. . ."; Third, there would be the "coercive phase.". . . [Hardin] wanted to get people "used to the idea of parenthood as a licensable privilege instead of a right. . . . There is only one way to eliminate the counterproductive effect of choice in population control, and that is to get rid of the choice itself."

The Club of Rome:

> [T]he Executive Committee of the Club of Rome [in *Limits to Growth*, 1972] made it clear that there would need to be . . . on a world scale: "Entirely new approaches . . . to redirect society toward goals of equilibrium rather than growth. . . ." the *Limits* team in 2004 urged that "Growth in population and *capital* must be slowed and eventually stopped by human decisions. . . ."

[*Comment:* In my view it is impossible to determine whether the effects of draconian policies by the elites to stop economic and population growth, or the ultimate effects of such growth if it remains unchecked, would represent the more destructive outcome. All we can say for sure is that the first option provides the greatest opportunity for the global elites to extend their oppressive rule over the whole earth, which is why they generally see it as *the better way*. Furthermore, in view of the above agenda, is it possible to simply brand as "paranoid" those who claim that our present world economic collapse has been engineered by interests who stand to profit by it? Before the reader answers this question, let him or her consider the fact that, according to Lee Penn, "The Club's full membership come from universities, UN agencies, and from other think-tanks world wide. Honorary members include Jacques Delors (the former president of the European Commission), Mikhail Gorbachev, Vaçlav Havel (former president of Czechoslovakia), Hazel Henderson (an "evolutionary economist"), the president of Sokka Gakkei International (a Buddhist "new religious movement" with a cultic reputation), Juan Carlos I (King of Spain) and his wife, three current and former high-level UNESCO officials, Prince Phillipe (the Crown Prince of the Netherlands), Beatrix (the Queen of the Netherlands), and former heads of state from Portugal, Georgia, and Germany."]

Lee Penn also lists among prominent depopulationists the Bush family, Hillary Clinton, John D. Rockefeller III, Ted Turner, Warren Buffett, George Soros, David Rockefeller Jr., Michael Bloomberg, Oprah Winfrey, Eli Broad, Peter Peterson, John Morgridge, Julia Robertson, Jacques-Ives Cousteau, Jan Fransen and Maurice Strong. Jacques-Ives Cousteau said: "World population must be stabilized, and to do that we must eliminate 350,000 people per day. This is so horrible to contemplate it that we shouldn't even say it" (just do it, apparently). Jan Fransen, demographer and former staff member for the U.N. Population Fund, believes that the earth's population should be reduced to between 700 million and one billion. Ted Turner wants to shoot for 2 billion; in 1999 he proposed before the U.N. a century-long one-child-per-couple policy, modeled on that of China, (Turner, we should remember, was so radical that his ex-wife, famous leftist activist Jane Fonda, became a born-again Christian on the rebound.)

Lee Penn's depopulation articles led me to do some research of my own. According to an article on the BBC website, Dec. 3, 2009, "The UK-based Optimum Population Trust ... is promoting a scheme in which wealthy people can offset their own carbon emissions by funding contraceptive programmes in the developing world." In other words, the rich should be allowed to continue with their "conspicuous consumption" as long as they are willing to prevent the poor from reproducing. On the board of the OPT sits Jonathon Porritt, whose Wikipedia article quotes him as saying: "I think we will work our way towards a position that says that having more than two children is irresponsible. It is the ghost at the table.... The trust (OPT) will release research suggesting UK population must be cut to 30m [a reduction of only around 29 million!] if the country wants to feed itself sustainably." The same article informs us that "Porritt acts as advisor to many bodies on environmental matters, as well as to individuals including Prince Charles." Charles' father, Prince Philip, is known for having expressed the sentiment that after he passes on he would like to reincarnate as a deadly virus so as to wipe out a large percentage of the human race.

But as Lee Penn warns us in his second article "Depopulation: Making the Abolition of Man a Reality", maybe we won't have to wait for that, since reliable methods for mass depopulation already exist. He also makes it clear that the idea of mass depopulation as one element of a "religious" belief-system is not as rare as one would think, or hope. Among depopulationist/eugenicists with religious beliefs or quasi-religious ideologies he names Theosophists Helena Petrovna Blavatsky and Alice Bailey, New Age teachers Robert Muller, Barbara Marx Hubbard and William Irwin Thompson, and also Christians: Teilhard de Chardin (a heterodox Catholic), Matthew Fox (Novus Ordo Catholic priest who converted to Episcopalianism), Bishop William E. Swing (former Episcopal Bishop of California and founder of the United Religions Initiative) and Rosemary Radford Reuther (Novus Ordo feminist theologian). Also on the list are James Lovelock (agnostic, anti-Christian, anti-Muslim and devotee of Gaia, as so many environmentalists are), and Ernest Callenbach (who authored "Earth's Ten Commandments").

Environmentalists who literally propose the destruction of civilization include Derrick Jensen and Keith Farnish, himself an advocate of ecoterrorism; among those who predict, and in some cases actually seem to propose (at least as *one alternative*), the extinction of the human race are to be found Matthew Fox, Robert Muller, LSD researcher Jean Houston, William Irwin Thompson and Alan Weisman.

Lee Penn makes the point that a society that could entertain "rational" plans for global nuclear and biological warfare—and who may still possess, and actually be disseminating, stockpiles of germ warfare agents—could also conceive of more "targeted" means for human depopulation. (After all, couldn't we describe the neutron bomb as an "anti-population bomb"?)

He quotes Earth First! Activist Christopher Manes to the effect that "If radical environmentalists were to invent a disease to bring human population back to ecological sanity, it would probably be something like AIDS.... I take it as axiomatic that the only real hope for the continuation of diverse ecosystems on this planet is an enormous decline in human population...." But such dark dreams are not the exclusive province of radical ecoterrorists of the lunatic fringe. Mr. Penn informs us:

> In 2005, researchers published the full genome of the deadly 1918 Spanish Flu on the Internet. Any terrorist group or rogue state now has the information needed to kick-start a new flu pandemic. Researchers have created hybrid strains of the flu that are (for mice) as contagious as human influenza, and as deadly as avian influenza (which killed 60% of its 442 human victims). The work was funded by grants from the U.S. National Institutes of Health, the Japanese government, and the Bill and Melinda Gates Foundation.
>
> In its 2001 report, the Project for a New American Century (PNAC), the influential conservative think tank, said that in the future, biological weapons could be designed to attack "specific genotypes", making biological warfare "a politically useful tool".

Population reduction, like many other aspects of the environmental movement, often tends to be advocated on a more or less "populist" basis (no pun intended). What many environmental populists may not realize, however, is that depopulation is being pushed by the global elites as a way to create a world more congenial to *them*, one less cluttered with depressing examples of lower humanity, and that their own work for environmental protection will not necessarily put them on the "fit to survive" list when "the survival of the fittest" begins to be enforced; to identify with the elites, serve them, take direction from them is a far cry from being one of them. Many in the environmental movement, as in the interfaith movement, are either unaware that the global elites are in some cases setting their agendas, or unwilling to face the full implications of this fact. When reduced consumption and human depopulation are advanced as a populist agenda by people who are willing to make personal sacrifices to further these ideals, then they present the appearance of legitimate goals. But when they are advocated by members of the elite who own many homes, travel the world and live in luxury—and who include members of royalty or nobility who must depend upon their bloodlines for their survival as a class—one is led to ask whether their real goal is to save the earth and the future of humanity, or simply to save the ruling class, retaining the earth as a kind of private park, and humanity be damned.

Some people who harbor the deep (and usually unconscious) fear of death that is inseparable from atheistic materialism will be induced to deny this fear by, in effect, *impersonating Death*. They will imagine themselves unleashing mass depopulation as a way of pretending that *they* will never die. Nonetheless—as we have already seen—some of the "populist depopulationists", given the suicidal element intrinsic to the depopulationist ethos, are apparently willing to sacrifice themselves, along with billions of their fellow human beings, in order to save the earth. The *elitist* depopulationists, however, have no such egalitarian sentiments; death, to them, is not the great Equalizer but the great Selector. With their life-extension technologies and their well-stocked underground cities, they fully intend to survive. As the "higher human beings", they—like the Aztec priests—plan to sacrifice to Gaia only the *plebs*. The populists are in many cases nothing but the pawns of these elitists, willing preachers of their gospel. The elites have the power to sacrifice others; the *hoi poloi* have no one to sacrifice but themselves.

Here we can see how human depopulation to make the world safe for the elites is a perfect example of the Luciferian aspect of the Counter-Initiation: If the global elites succeed in decreasing the population to the point where only they and a small class of human servants remain, and to "save the Earth" in the process, then they have fulfilled both the demands of "Gaian spirituality" and those of a predatory Luciferian worldview based on inverted hierarchy, which could be described as the transformation of social Darwinism into *spiritual* Darwinism: the Luciferian ideal posits predation as the sole and absolute engine of "evolutionary" change, and extends the concept of the food chain beyond the borders of the material world, up through the angelic hierarchies to the very throne of God. According to the Enlightenment conception of "Nature", which was a contributing factor in the American and French Revolutions, social hierarchies are artificial, human constructions, whereas Nature is the source of human equality; according to Thomas Jefferson, egalitarianism would survive in America only so long as Virgin Nature still remained for settlers to settle. Darwin stood this notion on its head by positing Nature, via "the survival of the fittest", as the principle of *in*equality—and if the elites succeed in ridding the world of "useless eaters" (a term attributed to Henry Kissinger), then they may justly claim that they were the fittest to survive, because they *did*. If animals have no compunction about fighting tooth-and-claw for their territory and food supply, why should they? Human beings, according to the materialist side of the ideology they hold, are nothing but animals after all, even if these particular animals aspire to overthrow God Himself.

The Aztec priesthood were degenerate even according to the degenerate canons of human sacrifice because, like the Nazis, they offered to the gods not "pure victims", representatives of the "higher human type" they considered themselves to be, but rather members of what they saw as a "lower" humanity, and did so in order to insure that *they* would never have to meet a similar fate. Likewise some among the global elites apparently want to "sacrifice" much of the rest of humanity to Gaia so as to secure their own position and future survival. And although a "human sacrifice by attrition" is obviously less radical than the more direct depopulation efforts of the Aztecs, the Nazis, the Stalinists, the Maoists and the Khymer Rouge, we must not forget that Thomas Robert Malthus (1766–1834), the "godfather" of the depopulationists, included war—the deliberate taking of human life—as one of the factors that would "naturally" limit the human population.

In conclusion, we must evaluate the dreams and plans of the depopulationists in light of The following admission by Paul Ehrlich himself, in his book *One with Nineveh* (2005): "... growth of the global population has slowed to about 1.2 percent per year, and it appears to be on track to continue slowing, according to the United Nations medium demographic projection".

V: Gaia vs. Kali

As we have seen above, the "return of the Goddess" is inseparable from the quality of the End Times, when the predominance of the Essential Pole, or Form, is replaced by that of the Substantial Pole, or Matter, leading to Matter's quasi-deification. The true *spiritual* quality of "the return of the Goddess", however, is not glamorized materialism; among traditional conceptions of the Divine it is perhaps best represented by the Hindu goddess Kali. Kali is primordial, not simply a reflection of the latter days, but Her particular quality assures Her a prominent role, whether or not this is recognized, at the end of the *manvantara*. Kali is the Absolute not as hierarchically exalted above conditional existence but as identical with it—the total unveiling of the Immanence of God, such that the polarity between God the Creator and Sustainer of the universe and the universe He creates and sustains is annihilated, resulting in the reabsorbtion of existence into its Principle: the *mahapralaya*, the end of the world. Seen in terms of the human microcosm, this appears as the "tantric" annihilation of the polarity between the purity of the Divine and the impurity of the passions, such that the passions are reabsorbed into their Divine archetypes; as the Buddhist *Guyasama Tantra* expresses it, "The conduct of the passions and attachments is the same as the conduct of a bodhisattva, that being the best conduct." This is not properly antinomianism, defined as the license to do evil, but rather a total purification from all evil of those actions that, before purification, formed the basis of the passions and attachments—not by suppressing them but by perfectly enacting them. This is what is called the "left-hand path"; needless to say it is filled with spiritual dangers, and should only be attempted by those occupying the highest spiritual stations (though why those occupying such stations would *need* to attempt it remains a valid question). When the left-hand path is literalized and externalized, however, it becomes totally profane, giving rise to a true antinomianism that ends by exalting the passions per se. The darkest expression of this impulse was undoubtedly the cult of the Thuggee, irregular worshippers of Kali, considered criminal even before the British Raj, who kidnapped and sacrificed travelers to the Goddess in the belief that they were propitiating Her, feeding Her with human blood to prevent Her from bringing even worse disasters. But in the properly esoteric worship of Kali—seeing that even the performance of passion-inciting acts in a passionless manner is relatively external—the subject of sacrifice is the *ego*, the self-concept. When Kali completely dawns, she demands of us all we are; in the face of the Goddess of Death, to hold on to self-definition is agony, while to release all attachment to self-definition is bliss. And since "This World" is nothing but a collective projection of the ego—the way we think things are, based on the way we think *we* are—She brings the "World" to an end as well. No longer can we say, like Job did before God tested him, "if I am good the Lord will protect me in my earthly life"; at this point, the only possible response left to us is, in the words of the Noble Qur'an: *There is no refuge from God but in Him.* Unfortunately, if the Great Goddess is conceived of as Gaia rather than Kali, the whole concept of self-transcendence through ego-sacrifice becomes obscured; we are left with a "religion" that does not satisfy the traditional definition of that word, a worldview totally devoid of spiritual hope.

The Divine hypostasis represented by the Goddess Kali is now being unveiled; this is one of the inescapable qualities of our time. Nor is it necessary to concentrate on its specifically Hindu manifestation to come to an understanding of it, though this manifestation is certainly the most explicit; the lineaments of Kali can be found in the apocalyptic prophesies of all the religions, including the Abrahamic ones— not always as explicitly or strictly identified, however, with the Divine Feminine. And because Kali is inescapable, those who are unaware of Her particular quality, and the specific spiritual opportunities She represents, will be unconsciously affected by Her presence. It is as clear as the setting sun that the depopulationists quoted above are *de facto* worshippers of Death. It is Death, not Life, that represents for them the sovereign rights of Absolute Reality, and summons them to worship Reality under that name and form. But since they are by and large materialists, they can neither worship nor realize the Absolute in a conscious manner, nor avail themselves of the profound opening to compassion and self-transcendence that the willing veneration of Kali can provide. And because they cannot be Her conscious devotees, they are forced to act as Her unconscious agents; as Seneca put it, "Fate leads the willing; the reluctant she drags."[3]

The foremost devotee of Kali in the 20th century was the great Hindu saint Ramakrishna, who saw Her largely in Her beneficent aspect. One element in of Ramakrishna's practice, fairly unique at the time, was that he reached God-realization not only as a Hindu, but also as a Muslim and a Christian, after temporarily adopting the prayers, the taboos, even the food and garb of these traditions. He was a true universalist—although in India, in the general context of Hinduism, this universalism could more easily be seen as an expression of the *sanatanadharma*, the Primordial Tradition, than in most other parts of the world. In the person of his successor Vivekananda and other *chelas* he became the source of much philanthropy and social service in India, inspiring the foundation of many hospitals, schools etc. Yet his universalism also had a weakening effect on Hinduism, especially in the context of the colonial and missionary influences of his time, the work of the Theosophical Society for Indian independence, etc.; the Vedanta Society that sprang from him cannot really be considered to represent orthodox Hinduism. Nor is it an accident, in my opinion, that a worshipper of Kali would assume the role of a religious universalist in our day. Kali symbolizes—and enacts—the dissolution of forms in the face of the Absolute; consequently Ramakrishna's own version of the Transcendent Unity of Religions represents both the unveiling of the Absolute Truth underlying all the faiths, and the dissolution of those faiths along with the earthly world they maintain. In both Ramakrishna and Frithjof Schuon we can thus understand the dawning of the Transcendent Unity of Religions as an eschatological sign.

3. The same is probably true of some serial killers and other perpetrators of "meaningless" vandalism and violence: they unconsciously intuit that dissolution is the central quality of our time and so start to feel that murder and mayhem are a kind of entitlement. The elites have the power to destroy whole nations and economies and ecosystems, but the sociopaths are out to rival the ruling class by proving that the "little guy" can also contribute his share to the general destruction.

VI: Naturalistic vs. Supernaturalistic Nature-Worship

Bron Taylor, in *Dark Green Religion*, makes a distinction between naturalistic and supernaturalistic nature-worship, between a veneration for the Earth that does not posit the existence of invisible intelligent forces and one that does. Naturalistic nature-worship blinds us to vast reaches of the universe of Divine manifestation and cuts us off from all non-material worlds, either imaginal or intelligible. It also suppresses all evidence, deriving either from revealed scripture, from philosophical speculation or from anecdotal accounts—including the experience of the Shamans—for both the reality of such worlds and the human survival of bodily death. It imprisons us in a cramped and truncated universe, far too small for the actual stature of humanity. And in teaching us to treat as eternal a thing that is always passing away, it produces a deep though largely unconscious anxiety that can only be escaped, temporarily, hopelessly, by denying our full humanity.

Supernaturalistic nature-worship, by denying the theistic conception of Absolute Reality in favor of pantheism (as well as, in many cases, polytheism or *Jinn*-worship), obscures and invalidates a true and necessary aspect of that Reality. The anthropomorphic image of God as a thinking, feeling and acting *individual*, albeit supremely wise, loving and powerful, does have certain limitations; nonetheless, it remains the best *concrete symbol* of Absolute Reality in terms of that Reality's specific self-revelation to humanity—and a divine symbol is not a mere human idea but an Idea in its own right, both a necessary concept and a conscious, living Person. Pantheism (and panentheism) seem to transcend the limitations of an anthropomorphic, personal God, but in so doing they deny the power of the Absolute to *act*, to author laws both religious and natural (as well as to suspend them), thereby invalidating all sacred codes of conduct as mere human inventions, and all *miracles* as either poorly-understood natural phenomena, magical actions by humans beings or spirit entities, or superstitious fallacies. Absolute Reality certainly transcends intent, but it also *embraces* intent; to deny to God the ability to intend specific things in relation to the relative world, either because He is beyond intent or because He intends *everything* (which are, nonetheless, two entirely valid views of His intrinsic nature), is to reduce Him to the level of natural law, to something amenable to human investigation and manipulative control. It is to make humanity active and God passive.

And both naturalistic and supernaturalistic nature-worship make it impossible for us to understand God as *merciful*, and thus to address petitions to Him. No one can pray for mercy to an abstract pantheistic force, any more than to the rocks or the stars; and though petitions can be addressed to a multitude of spirit beings, these beings are not independent powers capable of granting these petitions, but faces and emissaries of a Divine Reality that absolutely transcends them. Furthermore, to the degree that Transcendence is denied in the worship of visible nature, they can no longer fulfill this function.Thus we can conclude that nature-worship, in all its forms, effectively cuts out most of what has been meant by the word "religion", by most human beings and societies, throughout most of human history. Its widespread adoption is therefore a sign of the end of the present cycle-of-manifestation.

VII: The Secret Alliance Between Nature-worship and Technology

I have already alluded above, in the footnote on *Moby Dick* in Chapter One, to the secret affinity between nature-worship and technological destruction; I would now like to expand on this point. It is common nowadays to refer to human beings as "animals" (a dangerous half-truth if there ever was one), and to the human body as a "wondrous machine". (And if human beings are machines, certainly animals are also.) Both these "terminological inexactitudes" can be traced directly to the naturalistic worldview. To see human beings as animals has resulted in the attempt to extend "human rights" to our animal relatives, but it is also at the root of the much more powerful and widespread tendency to treat human beings as cattle—as, for example, through the spread of artificial insemination from animal husbandry to human reproduction, as well as the acceptance of abortion on demand and the ongoing campaign to legitimize euthanasia. And if we can genetically engineer crops and livestock, then why not human beings? [NOTE: The hidden relationship between nature-worship and *unnatural* technology is clearly revealed in the motion picture *Avatar*, where human beings can only interact with the ecologically pristine world of Pandora through computer-generated "virtual bodies".]

It is common for nature-worshippers to see the doctrine of a Transcendent God common to the Abrahamic religions as destructive to the earth, as if "transcendent" meant "distant", whereas what it really means "not limited by form and thus pervading all forms". The Transcendence of God guarantees that all things exist in relation to and draw their life from a Reality greater than themselves. If there were no Divine Transcendence, all entities would be purely material, sealed into themselves, totally cut off from living participation in anything ontologically superior to them—like the parts of a machine.

The Judeo-Christian-Islamic tradition is not the cause of our environmental crisis. The real cause is the materialistic side of Pagan Greek philosophy, which began to unduly influence the West when scholastic Aristotelianism won out over Neo-Platonism, and triumphed when, in the Europe of the Enlightenment, it gave birth to experimental science, and consequently to materialism and materialistic technology. The Roman Catholic Church tried to block this development. She failed, not because she was essentially anti-nature, but because she had lost the dimension of sacred science that might have allowed her to effectively oppose the growth of materialistic, secular science. Perhaps, given that she no longer had room for the full expression of her own tradition, especially after the Renaissance, this failure could not be avoided—but to blame her for the triumph of what she fought tooth-and-nail to prevent is historically ignorant to say the least. When the vision of Transcendence is blocked the material universe is ultimately seen as all there is, the result being that humanity, who is made for the vision of God, attempts to fulfill that function in a social and psychic environment that allows no room for God. It's as if an infinite desire were attempting to exhaust itself on a finite object, and so descending into lust and avarice—and, as an expression of its inevitable frustration, into anger, and finally sloth. When the human race, made for heaven, is confined to a conceptual earth become opaque to the light of God, we devour it like locusts.

VIII: Tafsir *of the Natural World*

Having presented such an extreme picture of what a perversion of the idea of the sacredness of the natural world can lead to, it is now my duty to right the balance by demonstrating how the vision of nature as sacred can take its place within a theistic worldview—specifically, that of the Noble Qur'an—and form part of the basis of a properly human morality. The following section appeared as an article in vol. 16, no. 2 of *Sophia: Journal of Traditional Studies*, 2011.

> *This is He who knoweth the unseen and the seen; the Mighty, the Merciful,*
> *Who hath made everything which He hath created most good.* [Q. 32:6 (Rodwell)]

The Meaning of the Earth in the Qur'an

The *earth* in the Qur'an has four basic meanings: 1) It is the field of human endeavor, both legitimate and corrupt; 2) It is an instance of Allah's generosity to humanity; 3) It is a similitude of Paradise; 4) It is something that should not be worshipped, because it will end. And according to meanings two and three, clearly we are required to care for the earth as part of our submission to Allah.

We can look at our human responsibility before Allah to care for the earth he has given us in two ways: In terms of *morality*—what we should do, and in terms of *meaning*—what we should know. Many Muslim writers have applied Islamic *fiqh* to environmental stewardship; this is the moral and legal dimension. Without the dimension of *meaning*, however, the *shari'ah* would be meaningless. The Qur'an opens us to an understanding that the natural world must be preserved not simply because we can't live without it, or because those who destroy what all must use are justly classed as criminals, but because it is made up of nothing but the signs of God—and to ignore, repudiate and destroy God's signs is to rebel against Him. According to the plain meaning of the Book, environmental destruction is precisely *sacrilege.* To knowingly engage in actions that result in the extinction of a living species is strictly equivalent to expunging a verse from the Noble Qur'an.

Every Created Thing is a Sign of Allah

> 2:159 *Assuredly in the creation of the Heavens and of the Earth; and in the alternation of night and day; and in the ships which pass through the sea with what is useful to men; and in the rain which God sendeth down from Heaven, giving life by it to the earth after its death, and by scattering over it all kinds of cattle; and in the change of the winds, and in the clouds that are made to do service between the Heaven and the Earth;—are signs for those who understand.*

All creatures are signs of Allah, even man-made objects. So are the elements, the plants, the animals, the cycles of time.

> 45:2–3 *And in your own creation, and in the beasts which are scattered abroad are signs to the firm in faith:*
>
> *And in the succession of night and day, and in the supply which God sendeth down from the Heaven whereby He giveth life to the earth when dead, and in the change of the winds, are signs for a people of discernment.*

The most familiar and easily available compendium of the signs of Allah is the human form itself—though we cannot really see what is in us unless we are also sensitive to the forms of the universe around us; an attentiveness to the forms of the natural world helps us to see ourselves objectively, to know ourselves as we really are.

> 30: 26–28 *If all the trees that are upon the earth were to become pens, and if God should after that swell the sea into seven seas of ink, His words would not be exhausted: for God is Mighty, Wise.*
>
> *Your creation and your quickening hereafter, are but as those of a single individual. Verily, God Heareth, Seeth!*
>
> *Seest thou not that God causeth the night to come in upon the day, and the day to come in upon the night? and that He hath*

> *subjected the sun and the moon to laws by which each speedeth along to an appointed goal? and that God therefore is acquainted with that which you do?*

This is not a mere hyperbole, though it *is* a metaphor: the trees of the earth *are* pens, in a sense; the seas *are* ink. Every living thing is composed of, and expresses, the Names of God; the voice of the wind in the trees is—like every other sound—the auditory expression of the action of Allah within creation, the action that we call *time*. The trees which are pens here represent the forms of the action of Allah, and the seas which are ink, the substance of creation upon which He acts. But material creation is only a tiny fraction of the cosmos created by God; the form and substance of the physical world cannot begin to exhaust the bounty of God's manifestation, any more than the spoken and written Qur'an exhausts the *Umm al-Kitab*, the Mother of the Book. The *Umm al-Kitab* is the "Guarded Tablet", the entirety of the words spoken and the thoughts expressed by Allah in eternity. Upon this Tablet—and out of it—the Pen, the *nafas al-Rahman* or "Breath of the Merciful", draws whatever is to appear, by the Will of God, in this or any world.

To be saved is to be integrated into the Archetype of Man, *al-Insan al-Kamil*; to be damned is to be separated from it. We are not saved through our individuality, though if we are saved our individuality is saved too: we are saved through our union with, and expression of, humanity as such. The human form was created by God as an epitome of all the Most Beautiful Names, in perfect balance and hierarchy and unity—a fact symbolized by God's command that all the angels make obeisance to Adam. As individuals we can express only a part of this unity; our partiality gains significance insofar as we recognize it as a necessary, though insufficient, aspect of a greater and more unified human form. We do not reach this unity by denying our individuality; if we deny who we are, we will have nothing to contribute to it. We reach it by transcending our individuality....and that is not the same thing at all. The necessary imperfections of our individual selves posit the necessity of *islam*, full submission to Allah. When the submission and offering of our individuality to Allah is completed, we are integrated into *al-Insan al-Kamil*; we return to the loins of Adam. When man is saved and reintegrated and unified, then God, Who is One, sees Himself *in* man, as in a mirror.

Because God holds the human Heart "between His two fingers, and turns it however He will", He knows us in all our actions, in all our changes and alterations. He knows that when we turn toward Him we are merely turning toward our idea of Him, and are thus also turning away from Him; He knows that when we turn away from Him we are only turning to our own poverty and nothingness, and are thus also turning toward Him, since our only avenue of relationship to God is our need. The day reveals all the forms of God's creation, His manifest Names, but at the same time it hides His Essence behind them. The night reveals His Essence, but reveals it only as darkness, as That Which Cannot be Known, upon the black surface of which appear all His Most Beautiful Names, symbolized by the stars. And the turning of the night and the day in *al-zahir* secretly arises from His turning of the human Heart in *al-batin*. The cosmos is the reflection of the Names of God insofar as they are dispersed and differentiated; the human being is the reflection of the Names of God insofar as they are gathered together into a single form.

> 30:19 *And one of His signs it is that He hath created you out of dust; then lo! you become men who spread themselves far and wide:*

Something that is "created of dust" possesses no intrinsic principle of life but what is given to it by The Living: man is no second God.

> 30:20 *And one of His signs it is, that He hath created wives for you of your own species, that you may dwell with them, and hath put love and tenderness between you. Herein truly are signs for those who reflect.*

God loves humanity as men love their wives; consequently for marriages to break up and married love to die is a sign of God's Wrath. A man who loves his wife wants to give her life and see her bring forth life, both physically and spiritually; thus loving marriage is both a metaphor of, and an actual occasion of, God's love for the human race; this is why the Prophet said, "Marriage is half the religion".

> 30:21 *And among His signs are the creation of the Heavens and of the Earth, and your variety of tongues and color. Herein truly are signs for all men.*

Human beings are created by God with various races and languages because Unity, *al-Ahad*, is a name of God, not a name of man or creation. If creation were One, if it lacked variety and differentiation, it would rival God; consequently it would exist in a state of *shirk*, which is impossible. If creation were perfectly One it would *be* God, and thus cease to exist as creation. Only as a multiplicity can it express God without being Him; the multiplicity of creation thus posits the Unity of God. Here we can see how the regimentation of humanity, as well as certain agricultural practices such as monoculture, which destroys biodiversity, are actually attempts to rival God.

> 24:43–45 *Hast thou not seen that God driveth clouds lightly forward, then gathereth them together, then pileth them in masses? And then thou seest the rain forthcoming from their midst; and He causeth clouds like mountains charged with hail, to descend from the Heaven, and He maketh it to fall on whom He will, and from whom He will He turneth it aside.—The brightness of His lightning all but taketh away the sight!*
>
> *God causeth the day and the night to take their turn. Verily in this is teaching for men of insight. And God hath created every animal of water. Some go upon the belly; some go upon two feet; some go upon four feet. God hath created what He pleased. Aye, God hath power over all things.*
>
> *Now have We sent down distinct signs.*

The clouds that Allah moves across the sky and gathers together are the subtle prototypes of material manifestation, the seeds of His Acts, which is why it is said that they are *made to do service between Heaven and Earth*, between spiritual Source and material manifestation; the rain and the hail are His mercy and wrath. And the lightning is the light of His Will, a light we cannot gaze upon without being dazzled, blinded. If we ask why God's Will is not always revealed to us, why it is not constantly laid bare for all to see so that (presumably) all would obey it, why it only appears—outside of the stability and constancy of the *shari'ah*—as momentary flashes of insight, Allah's answer is: Because you could not withstand such knowledge. Created forms can only remain in existence if they are veiled from the full light of their Cause; if this veil is rent, they are consumed. As Jalalluddin Rumi put it:

> If there were no heedlessness, this world would cease to be. Desire for God, memory of the other world, "inebriation", and ecstasy are the architects of the other world. If everyone were attuned to that world, we would all abandon this world and go there. God, however, wants us to be here that there may be two worlds. To that end He has stationed two headmen, heedlessness and heedfulness, so that both worlds will flourish. [*Signs of the Unseen* (*Fihi ma-Fihi*), p.114]

And whatever varied forms living things may take, they are created from a single substance: from water—that is, from Truth.

The Cause of Things Lies not In Them, but Above Them

30:22–26 *And of His signs are your sleep by night and by day, and your goings in quest of His bounties. Herein truly are signs to those who hearken.*

And of His signs are, that He showeth you the lightning, a source of awe and hope; and that He sendeth down rain from the Heaven and giveth life by it to the Earth when dead. Herein truly are signs to those who understand.

And of His signs also one is that the Heaven and the Earth stand firm at His bidding: hereafter, when with one summons He shall summon you out of the Earth,—lo! forth shall you come.

His, whatsoever is in the Heavens and on the Earth: all are obedient to Him.

And He it is who bringeth a creature forth, then causeth it to return again; and to Him is this most easy. To whatever is loftiest in Heaven and Earth is He to be likened; and He is the Mighty, the Wise.

Sleep is a great mystery; science has not yet determined exactly what its biological function is. But its spiritual function is clear: it exists to demonstrate to us, every night and often during the day as well, that this material world is not all there is. (Sleep during the night is life in death; sleep during the day is death in life.) Great bounties from God can be sought, and found, in sleep. In the words of the Prophet, peace and blessings be upon him, "dreams are the 46th part of prophesy". And the fact that we continue to breathe during deep sleep clearly demonstrates that we do not maintain ourselves in existence by our own will.

Lightning is awesome because of its destructive power and the thunder that accompanies it; but it is hopeful too because, like sleep, it is a door to the light of the heavens beyond the stars. No thing is stable by its own power, nor can it move by its own power from this world to another. No created thing possesses the power of either life or death in its own right; the destructive lightning and the life-giving rain come only from *above*. And what descends from above also calls us to ascend and meet it, where it began, in the chamber of the Secret.

All Things Submit to God

3:77 *To Him doth everything that is in the Heavens and in the Earth submit, in willing or forced obedience!*

It is only the human beings and the Jinn, beings endowed with free will, who are free to choose—and *must* choose—between willing or forced obedience, between being Muslims or being Infidels. The other beings God has created, sentient and non-sentient, all obey Him (as it were) "willingly"—which is why they can function, so to speak, as "angels" for us, bearers of messages from Allah. This is one reason why the contemplation of natural forms and cycles is both an act of piety and a way of knowing: If ants and horses, if mountains and stars obey their Creator perfectly, the least that humanity can do—as the bearer of God's Trust—is to follow suit. If we obey Him both consciously and willingly (as we and the Jinn alone can do), then we are greater than the stars, greater even than the angels; if we disobey, we are lower than the animals, lower even than the stones. The animals, the stones are not "low" in themselves;

a beast is what he is supposed to be, according to the will of Allah. Only a man who becomes *like* a beast can truly be called "bestial".

All Things are Subject to Man

16:12 *And He hath subjected to you the night and the day; the sun and the moon and the stars too are subjected to you by His behest; verily, in this are signs for those who understand.*

This is a rather mysterious verse—how can the sun and moon and stars be *subjected* to humanity? We certainly cannot control their development or their motions. In Genesis it is said that God gave man "dominion" over the animals, the fish and the birds; this is perhaps a bit easier to understand, since we can hunt them and eat them, and in some cases train and employ them. But how can man have dominion over the stars? Certainly the heavenly bodies are useful to us in that they provide light, help us tell time, and aid us in determining our direction of travel. But a deeper explanation lies in the concept of "the Trust" that God has placed upon man [cf. Q. 33:72 (Pickthall)]. The human race is greater than the sun and moon and stars because we can be conscious of them, while they cannot be conscious of us. The place of a given entity in the scale of existence does not have to do with its mass or energy, but with its *knowledge*; to know, in essence, is to be. And it is in order to express this truth that we say *Allahu Akbar*, "God is Greatest": *No vision taketh in Him, but He taketh in all vision* [Q. 6:103 (Rodwell)]. He, however, is not "Greatest" by His knowledge alone. It is possible for our knowledge to exceed our power, but His absolute Knowledge is always equaled by His infinite Power, in every way and at every point. Insofar as He creates all things by *naming* them, He creates all things by *knowing* them.

The Meaning of Creation in Relation to Man

10:5–6 *It is He who hath appointed the sun for brightness, and the moon for a light, and hath ordained her stations that you may learn the number of years and the reckoning of time. God hath not created all this but for the truth. He maketh His signs clear to those who understand.*

Verily, in the alternations of night and of day, and in all that God hath created in the Heavens and in the Earth are signs to those who fear Him.

People whose minds are modern and secular will see statements like *He . . . hath appointed the sun for brightness and the moon for a light* as a kind of naive foolishness, somewhat on the order of "God made elephants so we could have circuses and cockroaches so we would understand the consequences of poor housekeeping". But there's a lot more to it than that. Prof. Rodney Blackhirst has the following to say about the spiritual meaning of the earth and its place in the universe; it's written in the form of a dialogue with a student:

The geocentric view of the cosmos is right, is true. And so is the heliocentric view. The Ptolemaic model is right as far as it goes. And so too the Copernican. And the Newtonian. And the Einsteinean. These are not exclusive to each other. They are different orders of truth. But the geocentric world-view is especially important because it is what offers itself to our direct vision, our direct experience. It is especially real in that way. We experience the world, the cosmos, geocentrically, with the earth at the centre. It is what we see. It is what we experience. And we merely need to assume that there is purpose, or facility, in our experience. Whereas the modern models—true though they may be—are abstracted. Abstract models. You can't see them, or experience them, you can only think them.

But . . . the traditional outlook is not just geocentric but anthropocentric. It is assumes that man is at the centre of the universe.

Yes, and that man is the microcosmic reflection of the greater cosmos, of the macrocosm. That follows from the geocentric cosmology because it places man the observer at the centre of things.

How can you accuse modern man of self-flattery when traditional man thought that he was the pinnacle of the whole creation? Now we know that man is just a lucky primate on a tiny, unimportant planet.

These are ironies. Traditional man placed himself—or the human observer—actually the human consciousness—at the centre of creation, as man the microcosm, and yet maintained a human-scale world-view and a human-scale technology. Industrial man belittles himself on the one hand by insisting that he is just an animal and that the earth is just a speck of dust in a massive universe, yet this is cover for truly Promethean self-aggrandizement, conquering, raping nature. The traditional world-view is actually consciousness-centred. At the centre of the universe is human consciousness. In the modern world-view it is ironic—a tragic irony—that the same science that relegates man to an animal on a speck of dust promotes him to a god who sees fit to build nuclear bombs and splice fish genes into strawberries according to his whim . . .

Why should the earth be regarded as special? Science knows it is just a speck of dust, an insignificant satellite of the sun.

The answer to that question has exactly to do . . . with light. Because the most striking feature of light in the human macrocosm, in the cosmos, man's environment—the geocentric world—is *the proportion of reflected light to direct light.* Or moon to sun, sun to moon. In a relationship that is, as far as we know, unique in its freakish improbability. The strangest of coincidences. As far as we know, this is—in that respect—the weirdest place in the whole universe. The sun/moon polarity is the answer to this question. And then we remember that one of the first facts of human consciousness is that we experience it in two—at least two—main modes: waking and sleeping. Because dreaming is a mode of consciousness. This is the microcosmic parallel to the sun/moon polarity. Why do we need to sleep? Why is consciousness bifurcated like that? Why do we have cycles of sleeping and waking? Why that primal duality? Why is that duality built-in at such a fundamental level? In short, *because we are a product of a dualistic environment.* A dualistic environment of light. Night and day. But—equally important—direct light, reflected light. Sun and moon. The question is 'Why is this solar system special?' and, more especially, 'If man is the ontological axis of the universe, why is his home situated at some remote corner of an insignificant galaxy?' The first step in answering this question is to clarify the traditional position. The traditional assertion is that the earth and man are central in Creation because *both are paradigmatic*. That is, they express something *quintessential about the universe as a whole*. What might that be? Why is this particular solar system special? Because here something of an essential and paradigmatic nature takes place that is central in the totality of things though seemingly peripheral and insignificant on a physical, which is to say, cosmographical level. Scientific man, the industrial order, doesn't even have a *cosmology* as such—modern man merely has an extended, inexplicable cosmogeography. Which is really baffling for him. And in this vast cosmogeography—which makes no sense at all—he can make no sense of his own existence, least of all the very faculty of consciousness that he uses to explore this vast cosmogeography.

This dualistic environment Prof. Blackhirst speaks of, signified by the fact that the sun and the moon are almost equal in apparent size and move in orbits so close to the same plane that the moon can eclipse the sun and the earth eclipse the moon, is a fundamental aspect of God's creation; as it says in the Holy Qur'an, *And of everything have We created pairs: that haply you may reflect* [Rodwell 51:49]. And not only are night and day such a pair; even light itself, along with every other kind of electromagnetic energy, takes the form of waves that alternate between a "peak" and a "trough", just like the cycle of the day, the circuit of the year, the waves of the sea.

Satan Commands His Followers to Alter the Order of Nature

4:117–118 *They call, beside Him, upon mere goddesses! they invoke a rebel Satan!*

On them is the curse of God. For he said, "A portion of Thy servants will I surely take, and will lead them astray, and will stir desires within them, and will command them and they shall cut the ears of animals; and I will command them, and they shall alter the creation of God."

Satan says (referring to his followers, the Pagan polytheists, as well as to those Muslims and other Peoples of the Book he is able to pervert), *I will command them, and they shall alter the creation of God* [Rodwell, 4:119]. The Pagans who will change the order of nature are those who call upon secondary "gods" to do their bidding—beings who are actually what the Qur'an calls the *Jinn*, the "fairies" or "elementals". These beings are not gods in the same sense that Allah is, but only His creatures.

The Pagans of antiquity (like the Neo-Pagans of today) did not pray to the One God, but attempted to propitiate or control the lesser forces of the universe—the Jinn, in other words. Their method was not submission to Allah, but rather magic, including sacrifice performed with a basically magical (i.e., utilitarian) intent. And the basic worldview of magic is closely allied to that of technology. Both magic and technology seek to extend the power of human will rather than submitting to God's will, and both attempt to command the forces of nature. So it is not surprising that, according to the Qur'an, it is the *de facto* Pagans who will finally *alter the creation of God*. We should be quick to point out, however, that most of those who call themselves Pagans today have a great love for the natural world and are dedicated to preserving it, not destroying it, and that very few of them are overt Satanists. But to the degree that they operate according to the magical paradigm, they are unconsciously cooperating with the materialist/technological paradigm that is indeed destroying creation. We should further note that any so-called Muslim who seeks to wrest power from the forces of nature outside the will and law of Allah is a Pagan in all but name. To worship the natural world instead of Allah is to betray the human Trust, and in so doing transform humanity from the guardian of the earth into its destroyer.

This Quranic prophesy turns out to have been historically accurate. The technology and economy that is presently altering and destroying the earth—for example, by forcing farmers to use genetically engineered seeds which don't reproduce in the next generation, leading to widespread food shortages in the third world—was ultimately the product of the European industrial revolution. The industrial revolution grew out of the secular experimental sciences of the 17th century, which in turn were based on the rediscovery of the science and technology of the Greco-Roman Pagans during the Renaissance. Because this development took place partly outside the limits of traditional Christianity, the idea that nature is God's *creation* began to be replaced by the secular notion of nature as a "neutral" field in which the human race can exercise its powers according to our own willfulness without fear of transgressing the Will of God. Nor did the Church herself remain unaffected by these developments; Gregor Mendel, for example, the founder of the science of genetics, was a Christian monk. This does not mean, of course, that he was *necessarily* working outside the will of God. The American George Washington Carver, for example, was a horticultural genius who based his science on his ability to listen to the voice of God speaking to him through God's creatures, demonstrating that a truly pious science of genetics is not an impossibility. Those "technological wizards", however, who are dedicated to controlling the *elements* or forces of nature with no regard for the forms in which they have been created, have no intrinsic respect for God's universe because, by and large, they do not believe in Him—and even those who do believe in Him don't always see the natural world as composed of the signs of God as the Qur'an does. They will implant chicken genes in tomatoes, release deadly radioactivity into the atmosphere, and even clone human beings, with no sense that they are doing something horrendous, sacrilegious. And those Muslims who envy Western technology, with no sense that much of it (though certainly not all) is the product of Satan's command to his followers that they *alter the creation of God*, are directly opposed to Qur'anic norms. As the Book itself predicts: *O believers! if you obey some amongst those who have received the Scripture, after your very Faith will they make you infidels!* [Rodwell, 3:95].

In our own time we can discern a certain "counter-intuitive" alliance between ecology and technocracy. Eugenics, for example, wants to artificially reduce and genetically improve the human population in order to save the earth—and there is nothing less "natural" than eugenics. There are also various proposals to restore extinct animal and plant species through cloning or genetically engineering fossil DNA. To the degree that we deny that this world is a creation of God, we lose our ability to discern the Divine Order in nature—and as soon as we deny the existence of this Order, we free ourselves to alter the creation of God in any way we see fit—which in actual fact will be according to the desires inflamed in us by Shaytan. And insofar as the worship of a goddess represents a rejection of transcendence (which in most cases it does), and thus a denial of the reality of eternal form, of the existence of the prototypes of all things within the Mind of God, then it is opposed to nature in the name of nature. When goddess-worship, consciously or not, begins to replace the idea of creation with a sort of "glamorized Darwinism" where man's will to alter the creation of God is seen as an expression of the creative power of evolution working through him, then technocracy and goddess-worship are revealed as two sides of the same coin. Certainly many of those who worship a goddess are opposed to materialistic technocracy—but to the extent that they deny the reality of the Transcendent God they are left with nothing but matter, and so are effectively materialists whether they like it or not. And to be a materialist is necessarily to be a technocrat.

Many of today's Pagans literally worship the earth as an all-powerful goddess named "Gaia", while at the same time admitting that our planet is "fragile" and in need of our care; they would do well to emulate the Prophet Abraham who worshipped stars, moon and sun until he came to the understanding that they all pass away, that Allah alone is eternal. In the above passage, the Qur'an associates the worship of goddesses with the invocation of Shaytan, and both with the will to *alter the creation of God*. In there an inner logic to this, or is it simply a case of "male chauvinism"?

The archetype of the feminine principle is receptivity; the archetype of the masculine principle is action. Every human being possesses both capacities. If a man claims to act on his own authority, he is a tyrant; only if he submits to God's will, only if he is feminine in relation to God, can he act with true authority. Likewise, if a woman allows her receptivity to be transformed into a sullen passivity, if she refuses to submit to legitimate authority and act in line with it, with a masculine strength and vigor, but rather passively resists it, then she is a rebel. A goddess is not a human being, but a symbolic representation of the feminine principle. If the feminine principle, in either a man or a woman, refuses to receive and submit to the will and knowledge of Allah, the Source of its very existence, but arrogates to itself the right and the power to act on its own authority as if it were self-created, then it becomes destructive to the Divine Order.

The Creation is Perfect—But Can We See It as It Is?

> 67:3 *No defect canst thou see in the creation of the God of Mercy: Repeat the gaze: seest thou a single flaw? Then twice more repeat the gaze: thy gaze shall return to thee dulled and weary.*

The created world may not be perfect according to human desire—clearly most of us would choose to abolish suffering and death, if that were possible, and remain on earth forever, heedless of the fact that *unto Him shall all things return* [5:21]—but it is perfect in God's eyes. And as long as God, by His grace and generosity, allows us to see as if with His eyes—at least up to our limited capacity—then we will find no flaw in His creation; this is how those who are perfectly submitted to the Will of God contemplate the universe. But it is hard to maintain this exalted view, and to the degree that we try to perceive and evaluate the universe by our own efforts, we will lose sight of God's perfect creation, till finally we will be able to see nothing but our own passions and limitations projected upon the world around us. "Familiarity breeds contempt". And this kind of perceptual dullness and weariness leads to a heedless *identification* with the world; we take it for granted so completely that we no longer even see it. But if we want to show *respect* for God's Creation, we will have to break our sleepy, unconscious identification with it, wake up, and see it as it is, in line with the Prophet's prayer, "O God, show me things as they really are." If we know it as created by Allah and composed of only His signs, we will see it as an expression of the perfection of His will, and resist Shaytan's temptation to alter and distort it.

Natural Law and Intelligent Design

> 2:186–188 *For the Kingdom of the Heavens and the Earth is God's, and God hath power over all things.*

Verily, in the creation of the Heavens and of the Earth, and in the succession of the night and of the day, are signs for men of understanding heart;

Who standing, and sitting, and reclining, bear God in mind, and muse on the creation of the Heavens and of the Earth. "O our Lord!" Say they, "thou hast not created this in vain. No. Glory be to Thee! Keep us, then, from the torment of the Fire".

According to the Darwinian evolutionists and the secular cosmologists, the universe has no *purpose*. In their view, the heavens and the earth developed in vain; there is simply no reason for them. In terms of living species, the Darwinians speak of "the survival of the fittest", which is a tautology: all it really means is, "those who can survive, do". But if survivability is the criterion of life, if life has no intrinsic meaning beyond avoidance of death, then why did it not limit itself, for example, to the virus? Some viruses can survive in a latent state for aeons. If the avoidance of death and the ability to propagate are the only criteria, then how, for example, did the peacock appear? The magnificent tail of the peacock, and its dance, are explained by the Darwinians in entirely utilitarian terms, as being for the purpose of mating and reproduction. But cockroaches and mice and oysters can certainly propagate themselves without such a radiant display; and it is during their mating dance that peacocks are most vulnerable to predators. Only those *whose hearts are blind* could imagine a businesslike, utilitarian peacock! If reproduction and survival are the only criteria for life, surely the peacock, like so many other amazing and beautiful species, was created in vain. But the fact is, he was created for a purpose: to manifest in this world a certain aspect of the Beauty of God, a particular Name of God, just as the eagle manifests exaltation and swiftness of insight and the lion courage and nobility. And the less exalted animals manifest other aspects of Allah, including His willingness to extend His life and reality into every receptacle able to receive it, no matter how lowly; *Verily God is not ashamed to set forth as well the instance* [or *similitude*] *of a gnat as of any nobler object* [Rodwell 2:24]. The King grants a province to a great general; he also places a coin in the blind beggar's cup. But he does not grant the beggar a province

because he gives to each according to his or her capacity. Certainly life-forms change over time; only Allah is *as-Samad*, the Eternal. *Seest thou not that in truth hath God created the Heavens and the Earth? Were such His pleasure He could make you pass away, and cause a new creation to arise* [Q. 14:22]. But species do not appear and change and disappear for no purpose; Allah has not created this universe, nor this earth and all the living things within it, in vain. He has created it as a theophany, as a revelation of Himself.

As any intelligent person will immediately understand, the kind of atheistic, materialistic science that developed in the West is capable of great evil and destruction, largely because it sees creation as purposeless, and therefore meaningless. The worship of and/or the attempt to manipulate natural laws—as the Pagans both *worship* their "gods" and try to *use* them for their own ends—coupled with the denial that the universe is the creation of Allah, is the surest way of subverting and destroying the order of nature. And so it might seem that one way for Islam to take a stand against this evil would be for Muslims embrace the sort of theology developed by the Asharite school, which denies the reality of secondary causes—natural laws—entirely.

The proponents of Asharite *kalam* ("scholastic" theology) deny secondary causes in creation so as to preserve the absolute Omnipotence of Allah. If a rock falls or a fire burns, this has nothing to do with the physics of gravity or the chemistry of oxidation: the rock falls because Allah wills that particular rock to fall, right now; the fire burns because he wills it to burn in this moment. This unqualified loyalty to the notion of Divine Omnipotence led the Asharites to formulate their famous doctrine of "occasionalism", the idea that God recreates the entire universe in each separate moment—and, from one perspective, this is most certainly true. Most often, however, Allah does not recreate the universe arbitrarily or chaotically, but rather *rhythmically*; creative omnipotence is much more clearly expressed by harmony than by discord, which appears most particularly at the point when manifestation begins to dissolve.

Those theologians who deny secondary causes so as to assert the omnipotence of Allah seem to believe that if He were to establish a natural law, He would immediately become subject to it Himself;

He would be forced to obey it whether He liked it or not. This, however, is not the case. A powerful king may enact laws in order that his kingdom may operate harmoniously, but he in no way abdicates his power by doing so. To delegate power is not to abandon it, and if an omnipotent God is capable of ordaining events, then we are in no way justified in denying Him the power to ordain laws, as long as we also ascribe to Him the power to suspend those laws if and when He so chooses, thus producing what we term "miracles". *What He pleaseth will God abrogate or confirm: for with Him is the source of revelation.* [Rodwell 13:39]

The Asharites tend to deny both natural law and human free will, as if both of these would somehow necessarily be "partners" with Allah in the work of maintaining the universe, and thus fall under the heresy of *shirk* or polytheism. And it is certainly true that if Allah is seen as only *partly* responsible for the creation and governance of the universe and the events that occur within it, with natural law and human action also lending a hand so as to make up some kind of divine deficit, then His Omnipotence is indeed denied. But it should be obvious that the Qur'an itself implies the reality of free will whenever it warns or exhorts, which it does on almost every page; if human beings were no more than puppets of Allah, all warnings and exhortations would be meaningless. And, as we shall see, the Book itself accepts the reality of natural law—which is a far cry from making such law a partner to God. Natural laws and human choices certainly operate, but Allah encompasses all of them by His sovereign Command. When a rock falls or a fire burns, they do so only by That One's command, according to His established law; when a human being makes a free choice, he or she does so only by That One's will and power. [See Rodwell 4:80-8; 91:9–10]

The Qur'an does in fact clearly assert that Allah is the Author of the natural laws by which the universe operates. Although some English translations of the Qur'an—particularly that of Marmaduke Pickthall—speak as if Allah produces all natural events by His direct Command, others (those of Rodwell, Muhammad Asad, and Yusuf Ali) speak of Him as creating the natural laws by which the universe operates. Furthermore, there are two passages which, in all four translations, present Allah as setting the sun and moon to run for an appointed "term" or to an appointed "goal" (Rodwell 31:28 and 35:14; Pickthall, Yusuf Ali and Muhammad Asad, 31:29 and 35:13). In other words, they assert that Allah is in fact the Author of a particular set of *laws*—those that we have named "Newton's First Law of Motion", "Newton's Law of Gravity", and "Einstein's Special and General Laws of Relativity"—by means of which He commands the sun and moon to move in their courses. And if this is so, then scientific investigation of natural law is an integral part of Islamic piety, part of the recognition of all the forms and processes of the natural world as *signs of Allah*. Furthermore, the Qur'an itself exhorts us to reflect upon the spiritual meaning of the forms and periodic changes of the natural world: *And He it is who sendeth forth the winds as the heralds of His compassion, until they bring up the laden clouds, which We drive along to some dead land and send down water thereon, by which We cause an upgrowth of all kinds of fruit.—Thus will We bring forth the dead. Haply you will reflect* [Rodwell 7:59], and: *Verily, in the creation of the Heavens and of the Earth, and in the succession of the night and of the day, are signs for men of understanding heart; who standing, and sitting, and reclining, bear God in mind, and muse on the creation of the Heavens and of the Earth. "O our Lord!" say they, "thou hast not created this in vain"* [Rodwell 3:188].

So here we can begin to see how a "sacred science", a science that "bears God in mind", that recognizes the universe as an intentional *creation*, not simply a set of neutral "entities" or "facts" or "forces", is entirely possible. And, given the dire state of the natural environment, it would seem that such a science is becoming increasingly necessary. Such a discipline would certainly not be based upon a simple-minded mis-application of theological dogmas to physical facts, these being two very different levels of reality. Nonetheless, a logically and empirically rigorous science that accepts the natural world as the creation of Allah, fully granting Him the power and the right to intervene in His Own creation whenever He chooses, would be entirely valid, both theologically and scientifically.

Perhaps the closest approach yet made to such a sacred science in the modern age, though it grew up not in the Islamic world but in the Christian (or post-Christian) one, is the discipline known as

Intelligent Design. Intelligent Design uses strictly empirical methods, based largely on information theory, to detect degrees of purposeful complexity in the natural world, particularly on the biological level, that could never have been produced by natural law alone. Intelligent Design theory thus demonstrates that such designs must emanate from an Agent higher than, and therefore not subject to, natural law—though as soon as they have come into existence they must operate in terms of such law, unless Allah wills otherwise.

The two central books of the Intelligent Design movement are *Intelligent Design* by William Dembski and *Darwin's Black Box* by Michael Behe. Also important, though not strictly based on the theory of Intelligent Design, is William Denton's *Nature's Destiny*, a truly astounding account of the natural world as in no way a product of "chance", but as composed of interlocking levels of exquisite order that could never have arisen by chance. Muslims who wish to follow the Qur'an's exhortation that we reflect on the natural world as the ensemble of the signs of Allah should definitely read these three books.

The Meaning of Variety in Creation

16:10–17 *It is He who sendeth down rain out of Heaven: from it is your drink; and from it are the plants by which you pasture.*

By it He causeth the corn, and the olives, and the palm-trees, and the grapes to spring forth for you, and all kinds of fruits: verily, in this are signs for those who ponder.

And He hath subjected to you the night and the day; the sun and the moon and the stars too are subjected to you by His behest; verily, in this are signs for those who understand:

And all of varied hues that He hath created for you over the earth: verily, in this are signs for those who remember.

And He it is who hath subjected the sea to you, that you may eat of its fresh fish, and take forth from it ornaments to wear—thou seest the ships ploughing its billows—and that you may go in quest of His bounties, and that you might give thanks.

And He hath thrown firm mountains on the earth, lest it move with you; and rivers and paths for your guidance,

And way marks. By the stars too are men guided.

Shall He then who hath created be as he who hath not created? Aye! God is right Gracious, Merciful!

The rain Allah sends down is *al-nafas al-Rahman*, His general Mercy, the Mercy of existence itself. If God were jealous of His existence, He would harbor all possibilities without expressing them or letting the express themselves. But Allah is not one to retain existence for Himself, even though all existence is His by right; He is *al-Rahman*, the All-Merciful, and *al-Karim*, the All-Generous. Nor is His Mercy abstract and uniform simply because it is general; it produces different kinds of fruit for different needs, conditions and occasions, so much so that it is possible to say that He never repeats Himself, that *Every day doth some new work employ Him* [Rodwell, 55:29]. Each occasion has its unique and appropriate fruit, which ripens only in that moment.

Here again we hear how the sun and the moon, the day and the night, are subject to man. It is clear that they are not subject to us in the sense that we can change their courses or alter the length of night and day, but because sun and moon, day and night—as Prof. Blackhirst has pointed out above—*correspond* to him; they are the outer-world mirrors of what Allah has placed within him. This is what the Qur'an means when it says that it is man, not *the heavens and the earth and the hills*, who is bearer of *the Trust*.

The varying hues of the earth are the different qualities of creation, clearly visible to all. The sea, made up of water that has fallen from the sky, is the mystery of what has already been created but remains hidden; what fish or pearls or coral we may take from it remain invisible until they are lifted above its surface. The ones who sail in ships are those who have the power to tap the hidden potentials of life. They can fish; they can trawl; they can even dive. The land is what is known to all; the sea is what is known only to a few, but may be revealed to many through those few, if God so wills. So whenever we see a black or a white or a red cliff, we are reminded that Allah has ordained that our common life be made up of various ongoing, stable qualities—and whenever we gaze upon the sea and the ships that travel upon it, we are reminded that the visible surface of life hides many mysteries that are only rarely brought to light; Allah has ordained this as well. What is common to all and what is reserved for the few are both a part of God's creation; without both members of this pair—and without the clear distinction, the *shoreline* between them—God's creation could not stand.

The firm mountains Allah has thrown upon the earth to give it stability are the saints; the rivers and paths are the ways of those who follow them. The ways of Allah are both roads and rivers. In one sense we have to walk them by our own efforts, on our own feet, like roads; in another sense they simply carry us, like rivers. By His *baraka* they are rivers; by our earned and acquired virtue, they are roads; both are necessary to constitute any viable spiritual Path. The mountains are there to remind us what it is to be a human being, a bridge between heaven and earth; the roads, to remind us of the need for purposeful effort toward a goal in life; the rivers, to remind us that the paths created by God reach their appointed goals by His power, not ours, and that we can avail ourselves of that power by submission to the nature of things. Thus true science is not our conquest of nature based on rebellion against the nature of things as God created them, but our cultivation of natural world based upon our intelligent cooperation with it. Just as man either fulfills his nature as *khalifa* of Allah in this world, or else perverts it until he becomes worse than any *shaytan*, so he either perfects or perverts the natural order. We can easily see the truth of this when we consider the state of the world and what man has done to it; though he indeed is bearer of *the Trust*, nonetheless—as the Qur'an declares—*he hath proved a tyrant and a fool.*

The way-marks are the collected wisdom of the wise, who have walked the Path before and know the way.

The stars are the thoughts of God—His eternal Names or Attributes, not (like the clouds) His acts which appear and disappear in time. We can contemplate these Divine Thoughts only because they stand out against the blackness of Night: the Night is the Essence of God, which we cannot contemplate; That by which all things are known cannot be known in Itself.

All this is created by God, not by man. We can tap the potentials hidden within what God has already created, but we ourselves can create nothing. And when we begin to believe that we are creators in our own right, co-creators with Allah, His irrefutable answer is: *If you believe this, then raise your eyes and look at the stars.*

All Things Praise God

> 24:40–41 *Or like the darkness on the deep sea when covered by billows riding upon billows, above which are clouds: darkness upon darkness. When a man reacheth forth his hand, he cannot nearly see it! He to whom God shall not give light, no light at all hath he!*
>
> *Hast thou not seen how all in the Heavens and in the Earth uttereth the praise of God?—the very birds as they spread their wings? Every creature knoweth its prayer and its praise! and God knoweth what they do.*

A man cannot understand himself or the true nature of the world around him except by the light of Allah; *Allah is the Light of the heavens and the earth.* Man by his own efforts cannot illuminate the stormy sea of existence, nor understand his own form or condition; he must wait until Allah Himself dispels the clouds, until He illuminates both sea and sailor by His own light, in line with the prayer of the Prophet, "O Allah, show me things as they really are". Yes, he must wait; but he must also pray.

It's hard for us to understand nowadays what it means for all creatures to praise God; we even balk at the idea of praising Him ourselves. "God doesn't need our praise" we say; "if He did it would only show that He was lacking in self-confidence, that He was a petty tyrant dependent upon the flattery of others." Yes, we are actually capable of thinking this way! The ancient Pagans often saw their own "gods" in these terms, as beings who had to be "fed" with praise and sacrifice or they would eventually wither away. It is quite otherwise with the true and only Deity, whose Arabic name is Allah: He has no need whatsoever of creatures or their praise; *He is the Rich, and we are the poor.* When we wonder why we are commanded to praise Allah, this at least indicates that we see the hollowness of the Pagan idea that Allah might stand in need of the praise of man. But although Allah as-*Samad*, the Self-Sufficient, is absolutely independent of our praise, the creatures are in absolute need of their ability to praise Him; without this ability, they themselves would wither away. To praise Allah is not to give Him something He does not already possess, but to recognize Him as the Source of our existence, and thereby also realize what a miracle our existence is. If we fail to know Him as *al-Khaliq* (the Creator), *al-Mubdi* (the Producer) and *al-Musawwir* (the Fashioner), as the One Who conceives our eternal design within Himself, Who draws us into existence out of the night of the Unseen, and Who fashions us until we perfectly conform to that design, then we cut ourselves off from the Source of our own existence and life; like a branch torn from a tree, we quickly wither. To praise is to receive existence and mercy and virtue and knowledge from the Praised (*al-Hamid*). Creatures praise God by being transparent to His Light, and equally by transmitting it.

It is possible for man to choose not to praise Allah, or to forget to praise Him constantly; though in virtual terms we are host to all the names of God, it is up to us, by His Grace, to actualize them. It is otherwise with the other creatures of the earth: a rock or a tree or a lion is each an outer expression, as it were, of only a single name of God, or only a few of them; and yet that expression (at least in the case of a healthy tree or a healthy lion) is perfectly actualized. This is why all created things stand, in relation to man, as signs of Allah—and it is we alone, of all creatures, who can see them this way; this is what it means for the human form to be the bearer of *the Trust*. Since all creatures praise Allah *intrinsically*, we human beings—and we alone—can take spiritual guidance from them, insofar as we recognize them as reflections of the Names of God in this world.

The English poet Christopher Smart (1722–1771) expressed the truth that creatures praise God by their very nature in his poem "For I will Consider my Cat Jeoffrey":

> For I will consider my cat Jeoffrey.
> For he is the servant of the Living God, daily and duly serving Him.
> For at the first glance of the Glory of God in the east he worships in his way.
> For is this done by wreathing his body seven times round with elegant quickness.

For then he leaps up to catch the musk, which is the blessing of God upon his prayer.
...
For God has blessed him in the variety of his movements.
For, tho he cannot fly, he is an excellent clamberer.
For his motions upon the face of the earth are more than any other quadruped.
For he can tread to all measures upon the musick.
For he can swim for life.
For he can creep.

We should note here that Jeoffrey was in the habit of making seven circuits every morning, just as the pilgrims make seven circuits around the Kaaba. This leads us to ask whether Abu Huraira, "father of the little cat", remembered more of the words and actions of the Prophet than other people because his cat taught him to pay attention to many things that most people would consider small and insignificant, even if performed by a prophet.

Life and Death are Necessary to Each Other

> 30:18 *He bringeth forth the living out of the dead, and He bringeth forth the dead out of the living: and He quickeneth the Earth when dead. Thus is it that you too shall be brought forth.*

The natural world is the place where life and death are most clearly visible, both in terms of the clear distinction between them and of the many ways in which they cooperate; and natural life and death are perhaps the most potent and revealing symbols of the life and death of the Spirit. God separates those who are alive to the Spirit from the decay and death of *al-dunya*; He also separates from Life, from Himself as *al-Hayy*, those who are dead to the Spirit. The living also, by casting off whatever is dead in them by the power of the Spirit, "give birth" to the dead; likewise the dead "give birth" to the living by casting off spiritual life from themselves because they cannot stand the presence of this life, just as the Quraysh of Mecca cast off the Prophet and his companions, thus giving birth to *dar al-Islam* in Medina. The perpetual birth of the Spirit within the human heart casts off death just as the living body casts off excrement—and as Medina cast off the Jewish tribes who betrayed *dar al-Islam* to the Quraysh—while whatever is dead, by its very decay, supports the development of life, just as dung and rotten fish may be used to fertilize a field. It does so by being repellent to life and thus causing it to differentiate itself and separate itself from death. The growth and decay of life on earth according to the four seasons is thus a telling metaphor for the spiritual life, and even a power by which that life may be alchemically cultivated: as the Will of God operates in the seasons of organic life, so it also operates in the seasons of the soul. And the differentiation of life from death, so that death serves life by bringing it to life, and life serves death by sending it to death, operates in the next world as well, by the power of the Scales, which send the spiritually living to the Garden and the spiritually dead to the Fire. The Scales will complete their operation when the two worlds become one at the arrival of the Hour—and they complete their operation just as definitively in the case of any human being who is annihilated in God, and consequently subsists in God, not in himself, though here the meanings of life and death are reversed: in annihilation, the friend of God is brought forth dead from the living; in subsistence, he is brought forth alive from the dead.

Creation is the Realm of Choice

> 7:55–56 *And He it is who sendeth forth the winds as the heralds of His compassion, until they bring up the laden clouds, which We drive along to some dead land and send down water thereon, by which We cause an upgrowth of all kinds of fruit.—Thus will We bring forth the dead. Haply you will reflect.*
>
> *In a rich soil, its plants spring forth abundantly by the will of its Lord, and in that which is bad, they spring forth but scantily. Thus do We diversify Our signs for those who are thankful.*

We are sown here like seeds by the hand of Allah, and after our lives here we will be harvested and taken elsewhere, just as the crop after harvest is taken to the threshing-floor (Judgment) and gathered into the barn (Paradise), while the husks of the grain are carried away by the wind and remaining stubble piled up and burned (the

Fire). This, not permanent residence on this earth, is the purpose of human life, seeing that *All is perishing but His Face.* And just as the human form is sown on earth like a seed, so virtues and spiritual insights are sown by Allah within the human heart. If the heart is well-cultivated it will bring forth an abundant harvest of virtue and knowledge; but if we are "hard-hearted", if the potential for virtue and knowledge within us is resistant to the seeds sown by Allah and the rain He sends to nourish them and give them life, our crop will be scanty or deformed; it will weigh lightly in the Scales, and so destine us for the Fire. It is clear that Allah sows his seeds within all fields and sends his rain upon all creatures; as *al-Karim*, the Generous, He wills to do nothing else. The kind of crop we bear depends upon whether or not we are open to His gift of life to us, and His second gift of knowledge and virtue once we have attained to life. He knows who will bear and who will be barren, but He does not take away from us our power and our duty to choose which we will be; if this were so, why would the Qur'an be filled with warnings and exhortations on almost every page? Our choice is not *forced* upon us by His choice: our choice *is* His choice. Choice, like existence, belongs to Him alone; human beings, as creatures and slaves of Allah, possess neither any existence nor any power of choice on their own. As he lends us His existence, so He lends us His choice. Our wills are certainly free—and yet we possess, and exercise, no freedom but His. But only *the thankful* know this; only they know that their free choice as well as their very existence belong to Allah alone. To be thankful means to know the true identity of *al-Karim*, to know Who *the Generous* really is. Those who are not thankful either take Allah's generosity for granted, thus making it only a source of corruption, or else complain of His stinginess, failing to realize that they alone are responsible for their state. Shaytan, in the Qur'an [Rodwell 14:27–28], speaks as follows: *Verily, God promised you a promise of truth: I, too, made you a promise, but I deceived you. Yet I had not power over you: But I only called you and you answered me. Blame not me then, but blame yourselves....*

To Fulfill our Function on Earth We Must Not be Bound to It

25:64 *And the servants of the God of Mercy are they who walk upon the earth softly. . . .*

The servants of Allah are not dominated by matter, weighed down by the gravity of materialism: The Prophet Muhammad, peace and blessings be upon him, could fly from Mecca to Jerusalem, ascend through the celestial spheres and return to his starting point in less time than it takes for a pitcher of water that's been upset to empty upon the floor. Those who are involved with material concerns are burdened by them because matter means "reality" to them; they *believe* that they believe in Allah, but actually they are *kafirun* without realizing it. Can a stone lying in a field plow and seed and fertilize and cultivate a garden? Certainly not. Only a man, who can see the state of the garden because he can move about freely within it, can cultivate it, defend it from pests, and raise a healthy crop. Likewise man is the *khalifa* of Allah in this material world because he transcends matter, while at the same time being fully "expressed" by Allah in material terms. By the will of Allah he is related both to *al-zahir*, a part of the material world, and to *al-batin*, a resident of the spiritual world. It is precisely this that fits him to bear *the Trust.*

All Things Return to Allah

24:42 *God's, the Kingdom of the Heavens and of the Earth: and unto God the final return!*

All things return to Allah because they have no existence of their own. If they did, they would be eternal like Him, consequently God would have partners—which is impossible. But since they do not, this truth must be expressed by the dissolution of their existence and their return to their Essence, which is He. They are annihilated in the world of existence. But because Allah, the Infinite Reality, embraces all possibilities, they remain within Him, within the world of the Essence, forever. Their existence is intermittent; His Being and Essence are Eternal. He does indeed create all things out of nothing, because in Him they *are* nothing. He does so by *calling* them; all *He needs do is say to a thing be!* ("kun!") *and it is.* He calls non-existent things into existence by asking them *am I not your Lord?* The moment they answer *Yea!*, they exist.

The Meaning of the Garden

Paradise in the Qur'an is pictured as a *garden*. What is a garden? It is a place where nature and human labor come together, just as Allah's guidance and human labor must come together in a soul working toward holiness. In the soul, God provides the basis for sanctification—the soul itself—as well as the Law that guides it and the Grace that inspires it. But this Law and this Grace must be made effective by human work: obedience to the law, submission to the will of God and receptivity to His Mercy. Likewise, in a garden, God provides the ground to be cultivated, which is like the human body and soul; the seed, which is like the human spirit or essence; and the air and sun and rain the seed requires in order to grow, which are like the God's Spirit and Law and Grace. But for a garden to flourish, humanity must provide the work: tilling, planting, fertilizing, combating pests, and harvesting the crop. (A similar kind of work is necessary for the soul, too—especially when it comes to combating pests!)

If the best similitude of Paradise is a garden, then a garden may well be the closest thing on earth to Paradise.

4

Magic and *Tasawwuf*

THE BASIC APPROACH of Perennialists René Guénon, Ananda Coomaraswamy and Frithjof Schuon to the Spiritual Path was as far from magic as can be imagined, although Baron Julius Evola practiced something he called by that name. Prof. Patrick Laude, however, in his *Frithjof Schuon: Life and Teachings*, characterized Schuon's Native American practices as "Shamanism" (incorrectly I believe), while the late Algis Uzdavinys, that incomparable scholar of archaic spiritualities who is unfortunate no longer with us, seemed to call for a renewal of Neo-Platonic and/or Egyptian theurgy in his *Philosophy and Theology in Late Antiquity*. Theurgy, being a sacred art (as Shamanism also is, or was), is certainly not to be simply identified with magic or thaumaturgy; the Sun Dance rite of the plains Indians is a case in point. Nonetheless, archaic forms of theurgy in their decadence undoubtedly contributed to the growth of various types of subversive thaumaturgy, a counter-initiatory influence which, like that of degenerate Shamanism (though legitimate Shamanism, God willing, is still in existence) has lasted into our own times. Sufism too has its thaumaturgic practices, some of them undoubtedly of great antiquity. And in view of the fact that many people who are attracted to esoteric spirituality do not always clearly differentiate between esoterism and magic, this chapter, in which I do my best to make the difference between them crystal clear, may be timely:

> [*They*] *follow that which the devils falsely related against the kingdom of Solomon. Solomon disbelieved not; but the devils disbelieved, teaching mankind magic and that which was revealed to the two angels in Babel, Harut and Marut. Nor did they* (*the*

angels) teach it to anyone until they said: We are only a temptation, therefore disbelieve not. (Qur'an 2:102)

In our time, the great resurgence of interest in the magical arts, both traditional and innovative, should be obvious to all. In the minds of many people, magic and occultism, mysticism and esoterism—anything in the spiritual field outside of strictly moralistic religion—are seen as intrinsically similar, if not identical. And while it may be true up to a point (and ironically so) that an interest in both legitimate esoterism and magic are shared by certain groups and subcultures who are fundamentally opposed to mainstream religion, in metaphysical and cosmological terms the magical path and the esoteric spiritual Path lead to radically different destinations. As many religions teach, while paranormal powers or *siddhis* (the Hindu term) may or may not develop as an accidental result of progress on the Path, to *seek* such powers is always detrimental to the spiritual life; and this is certainly true in terms of *tasawwuf* or Sufism. Although historical Sufism embraces (legitimately or otherwise) certain thaumaturgic practices which when deviated may tend toward the magical, the truth is that magic and *tasawwuf*, in essence, are poles apart. [NOTE: The first step, though certainly not the last, in determining the legitimacy of any form of thaumaturgy or theurgy or spiritual practice is to ask whether or not it forms an integral part of a Divine revelation that is presently in force, and consequently enjoys God's favor. Forms of magical or spiritual practice based on the mere literary or archaeological resurrection of dead religions will be useless as best, and at worst make us vulnerable to the toxic psychic residues of forms of the Spirit that have departed this world. Consequently when Algis Uzdavinys says in *Philosophy and Theurgy in Late Antiquity* [Sophia Perennis, 2010], "if the summit of perfection is achieved only through the union with the divine principles themselves and, if they are called 'gods', the traditional means of ascent should be rehabilitated and reused" —thereby apparently calling for a return to polytheistic theurgy—I cannot go along with him.]

According to Islamic lore, the one who has been opened to the psychic plane but has been unable to transcend it and make contact

Psychic vs. spiritual plane

with the Spiritual plane, as well as anyone who has *broken into* the psychic plane on his own initiative instead of allowing God to open it in His own time, is in danger of becoming a *saher*, a sorcerer; the same destiny may lie in wait for the Sufi who abandons the Path after having made a certain degree of progress. The *saher* becomes subject to various psychic influences he may believe he can dominate, but which in reality dominate him. The essence of Sufism is to choose God's will over one's own, until it is realized that only God's Will exists; consequently *tasawwuf* precludes magic definitively and from the outset (though the *saher* may sometimes feed himself on the crumbs that fall from the Sufis' table; cf. Qur'an 20:85–96, verse 96 in particular). There are also many stories in Islam of human interactions with those subtle beings of the psychic plane known as the Jinn, stories involving poets, warriors, sorcerers, physicians, Sufis and others; some of them are undoubtedly true. Islam, unlike Christianity, but in line with many archaic religions, sees the Jinn—whom we in the west call the "fairies"—as made up of both good and evil spirits, both Muslims and unbelievers. However, the Qur'an is clear on the fate of those human beings who conclude alliances with them: *In the day when He will gather them together (He will say): O ye assembly of the jinn! Many of humankind did ye seduce. And their adherents among humankind will say: Our Lord! We have enjoyed one another, but now we have arrived at the appointed term which Thou appointedst for us. He will say: Fire is your home, abide therein forever, save him whom Allah willeth (to deliver). Lo! thy Lord is Wise, Aware* (Q. 6:129). Some claim that this applies only to the evil Jinn; nonetheless it is recognized by the Sufis that human intercourse with even the Muslim Jinn can have a deleterious effect; they can be highly fascinating and *distracting* to the person attempting to fulfill the Trust by conforming his humanity to Allah (cf. Qur'an 33:72) because they are not on the "human stem". A story is told of one Sufi saint who, whenever he performed his daily prayers, was joined by a group of the Jinn, obviously the Muslim Jinn; as soon as he realized this, he asked them kindly to find another place to pray. And there is little doubt that many magical operations are based on human interaction with the Jinn and their powers.

Magic, though it certainly leads to delusion and is based on delusion, is itself quite real. It is an actual psychic "technology" that can produce real psychic and physical results. Every human civilization throughout history, except for the most recent and the most materialistic, has known this, and nearly every sacred scripture, including the Bible and the Qur'an, attests to it. And as long as we see things from the psychophysical level alone, according to a worldview based on the essentially profane root-assumptions of that level, we are justified in defining magic as a power that can be used either for good, or for evil, or to secure useful information, or simply for entertainment and diversion.

When viewed from the Spiritual or Metaphysical level, however, the practice of magic, no matter what phenomena it is apparently able to produce, is seen as based upon a fundamentally false assumption. It's as if someone knew everything possible about operating a computer, but labored under the delusion that in operating it he was actually designing and building it. The magician may feel that he has the power to operate upon reality up to a certain point, and that he has had this assumption apparently confirmed innumerable times by concrete phenomena. But the fact is, reality was designed by Someone Else, and *is* Someone Else. Whoever thinks that he is the ultimate Doer, that he has the power and the right to both propose and dispose, is totally involved in illusion.

Yes, the will is free, but it is only *totally* free at one point: the point of the choice of masters. If you choose Reality as your master, then the notion that you are the ultimate Doer of anything whatever is totally dispelled. If you choose *any other* master, then you are essentially a magician, whether you deal with "occult" forces or simply with "ordinary" psychological or material forces. Ultimately, what makes a magician is not access to the realm of psychic or unseen powers; what makes a magician is the simple belief, the root illusion from which all other illusions spring, that he is the Doer. Once you fall under the power of this error, everything else follows, every other conceivable delusion. And if you believe that you are the Doer, then your intentions, "good "or "bad", "selfish" or "altruistic", ultimately come down to the same thing. This "ultimately" may take a long time to arrive, but direction of the road you have taken according to either the pursuit or evil or the *egotistical* pursuit of "good" is toward the creation of a world other than the one created by God, a non-existent world, a world which may be termed "total egotism" or "the pit of Hell" just as you please. If you believe that you are the Doer, the intent to do "good" and the intent to do "evil" both lead, slowly in the one case, swiftly in the other, to the same destination: the frozen paralysis of Hell. (In the words of William Blake, "Caiphas was in his own mind a benefactor to mankind".) That's part of what we mean when we say, usually without grasping its full implications, "the road to Hell is paved with good intentions". As a laughing, Mephistophelean hippy once told me in the 1970's in the mountains of British Columbia, before one of the "excursions" we used to take in those days, "Let me clue you in: *all* magic is black magic".

In the words of the Peter O'Toole character of Lawrence of Arabia from the movie of the same name: "You can *do* whatever you want, but you can't *want* whatever you want." That's the crux. Let us say that a magician forms his intent, undergoes preparatory austerities, draws his magic circle, performs his invocations, summons his forces, produces his visions or his phenomena, and then succeeds in withdrawing from his "voluntary madness" and re-establishing his personality again in stable form in "ordinary reality". Quite a tour-de-force! He has ridden the tiger, once again, and once again survived. And perhaps he can even see that his actions apparently had a good ongoing effect—or an evil one, if that's more to his taste. So it looks to him like he has covered the whole territory of reality pretty thoroughly, within the limits (of course) of his intent and his operation; like Satan in the *Book of Job*, he will be able to say that he's been "going to and fro in the earth and walking up and down in it". Little, apparently, has escaped his attention. [NOTE: "Voluntary madness" is a term coined by Peter Levenda, who presents, in his trilogy *Sinister Forces: A Grimoire of American Political Witchcraft*, much well-researched and documented evidence of the great affinities and bleed-throughs and conscious alliances between the world of the occult and that of the U.S. intelligence community, a milieu that also involves many prominent figures of the ruling elite; his work exposes levels of evil that most of us have never dreamed of. His "metaphysic", based on magic and occultism, is erroneous and subversive, but his findings are of the greatest value for our understanding of "the rulers of the darkness of this world" and the Counter-Initiation that is their most direct expression.]

But the one thing that the most dedicated Shamanic healer (unless he is truly a holy man, truly *wakan*), or the most evil CIA brainwasher of the infamous MK-ULTRA mind-control program, forgets to ask, is: *where did that intent come from*? Is he actually deluded enough to believe that he has summoned it out of nothing? On the basis of what intent might he have been able to do that? The magician is like powerful, skilled and courageous warrior who confronts the enemy and triumphs (or is killed or captured, but for the sake of the argument let us say he triumphs). He feels powerful, successful, and seems entirely justified in this feeling. But zoom out to the next larger frame of reference and what do we see? This warrior is now revealed as nothing but a soldier acting under orders. Whose orders? Along what chain-of-command? In the service of what overall strategy, what political agenda? The soldier sees and knows next to nothing of this; that's not his business; his business is simply to do what he's told. And the same is true of the magician. He may be imminently successful in enacting his intent—but as to where that intent came from, he is in total ignorance. He never asks that question, never looks in that direction, because he believes *he* is the Doer. To obey your own intent is to act under the command, under the tyranny I would say, of forces you will *never* see as they are, or understand, or be able to name. You may come up with some sort of psychological insight into patterns of intent you take as causal, or into the nature of the spirit beings to whom you attribute them, but the true origin of these patterns is completely hidden from you. Why? Because if you are the Doer, your knowledge, for all your excursions into the grim, fascinating, multifarious worlds of the Unseen, begins and ends with you yourself. The only way to even begin to see the real patterns that lie behind your intent is to recognize that the Doer is Allah—no-one else, because there IS no-one else. Instead of obeying our own intent, it is our duty, by the Trust that is laid upon us, to intend to obey Reality alone: "There is no power or might except in Allah". This is the precise point where our true freedom lies—the point where our intent to submit to

Allah is the actual presence of Allah.

That's *tasawwuf*; that's the essence of the spiritual Path in every tradition. Everything else, every political strategy, every psychological manipulation or evasion, every buy or sell order on the stock market, every twisting of, or letting yourself be twisted by, occult forces, is in some sense magic. That's why must I reiterate, and insist: Sufism and magic are poles apart. Where there is Sufism, there is no magic. Where there is magic, there is no Sufism. Those adepts of *ruhaniyyat* (Sufi thaumaturgy) who think that they—by the wonderful power of Allah, of course!—are producing this or that phenomenon, are (in Rumi's simile) like children riding hobbyhorses and playing at war.

A story may illustrate this point: Abbas Hussein calls the *adab* of the Prophet Muhammad (peace and blessings be upon him), his constant and never-failing courtesy, the *ultimate miracle*. Now calling the courtesy of the Prophet "the ultimate miracle" may seem like only a figure of speech, an exaggerated way of expressing admiration for a figure universally admired. But in another way it is the simple truth. A true story is told of a dervish who was visiting other dervishes belonging to a different group. These dervishes were known for indulging in *karamat* or wondrous feats. One of these *karamat* was to cut themselves with knives and swords while under the influence of a spiritual state (*hal*), without drawing blood or leaving any wound. While the visiting dervish looked on, one of the dervishes of this group drew a razor-sharp sword, then leaned against it until it cut deeply into his belly. The visiting dervish, not being used to paranormal occurrences, jumped up and ran over to his brother dervish, anxiously asking him if he was injured, if he needed help. "Fool!" said the wonderworker. "Of course I am not injured! Have you no experience of such things in your order? I need fear nothing, the power of Allah has protected me." And so it was; when he withdrew the sword, no blood appeared, neither was there any wound.

What can we learn from this story as it relates to *adab*, and to the difference between magic and Sufism? Perhaps the lesson is that although the wonderworker had enough power to plunge a sword into his belly and remain uninjured, he did not have enough to avoid injuring his brother through discourtesy and arrogance, demonstrating that the power it takes to be courteous is greater than the power required to produce wonders. And the truth is, while magicians may perform wonders, only Allah can perform miracles—and the *adab* of Allah is necessarily perfect.

As soon as you let go of the illusion that you are self-created (which is easier said than done!), you will see God creating you in this instant—you and the entire universe. You will see with His Eye—or rather, He will see with the Eye of the Heart, that Eye occupying the center of the place now vacated by the mother of all illusions, the illusion of the self-created, self-defined, self-determined ego: the *nafs al-ammara*. And what He will see, whatever may be the patterns that manifest it, will be Himself Alone.

What, after all, are "phenomena"? What are these "significant coincidences" that so amaze the would-be magician that he dreams of one day being able to manipulate them by some sort of subtle occult bridge between the inner self and the outer world? In the words of the Holy Qur'an (41:53), *We will show them Our signs on the horizons and in themselves, till it is clear to them that it is the truth. Suffice it not as to thy Lord, that he is witness over everything?* This verse reveals the true nature of the phenomenon that Jung named *synchronicity*, which is not based, as he and physicist Wolfgang Pauli speculated, on some mysterious affinity between mind and matter that might be explained by the "non-locality" principle of sub-atomic particles, but which simply reflects the truth that only God is the Real; consequently the world of subject-object polarities that both veils and reveals Him, that He both pervades and transcends, is ultimately unreal. To the degree that we believe it is real, however, an act of God that is one in essence, just as He is One, will falsely appear—through the distorting prism of the ego—as refracted into "inner" and "outer" events. If we were completely free of the delusion of the ego, the *nafs al-ammara*, *all* events would appear as synchronicities. We would witness them not as products of antecedent causes in time but as eternal acts of God that send their waves through psyche and world simultaneously, because the subjective self and the world it sees are two inseparable designs woven into the one pattern of existence.

The illusion that I am the Doer, the illusion of personal power, is doom. We may think of the evil black magician or CIA brainwasher of MK-ULTRA as "powerful"—and yet, as Peter Levenda points out in *Sinister Forces*, the CIA interrogation manual (retrieved, heavily censored, via the Freedom of Information Act), whose methods he compares quite convincingly to magical techniques from many cultures, requires that the interrogator split himself in two, that he "sincerely" act as a "true friend" and a "real enemy" at the same time: in order to dominate the soul of his victim, in other words, he must effectively destroy his own soul. [NOTE: This apparently validates my contention, in *The System of Antichrist: Truth and Falsehood in Post-modernism and the New Age* (Sophia Perennis, 2001), that one of the central techniques of individual or mass mind control is "unconscious contradiction", though in terms of the interrogation technique here in question the contradiction is conscious in the sense that it is overt, while still remaining unconscious in the sense that the broken mind of the victim can no longer understand that for one's torturer to be one's true friend "does not compute".]

And lest we fall into the error of seeing only those magical or occult operations based on the most obvious sort of evil intent as capable of splitting the soul, we must realize that even the most altruistic act of "white magic" is also based on a split—the fissure between the human soul and the will of God, followed by the false identification of the soul *with* God, according to the illusion "I am the Doer". Once this primal alienation occurs, every other type and degree of psychic fragmentation will eventually follow.

If personal power is divorced from the Good, and consequently also from the Real, is it really power? Power and the *feeling* of power are often poles apart; in the words of St. Paul, "our strength is perfected in weakness". Those who act against their own best interests in pursuit of the mere feeling of power, and who ultimately destroy themselves in the process, can in no way be considered powerful, any more than a psychopath who sets fire to a forest and then perishes in the blaze. A tiny act on his part, the mere striking of a match, ends by producing a massive effect, changing lives, setting hundreds or thousands of people into motion at his command; how powerful he must be! Likewise it may seem to a genetic engineer tinkering with human genes that he has matched Allah himself in creative power, whereas all he has really done is deconstruct the human form, ultimately including his own. In the words of the Holy Qur'an, *It is not their eyes that are blind, but the hearts in the breasts are blind.* Does the CIA brainwasher ever ask: "What terrible forces beyond my control have rendered me subhuman, made me their puppet, and destined me for the Fire?" Rarely, I would guess. More often he simply thinks that he is powerful both in himself and in the forces that "back him up". He is powerfully deluded.

And the most deluded of all are those global elites who, with almost inconceivable "power" and "intelligence" and thoroughness and ruthlessness and subtlety and reach, are on their way to turning this world—meticulously, deliberately—into a living Hell, a Hell from which there can be no escape for them because it will be peopled only by fiends like themselves, or suffering victims who could only bathe them in an atmosphere of pain. What could be more idiotic than pressing all the powers of the human mind and soul and all the technologies the human mind and soul can invent into the service of a negative result? And that's precisely what evil is: the synthesis of immense cunning and immense stupidity. [NOTE: 17,000 farmers committed suicide in India in 2010 because they couldn't pay their debts, a trend that's been going on for quite a while. Globalized agribusiness forces them to buy hybrid and/or genetically engineered seeds that don't reproduce in the next generation so they can't save any seed corn for next year's crop. And as traditional agriculture goes, so goes Hinduism, which requires the rhythms of village life for its *pujas*; as one Indian computer tech-support agent told me during a long download, "nobody has time for Hinduism nowadays". When my wife and I visited Rama Coomaraswamy in 2005 he told us: "No more than 5% of the population of India actually practices Hinduism anymore; if my father had made good on his plan to move there and try to live as a forest sage, it would have broken his heart."]

Sufism and Shamanism

At this point we need to address the question of Shamanism, and other ancient forms of thaumaturgy that have survived as remnants from previous world ages. Does our condemnation of magic apply to every practice of one of the "primal religions "that manifests some thaumaturgic element? In terms of the Native American spirituality of North America, must we condemn Black Elk and Thomas Yellowtail along with Harley Swift Deer and Carlos Castaneda?

René Guénon, in *The Reign of Quantity and the Signs of the Times* [Sophia Perennis, 2001] had the following to say about Shamanism, which, in my opinion, is most likely applicable to all forms of traditional magic that have survived into our times:

> If we consider "Shamanism" properly so-called, the existence of a highly-developed cosmology becomes apparent, of a kind that might suggest concordances with other traditions in many respects, the first with respect to a separation of the "three worlds", which seems to be its very foundation. "Shamanism" will also be found to include rites comparable to some that belong to traditions of the highest order: some of them, for example, recall in a striking way the Vedic rites, and particularly those that are most clearly derived from the primordial tradition, such as those in which the symbolism of the tree and the swan predominate. There can therefore be no doubt that "Shamanism" is derived from some form that was, at least originally, a normal and regular traditional form; moreover it has retained up to the present day a certain "transmission" of the powers necessary for the exercise of the functions of the "Shaman"; but as soon as it becomes clear that the "Shaman" directs his activity particularly toward the most inferior traditional sciences, such as magic and divination, a very real degeneration must be expected, such as may sometimes amount to a real deviation, as can happen all too easily to such sciences whenever they become over-developed.

In view of this, the least that we can say is that Shamanism in our time, even in its most traditional forms, is an extremely uncertain proposition. Perhaps powerful, balanced and good-willed Shamans working directly under the command of the Great Spirit still exist; I hope they do. Nonetheless, the likelihood of our ever encountering one decreases with each passing year.

As Mircea Eliade points out in *Shamanism: Archaic Techniques of*

Ecstasy, the Shaman is usually "summoned" to his role and his powers by a spirit being; and the psychophysical death-and-resurrection by which he claims them does seem analogous in some ways to the *fana* and *baqa* of Sufism: annihilation in God followed by subsistence in God. But if the Shaman is not also a holy man, if he does not possess the ability to view things from the standpoint of *Wakan Tanka*—or to fully submit to the will of *Wakan Tanka* whether or not he can see with His eye—then he is limited to serving the "agendas" of his spirit helper, which he has no way of investigating or evaluating with any certainty since he cannot stand "behind" them; this is something that only God can do. As for the *fana* and *baqa* of *tasawwuf*, these are produced not by fierce austerities undertaken on one's own initiative, by a self-willed psychophysical suicide and self-reconstruction, but precisely by the will of God. In the words of Jesus, "he who seeks to keep his life shall lose it, but he who loses his life, for my sake, shall find it."

An inescapable ambiguity crops up, however, when we recognize that it is possible to become more deeply receptive to the will of God through various techniques that include a psychophysical element, such as the Sufi *dhikr* (invocation), *sama* (spiritual concert), dance, or *khalwa* (spiritual retreat). That's why it's important to undertake these things only by the order or permission of one's *shaykh*, and why there is always a danger in Sufism, or in any heavily technique-laden spiritual way such as yoga, that the practitioner will fall into the illusion that he is reaching or summoning God on his own initiative, in which case everything is lost. In the case of *dhikr*, for example, the Sufi is not commanding God's presence by pronouncing His Name considered as a magical "word of power"; rather, God is speaking His own Name, on His own initiative, within the Sufi's heart. The path of *tasawwuf* is not traveled by the power or plan or intent of the traveler, but by that of Allah: "Not my will but Thine be done."

The Addiction to the Psychic and the System of Antichrist

But why the great *attraction* to magic in our times? There is a dialectic to it: The "solidification of the cosmic environment" under the regime of materialism that Guénon spoke of in *The Reign of*

Quantity produces, on the psychic level, a feeling of stagnation, dryness, petrification. Conscious access to God and the celestial world is largely blocked; the universe becomes "material, all-too material". When materialism is new it expresses itself as triumphalism, the excitement of innovation, the "conquest of nature", the belief in progress; (this, apparently, is the phase China is in now). When it grows old, however, and when the negative consequences of such triumphalism—social, psychological and environmental—become apparent, the opacity and solidification of the universe, and the human soul, become terribly oppressive. That's when the "cracks" Guénon speaks of begin to appear in the solidity of cosmic environment, cracks that open in the direction of the "infra-psychic". And the Jinn know all-too-well how to exploit these cracks, since some among them have also been working to open such fissures from the other side. The dryness and deadness of materialism make the glimmering antics of the Jinn highly attractive to a jaded humanity; consequently magic, spiritualism and interest in the paranormal appear as an alternative to the materialist worldview, one that is vital and imaginative as opposed to dry and dead. They promise relief from oppression; but as with any addictive drug, the oppression that's temporarily relieved is in large part produced by the drug itself. As Hamlet said, "I could be bounded in a nutshell and count myself king of infinite space, were it not that I have bad dreams." And once the soul becomes addicted to the sort of psychic experience the Jinn can provide, or simply to the hidden powers of the psyche itself, access to God and the celestial order is doubly veiled: first by material opacity; secondly by a psychic counterfeit of spiritual realities. This, in Guénon's terms, marks the passage from "Anti-Tradition" to "Counter-Tradition". The deep emotional glamors (the Water element) and/or the sparkling multidimensional agitation (the Air element) that a person's psyche becomes subject to when under the influence of the Jinn will seriously compromise his or her ability to attain what the Sufis call *'jam*, "recollection", the sort of spiritual sobriety that allows one to concentrate one's attention upon God and the Path. (The "drunkenness" spoken of by the Sufis is not, if you will pardon the pun, Jinn-drunkenness; drunkenness with God does not disperse the psyche but recollects it, which is why it can function as the polar complement to contemplative sobriety, as when St. Augustine speaks of "sober inebriation".) The steady, solid light of the celestial order—so well represented by the gold leaf used in Eastern Orthodox iconography—is replaced by the sparkling "pixie-dust" of the Jinn-world, in comparison to which anything else will seem painfully boring and uninteresting. Furthermore, just as in the case of psychedelics, alcohol and addictive drugs, the more we open ourselves to the Jinn and the sorts of experience and information they can provide (leaving aside for now the whole question of whether the Jinn we happen to be dealing with are Muslim or *kafir*, good fairies or demons), the drearier everything else becomes to us; we literally become addicted to psychic experience, and must endure all the jadedness and desiccation that goes along with it. And so we need more and more of it all the time, this being one of the lesser-known aspects of "the reign of quantity" (as well as, I would add, of our wonderful "information culture "with its "weapons of mass distraction"). However, according to a couplet I composed quite a few years ago,

> Better the Wine of the Desert
> Than the desert born of wine.

Once we have fallen into this sort of psychic addiction, the felt presence of God will become painful to us; we will tend to flee from it. God will seem to bring with Him a whole world of hopeless psychic deadness, burden, even cruelty. What we are actually going through in experiences like this, God willing, is a purgative withdrawal from our addiction to psychic experience—in the face of which, however, we will be tempted to see Allah as not a merciful Sustainer but a cruel torturer; only those recovering addicts who (by His Grace) love Him above all else will be capable of choosing the pain of the Real over the pleasure of illusion. In the words of St. John Chrysostom, "prayer is a torture-chamber"; or as St. Silouan of Mt. Athos put it, "Keep your mind in Hell and don't despair".

In strictly Islamic terms, the solidification of the cosmic environment is represented in part by the fundamentalist terrorists. Only someone whose soul is so painfully constricted that it seems to be choking the Spirit out of him will be attracted to meeting his Maker by blowing himself up. Thus suicide bombing is not only a tactic; it is also a passion. And in the face of such constriction, desiccation and cruelty, the betrayal of Islam via dealings with the Jinn and their world will become increasingly attractive to those who are repelled by the opposite and equal betrayal, that of the fundamentalists, as will those Sufi groups who habitually interact with the Jinn (whether or not they know it), practice *ruhaniyyat* and indulge in *karamat.* Nor is the meeting of the two apparent extremes of magic and warfare beyond the realm of possibility. Wizardry was a common weapon in the arsenals of the ancient world (as psy-ops is in ours), and the individual soldier of today will often seek magical protection from enemy bullets; this is one reason why Wicca is becoming increasingly prevalent in the U.S. military (cf. Qur'an 13:16). To the degree that Allah withdraws His Spirit from visible, historical Islam—as He is now withdrawing it, up to a point, from every religion, to the precise degree that its adherents have fallen away from Him—the *psychic* element of Sufism, valid and necessary though it is for the viable existence of *tasawwuf* in this world, will increasingly be reduced to the level of those "psychic residues" that Guénon saw as inhabiting the shells of dead religions—and the mass of psychic material collected by Sufism over its history is truly vast, vaster than the treasures of a thousand caves of Ali Baba. Such psychic residues, as Guénon pointed out, can be exploited by magicians. To the degree that established Islam rejects Sufism, Sufism will be tempted not only to depart from Islamic norms in the direction of magic, but also to throw in its lot with those globalist forces who want to groom *tasawwuf* as a benign (or *compliantly* militant) alternative to the Islamicists. And as Lee Penn has amply demonstrated in his *False Dawn*, and Peter Levenda in *Sinister Forces*, Jinn-worship under one name or another, and according to the widest possible definition of this tendency (including adherence to a basically New Age or Neo-Pagan worldview), is far from uncommon among the intelligence communities (Levenda) and the national and/or globalist ruling elites (Levenda and Penn). [NOTE: As examples of this I can point to the acceptance of New Age teachers Barbara Marx Hubbard and Robert Mueller (former Assistant Secretary General of the U.N.) in the world of globalist institutions, as well as to Mihkail Gorbachev's revelation that he worships the "nature" [see *False Dawn*]. Consequently, there is a danger that certain elements of Sufism, or what once was Sufism, will become further jinnified, further veiled from the Light of Allah, further attracted to the practice of magic, as they are drawn into the gravitational field of globalism and its agents.

The "Great Goddess"

Both the cosmic environment and the collective psyche, at this extreme tail-end of the Kali-yuga, are haunted by the Jinn. And given that these beings include among their many nations the elementals or nature spirits (the Gnomes of Earth, the Undines of Water, the Sylphs of Air and the Salamanders of Fire, according to Paracelsus), and that the entire psychophysical world is feminine in relation to the Spirit, just as universal manifestation itself is feminine in relation to the Creator—Allah in His Name *al-Khaliq*—the world of the Jinn is in many ways the world of Mother Nature, the Great Goddess who, when no longer recognized as *Shakti* to the Absolute Divine Witness, is transformed into that regime of hopeless Fate that so oppressed the Pagans of late antiquity, and from the power of which—also (ironically) *by* the power of which—many blindly sought the protection of magic. For Shakespeare in *A Midsummer Night's Dream*, the Fairies are ruled by a feminine power, Queen Maeve; and it is obvious that the whole "return of the Goddess" in our time has gone hand-in-hand with a mass resurgence of the interest in both Paganism and every form of magic. [NOTE: The openness of the Traditionalist School to the Divine Feminine outside the bounds of a single tradition is one of the things that has made it possible for various intellectual Neo-Pagans to identify with certain elements of Traditionalist doctrine and integrate them into their own worldview—something that Schuon himself, judging from his highly critical attitude toward Paganism, would have been flatly opposed to. The magazine *Primordial Traditions* out of New Zealand, for example, has drawn heavily on the ideas of René Guénon, Frithjof Schuon and Huston Smith, as well as Nietzsche, Julius Evola and Aldous Huxley; its past editor, Gwendolyn Toynton, though opposed to Wicca and "non-traditional" Neo-Pagan-

ism, believes that revived forms of ancient Hellenic or Northern European Paganisms such as Hellenismos or Asatru, based on traditional texts, can be viable spiritual paths in our times.] Consequently it behooves us to be very clear on exactly what the Divine Feminine is, and what She is not. And those of us who identify (as I do) with the Traditionalist School founded by René Guénon and brought to its highest point of development by Frithjof Schuon will be hampered to a degree in this study by the fact that Guénon hardly mentioned her, while Schuon by and large emphasized only her positive aspects, in both his books and in the radiant female nudes of his "shakti" paintings (though he did speak of the rigorous aspect of the Virgin Mary in his chapter "The Wisdom of Sayyidatna Maryam" in *Dimensions of Islam*). Simply put, if this Kali-yuga, then where is Kali? Where is the bloody-mouthed hag with the necklace of human skulls? Without an honest presentation of the dark side of the Divine Feminine, including the dark side of Eros, the image of the paradisiacal Feminine, erotic or otherwise, remains vulnerable to the insidious influences of what is denied. [NOTE: Patrick Laude in *Frithjof Schuon: Life and Teachings* sees Schuon's aesthetic/erotic/contemplative relationship to the Divine Feminine as an example of Shamanism—incorrectly I would say—and understands the goal of Shamanism as the integration of the body and the lower aspects of the psyche into the spiritual life. He says: "The matter is not to cultivate powers for the sake of power—for, as Schuon has judiciously and vigorously stated, one can go to Hell with all the powers one wishes—but rather to integrate the various levels of one's being so as to know God with all that one is." Point well taken. But to consider magic of any kind, even the most traditional and altruistic forms of Shamanism, as a reliable method of integrating the psychophysical individuality into the spiritual life, especially in these darkest of times—and for people whose cultural background is derived from western civilization—is ill-considered. Those whose psychophysical nature is not already fully integrated into the Spirit, or at least fully submissive to It—a condition extremely rare in our time—should never touch Shamanism, the exceptional case being that of the person (if he lives in the Americas) who, by the grace of God, has found and been accepted not simply by a working traditional Shaman or medicine man, but a true holy man of the Native American way.]

Every rose has its thorn, every paradise its angel with a flaming sword; they are there to protect "the soul of sweet delight" (Blake) from the crassness and lust of this world. Schuon is entirely right in saying the physical beauty of the human body testifies to Divine Beauty as such, independent of the spiritual state of the soul occupying that body. But without a teaching which elucidates Femininity and Eros in their false forms as well as their true ones—and in their rigorous forms as well as their merciful ones—a strict Puritanism, in my opinion, would be the wiser course. There are plenty of traditional sources (Grimm's fairytale "The Goose Girl", for example) which remind us that the outwardly attractive woman is not always the true bride, a doctrine which is valid in gnostic as well as emotional terms. Popular culture also recognizes this truth, its classic cinematic statement being *The Blue Angel*, starring Marlene Dietrich. But it is Shakespeare, not surprisingly, who ultimately says it best.

In *The Merchant of Venice*, Portia—Divine Wisdom—has concealed her portrait in one of three caskets—of gold, of silver, and of lead. She is then approached by three suitors. The expansive, foolish one chooses the gold casket: wrong. The cold, calculating one chooses the silver casket: wrong again. But the true bridegroom, Bassiano, chooses the leaden casket, and in so doing becomes a type of Christ, who endured the *tamasic* heaviness of the material world, death on the cross, and the harrowing of hell to save the human soul. Within the lead of radical *kenosis*, Bassanio finds the portrait of the True Bride. "You that choose not by the view" says Portia, "chance as fair, and choose as true!" And we need to listen as well to her verse dismissing the Prince of Morocco, the vain, inflated suitor, whose character reminds one of the Islamic legend that it was the peacock—narcissistic aestheticism—who introduced the serpent into Paradise:

All that glisters is not gold,—
Often have you heard that told:
Many a man his life hath sold

But my outside to behold:
Gilded tombs do worms infold.
Had you been as wise as bold,
Young in limbs, in judgement old,
Your answer had not been inscroll'd:
Fare you well; your suit is cold.

Only the man, or woman, who thoroughly understands this can look upon Beauty naked, and know it as Wisdom. To teach "Beauty is the splendor of the True" without at all points immediately balancing it with "all that glisters is not gold" is to invoke *avidya-maya,* ultimately leading to the veiling of the Intellect and the corruption of the will. And one of the most common doors to the world of the Jinn (the other being the Promethean power-motive) is this very relationship to the Divine Beauty, something Jean Borella in *Guénonian Esoterism and Christian Mystery* criticizes as "the aesthetic identification with the Essence". To fail to grasp the truth that Beauty too has its rigorous side—something that the Troubadours and the Arthurian Romancers well expressed by their theme of the "Noble Lady Hard-to-Attain"—is to ask to become *pixilated* ("pixie-led"), *majnun* (Jinn-possessed). And the one who chooses the glamors of the Jinn over the rigors of Truth has picked the golden casket, wherein the true semblance of the Beloved will never be found. But the one who has endured the dryness of death to the world, death to the "soul commanding to evil", who has withstood the Jinn and all their blandishments, and has consequently chosen the leaden casket, will find that semblance, that *imago dei—insh 'allah*—and be granted not only the power, but also the *right*, to look upon Beauty naked.

The Ambiguities of *Ruhaniyyat*

Be that as it may, Sufism, as we have seen above, does include its own form of thaumaturgy, known as *ruhaniyyat* (a name which, however, is applied in several other senses) which we may criticize but cannot absolutely exclude. If in his practice of this thaumaturgy the magus taps the power of Allah, and if he understands that he is working not with his own personal power but with that of the

Deity, then well and good. But again, where did the *intent* to employ the power of God for this or that purpose come from? Who issued the *commission*? Say a young woman comes to a *ruhani* magus and says, "Please, shaykh, invoke the power of Allah to heal my mother, who is quite ill." Does this magus know for sure, simply because he has received that request, that it is God's will that the girl's mother be healed? I myself want many apparently benign things that God may not want. Or is the very fact that the girl has arrived and made this request sufficient proof that Allah desires it to be granted? If God has told the magus in no uncertain terms, "those who apply to you have thereby applied to Me", then well and good; if indeed the shaykh in question has reached absolute certainty as to God's commission to him, and labors under no delusions, then he may do as he pleases. But if he simply says to himself (most likely without being fully conscious of it), "God is merciful and I am a man of good will; therefore I have a right to invoke the power of Allah to fulfill any petition that seems to me benign", then things are much less certain. Such a magus who has not been informed by the Deity in no uncertain terms that "your wish is My Command" must first submit that petition to Allah, stand in wait for His answer, and then *accept* that answer, whatever it might be, on pain of acting as a *saher.* Because the truth is, Allah only fulfills petitions that are brought to Him in response to His command "petition Me". A petition truly invited by Allah will be based on a desire formed by Allah Himself in the heart of the petitioner—and if the petition is not only granted by Allah but also in effect issued by Him, then of what use is *ruhaniyyat*? If the King offers me a precious gem with his own hand, do I send a carrier pigeon to retrieve it, and then hope the pigeon will be able to find its way home? At one point *ruhaniyyat*, like all other forms of thaumaturgy, or even theurgy, simply gets in the way—though without it (if, that is, we have been called to it by Allah, rather than entering it on our own initiative)—and, of course, in the absence of perfect *islam*—we may never be able to see exactly where that point is; as William Blake expressed the matter, "If the Fool would persist in his Folly he would become wise" (*insh'allah*).

The Prophet Solomon, peace and blessings be upon him, was

given the power by God to command the Jinn and the physical elements, but according to Ibn al-'Arabi in the *Fusus al-Hikam*, he was the only prophet commissioned by God to do so, or rather the only one given both the power and the right to issue such commands on his own initiative; and the specific power he received was given to no one after him. God may perform miracles through His saints, but even the Prophet Muhammad, peace and blessings be upon him, was reminded by the Holy Qur'an that the power he manifested when, at the battle of Badr, he threw a handful of pebbles in the direction of the enemy after which the tide turned in favor of the Muslims, was not his own power, but God's: *You did not throw when you threw, but God threw.* (Q. 7:180)

I will end with a highly relevant account of "wisdom after foolishness" given by the great Shaykh Ahmed al-Alawi, as recounted in *A Sufi Saint of the Twentieth Century* by Martin Lings:

> My first leaning [in the direction of Sufism] was marked by my attachment to one of the masters of the 'Isawi Tariqa who impressed me by his unworldliness and evident piety. I made every effort to comply with the requisites of that order [known for its practice of wonderworking], and this came quite easily to me on account of my youth and the instinctive attraction for wonders and marvels which is a part of human nature. I became proficient in these practices, and was well thought of by the men of the order, and I believed in my ignorance that what we did was purely and simply a means of drawing nearer to God. One day when God willed that I should be inspired by the truth we were at one of our gatherings and I looked up and saw a paper that was on one of the walls of the house we were in, and my eye lit on a saying that was traced back to the Prophet. What I learned from it caused me to give up what I had been doing in the way of working wonders, and I determined to limit myself in that order to the litanies and invocations and recitations of the Qur'an. From that time I began to extricate myself and make excuses to my brethren until I finally gave up those other practices altogether. I wanted to drag the entire brotherhood away from them also, but that was

not easy. As for myself I broke away as I had intended, and only retained from that contact the practice of snake-charming. I continued to charm snakes by myself or with some of my friends until I met Shaikh Sidi Muhammad al-Buzidi. . . .

One day, when he was with us in our shop, the Shaikh said to me: "I have heard that you can charm snakes, and that you are not afraid of being bitten." I admitted this. Then he said: "Can you bring me one now and charm it here in front of us?" I said that I could, and going outside the town, I searched for half the day, but only found a small one, about half an arm's length. This I brought back and putting it front of me, I began to handle it according to my custom, as he sat and watched me. "Could you charm a bigger snake than this?" he asked. I replied that the size made no difference to me. Then he said, "I will show you one that is bigger than this and far more venomous, and if you can take hold of it you are a real sage." I asked him to show me where it was and he said: "I mean your soul which is between the two sides of your body. Its poison is more deadly than a snake's, and if you can take hold if it and do what you please with it, you are, as I have said, a sage indeed." Then he said: "Go and do with that little snake whatever you usually do with them, and never go back to such practices again."

And Pharaoh said: Bring every cunning wizard unto me.
And when the wizards came, Moses said unto them, Cast your cast!
And when they had cast, Moses said: That which ye have brought is magic. Lo! Allah will make it vain. (Q. 10:79–81)

5
The Fall of the Jinn

for Amira El-Zein

IN REALITY, there is no god but God; a plurality of Absolutes is absurd. God's Names are not gods in their own right, nor are they "parts" of God; to say "God is One" is to say that He is both unique and indivisible. His Names, as Ibn al-'Arabi teaches, represent His relations to His creatures, to each of which He presents a different face, corresponding to that creature's qualities and limitations. The highest creatures in the hierarchy of being have as their respective "lords" the most comprehensive and essential Names of the One God—though Man, since he represents a synthesis of all the Names, is potentially even greater than they. These creatures are the highest angels, whom the Pagans mistake for actual gods or independent principles. Every true religion begins with a revelation of the One God, of the Transcendent Unity of Being. As the vision of this Transcendent Unity decays over time, God becomes less accessible, and finally less plausible. Human beings begin to relate to God through intermediaries, and end by worshipping these intermediaries as if they were gods in their own right, which they most certainly are not. So when the term "gods" appears in this chapter, the reader should understand it according to this definition—as designating something real, the true nature of which is misunderstood.

The Jinn, the "fairies" of Islam and pre-Islamic Arabia, are roughly equivalent to the Greek *daimones*, powers of the intermediary or psychic plane who once served as links between the gods—the Platonic intelligibles, equivalent in Islamic terms to the Names of Allah—and the material world. When classical Paganism was in force as a spiritual dispensation, the *daimones* carried petitions from men to the gods and answers from the gods to men, like the

Python vis-à-vis Apollo in the system of the later Delphic Oracle—the Python being a *daimon*, Apollo a god. The Jinn of the Arabs, however, had largely lost this "angelic" function even before the advent of Islam; and so it is possible to assert—at least according to the myth we are presently weaving—that at one point a split developed (due, as René Guénon would say, to cyclical degeneration) between the *daimones* and the gods, after which the *daimones* could no longer carry men's prayers to the higher worlds. At this point a second division occurred among the *daimones* themselves, a split reflected in the Islamic doctrine that some of the Jinn are Muslims and some unbelievers. The *kafir* or unbelieving Jinn, like the *daimones* of Greco-Roman Paganism after God's favor passed from Paganism to Christianity (and, to a degree, even before), said to themselves: "All these prayers and sacrifices that men make—since we can no longer carry them to God, let's just accept them for ourselves, live off them, and become gods in our own right."

That's the point at which the Pagan gods began to be progressively transformed into demons, or rather were replaced by demons—demons being *daimones* masquerading as gods, or ones who (like the Gnostic *archons*) believe that they *are* gods. This process of spiritual devolution is what justified Christianity and Islam in destroying the degenerate remnants of Paganism in the Mediterranean lands and Arabia. After these new revelations had done their work, those demons could no longer pretend to be gods, but were revealed in their true nature; they became more purely "demonic". (It is likely that the *kafir* Jinn are the ones most open to having dealings with men, whereas the Muslim Jinn are more discrete, not wishing to tempt us to polytheism and magic, or themselves to the acceptance of human worship. It is nonetheless certainly possible for an unbelieving Jinn to *pose* as a believer.)

Still, the question arises: Are there any archaic systems, forms of shamanism perhaps, where the *daimones* can still act as mediators between earth and Heaven? This is highly uncertain, but not entirely impossible. In the world of Shinto, for example (assuming it is still spiritually in force), where the *kami*, at least the lower ones, are a class of *daimones* roughly equivalent to the Jinn, the worshipper "makes friends" with a minor *kami* at a local shrine, who will, if all goes well, introduce him to more important *kamis*, and so on up the Great Chain of Being until the highest *kami* is reached, Amaterasu Ōmikami, Goddess of the Sun. So it is just possible that in Japan and other parts of Asia, as well as among some Native Americans, the role of the *daimones* as mediators between humans and the gods, and ultimately the Absolute Principle, is still partly in force, as it most certainly is not in the various contemporary revivals of Neo-Platonism or Northern European Paganism, nor under the dispensations of the living Abrahamic religions.

In Islam the Jinn are often considered to be a race that inhabited the earth before humanity was created. But if so, what are they now? They are seen as associated, albeit invisibly, with certain geographical areas, so in that sense they are still on the earth alongside men. Are they the remnants, the ghosts as it were, of "pre-Adamite men", or are they actually fallen gods? This question, though apparently clear-cut, is difficult to answer, given that the terrestrial environment was less "material" in earlier ages than it is now, less radically alienated from the celestial worlds. Gods walked among men, and men were like gods. "There were Giants in the earth in those days" according to the book of Genesis—the *Nephilim*.

In Indo-European mythology we encounter a race of beings known to the Hindus as the Asuras, to the Norse as the Jötun or Giants, to the Greeks as the Titans, who are universally considered to be the enemies of the gods. The Titans were an earlier race of deities who were conquered and exiled by the gods of Olympus, ruled by Zeus. The Giants are the enemies of the Norse gods, the Aesir (though a few of the Jötun, Loki for example, were included among the gods), just as the Asuras or warrior-demons are shown as in perpetual war against the Hindu gods, the Devas. (In Zoroastrianism the attributions of these beings are reversed: the Daevas in the religion of Zarathustra are the devils, the Ashuras the gods or angels.) And Islamic legend tells of a war between the Angels and the Jinn before man appeared on earth in which the Angels were victorious; it also recounts an incident where a child of the Jinn was adopted by the Angels, just as certain of the Jötun were admitted to the company of the Aesir in Valhallah. Furthermore, one of the tribes of the Jinn was named the *'Asr*, a name that is clearly echoed in "Asura", "Ashura" and "Aesir".

According to the Hindu and Greco-Roman doctrine of the cycles of manifestation, the earlier ages of a given cycle are spiritually higher than the later ones; and certainly both the Bible and the Qur'an speak of the present age as ending in spiritual degeneration and destruction. In line with this doctrine, we should expect both the deities and the earthly inhabitants of the world-age preceding our own to have been wiser, more powerful and more integrated than the Men and Gods (or in Abrahamic terms, the Angels) of our own time. And yet the triumph of the Gods over the Titans or the Angels over the Jinn is considered to be entirely positive and in line with the Divine Will. Why is this?

The Titanic or Promethean transgression is based on an attempt to live according to the norms and assume the rights and powers of a higher age that is now past. The Asuras are in continual war with the Devas because they remember how, in their former glory, they were higher beings than the Devas are now; they are like disinherited nobility living among an ascendant bourgeoisie and plotting their return to power, meanwhile taking refuge in some cases as Bohemians of the *demimonde*. Likewise when (according to the Qur'an) the Jinn were in the habit of flying up to heaven to eavesdrop on the councils of Allah and His Angels, this was because they remembered their status as the "Angels" of a former age.

But how can a God or an Angel be "demoted"? The Jinn are considered to be mortal, though they live for a very long time; they share this with both the Buddhist version of the Devas and the Medieval Christian idea of the fairies, who were called the *Longaevi*, the "long-lived ones". The Norse Aesir were expected to pass away at the end of this world-age in *Ragnarök*, "the twilight of the gods"; the Angels of the Abrahamic religions, however, are immortal, as were the Gods of the Greeks.

These ambiguities can perhaps be resolved by considering René Guénon's doctrine that sacred places and objects and ritual forms pertaining to dead religions retain the "psychic residues" of those religions. The Spirit or Archetype of these earlier dispensations has returned to its Divine Source, but the psychic "materia" magnetized by that Archetype over the period of its earthly sojourn remains clinging to its material relics. Thus we are led to ask whether the

Titans or the Asuras or the Jötun or the Jinn are simply the psychic "husks" of an earlier race of gods, something on the order of the Kabbalistic *qlippoth*. These beings, however, are not presented as mere ghosts or wraiths; they appear as conscious, acting individuals. And according to the Qur'an, the Jinn, like human beings, possess free will; consequently they must retain some contact, however attenuated, with the Spiritual domain.

My solution to this dilemma is to speculate that the Gods, the Giants, the Titans, the pre-Islamic Jinn are subtle beings who have "lost their religion", who are cut off from the Spiritual Archetypes or Platonic Ideas or Names of God to which they owed their elevation and their immortality. Like all immortal beings unless and until they fall, the *daimones* in their former godhood were immortal only by participation in the immortality and eternity of God; once that participation failed, once that connection was broken, they had to "die" for it to be restored, just as fallen humanity cannot retain the immortality of both body and soul enjoyed by Adam and Eve in the Garden of Eden, but can only look forward to it as a posthumous state. We no longer live in an Earthly Paradise, like the men and women of the Golden Age, but now must physically die in order to regain our *physical* immortality, though we may realize spiritual immortality even in this life. The Titans, Asuras, Jötun, Jinn may thus be considered as beings who reside in a kind of Limbo, like the Celtic Land of the Ever-Young—not in Hell, but in a sort of fallen Paradise. They are psychically more powerful than "average" humanity due to their descent from an earlier and higher age, but spiritually speaking they are disinherited, which is why the Prophet Muhammad, peace and blessings be upon him, was given the Qur'an by Allah for the salvation and enlightenment of both men and Jinn. Just as the Jinn had lost their own religion, which is why they adopted the role of "gods" and accepted the worship of men, so the human beings of the Prophet's place and time had lost their primordial Abrahamic faith, and consequently worshipped various of the Jinn as deities. The Qur'an speaks both of prophets sent to the Jinn *from among their own number*, and of the Jinn as following various human prophets—Moses, and later Muhammad. This ambiguity is resolved if we understand the Jinnish prophets as being sent to the

Jinn as they were in an earlier world-age, whereas in our age, the age when the Trust is born by man, not by the Jinn or by any other created beings, these *daimones* must follow and be taught by human prophets. (It has always been my impression that Christ's harrowing of Hell included a passage through, and partial redemption of, the realm of Faerie, the homeland of the disinherited gods of the Celts, which would explain why the later Celtic Christian monks could, up to a point, live on earth as if it were the Garden of Eden.) Islam, in common with the other Abrahamic faiths, does not emphasize the doctrine of earlier world ages and cycles-of-manifestation as do Hinduism and Buddhism; Ibn al-'Arabi, however, speaks of his imaginal meeting with a figure who claimed to be one of his own ancestors who lived in a remote time whose humanity were descended from a "different Adam", and the Qur'an itself implies this possibility when it mentions the ruins of ancient great works built by tribes of men who have passed away. Q. 4:133 also posits the possibility of future cycles of manifestation: *If He pleased, He could cause you to pass away, O mankind! and create others in your stead: for this hath God power.*

In Islamic belief, as I already mentioned, the Jinn were once in the habit of "eavesdropping" on the heavenly councils—a practice that was terminated by the sending of the Qur'an to Muhammad. After the Book was in force they found their way blocked: *And we stretched towards heaven, but we found it filled with terrible guards and meteors. We would sit there on seats to hear; but any listening now finds a meteor in wait for him* (Q. 72:8–9); they could no longer overhear the speech of the Angels. This story indicates that the Jinn had already lost their proper function as *daimonic* intermediaries between human beings in the terrestrial world and the Gods in the celestial one—or in Abrahamic terms, the Angels, the intimates of Allah. Now in their fallen state they were capable of maintaining no more than a ghost of their former function, and that only by stealth; their practice of "stealing" intelligence from the heavenly worlds is thus strictly comparable to Greek myth where the Titan Prometheus steals fire from Zeus. Muhammad simply terminated the vestiges of an earlier relationship between the Jinn and Allah that had already decayed, and gave them a new and more effective Path, that of the Qur'an, a Path that was in line with the Will of Allah for the present age. In order to accept the prophethood of Muhammad and the primacy of the Qur'an, however, they had to abandon all hope of returning to their former glory, to that earlier age when they were the bearers of the Trust, and accept their subordinate status under the present dispensation when the Trust, by God's will, had passed to man.

Not all the Jinn, however, were willing to undergo this "humiliation". The Qur'an recounts that when the Angels were commanded to bow down to Adam in the celestial world before his creation on earth, Eblis, who was apparently a Jinn admitted among the company of the Angels like Loki among the Aesir, refused. As punishment he was exiled from Paradise and became Shaytan—just as Lucifer in the Christian account became Satan after his fall—and later functioned as the leader of those *kafir* Jinn who refused to accept the Qur'an and the prophethood of Muhammad. In all this we can see how God's appointment of man as His viceregent on earth ended the regime of the earlier gods; Eblis (unlike the eternal Angels) refused to bow down to Adam because he understood Allah's creation of the Primordial Man to represent the passage of the earthly viceregency from the Jinn to the human race. In the Greek universe the Olympians, though lower than the Titans as these had been in their original glory, were the gods of *man*; only under their regime—presuming that the sense of an Absolute Divinity was not eclipsed by them, as it certainly was by the Olympian gods in their later degeneracy—and not under the regime of those earlier Powers whom William Blake called "the Antediluvians who are our Energies", could man assume his full viceregal status as bearer of God's Trust in this terrestrial world. And this is precisely why the *surah an-Naas*, the last *surah* of the Qur'an, invokes *the Lord of mankind, the King of mankind, the God of mankind* against *the evil of the sneaking whisperer, who whispers in the hearts of mankind, of the Jinn and of mankind.* The *God of mankind* is the particular face that Allah presents to humanity alone—not to the animals, not to the Angels, not to the Jinn—and which consequently harbors within it the Archetype of Man *in divinis*, in terms of which we are all still *in the loins of Adam*. The *sneaking whisperer* is the temptation to approach Allah through a channel not sanctioned by Him in the present age: for the Jinn, to resurrect their own dead religion and its prophets; for mankind, to worship God through the Jinn considered as mediating gods, not directly through the Holy Qur'an. And Eblis could certainly be considered a *sneaking whisperer* for both men and Jinn: if all men were to worship the Jinn, along with Eblis their king, we would thereby abandon the Trust and posit the Jinn as the bearers of it, as they were in an earlier world-age—something which is both the essence of impossibility and the essence of destruction, for both man and the earth. (Such figures as Eblis and Loki may represent those relics of a previous world-age that can be of use to the present one, though in both cases they appear as principles of disorder. An element of disorder is apparently necessary to prevent a particular spiritual dispensation from petrifying, and allow for the exercise of free will.)

But what exactly did William Blake mean when he said spoke of the "Antediluvians" as "our Energies?" The Jinn, the Jötun, the Asuras, the Titans are essentially psychic powers. Insofar as they are conscious individuals with free will they also possess spirits, but their *function* in this age is entirely on the *psychic* plane; the *spiritual* function of the Trust has passed to man. And just as man, in fulfilling that spiritual function, has precedence over the psychic powers of the Jinn—which is why Ibn al-'Arabi, for one, teaches that human knowledge is superior to Jinnish knowledge, which is simply to say that Spiritual insight is higher than psychic "information"—so the Spirit in man, *al-Ruh*, has precedence over the human soul, *an-nafs*. The world of the *nafs* is the world of the human psyche, which is in some ways continuous with the psychic and subtle-material environment as a whole, the home of the Jinn. Consequently the Jinn, from a certain perspective, can be seen as *the psychic powers of man*. By this I do not mean to limit them to the "merely psychological" or deny their power to act independently within the psychic plane, and sometimes even affect the material plane. It is nonetheless true that the human being whose spirit has dominance over his psychic powers is analogous on a certain level to (though certainly not to be identified as) a prophet who is given power over the Jinn by God, as the Prophet Solomon was. Thus it should be at least virtually possible for every human being who is perfectly submissive to God to have absolute power over the Jinn, and this was the indeed case in earlier times; it appears that even certain North American shamans still retain the ability, or did until recently, to influence the weather, which would indicate power over the *spirits of the elements* who form one class of the Jinn. The Bantu say that every *muntu* (the singular of *bantu*)—every being, that is, who is endowed with the power of speech, which in Islamic terms would include both men and Jinn—possesses the power to say "sun, fall from the sky", and see it fall. And if it does not fall, that is only because other *bantu* are saying "sun, remain in the sky" at the same time. This recognition of the virtually absolute viceregency of Man vis-à-vis the terrestrial world is the origin of many of the ideas of "High Magic" that were abroad in the West during the Renaissance (and certainly also today), as well as of the Sufi thaumaturgic practice of *ruhaniyyat.* This pan-human thaumaturgy, however, is neither possible nor lawful in our own time; according to Ibn al-'Arabi, only Solomon among all the prophets was given this power, though other prophets, as well as certain saints, may exercise a certain limited power over the Jinn, particularly in terms of exorcism and spiritual healing. The situation of the present age is expressed by the Qur'an in the story of Abraham, who abandoned the worship of (and thus also, by implication, the power to invoke) the created elements of star, moon and sun, all of which pass away, in order to worship Allah as *as-Samad*, the Eternal. The only legitimate right and duty granted by God to the human race as a whole in this age—though we must exercise human labor and free will in order to avail ourselves of it (and many do not)—is sovereignty over our own *energies*, our own psychic powers. Without effective spiritual viceregency over the human microcosm, which is rare enough in our time, the dream of thaumaturgic viceregency over the macrocosm is a chase after the wind.

The futility of such thaumaturgic power in our times, however, is not recognized by those whom René Guénon, in *The Reign of Quantity and the Signs of the Times*, called "agents of the Counter-Initiation", but is being actively sought. These occult forces, who are progressively coming out of the closet as organized groups operating within the globalist elites, are dedicated to the destruction of every true religion, the perversion of all esoteric spiritual paths, and the creation of a One-World Religion, or at the very least the federation of the world's religions under a non-religious authority. And one of the most significant trends that demonstrates the influence of these "change agents" is the contemporary resurgence of invocation of psychic forces, the worship of the Jinn. Their intent is to produce psychic counterfeits of traditional religious doctrine and practice, to drag all true spiritual traditions down to the psychic level where magic and other "psychic technologies" will replace the sacred sacramental and contemplative theurgies provided to humanity by God as paths back to Him. Such New Age "channeled" philosophies as those of Seth, Michael, Ramtha, the Pleiadians, and their various successors—along with various Neo-Pagan revivals—represent false psychic religions disseminated by the *kafir* Jinn; their currency among certain sectors of the global elites is much wider than is commonly thought. [See *False Dawn.*]

Nor are these subversive influences limited to the conscious agents of the Counter-Initiation; virtually no-one in today's world is entirely immune to the influence of the *kafir* Jinn and the general psychic permeability and "jinnification" of the human soul in the latter days, when, according to the Qur'an, *men . . . shall become as scattered moths.* And those who have been granted a certain intuitive insight into the qualities of the earlier and higher ages of this cycle of manifestation may be seized by a nostalgia for those august and ancient worlds; but this nostalgia is barren. If we are serious about following the Will of God in intimacy and faith, we will not dream of older and higher times, but will squarely face, and responsibly deal with, our own times. Certainly we live in the Dark Age, the Kali-yuga—but what of that? Because the truth is, each successive world-age is not only a fall of both the cosmic macrocosm and the human microcosm to a lower ontological level, but also a secret, inner restoration of an earlier and higher world-age in a dimension that is not only lower, but also *deeper.* The function that Adam fulfilled effortlessly, in the Eden of the Golden Age, could only be fulfilled by Christ through the *agon* of the Cross. But as the attainment of a given level of spiritual realization becomes progressively more difficult, and consequently rarer (according to the Qur'anic *surah The Calamity*, the spiritually *foremost* are *a multitude of those of old and few of those of later time*), its achievement under these more rigorous cosmic conditions represents a deeper, and thus more quintessential, manifestation of God. This is precisely why St. Augustine characterized the sin of Adam as a *felix culpa*, a "fortunate fault". Spiritual values can be forged in the infernal darkness of Kali-yuga that the "mass theophanic consciousness" of the Golden Age could never produce; necessity is the mother of deification. As the Christian Desert Father

Abba Moises said, "In the latter days people will be much weaker than we are. Austerities will be largely impossible for them due to this weakness. But they will be better men than we are, because they will be given the opportunity to battle Satan face-to-face." This is one of the things Jesus meant when he said "and greater things than these [things I have done] will you do." And in the words of the Prophet Muhammad, peace and blessings be upon him, "Islam began in exile and will end in exile—blessed are those who are in exile!"[4]

4. There is a question among Islamic scholars as to whether demons (*shayatin*) form a separate class of beings from the Jinn, or whether they are simply those among the Jinn who are unbelievers. Some make a sharp distinction between the Jinn and the *shayatin*, but the Qur'an itself does not. In Q.18:50, Iblis, the Muslim Satan, is said to be *of the Jinn.* In Q. 2:81–82 the Prophet Solomon is described as having been given power over the demons*: And unto Solomon . . . the evil ones (shayatin), some of whom dived for him and did other work,* whereas 27:17 tells us *And there were gathered together unto Solomon his armies of the jinn*; the Qur'an seems to be implying here that the *shayatin* who labored for Solomon were of the Jinn. Q. 26:221–227 deals with the question of poetic inspiration: *Shall I inform you upon whom the devils (shayatin) descend? They descend on every sinful, false one. They listen eagerly, but most of them are liars. As for the poets, the erring follow them. Hast thou not seen how they stray in every valley, and how they say that which they do not?* Since it is well known that some Arab poets both before and after the coming of Islam claimed to be inspired by the Jinn, it is clearly implied here that these inspirers are *shayatin*, demons. And in Q. 6:113, all uncertainty is dispelled. This passage speaks of *devils (shayatin) of humankind and jinn* as being the adversaries of the prophets; in other words, the *kafir* Jinn are clearly identified in the Qur'an as devils or demons. The Christian bias which portrays all denizens of the intermediate plane, all the "Powers of the Air", as demons is extreme and not strictly true, though it is nonetheless wise from the standpoint of spiritual direction: not every fish in shark-infested waters is a shark, but this does not mean that one can swim in such waters with impunity. But to make a strict distinction between the Jinn and the demons is to fall into the opposite extreme: if demons are beings of the intermediate plane who possess free will—and no intelligent being, without exercising free will, can be disobedient to God—then they fit the definition of the Jinn. Certainly there are different nations of these beings; the Jinn of the Arabian deserts, for example, will exhibit different characteristics than the Fairies of the northern forests. Some are less geographically identified than others, and the Jinn as a whole occupy a hierarchy of their own that mirrors the ontological hierarchy of the Celestial, Psychic and Material worlds, though in psychic terms alone. But all intelligent beings with free will who reside in the intermediary plane between the celestial and the terrestrial worlds may be called Jinn according to the most common and most useful meaning of that name.

6

UFOs, Mass Mind-Control, and the *Awliya al-Shaytan*

[NOTE: This chapter expands the argument presented in my book *Cracks in the Great Wall: UFOs and Traditional Metaphysics*, Sophia Perennis, 2005]

ACCORDING TO the best available evidence, the UFO phenomenon has three separate yet intimately related aspects: (1) It manifests in terms of real material-world events, detectable by radar and sometimes leaving behind physical traces, events that are inexplicable according to mainstream science, though certain theories of post-Einsteinian physics might be able to speculate legitimately on some aspects of them; (2) It is also a psychic phenomenon that profoundly alters the consciousness of those exposed to it; (3) It is apparently surrounded by deception activities which mimic it, produced by actual human groups, as Jacques Vallee has demonstrated in his book *Messengers of Deception*.

My central thesis regarding the UFO phenomenon is as follows: The UFO "aliens" are beings from another "dimension"—the world called in some systems the *etheric plane*, situated on the "isthmus" between the material world and the world of dreams and mental imagery. The etheric plane is home to the Jinn, the elemental spirits, the fairies, the Powers of the Air mentioned in Ephesians 2:2—the "air" in this sense denoting the subtle-material dimension. (The "border" between the etheric plane and the world defined by the five senses apparently has something to do with the electromagnetic spectrum, as evidenced by the fact that the proximity of a UFO will often cause electronic equipment to malfunction.) Some of the denizens of that world are best described as demons. Not all etheric "nations" are demonic, just as not every fish in shark-infested waters is a shark; nonetheless the early Christian Fathers were very wise to counsel strict avoidance of that realm, especially since the people who most commonly interacted with it in their time—and are still doing so today—were (and are) the Pagan magicians. The prime enigma is: How do the three aspects of the phenomenon relate to each other? Aren't they mutually exclusive? If UFOs are a real physical phenomenon, doesn't that mean that they have to be alien spaceships? If they are a psychic phenomenon, doesn't that mean that they *couldn't* be physical craft? And if the phenomenon is shown to be surrounded by human deception activities of the "Mission Impossible" variety, doesn't that mean that the whole thing is a hoax? *No* on all three counts. Demons are subtle beings inhabiting the psychic or etheric plane who can temporarily materialize themselves and various objects in this world, but who cannot remain on our material plane in stable form for very long—if they could, they wouldn't have to *possess* people in order to work their evil in this world. (See Seraphim Rose, *Orthodoxy and the Religion of the Future.*) And the deception activities of human groups, besides being attempts to piggyback on and use a phenomenon that the deceivers didn't originate and can't control (the same can perhaps be said for various human attempts to mimic alien "technology") may actually be—or also be—acts designed not simply to deceptively imitate the "aliens" in order to influence mass belief, but to actually *invoke* them, in line with the practice of "sympathetic magic" as described in the classic work on mythology and primitive belief, *The Golden Bough* by Sir James Frazer. This depressing thesis leads us directly to the question of the possible involvement of the intelligence community and various arcane technologists, whose connection to the UFO phenomenon have been documented both by Jacques Vallee in *Messengers of Deception* and Peter Levenda in *Sinister Forces: A Grimoire of American Political Witchcraft*, in outright Satanism. (Levenda, for one, gives much well-researched evidence in support of this thesis). The case of pioneer rocket scientist Jack Parsons comes immediately to mind. Parsons was a follower of black magician Aliester Crowley and an associate of L. Ron Hubbard, another follower of Crowley who founded the Church of Scientology and who also (according to my correspondence with Beat Generation writer William Burroughs in the late 1960's, when Burroughs was in the process of breaking with Scientology) had a background in Naval Intelligence, something confirmed by Levenda. Parsons (according to Vallee) claimed to have met a "Venusian" in the Mojave Desert, performed Pagan rituals at his launchings (as recounted by Levenda), and went on to co-found the Aerojet Corporation and the Jet Propulsion Laboratory. He provided early designs for the Pentagon; a crater was named after him on the dark side of the Moon. Parsons' rituals appear to be a continuation of a series of magical invocations performed by Crowley in 1918 called the "Amalantrah Workings" whose purpose was to open an interdimensional portal that would allow him access to beings from other worlds; one of the spooks that came through this portal was a generic or collective entity named "Lam". The sketch Crowley made of this being bears a striking resemblance to the "Gray", the standard contemporary image of the extraterrestrial popularized by Whitley Strieber.

In light of these revelations, I believe we should take seriously Eastern Orthodox priest Seraphim Rose's assertion, in *Orthodoxy and the Religion of the Future*, that the great expansion of the UFO phenomenon after WWII was in order to lay the psychic groundwork for the advent of the regime of Antichrist, particularly since there is no question that the mass belief in UFOs, whether conceived of as alien spacecraft or as "interdimensional" manifestations, has been an important element in the widespread pagan/occult revival that has so obviously weakened and undermined the world's religions. The French metaphysician René Guénon, *The Reign of Quantity and the Signs of the Times*, provides a solid metaphysical basis for idea of Antichrist by demonstrating that this figure (whom Muslims call *al-Dajjal*, "the deceiver") is not simply a just-so fable that we must take on blind faith, but represents a necessary dialectical phase in the dissolution of the present cycle-of-manifestation, and the ultimate re-creation of the world. Guénon also provides a cosmological context for the UFO phenomenon, though he does not mention it by name, limiting himself to describing the breakthrough of "infra-psychic forces" due to the hardening of the cosmic environment under the regime of materialism (the phase he calls "Anti-Tradition"), followed by the psycho-physical fracturing of that environment in our own time (the phase of "Counter-Tradition", i.e. false religion). Anti-Tradition peaked in the 19th Century under the regime of "classical materialism", while Counter-Tradition expresses itself in terms of our present postmodern worldview, one that might be termed "magical scientism". The upshot is that fissures are now starting to appear in the "great wall" separating the material world from the subtle-energy dimension, home to those entities that we regard, according to the scientistic paradigm, as "extra-terrestrial entities". Seraphim Rose, citing many of the Eastern Orthodox saints and the Greek Fathers, as well as Guénon himself, draws many exact parallels between the UFO phenomenon and the experiences of the early Christian saints with the demonic powers, in the days when Christians were still a small minority within a largely Pagan society where the practice of magic was commonplace. Jacques Vallee, in *Messengers of Deception* and his other books, provides much evidence to support this thesis, though he himself does not assert it; and if Peter Levenda's well-documented findings are accurate—findings that demonstrate the massive cross-pollenization since WWII between the military, the intelligence community and the power elite on the one hand and the world of the magicians and the occultists on the other—then we can say without fear of exaggeration that elements of the CIA and the "military-industrial complex" are involved in practices that can be accurately described as Satanism, whether or not it goes by that name. If Jack Parsons, as Levenda shows, identified himself with Antichrist and dedicated himself to the destruction of Christianity, and if prominent psychic researcher Andrija Puharich, with all his connections to the intelligence community, was involved in channeling so-called "Extra-Terrestrial Intelligences", for which read The Powers of the Air (see below), then is Seraphim Rose's thesis, and mine, really that far-fetched? It will only seem far-fetched to those who do not accept the reality of the paranormal.

In his book *The Nine* (the first in the *Sinister Forces* trilogy), Levenda provides hard documentary evidence in support of many conclusions I myself had earlier reached, based mostly upon intuition and logic, and supported by only a few pieces of data I took as factual. For example, when I considered the information provided by Jacques Vallee that the UFO phenomenon is physical, *and* psychic, *and* also sometimes a product of human deception, I simply drew a logical inference: that if it is both psychic and physical, then it might well be a *materialization* (usually short-lived) of psychic realities in the form of physical objects and events, such as magicians have always reputedly been able to produce. And if it is also surrounded by human deception activities, I asked myself if such activities, at least on one level, might be *invocations* designed to catalyze these very materializations. This is the basic premise of the practice of "sympathetic magic" that was universal in the ancient world, and in the world of primitive tribes up to our own time: that in order to produce a phenomenon, the magician (after preparing suitable conditions) imitates it, as a Voudoo practitioner will stick pins in a doll so as to injure the person it represents. Anyone who has handled or bought a "rain stick" at their local health food store or Pagan Shoppe has come into contact with a traditional tool of sympathetic magic.

I further conjectured as follows: That certain magicians found they were able to produce actual preternatural phenomena through autosuggestion; as with the Tibetan practice of psychically materializing a *tulpu*, their ability to alter their psychic state also ultimately altered their physical environment as well: the premise of all magic. And then, in the early 20th century, as studies of the effect of propaganda on entire populations in the "radio age" advanced and became better known, certain black magicians came to an obvious and horrible conclusion: that if changing their own consciousness could produce *local* manifestations of the preternatural, *changing the consciousness of the mass could produce global ones.* (The *mass* dissemination of LSD likely sponsored by the CIA in as part of their MK-ULTRA mind control program might well have been an expression of this agenda.) Consequently the "cracks in the great wall" were immensely widened, and in flew the UFOs, and all the other spooks and demons and sinister forces that beset postmodern humanity. Certainly such entities have a long history of intervention in our world, but today's *mass* interest and belief in them, and mass *experience* of them, has probably not been so widespread since late antiquity. Perhaps it was the Nazis, who, as Peter Levenda demonstrates in his book *Unholy Alliance*, placed all of Germany and much of Europe under the power of a Satanic cult dedicated to invoking the Powers of Darkness, who first got their foot firmly in the door in terms of the modern world; this would explain the "foo-fighters" (early "flying saucers") encountered by the allied air forces in their bombing runs over the dying Reich. After all, what is the literal meaning of *holocaust*? It means: a mass immolation of human victims in the cult of a Pagan god. And as the Argentine writer Jorge Luis Borges pointed out in his story "Deutches Requiem", the Nazis did not only immolate the Jews, but ultimately offered Germany itself as a living sacrifice on the altar they raised to the birth of the New Man and the New Age of Darkness. (NOTE: Certain of the secret "experimental aircraft", some of them disc-shaped, produced by the Nazis, and later by the Americans, during and after the war—the United States "inherited" many Nazi scientists through Operation Paperclip—were probably attempts to imitate the aeronautical abilities exhibited by UFOs, on the theory that these were highly-advanced technological devices built either by the human enemy or an extraterrestrial race. But some of the more "esoteric" of those involved in their production may have understood them on a different level: as another instance of sympathetic magic, one more highly concrete act of *invocation*.)

As Levenda has amply demonstrated, Jack Parsons was at the center of all these vectors of dark force: scientist, close associate of intelligence agents, Pagan magician. He is one of the ones who let the cat out of the bag in terms of the possibility of a literal synthesis between Satanism and modern science. But an even more interesting cat is the one released by Arnold Dahl, Fred Crisman and Kenneth Arnold.

The story, recounted in Levenda's *The Nine*, is as follows: On June 21, 1947, harbor patrolman Arnold Dahl spotted six UFOs hovering over his boat anchored at Maury Island in Puget Sound, this being the first major civilian UFO sighting after WWII. A slight explosion occurred on one of the objects, after which hot metal rained down upon and damaged Dahl's boat, killing his dog and injuring his teenage son. He had a camera on board and was able to photograph the objects. After returning with his boat to Tacoma he told his boss, Fred Crisman, of the strange event, and turned over to him his camera, the photographs and a sample of the metallic slag that had fallen from the sky. (More than 20 years after this event, Crisman was subpoenaed by Jim Garrison in the course of his investigation of the Kennedy assassination, and was found to be an ex-OSS officer with CIA connections, as well as a friend of Clay Shaw!) The next evening, Arnold Dahl was visited by the 20th century's first recorded "man in black", who advised him to forget the whole incident. The following day Crisman went to Maury Island, retrieved some more of the material that had fallen on Dahl's boat, and spotted another UFO. A day later, on June 24, one Kenneth Arnold, a deputy federal marshal and member of an Idaho search and rescue team, while piloting his aircraft near Mt. Ranier in Washington State in search of a missing transport plane, spotted a formation of nine UFOs flying in formation. His subsequent description of them gave us our term "flying saucer"; it was these two sightings that began the first American "saucer scare" of the postwar era. Arnold's account was published in an Oregon newspaper; then, in early July, he was visited by two Air Force intelligence officers from California who were interested in hearing his story. Next, Fred Crisman contacted Raymond Palmer, editor of *Amazing Stories* magazine, with Arnold Dahl's story of the Maury Island encounter, but not before Palmer himself got in touch with Kenneth Arnold about the Mt. Ranier sighting. Palmer then suggested that Arnold meet with Dahl, a meeting that took place in Tacoma on July 30.

Flying to make that meeting on July 29, Arnold saw another, larger fleet of UFOs. And when he arrived in Tacoma, he found that no hotel rooms were available—except for a room in the most expensive hotel in town that had already been reserved in his name by person or persons unknown. Arnold and Dahl came together in that room to compare notes about their strange experiences—after which United Press International apparently received a verbatim transcript of the entire meeting!

Arnold Dahl was visited by his "man in black" a mere 24 hours after his UFO sighting and the explosion that killed his dog—and this at a time when UFOs did not loom large in the public mind, as they certainly were to do in short order, due in great part to the revelations of Dahl and Arnold themselves. How is this to be explained? In the absence of a mass paranoia about UFOs, why would a presumed government agency already have in place a system apparently designed to suppress evidence for the existence of extraterrestrials? That evidence, by and large, had not yet appeared, at least to the public at large. And though it may be true that the government and the intelligence community feared that the open appearance of such evidence was imminent and had taken steps to cushion the blow of these revelations on the public mind, another and equally logical explanation is that the man in black and his superiors *knew that the UFO apparition over Maury Island was about to take place*—and they could only have known this, 1) if they themselves produced the phenomenon, or 2) if they were in touch with those entities who planned to, and had received advance warning. Since it strains credulity to believe that any terrestrial technology available at that time, or even today, could have produced fleets of craft that were both undeniably physical objects, and also capable of feats no human aircraft could remotely duplicate, one *logical* (which certainly does not mean *conventional*) explanation is that the beings in control of those craft had communicated with their human agents to the effect that: "We are going to appear at such and such a place on such and such a date; get ready to put into action the follow-up plan we discussed." Likewise the mysterious advance booking of the hotel room where Kenneth Arnold met with Arnold Dahl, the apparent bugging of their room, and the release of the transcripts of their conversation to UPI, are extremely good evidence in support of the hypothesis that both Dahl's and Arnold's UFO sightings were somehow arranged or known about in advance; if this were not the case, how could such a well-designed plan to exploit their reactions to those sightings, obviously requiring extensive resources and a great deal of coordinated effort, have been put into action so soon after the events themselves? One point on which I disagree with Peter Levenda is where he assumes the appearance of the "man in black" to Dahl and the recording and release of Dahl's and Arnold's conversation in the hotel room were part of an effort to *discredit* their reports. Certainly the threats made by the "man" would make anyone think twice about revealing what he'd seen, but could this messenger's appearance not be equally well explained as an attempt to *lend credibility* to those reports? What could be more likely to convince someone of the reality and serious import of a particular experience than a threat by a mysterious stranger of unfortunate consequences if that experience were ever revealed? And why leak the conversation of Dahl and Arnold to the *UPI itself* unless the intent behind the leak was not to debunk UFOs but to influence the public to believe in them? A major *myth* of the UFO belief-system is that "the government knows everything, or at least an awful lot, about UFOs, but it is hiding all this data from us because it wants to convince us that UFOs—who are probably extraterrestrials—don't really exist." One way mind control works, however, is through the implanting of *assumptions* like this in the public psyche. Beliefs that, because they deal with the fringes of consensus reality, are rarely subjected to logical analysis, often become the focus of both "true belief" and "cynical debunking"—two equal and opposite departures from logical objectivity—two sides of the same coin. And to the degree that the effort to make sense of the UFO phenomenon is limited to the question "are they real or only an illusion?", all questions of their spiritual *quality* or their possible use as a vector of mass mind-control are pushed into the background. You are either a true believer or a cynical debunker; the purpose of the cynical debunker is in fact to *create* the true believer, to separate the knowledge that he or she possesses of the reality of the UFO phenomenon, based on painstaking research if not personal experience, from the collective validation that such knowledge would normally enjoy, thus producing a state of *paranoia*. Undoubtedly those who are working to influence mass belief well know that an individual laboring under this kind of oppression will desperately seek to overcome his schizophrenic split from consensus reality by finding or developing an explanation for his experience that consensus reality will accept. Consequently he or she will be apt to accept uncritically whatever explanations the social engineers may wish, for their own purposes, to provide; see my account of the mind-control technique of "deferred closure", below. And just as the cynical debunker causes the true believer to harden his position, so the believer has the same effect on the debunker.

Harvard psychiatrist, UFOlogist and Pulitzer Prize-willing author John Mack (he won his Pulitzer for a book on T. E. Lawrence, who was a British Intelligence asset; his UFO book is entitled *Abduction*) gained influence over his clients, most of them "alien abductees", by taking their side against their cynical friends, relatives and employers, many of whom thought they were crazy. But Dr. Mack was their friend; Dr. Mack *believed* them. His job was to help them to *accept* their experiences—to "accept" them as real, certainly, but also to "accept" the terroristic violation and *indoctrination* that such experiences usually involved—two very different meanings of the same word. Mack's job, apparently, was to solidify and exploit the alien control that first penetrated the souls of his clients during their abduction experience, in a perfect example of well-known brainwashing technique of alternating terror (the abducting, violating aliens) with relief (the helpful, understanding Dr. Mack).

There has definitely been a concerted government effort to debunk the reality of UFOs; I certainly don't want to deny this obvious fact. But as I have stated, I believe there has also been a parallel attempt to plant the idea of their reality the public mind. It is possible that these seemingly opposed efforts may represent different factions within the power elite, but it is equally possible that both are part of a single overall strategy. In the 1997 UFO documentary *Area 51*, one of the interviewees makes the claim that as the human race entered the space age, the U.S. government and the military confronted the following question: What if in our exploration of space we encounter intelligent, technologically-advanced aliens and establish their reality? What effect would this have on human society? The conclusion was that it would create social chaos, so the Rand Corporation and the Brookings Institute were hired to develop a plan to head off this potential chaos. The result was a proposal that the public be slowly acclimatized to the notion of human encounter with extraterrestrial aliens over a 30 year period. Clearly the planting of evidence (spurious or otherwise) pointing to the reality of aliens, and the debunking of evidence in favor of that reality, would both find their place in such a plan.

But this begs the question: what was supposed to happen at the end of those 30 years? The Rand/Brookings social engineering plan may or may not actually exist, but if it does, it could have started out as described, and then progressively morphed into a plan to *produce* incontrovertible evidence of alien/human interaction (spurious or otherwise) after the 30 years were up, for specific social engineering purposes—perhaps in order to create the "united earth" that must ready itself to encounter an enemy from another galaxy. This, incidentally, would go a long way toward explaining the heavy and overt military and intelligence involvement in the Disclosure Movement (see below). As Peter Levenda recounts in his book *The Nine* (the first in the *Sinister Forces* trilogy), the relationship between the UFO phenomenon and the push for a One-World Government was clearly expressed by General Douglas MacArthur in a speech to the cadets at West Point on May 12,1962:

> We deal now, not with the things of this world alone, but with the illimitable distances and as yet unfathomed mysteries of the universe... of ultimate conflict between a *united human race* and *the sinister forces of some other planetary galaxy*; of such dreams and fantasies as to make life the most exciting of all times. And through all this welter of change and development your mission remains fixed, determined, inviolable. It is to win our wars [emphasis mine].

Returning now to *Area* 51, I would suggest that anyone viewing this documentary (it is available through Netflix) should direct his or her attention to one scene where, in a supposed video of a UFO, the object in question is described by the narrator as entering the field of vision "from the lower right", whereas the actual image we see is in the upper half of the screen. This disconnect between word and image is one form of the mind control technique I have named "subliminal contradiction". If the viewer accepts both the message received by his eyes and the opposite message received through his ears unconsciously, without noting the contradiction, his critical faculties are at least partially disabled and he becomes highly receptive to suggestion. (The "lower right quadrant" element also suggests a Neuro-Linguistic Programming technique.) This "error" in the documentary does not appear in the (supposedly unrehearsed) accounts of the interviewees; it appears in the composed narrative of the voice-over—and if it were an actual error it would certainly have been caught and corrected in the editing process. So we must conclude that it was deliberate, and thus that *Area* 51 as a whole is a mind control production, possibly to further prepare us for the "disclosure" to come. And as for the revelation (if legitimate) that Rand and Brookings produced a report recommending that the belief in UFOs be slowly engineered into the public mind, this could be an example of the mind control technique Michael Hoffman calls "revelation of the method", as well as an attempt to depotentiate and co-opt any glimmer of realization on the part of the public that the belief in UFOs is being *promoted* as well as debunked. This could be done by admitting that the promotion is taking place while at the same time explaining it in such a way as to further the ultimate ends of that promotion rather than undermining them: "Certainly we are covertly promoting the belief in UFOs—not to delude you, however, but to prepare you to accept *the truth*." (This assertion appears not only in *Area* 51, but in the 2000 documentary *Close Encounters: Proof of Alien Contact*, also available through Netflix.) And to both promote and debunk the existence of alien-human contact could certainly represent the technique of subliminal contradiction applied on a mass level. This technique even seems to form part of MacArthur's speech in 1962: what could be more contradictory than for the cadets at West Point to be asked to steel themselves to fulfill a "fixed, determined, inviolable" mission in a war against "fantasies and dreams"? As I have already made clear, I entirely accept the reality of the UFO phenomenon and the existence of "aliens", but I see the aliens as demons and the true reality of ongoing alien-human contact as the systematic invocation of such demons by elements of the military and intelligence communities operating under deep cover, an alliance that may have begun in some cases—as Peter Levenda and others have speculated—when scientists in Russia or at the Stanford Research Institute or the Lawrence Livermore Laboratory inadvertently broke through, in the course of their various psycho-technological tinkerings, into the dimension the demons inhabit. (See *The Manson Secret*, the third book in the *Sinister Forces* trilogy, for accounts of the harrowing

praeternatural apparitions that dogged the scientists from Lawrence Livermore after they undertook to test the psychic powers, including psycho-kinesis, of famous Israeli psychic Uri Geller in 1974–75.) And it is highly likely that such experiments in arcane science would have been inspired, in some cases at least, by the demons themselves.

"Mind control" techniques of various descriptions also operate in ordinary social situations. Anyone who has a basically manipulative way of relating to others is, if successful, a junior grade mind-controller; such people often gravitate to intelligence work where they can hone their skills and bring them to a more professional level. I personally experienced the effects of the revelation-of-the-method technique at the hands of a "friend" with whom I was involved in a certain church project. For quite a few years this man had been a management consultant with an impressive portfolio of past work in the world of multi-national corporations, teaching various meditative and cognitive techniques to upper management and applying them to conflict resolution and organizational development; his ex-wife had a background in undercover work with the Pinkerton Detective Agency. On one occasion I told him, "I feel like I'm being used"—to which he replied: "But you *want* to be used, don't you? Don't you want to be useful?" Today my answer to that question would simply be "no—at least not by, or to, you"; but at that time I only replied, "Uh, yeah, sure, I guess. . . ." In like manner, when Americans are told "your mass consciousness is being manipulated—but you already suspected that, didn't you?", our answer often is not "You bastard, are *you* one of the manipulators?", but "Hey! We were right!"—a much pleasanter sentiment, a much less frightening concept than the idea of total helplessness.

Since my main area of expertise is traditional metaphysics, let us now take a look at how various mind-control techniques, or those events and processes I believe might represent them, would look from a metaphysical perspective. To begin with, the use of the "revelation of the method" technique to demoralize the public by nonchalantly letting them know that they are (perhaps) under total control, is in fact based on a satanic inversion of the metaphysical principle that God is both Absolute Good and Absolute Power, an inversion that produces the counter-proposition: *whatever is inevitable must therefore be good*—the same principle that leads some voters to "back the winner" even if he or she is opposed to everything they claim to hold sacred. And subliminal contradiction itself is the satanic inversion of another metaphysical principle which holds that "God is beyond the *dvandvas*, the pairs-of-opposites"; to employ subliminal contradiction is thus to imply that whatever reality may lie beyond consensus reality ("the truth is out there!" as the *X-Files* mantra has it) must necessarily be Absolute Truth and Absolute Power. These inversions of universally accepted metaphysical principles are so precise and so word-perfect that one is led to ask whether or not certain Satanists, or mind-controllers trained and employed by the military or the intelligence services, may have in fact studied metaphysics so as to put it to use, in inverted mode, as the highest form of the "magical" manipulation of consciousness. (Anyone who has read *The Screwtape Letters* by C.S. Lewis will be familiar with the idea of the demonic manipulation of mass social attitudes—a manipulation that we might ascribe, under the theory that devils are rebel angels, to the "fallen cherubim". The cherubs appear in the Book of Ezekiel as flying-saucer-like aerial wheels whose rims are studded with eyes, symbolizing an *aeonian* knowledge that is both global in space and simultaneous in time. And the inverted, satanic metaphysicians who may be inspired by these fallen cherubim could be those to whom René Guénon, in *The Reign of Quantity and the Signs of the Times*, applies the Islamic/Sufic name of *Awliya al-Shaytan*, "saints of Satan".)

I would also like to draw your attention to what I believe could be another mind control technique that appears from time to time in the various UFO videos available on YouTube: A video with a caption like "Huge Amazing Mothership Appears over El Paso!" is followed by a video of a sky with clouds, and nothing else. This is similar to subliminal contradiction, but it is also apparently an attempt to suggest that the viewer sees something that he in fact does not see—in other words, to set up a hallucination. (It would be interesting to know whether subliminal images form a part of this process.) This technique is also based on an inversion of a particular metaphysical principle that lies at the heart of Christian theology, in this case the principle that God the Father, Who is Reality Itself, is invisible ("None has seen the Father at any time" said Jesus in John 1:18). In other words, the UFO that is invisible, but actually there, is identified with God Himself, the corollary being (again in Christian terms) that the UFO that *does* appear is equivalent to Christ, who is the manifestation or *icon* of the Father. And a UFO that is considered equivalent to Christ is nothing less than a sign of the Antichrist.

In any case, I believe that the evidence is quite strong that elements of the U.S. government and the governments of other nations have been doing all they can to implant the idea of the reality of UFOs as extraterrestrial spacecraft in the public mind while simultaneously debunking this belief; why else would Douglas MacArthur have come right out and told us in 1962 that the next world war—or the next war of the worlds—will be between a *united humanity* and invaders from *another galaxy*? In doing so he may have in fact revealed that the ultimate goal served by the inculcation of a belief in extraterrestrials in the public mind is to create a One-World Government by uniting the peoples of the Earth against a (real or imagined) common enemy—a speculation Jacques Vallee also put forward in *Messengers of Deception*. And if a united earth is the goal of such propaganda and mind control, then it stands to reason that the impetus and resources necessary to carry on such a massive social engineering campaign—which I believe includes the production of such motion pictures as *ET* and *Close Encounters of the Third Kind*, (both directed by Steven Spielberg), the docudrama *Roswell*, and television series' like *The X-Files*, as well as well-timed public releases of classified UFO files by the governments of Mexico, France, the United Kingdom, and more recently both New Zealand and the U.K. again—likely emanate from a power bloc that transcends the national governments. In *Cracks in the Great Wall*, in the section entitled *Mind Control and Roswell: The Spielberg Agenda?* I commented on the mind control-like qualities of Spielberg's UFO productions. I subsequently learned from *Sinister Forces* that a nuclear physicist named Jack Sarfatti, a colleague of psychic investigator Andrija Puharich and also of Uri Geller—Sarfatti was involved in the "remote viewing" experiments at the Stanford Research Institute (a group that also studied the powers of Geller), experiments that involved the U.S. Army, the CIA, the NSA, the DIA, and the National Security Council—on one occasion introduced Uri Geller to Steven Spielberg. So it would seem that a U.S. intelligence influence operating through some of Spielberg's movies is not beyond the realm of possibility.

Several motion pictures beyond those produced by Spielberg appear to be attempts to build and manipulate the "alien" myth. Leaving aside the more obvious candidates for this role such as *The Day the Earth Stood Still*, the 1952 science fiction movie *Red Planet Mars*, directed by Harry Horner and produced by Anthony Veiller, who also wrote the screenplay, seems to fit this description. It is interesting, from a synchronistic point of view at least, that the motion picture was released in the same year that massive UFO fleets made their appearance over Washington, D.C.; even more interesting is the fact that *The Day the Earth Stood Still*, screenplay by Edmund H. North who made training films for the U.S. Army Signal Corps during the Second World War, was released a year earlier; it certainly seems to have predicted (if not actually catalyzed) the D.C. sightings.

Red Planet Mars presents itself as a simplistic piece of Cold War propaganda with a rather absurd plot—but an entirely different text is evident just beneath the surface. During World War II Horner worked on a U.S. Air Force propaganda film by Moss Hart called *Wingéd Victory*, based on Hart's play of the same name; simultaneously Veiller was working with Frank Capra on several films in the documentary/propaganda film series entitled *Why We Fight*. When Horner made his directorial debut with *Red Planet Mars*, starring Peter Graves, this got him in on the ground floor of an American postwar trend, or program, of using science fiction movies to posit new social paradigms and belief-systems, movies sometimes drawing upon the expertise of WWII cinematic propagandists trying to reinvent themselves in a Cold War context, possibly under continued government patronage. All of them were following more or less in the footsteps of H.G. Wells.

The basic story-line is as follows: An independent American scientist begins sending radio messages to Mars and picking up replies suggesting intelligent life; these exchanges are also being monitored by a Nazi scientist in South America working for the Russian Communists. The communiqués, detailing the advanced technology and high quality of life on the Red Planet, cause global chaos and economic breakdown, especially in the West, which leads Russia and the Soviet Block to believe that they have won the Cold War. But then messages with a religious content begin arriving, messages that suggest that God, or Christ, is the "supreme ruler" or "supreme being" of Mars. (The Mormons actually hold a similar belief.) This precipitates a worldwide religious revival, which the President of the United States interprets as heralding the advent of a new universal faith, based on the most ancient truths, one that encompasses and transcends all the traditional religions. This revival culminates in a Christian uprising in Russia that overthrows the Soviet system and installs the Patriarch of Moscow as the new head of state. The world rejoices. All this appears on the surface to be simply another example of the "Christian anti-Communism" of the Cold War, but since the religious world revolution is shown as based on the revelation that Jesus is not God but really only a Martian, leading to the inescapable conclusion that there is no God, it's obvious that a radically different worldview and agenda are being promoted: what appears to be a Christian revolution against dialectical materialism is really a *materialist* revolution against every religious faith—and the new universalist religion based on ancient truth is clearly the regime of Antichrist.

Then things take a turn: the Nazi scientist shows up at the American scientist's laboratory, and reveals that he was the one who transmitted the messages supposedly coming from Mars; he shows them the original texts in his notebook. He threatens to tell the world of his deception and destroy the new-found peace. The American scientist and his wife realize that the later religious messages aren't in the notebook, so they must have come from another source. At this point the American scientist begins to "lose his faith in Mars" and believe that the messages might have been a deception planted by the U.S. government to bring down the Soviet system; the Nazi agrees.

The picture now reaches a Luciferian/nihilist crescendo. The Nazi starts quoting Milton's "Paradise Lost": "Better to reign in Hell than serve in Heaven . . . the unconquerable Will,/And study of revenge, immortal hate, /And courage never to submit or yield . . ."; he declares that he worships Lucifer. Then, unbeknownst to the Nazi, the American scientist releases explosive gas into the laboratory, planning to blow him up along with himself and his wife in order to preserve the deception that has brought peace to the world; his wife sees what he has done, agrees to die with him, tells him she loves him and says that what they are doing is good; the Nazi still doesn't realize what is afoot, but he pulls a gun and holds them captive. The scientist's wife asks him to light a cigarette for her which will touch off the explosion, but he resists. She says to the Nazi, immediately after she has chosen to commit murder and double suicide in order to protect a global deception: "God gave us free will, that's what distinguishes us from the animals. But if we choose evil now, that's the end of the human story." Then the Nazi realizes that the room is filled with explosive gas. He struggles to prevent the American from lighting his lighter, but at the last moment a *real* message starts coming in from Mars, indicating that the earlier religious messages were genuine, so the Americans no longer need to blow up the laboratory. The Nazi, however, in an attempt to suppress the message, fires at the transmitter and the laboratory blows up anyway, killing all three.

The eulogy for the scientist and his wife is delivered by the President of the United States, who talks about their being caught up to God in a fiery chariot (the lab explosion), but then contradicts himself, rather eerily, by saying "the whole earth is their sepulcher". Apparently no more messages will be coming from Mars because only the dead couple (and the Nazi) knew how to receive them. But the last message has been preserved: "Ye have done well, ye good and faithful servant." The movie ends with a view of churches all over the world filled with the faithful giving thanks to God for their salvation in a world of peace. In the last scene a Pentagon general embraces the American scientist's two orphan sons, as if he were their father now. The whole idea that Jesus was a Martian is never denied, just drowned and suppressed in a wave of "Christian" piety.

So here we see God's salvation of the world identified with murder and suicide, perhaps in a Luciferian inversion of the Crucifixion and the suicide of Judas; we see the "good" American scientist and his wife and the "evil" Nazi united in choosing to commit a capital crime and mortal sin; we see *telling the truth to the world* associated with Nazi *evil*, and *deceiving the world* identified with upstanding American Christian (or upstanding American Martian) *good*; and we see the military taking over the protection and raising of our children. The effect of this motion picture in terms of social engineering is to deny the existence of God but retain religious sentiments while diverting them to an inappropriate, material object (i.e., an idol), and to represent deception and crime as the only way to world peace and global unity: if the people would only forget God, make a god out of science, happily allow themselves to be deceived and call evil good, all would be well on planet earth. I have absolutely no doubt that these are the precise social engineering goals of some in the power elite, who may well have hired Horner and Veiller, these makers of propaganda films, people who had already worked under their direction during the war, to implant these notions—under cover of cheap cinematic fiction that need not be rigorously analyzed because it is not expected to be taken seriously—in the mass mind.

Postwar cinema presents us with two basic images the "extraterrestrials": they are either a technologically advanced and spiritually enlightened race whose intentions toward humanity are good, or a race of evil monsters bent on enslaving or destroying us. *Red Planet Mars*, *The Day the Earth Stood Still*, Carl Sagan's *Contact* and (in some ways) Steven Spielberg's *Close Encounters of the Third Kind* present more or less the first view—although *The Day the Earth Stood Still* portrays the aliens as interstellar policemen who will destroy us if we do not renounce war as they have—except, apparently, when they opt to destroy entire races and planets from time to time—while *The War of the Worlds*, the television miniseries *V*, *Independence Day* and a whole slew of grade B space operas present the aliens as enemies of the human race. However, both these versions of the aliens have one thing in common: they both call for *global unity*, either as the crowning "evolutionary" achievement of humanity as helped and guided by the "space brothers", or (as Douglas MacArthur warned us) the necessary united front against an enemy from beyond the stars. And given the nature of the mind-control technique I have named "unconscious contradiction", it is not inconceivable that both views of the space aliens were designed to work together; in any case they *do* work together *de facto*. It is quite likely that H.G. Wells, as a Fabian Socialist and an unashamed technocratic globalist, intended *War of the Worlds* as a propaganda piece promoting global unity; he certainly presents space travel as part and parcel of a politically united earth in his *Things to Come*. In the first book he paints the aliens as enemies of the earth; in the second, it is the higher caste of technocratic globalists who initiate space travel, as against the bigotry and superstition of the ignorant masses who want humanity to remain earthbound. In *The Day the Earth Stood Still* the aliens act as a sort of United Nations peace-keeping force; in *Red Planet Mars* and *Contact* they are revealed as the actual *material* reality behind the human belief in God. But despite their differences, every one of these motion pictures is a clear apology for political globalization. A question I can't answer with any certainty, but one that definitely needs to be asked, is: could this unanimity be nothing more than an accidental reflection of the *zeitgeist*, or is it, at least in part, the product of a deliberate program of social engineering?

A more recent example of this kind of engineering is the book *Challenges of Change* (2008) by "retired NORAD officer" Stanley A. Fulham, which is supposed to be based on revelations made by an "intelligence officer connected with NORAD" of a great deal of UFO information that has been kept secret from the public by the U.S. government, and which predicted that UFOs would appear in the skies above earth's cities on Oct. 13 of 2010, in a sort of real-life version of a similar episode from science fiction writer Arthur C. Clarke's book *Childhood's End*. The UFOs dutifully appeared, right on schedule (you can see the videos on YouTube), although the ones that took their place in the sky above New York's Central Park gave more the impression of illuminated helium balloons than of the more spectacular and convincing types of UFO phenomena.

Retired astronaut Edgar Mitchell, in a 2008 interview, made a "startling new revelation" about UFOs, claiming that the U.S. government has been trying to hide their existence for years but that the truth finally leaked out despite their best efforts. He also revealed that he had been briefed by the Pentagon on several occasions—one of these briefings, he implied, being fairly recent—to the effect that the UFO phenomenon is real, and the government is in ongoing contact with the extraterrestrials. We know, however, that Mitchell has been making claims like this for many years; why would the Pentagon reveal information to him that they hoped would never be made public when, judging by his past statements, he was all but certain to make it public, as he in fact did? And why was he never subject to persecution or legal action for revealing classified information? This makes no sense—unless the true intent of the unknown source of this "information" (and of Mitchell himself), is to implant the belief in UFOs in the public mind. As Levenda points out, Edgar Mitchell (who also happens to be a Freemason) has a long-standing involvement in paranormal research; he was the one who was on hand to welcome Uri Geller to the Stanford Research Institute.

One of the methods employed in this mass social engineering campaign is illustrated by the following anecdote: *Someone admitted to an American Air Force base catches a glimpse of an object resembling a UFO through an open hangar door. As soon as he sees it, the door is closed and he is told "You weren't supposed to see that". Then, a few days later, the proverbial "men in black" arrive at his house, threatening reprisals if he tells anyone what he saw.* This is a classic case of psychological manipulation, where an event that might have made little impression on him suddenly, through the use of terror, assumes the status of a dark revelation: "If these people are desperate enough to threaten to harm me or my family if I reveal what I know, THEN WHAT I SAW MUST BE REAL."

So it appears that various governments, possibly taking their orders from an authority that transcends the national state, have been trying to capitalize on the UFO phenomenon by *officially* denying that it exists (against massive and mounting evidence) while at the same time clandestinely leaking stories confirming that it does exist. Why would they do this, other than as an opportunity to employ the subliminal contradiction technique on a mass level, or as a way of "easing" the public into an acceptance of the reality of extraterrestrials so as to minimize social chaos when the big "disclosure" arrives? For one thing, if they were to officially admit the existence of the UFO phenomenon, they would either have to say "we don't know what it is and we can't control it"—thus undercutting their own authority—or else they would have to produce the alien diplomats they are claiming to be in contact with so they could appear on the Oprah show. Since they can't produce those diplomats, they would rather let a growing segment of the population believe that they *are* in contact with extraterrestrials, but that they must hide this to prevent mass panic. By acting in this way they are suggesting to the populace that they have immensely powerful allies, and at the same time preventing their lack of a full understanding of the UFO phenomenon (which Jacques Vallee believes to be the case) from being publicly exposed. So what we have is a mass mind-control project piggybacking on a real phenomenon, which would explain why some UFO encounters are truly inexplicable, while others appear to be deceptions most likely produced by human action.

This social engineering program has already produced, among other things, the Disclosure Movement, many of whose sponsors have military or intelligence backgrounds (they are quite open about this), which is dedicated to pressuring the U.S. government to come clean on what it knows about UFOs and alien contact. And every time they "force" the government to reveal another item of data about the "reality" of this contact, the greater their sense of triumph after so many years of social marginalization, of being typed as mentally imbalanced cranks. In view of this long-delayed "success" it is highly unlikely that most Disclosurites would be willing to consider the possibility that they are being manipulated by the very people they believe they are finally triumphing over after a lifetime of lonely struggle.[1]

The program has also given rise to the "discipline" known as *exopolitics*, whose proponents believe that they are in ongoing, diplo-

1. From a correspondent: "Bill Cooper saw classified gov[ernment] doc[ument]s on aliens which he said were planted to generate 'insider' accounts for 'disclosure.' These 'secret' doc[ument]s were circulated to officers with 'access' to create leaks from 'insiders.'"

matic communication with the aliens via an extraterrestrial organization or organizations somewhat on the order of the United Federation of Planets from the Star Trek mythology. In this they are imitating what they believe the Federal Government is capable of; according to them, the Feds don't have the monopoly on extraterrestrial contact, by golly! They too have made an alliance with the Powers of the Beyond. This leads us to ask how this "communication" with the aliens might be accomplished. Are their "allies" from the intelligence community feeding them all the latest diplomatic communiqués? Or are they in direct contact with the demons themselves through channeling and mediumship? This second possibility is far from unlikely, given that the well-known psychic researcher Andrija Puharich, associate of Aldous Huxley, the man who introduced Uri Geller to American audiences, consultant to the Pentagon on the military uses of parapsychology, participant in the MK-ULTRA mind control experiments conducted by the CIA, was also involved, along with a group of eight colleagues that included members of some of America's first families, in channeling (through an East Indian medium) a group of "extra-terrestrial entities" known as *The Nine*; the story is recounted in Peter Levenda's book of the same name. This project would appear to be the ancestor of various later New Age alien channelings, such as *The Pleiadian Agenda* by Barbara Hand Clow (1995). Furthermore, when I contacted the Exopolitics Institute in Hawaii, founded by Dr. Michael Salla, who once received a Ford Foundation grant and who has a history of connection with the Center for Global Peace at the American University in D.C., I made some very interesting discoveries. I asked someone on the staff if they were in touch with extraterrestrial organizations representing a consortium of planets, something like the Intergalactic Council the hippies believed in, and he said "yes". Then I asked him if 2-way communication was ongoing between the Institute and the extraterrestrials; he said "yes". Then I asked him by what means; he answered, "telepathy".[2]

2. From a correspondent: "An expolitics leader claims on mass media to have encountered Jesus Christ. There is the religious angle, roping Christians into UFO belief. Why, Jesus confirms exopolitics!"

To sum up, the "outer" explanation of the UFO phenomenon and the human activities surrounding it is as follows: The phenomenon is real, and largely inexplicable according to conventional science, though theories abound. In view of this, national governments, or cabals within them, or various extra-governmental power blocs, have said to themselves: "If we can't explain or control the UFO phenomenon, we can at least use it to our benefit." Consequently they have been playing a game with the public of issuing both official denials that the phenomenon exists, or is inexplicable, or is in any way significant, while at the same time planting spurious evidence that suggests it is all too real—evidence to which are attached various items of belief, or various *commands*, that they wish to disseminate. In particular, they apparently want to spread the belief that national governments know a great deal about the phenomenon and what's behind it, and that such governments are in fact in ongoing contact with intelligent extraterrestrial beings, but must officially deny this for obvious reasons. In other words, the actual dis-information being disseminated is not in service of the alleged Massive Government Coverup, which in practical terms would be almost impossible to pull off, but rather a highly successful attempt by some group or groups to make the population *believe* that a Massive Government Coverup exists, that the government wishes above all things to debunk the UFO phenomenon—a much easier task. (This is not to say that the military and the intelligence community do not possess great masses of classified data on UFOs and alien contact, simply that they do not necessarily understand what they are or why they are appearing; this, at least, is Jacques Vallee's belief.)

The effect of this affirmation/denial technique in terms of the more "exoteric" aspects of social engineering is five-fold:

(1) It protects the national governments from being called upon to actually produce the alien diplomats they are supposedly in contact with;

(2) It lends such governments an aura of preternatural power, and terror, since they appear to have as allies highly "advanced" beings, beings from Beyond, who certainly do not rule by the will of the people;

(3) The practice of openly denying while covertly affirming the

existence of extraterrestrials is an example of two mind-control techniques. The first, detailed above, is the one that I have termed "subliminal contradiction": Contradictory bits of information are proposed to the human mind as equally true, and the contradiction between them carefully kept from rising into consciousness; this technique stuns the critical faculties and put the mind of the individual or collective subjected to it into a highly suggestible state. The second technique, which I call "deferred closure", by continually promising to satisfy and at the same time continually frustrating the innate need and function of the human mind to come to a consistent view of reality, produces a state of "closure-starvation", after which almost any belief that promises to provide the desperately needed closure will be seized upon as true, and believed implicitly, like a straw clutched by a drowning man. It will be believed because it is seen not as an alien notion that is being imposed upon the subject against his will, but as the product of his own creativity, insight, perseverance, and self-sacrifice.

(4) It makes the true UFO believers feel as if they are part of a growing and increasingly successful campaign to force the hand of the U.S. government, that they are both persecuted martyrs and victorious heroes. This is a perfect example of *the government co-optation of anti-government action*, the creation of a "controlled opposition"—a method of social engineering that is certainly not limited to the UFO field;

(5) By fostering the mass belief in alien contact, it acts to break down traditional paradigms of reality, including religious worldviews, in order to make the imposition of a One World Government, and possibly a One World Religion, easier to swallow—a religion that must appear to any well-informed believer of the Abrahamic Religions as the regime of Antichrist. As General Douglas MacArthur (who happened to be a Freemason) said on Sept. 2, 1945 (recounted by Peter Levenda in *A Warm Gun*, the second book in his *Sinister Forces* trilogy):

> We have had our last chance. If we cannot devise some more equitable system, our Armageddon will be at our door. *The problem basically is theological* and involves a spiritual recru-

> descence, an improvement of human character that will synchronize with our most matchless advances in science, art, literature and all the material and cultural developments of the past two thousand years. It must be of the spirit if we are to save the flesh [emphasis mine].

It is possible to see this as a call for a Christian revival in western civilization. The general, however, does not appeal here to Christian tradition, but to science, literature and art. His pronouncement is also a succinct statement of the basic premises both *The Day the Earth Stood Still*, whose theme is in no way Christian, and *Red Planet Mars*, whose premise pretends to be Christian but is in fact materialist and atheistic; it almost fits him to be considered one of the ideological founders, the "grand old men", of the New Age Movement! Furthermore, as I have already pointed out, the human activities surrounding the UFO phenomenon have an "inner" or "esoteric" explanation as well: Certain individuals and groups within national governments and/or the intelligence community and/or various extra-governmental power blocs actually *are* in touch with "extraterrestrial intelligences", but in much different way than they wish the public to believe. These "intelligences" are demons, and those in touch with them, black magicians. What to the "exoteric" social engineers are deception activities designed to alter mass belief, to the "esoteric" magicians, the "metaphysicists" are acts of demonic invocation: the mass belief in extraterrestrials, and the *mass suggestion programs* that foster this belief, actually aid these *awliya al-Shaytan* in their attempt to contact those entities, and release their baleful influence upon an unsuspecting world.

The esoteric dimension of the UFO phenomenon and the human activities surrounding it also manifests in terms of an inverted metaphysics. As subliminal contradiction is the satanic shadow of the Absolute, so deferred closure is the satanic shadow of the metaphysical principle, enunciated by metaphysician Frithjof Schuon (who was in some ways a "successor" to René Guénon) that God, as Absolute Reality, is necessarily also Infinite Possibility—which is why Scripture informs us that "with God all things are possible" (Matthew 19:26). If the intuitive sense of Infinite Possibility becomes alienated from the intuitive sense of Absolute Reality, the Absolute will falsely appear not as the inviolable source of all stability, security and certainty, but rather as a kind of "Absolutist," a Divine Tyrant. At the same time, our perception of the Divine Infinity will be transformed from a vision of Infinite Life into an endless pursuit of an elusive wholeness that always escapes our grasp, one that leads only to the dissipation, and ultimately the destruction, of the soul that attempts it, or is lured into it. It is this deluded quest that led William Blake to say, "More! More! is the cry of a mistaken soul; less than All can never satisfy man." If subliminal contradiction is the satanic inversion of the Absolute, and consequently of the masculine aspect of the Divinity, deferred closure is *avidya-maya*, the satanic inversion of the Divine Feminine. Subliminal contradiction stuns and oppresses us with a heavy hand; deferred closure teases us, drains our vitality, until we become its slaves, its eunuchs.

One final and highly interesting piece of the UFO puzzle may have been provided by a strange figure known as Prophet Yahweh—a Black man who dresses a bit like a Muslim and who claims to be able to summon UFOs at will. In a 2008 news editorial on ABC Channel 13 in Las Vegas, Nevada (available on YouTube at *http://www.youtube.com/watch?v=ObD_ujSot9E*), he was shown as apparently able to induce a swift, high-flying orange sphere to materialize on command, which was filmed by the startled news crew. Prophet Yahweh had issued a challenge to the media, claiming that he possessed this ability; Channel 13 responded by naming the place, date and time when the UFO was to appear, apparently hoping to produce an entertaining segment debunking an inflated but harmless crank. But when the UFO actually did appear, they were (apparently) non-plussed. It is possible of course that Channel 13 was in on the stunt. But if they weren't, a couple of other scenarios suggest themselves: either the Prophet was in radio contact with human agents able to produce the phenomenon at will, or he did in fact possess the psychic ability to invoke the apparition of UFOs. In other words, he was either a disinformation agent or an actual magician—possibly both (though he has more the demeanor of a victim, possibly a victim of mind-control, than of a powerful and self confident Magus). I remember when, as a child in the late 1950's, my family and I used to gather on our patio at night overlooking San Francisco Bay to view the Perseid meteor shower, which takes place in August. Gazing up at the starry sky for hours, my mind would wander to the subject of flying saucers; I had the distinct feeling that if I wished hard enough I could make one appear—and I don't think I am alone in this fantasy, which seems to be one aspect of the "UFO archetype" in collective belief.

In conclusion—leaving aside for now the possibility of organized demonic invocation to usher in the Antichrist, which not every reader will accept, to say the least—I believe that UFOs and alien contact are both very real phenomena and elements of a modern myth that has been partly created, and certainly widely manipulated, by various governmental and globalist forces for their own purposes. Until the UFO debunkers take the hard evidence for the reality of UFOs seriously, and the UFO believers do the same with the hard evidence that their conception of the manifestation is being manipulated by people who do not have their best interests at heart, no sort of scientific, or psychological, or political objectivity will be possible with regard to the UFO phenomenon and its profound effects upon the human race.

Addendum

It is important to realize that, among what used to be called "the educated classes", a belief in the reality of extraterrestrial life is not limited to a few scientists and a handful of psychiatrists. Monsignor Corrado Balducci (1923–2008), a Roman Catholic theologian of the Vatican Curia, long time exorcist for the Archdiocese of Rome, and a Prelate of the Congregation for the Evangelization of Peoples and the Society for the Propagation of the Faith, became well-known in UFOlogist circles for his belief in extraterrestrial life. In his Wikipedia article he is quoted as maintaining, on the one hand, that "As God's power is limitless, it is not only possible but also likely that inhabited planets exist" (in other words, that physically-embodied extraterrestrials are likely a reality), but also that "It is probable that there are other beings . . . because there is too much discrepancy between human and angelic nature, of which we have the theological certainty. And since in man, the spirit is subordinate to matter, and since the Angels are alone spirit, it is probable that beings exist with very much less body and matter than we have. They could be those that we call UFO [aliens], these persons that would appear with these wagons [i.e., vehicles] and that also have not only one science, but a natural ability to be our guardians." In this second quotation he is approaching the Greek notion of the *daimones* and the Muslim doctrine of the Jinn. He also maintains that extraterrestrial encounters "are not demonic, they are not due to psychological impairment, and they are not a case of entity attachment" [apparently a non-traditional Novus Ordo Catholic term, derived from Spiritualism, denoting demonic possession]. At this point Monsignor Balducci exhibits the effects of both an incomplete cosmology and a lack of "discernment of spirits". Anyone who has read Dr. John Mack's book *Abduction*, and who also both believes in demons and understands their nature, will be forced to conclude that the majority of the terrifying encounters he reports have to do with the demonic and nothing else. Many of these encounters appear to be cases of obsession (external attack) rather than full possession (internal control). And yet the fact that, as Dr. Mack informs us, many of the "entities" who end by abducting their adult victims began as "imaginary playmates" during the victims' childhoods, is evidence that demonic possession is also a distinct possibility in some cases, as least insofar as we can define "familiar spirits" as possessing demons, not merely obsessing ones. If this exorcist for the archdiocese of Rome had been able to survey thoroughly and dispassionately his Church's archives relating to demonic activity, he would have seen that his description of the UFO aliens as possessing a kind of semi-material body, subtler than the human but grosser than the angelic, can certainly be applied to demons; as Fr. Malachi Martin (himself an exorcist) points out in *Hostage to the Devil*, demons are often associated with specific localities in the physical world, as angels never are. It is possible that Msgr. Balducci shied away at this point from allowing that the UFO aliens (or some of them) might be demons because he encountered certain manifestations that seemed generally benevolent, or at least neutral; at this point he might have profited from the Muslim doctrine that "some of the Jinn are Muslim and some are *kafirun* (unbelievers)", the unbelieving Jinn being precisely demons, *shayatin*. Furthermore, to maintain that any subtle but not fully spiritual being can be a *guardian* to humanity is a strictly Pagan belief; according to traditional Catholic doctrine, our guardians are necessarily *angels*, not *daimones*. That a high-ranking Catholic exorcist was apparently unable to tell the difference between a guardian angel and a familiar spirit is one more glaring indication of the tragedy of the Novus Ordo Church since the Second Vatican Council. It is possible that, due to the weakening of the theurgic powers of the Novus Ordo stemming from the virtual deconstruction of the sacramental order, certain Catholic exorcists who came into intimate contact with demons, not realizing that they now lacked the spiritual potency that would protect them from these beings, and also in view of the fact that Catholic doctrine has been rendered relatively vague and ambiguous since Vatican II, may have become deluded by them, if not actually possessed. This possibility is rendered all the more likely in light of the recent announcement by the present exorcist of the Diocese of Rome, Fr. Gabriele Amorth, that the new rites of exorcism are basically ineffective.

7

The Real Rumi

JALALLUDDIN RUMI is without a doubt one of the most misrepresented figures in the history of religion. There is the Rumi of Valentine's Day, the Rumi of interfaith amity and universal peace, the alcoholic Rumi, the gay Rumi, the lighthearted hippy Rumi opposed to humorless Islamic orthodoxy, not to mention the politicized Rumi (who shows every sign of having been cooked up in a State Department think-tank somewhere), poster-boy of the Iranian opposition, as well as the standard-bearer of the kind of harmless, universalist, hardly-Islamic Islam now openly patronized by the forces of globalization because it is seen as more easily integrated into the New World Order than either the Islamicists or the traditional Muslims. As *dar al-Islam* is relentlessly pounded by military force from without, *al-Din* is being subtly undermined from within by the sentimental and degenerate falsification of Sufism, in part attributable simply to the negative side of promiscuous cultural diffusion, in part deliberately engineered. This falsification has been greatly aided by certain western poets who have done all in their power to separate Rumi and other Sufi poets from their proper Islamic context, thus completing the work of earlier "Sufi" de-Islamicizers like Hazrat Inayat Khan and Idries Shah (whatever may be the real merits of their work in other respects). A shallow aestheticized Sufism cut off from its Islamic roots, one that defines the spiritual path as a kind of sentimental fantasy rather than as a hard-edged and acutely intelligent struggle against the passions of the lower self, a struggle the Prophet called "the war against the soul" or "the greater *jihad*" because physical combat itself is tame by comparison—such emasculated pseudo-Sufism can only tempt Muslim youth, seeking the essence of Islamic manhood, to polarize against it in the direction of the Islamicists, those heartless betrayers of their religion and haters of the Prophet Muhammad and his *sunnah* who, when the Wahhabis (backed by the British Empire) conquered Medina in 1925, obliterated the tombs of the Prophet's companions, and nearly destroyed that of the Prophet himself. As opposed to the growing willingness on the part of these false *mujahidin* to kill anyone, innocent or guilty, soldier or non-combatant, Muslim or *kafir*, simply because they have no more respect for their own lives than they do for the lives of others, the inner, spiritual *jihad*—a pitched battle, by the power of God, against one's very sense of separate existence—may be the only way to come to grips, without dishonest and nihilistic evasions, with the real enemy.

Unfortunately, given that true Sufism is of no use to the global powers that be (both the pseudo-Sufis and the Islamicists being of definite use, since they tend to create each other and thereby work together to advance and justify global pacification), the "Rumi industry" continues to grow. My wife and I were recently invited to an interfaith banquet at the local university, sponsored in part by a Rumi organization based in Washington, D.C. The mayor was there; the chief of police was there; a representative of the governor was there. The organization in question had nothing to do with Islam, with Sufism, with questions relating to the spiritual path; it was not even an art organization interested in poetry. No: It's sole function was to present Rumi as the patron of interfaith unity and global peace. Suspecting that this would be the general drift of things, I prepared a page with a couple of quotes from the Mevlana; after the event was over I approached the woman who had spoken on behalf of the Rumi organization, and showed her the page, which contained the following texts:

> When has religion ever been one? It has always been two or three, and war has always raged among coreligionists. How are you going to unify religion? On the Day of Resurrection it will be unified, but here in this world that is impossible because everybody has a different desire and want. Unification is not possible here. At the Resurrection, however, when all will be united, everyone will look to one thing, everyone will hear and

speak one thing. [Jalalluddin Rumi, *Signs of the Unseen* (*Fihi ma-Fihi*), Threshold Books edition, p.29].

I am the servant of the Noble Qur'an as long as I draw breath;
I am dust on the path of Muhammad, the chosen of God.
If any man claims he's found something else in what I have written
I am disgusted with him—and finished with him.
[Quatrain No. 6: F–1173]

She was deeply shocked. Her eyes widened, her mouth dropped open, and when she was finally able to stammer a few words, she said: "I guess that even *Rumi* could have a *bad day!*" [NOTE: Rumi's appropriation by today's globalists as a patron of religious universalism is right in line with the false claim made by some Islamic Freemasons that Jalalluddin Rumi was one of their predecessors; see Hamid Algar in "An introduction to the History of Freemasonry in Iran" *Middle Eastern Studies*, vol. 6., no. 3; 1970]

Patron of interfaith; homoerotic troubadour; alcoholic; hippy; heterodox aesthete—the real Rumi was none of these things. He was a spiritual poet and contemplative working within a long tradition of *tasawwuf* (Sufism), which, though not always accepted by all Muslims, and sporadically persecuted by the exoterics, was and is intrinsic to the Islamic revelation as its true spiritual heart. Though the Prophet Muhammad, and his son-in-law and esoteric heir Ali Ibn Abi Talib (peace and blessings be upon him) lived in the age of "primordial Islam" where the differentiation and self-identification of Sufism as a separate spiritual stream had not yet become necessary (though the contemplatives attached to the Prophet's household, the *ahl al-suffa* or People of the Bench, may be seen as precursors), still it is not untrue to say that Muhammad was the "original Sufi"; and Ali is recognized by most Sufi orders active today as the first "Pole" or *qutb*. If the cycle of Prophesy is that of Divine Revelation, the cycle of *Walaya* or Sainthood, the special province of the Sufis, pertains to the exegesis and interiorization of that Revelation, the spiritual Path. If Revelation is the flow, *Walaya* is the ebb—and the center of that current of return-to-God, the magnetic lodestone of it (so to speak), is the one called by the Sufis "the Pole of the Age," of which Ali was the first.

The Mevlana may himself have been the Pole of his own time; in any case he is often referred to as "the Pole of Love", in some ways the complementary opposite to Muhyiddin Ibn al-'Arabi, the *Shaykh al-Akbar* (the Greatest Master), who is called "The Pole of Knowledge." And just as there is more love in the encyclopedic "theosophical" works of Ibn al-'Arabi than in the whole world of sentiment and aesthetic romanticism (though he also wrote exquisite spiritual poetry), so there is more knowledge in the poems and discourses of Jalalluddin Rumi than in the whole universe of philosophy, considered as the product of mere human mentality.

Rumi's only peers in the West are Dante, Blake and Shakespeare. And given that he worked as a poet within an established spiritual tradition, he is better compared to Christian poets such as Dante and Angelus Silesius and San Juan de la Cruz (whose work shows many Sufi affinities in both form and content) than to spiritual freelances like Keats or Shelley or Ralph Waldo Emerson or Walt Whitman. When God, speaking to St. Catherine of Siena, said "I am He who is; you are she who is not", this audition was much closer to Rumi and *tasawwuf* than anything in Goethe or Rilke or Emily Dickinson.

Rumi's poetry was essentially "bardic", by which I mean that he drew upon a vast store of tradition—memorized Qur'anic allusions and conventional poetic tropes and symbols, both Persian and Arabic (though he wrote almost entirely in Persian)—much as the Celtic bards employed the myths and symbols of their own tradition. As with any traditional art, his poetry was not so much the work of an "original genius" as the that of a master craftsman working within the limits of traditional themes and prosody, capable of bringing them to an unparalleled "vertical" height partly because a "horizontal" wandering outside that tradition would have been neither desired by the poet nor acceptable to his audience. This is not to say that Rumi's poetry was repetitive, derivative or stilted; as with religion, as with marriage, as with true science, great freedom is possible within strictly-defined limits—limits that also work against the dissipation of effort and the weakening of imaginative force.

As is true of every poetic tradition at its origin, Rumi's Quatrains were meant to be sung, which is why allusions to the musical instruments proper to traditional Persian music (the hand-held drum or *daf*, the *setar*—something like a percussive lute or base mandolin—the *ney* or reed flute, etc.) appear so often in these *rubaiyat*. And it is a common poetic trope in these poems to compare the poet/singer, or his heart, to these instruments; God (in His Majesty) beats the poet's heart like a drum, or strums upon him or his heart like a lute, or (in His Beauty) blows upon him like a flute. On the mystical level, this represents the realization that if *la illaha illa' La*, "there is no god but God", then there is no being but His Being, and consequently no Doer or Performer but He. And on the musical level, this realization is concretely experienced during those moments when the musician or singer disappears, leaving only Music beating the drum, vibrating the vocal cords, or striking the strings; this is one of the ways in which the *sema* or mystical concert of the Sufis transmits esoteric truths directly, beyond explanations.

It is interesting to note that the same comparison of the heart to a musical instrument appears in English and French poetic/musical tradition via the trite term "heart-strings", just as the common trope in Sufi poetry, "the lane of your love", referring to the romantic glamor cast by the presence of one's beloved over what might otherwise be a rather shabby neighborhood of back streets and balconies and clothes-lines, appears again in the song "The Street Where You Live" from *My Fair Lady*. And just as Rumi speaks of the musical instruments crying out as if with human voices, so George Harrison sings "As My Guitar Gently Weeps". (Not for nothing are the posts of harps sometime carved with the torsos of women, or the shape of violins compared to the feminine figure.)

"Classical" Persian music reached great heights of subtlety and elaboration, but it never really departed from what we might call its "folk" roots. Instruments were never dizzily multiplied as in western classical music; the players sit on the floor as if under the open sky; the sort of swaying and hand-clapping one might encounter around a tribal campfire on a desert night are often in evidence and never far away. The music exhibits a kind of deep unsentimental passion, a profound intoxication in the very fist of sobriety—one that, even though sugar is so often mentioned in the Quatrains, reminds one more of the sharp tang of salt. (Those who know Persian food will recognize this same quality in the sour pomegranate for example, so different from the lushness of peach or papaya, as well as in those exquisite Persian candies, seasoned—like some kind of delicious edible soap—with rosewater or cardamom, confections that transmit a *knowledge* of great sweetness, without totally giving way to it: indulgence in the midst of restraint, and restraint in indulgence.)

Arabo-Persian music and poetry exerted a great influence upon European art, culture and spirituality, and became one of the central tributaries to the western Romantic tradition. (By "romantic" I am referring, in literary terms, not to the English and German poets of the Romantic Era, but to the original *romances* dedicated to chivalric love and the Grail quest, by such authors as Robert de Boron, Chrétien de Troyes, and Wolfram von Eschenbach, in which human love was often taken as both a symbol and as a concrete expression of Divine love and the spiritual path.) The very concept of the western "love-song" may ultimately be of Sufi origin, and the troubadour convention of the beloved but unattainable Lady was clearly foreshadowed by the *udhri* poets of 11th century Islam, who deferred to and idealized their chosen Ladies in terms nearly identical to those used by the western troubadours, and considered romantic love as one of the most powerful ways of developing and refining the human character. (The Lady cannot be attained on the lover's own initiative. She must *grant* her favors, and she remains entirely free to grant or to withhold them; she is legitimately comparable to God in this respect.)

The Arabo-Persian-Sufic literary influence that was essential to the development of the troubadour tradition in the west, and which influenced the chivalric romances as well, entered Europe through several doors: through the crusades, through the culturally Islamicized imperial court of Frederick II in the Kingdom of Sicily (which included much of the Italian peninsula), and through Muslim Spain. A system of sentiments with affinities to that of the *udhri* poets was expressed by the Andalusian writer Ibn Hazm in his book *The Dove's Neck-ring*, which is thought to be the direct ancestor of *The Art of Loving Honestly* by Andreas Capellanus, the central prose textbook of the western romantic tradition, commissioned by Eleanor of Aquitaine herself. Capellanus, Dante, Boccaccio, Guido

Cavalcanti, the painter Pedro de Pisa, Petrarch, Cardinal Francesco Barberino, Dino Compagni, and Brunetto Latini are thought by some scholars to have been members of the Fedeli d'Amore or Fede Santa, a secret initiatory order which used both the allegory and the actual practice of romantic love as a spiritual method. Such great figures in Sufism as Ruzbehan Baqli have been classed by some (Henry Corbin, for example) as among "the Fedeli d'Amore of Islam," while affinities and possible ties have been discerned between the western Fedeli d'Amore and both the Knights Templars, the flower of western chivalry, who respected Islam even while fighting against it in the Crusades, and the Sufi order known as the Shadiliyya.

But one of the most direct encounters between the Arabo-Persian poets and singers and the western troubadours, and thus the world of western romance, came about in the following way. The father of "the first troubadour", Guillem de Poitiers, Duke of Aquitaine—himself grandfather of Eleanor of Aquitaine—won from a Spanish emir in one of the many feudal skirmishes of the time a troupe of singing-girls, who would have known, between them, hundreds of songs at the very least. Guillem grew up in a palace surrounded by these women; in effect, they were his nannies. This is the most direct link we know of between the poetry of the troubadours and the Arabo-Persian tradition, filled with Sufi lore, that it so closely resembles. (Guillem was also interested in Neo-Platonism, a tradition that greatly influenced Sufic modes of expression, though their doctrine and practice remained for the most part firmly rooted in Islam.)

In any case, the influence of Arabo-Persian Sufi poetry upon the western romantic tradition was deep and widespread, and it certainly entered the west before Rumi; the Mevlana died in 1273, Guillem de Poitiers in 1126. Elizabethan poetry was greatly influenced by it, partly through the poetic tradition of Italy; some of the sonnets of Shakespeare, though in general a bit more elegaic in tone, read like Sufi *ghazals* (lyric poems), a form that may in fact have been the ancestor of the Petrarchian sonnet. And as late as the 20th century, Sufi themes (though probably not recognized as such) still appeared in the Spanish poetry of Juan Ramón Jiménez and Antonio Machado.

Before the "discovery" of Rumi by Reynold Nicholson, translator of the *Mathnavi*, and his later popularization (in partly bastardized form, at least to begin with) by such American poets as Robert Bly and Coleman Barks, the Mevlana was known to Goethe (1749–1832), Persian poetry being the main influence upon his collection of poems *West-Oestlichen Divan*; Emerson (1803–1882) and the New England Transcendentalists were familiar with this poetic tradition as well. In many ways it was among these largely de-Christianized poets that the de-Islamicization of Rumi and his compatriots began in the west—a trend now being put to extremely destructive use by the globalists as a way of undermining dar al-Islam, the last still-partly-traditional civilization in the world based upon a Divine revelation.

Apart from these well-known writers who consciously turned to Sufi works for spiritual sustenance, the unacknowledged influence of Sufi poetry also persisted in the west far into the 20th century through the "literary ballad" tradition and its influence on popular song. A good example is the song "Plaisir d'Amour", written in 1780 by Jean Paul Égide Martini, and recorded, partly in English translation, by Joan Baez:

The joys of love
Are but a moment long;
The pain of love endures
The whole life long.

Your eyes kissed mine
I saw the love in them shine;
You brought me heaven right there when
Your eyes kissed mine.

My love loves me,
A world of wonder I see;
A rainbow shines through my window;
My love loves me.

And now he's gone,
Like a dream that fades in the dawn;
But the words stay locked in my heartstrings:
My love loves me.

Compare this song to the following quatrains:

Remembrance of you only hides you from me, Beloved.
The lightning of your face only veils that face, Beloved.
Remembering your lips, I know I am without them;
To remember your lips is to lose those lips, Beloved.

I am Love's Lover—and Love? He loves me too.
Flesh is lover to soul, and soul to flesh.
Sometimes I circle his neck with my two arms;
Sometimes he pulls on my coat, as lovers will.

By your step the dust of earth became green and happy;
Pregnant with joy, a hundred buds were born.
By your step the stars and the heavens all shouted together;
Inside that clamor, a star caught a glance from the Moon.

Since God has written "soon we will part" on the Tablet,
Then why all this conflict and violence, my friend?
If I've been bad for you, soon you'll escape that annoyance—
And if I've been good, our love will live in your memory.

Another example is the poem "I Shall Not Care" by Sarah Teasdale (1884–1933), set to music and recorded in 1967 by Tom Rapp of the folk-rock band Pearls Before Swine:

When I am dead
And over me bright April
Shakes out her rain-drenched hair,
Though you should lean
Above me broken-hearted,
I shall not care
(I shall not care.)
. . . .

I shall have peace
As leafy trees are peaceful
When rain bends down the bow;
And I shall be
More silent and cold-hearted
Than you are now
(Than you are now.)

Compare these quatrains of Rumi, where (given that God is better than any of us at playing hard-to-get) the same sentiment is expressed, but not the same conclusion:

Though love and faith bind me to you
—you endlessly tormenting beauty—
Still, I am patient. But aren't you ashamed,
Even for one day, of the pain you've dealt my heart?

"If I keep apart from my beloved", I said to myself
"Maybe he will miss me".
I strove much and endured much, but failed in everything:
How can I ever hide myself from You?

The heart that's ruined by those lips
Will never wander in the garden, in springtime, again.
The branches of the trees prostrate, endlessly, endlessly,
To the power of the wind.

The day you pass by my tomb, sit down and admit
That by making me want you, it was you who killed me.
Then I can shout from the earth with which I am blended:
"O my lost one! O Joseph of the age!"

Romance in the west always had an uneasy relationship with the Catholic Church, just as Sufism did with exoteric Islam. The Sufis were almost always orthodox Muslims, whose spirituality was the sometimes unrecognized but always legitimate expression of the central truth of the Islamic religion, based in large part on an esoteric hermeneutic of the Noble Qur'an. Romance in the west, however, was less fully Catholic than Sufism was Islamic, at least before Dante ultimately synthesized them. To take one example, it formed an integral part of the culture of southern France which spawned the heretical Cathars or Albigenses; it was only after Provence was forcibly re-Catholicized by the Albigensian Crusade—the only crusade launched against an entirely European enemy—that the troubadours took the Blessed Virgin, not the wife of some local lord, as their Lady. And it is important as well not to identify Sufism with "spiritual romance" exclusively, since philosophical or metaphysical intelligence, as well as rigorous ascetic sobriety, were and are equally integral parts of that tradition.

It may be because of the uncertain relationship in the west of romance—spiritual or humanly erotic—to Christian orthodoxy that we tend to see Rumi and his compatriots as rebels against orthodox Islam; however, this is almost entirely false. Persian poetry, like the Song of Solomon, was capable of employing human eros as a metaphor for the love of God in a way and to a degree that is almost inconceivable to us in our own secular, post-Christian society. It is we who can hardly imagine any more a love that is not immediately reducible to sex, not Jalalluddin Rumi. His love for Shams Tabrizi, his spiritual master, was both unashamedly passionate and almost entirely transpersonal; Rumi mourned his disappearance not because he had lost a love-object, but because he had lost the mirror within which, whenever he chose or was permitted to look, he might see the face of God. If the troubadours had all been monks instead of philandering aesthetes, they would have been much closer in terms of Christianity to what the Sufis were, and are, in terms of Islam.

It remains only to say that poetry, to Jalalluddin Rumi, was really not that important. He was a contemplative, saint and spiritual master first, and only secondarily an artist. We are reminded here of the words of the Noble Qur'an from the Surah of the Poets:

Shall I inform you upon whom the devils descend?
They descend upon every sinful, false one.
They listen eagerly, but most of them are liars.
As for the poets, the erring follow them.
Hast thou not seen how they stray in every valley
And how they say that which they do not?
Save those who believe and do good works,

> *and remember Allah much, and vindicate themselves*
> *after they have been wronged.*

Rumi himself expressed his own opinion on the art of poetry in the following terms [*Signs of the Unseen* (*Fihi ma-Fihi*), Threshold Books edition, p.77]:

> My disposition is such that I don't want anyone to suffer on my account. . . . I am loved by those who come to see me, and so I compose poetry to entertain them lest they grow weary. Otherwise, why on earth would I be spouting poetry? I am vexed by poetry. I don't think there is anything worse. It is like having to put one's hands into tripe to wash it for one's guests because they have an appetite for it. That is why I must do it.

This is the real Rumi. The shameless use made of him by those who only want to admire themselves in the glass of his fantasized image, and give aid and comfort to the common enemies of the true spiritual life in doing so, will one day awake to see what they really look like in that uncompromising mirror. That day will be a day of repentance—or else despair.

8

A Chink in the Perennialist Armor—Uncertainty as to the Principial Unity of Knowledge and Love

for Marty Glass

IT IS ESSENTIAL to make a clear distinction between spiritual devotion and intellective intuition, between *bhakti* and *jñana*; René Guénon and Frithjof Schuon between them have established sound criteria upon which such a distinction can be based, and according to which it can be clearly understood. However, to misapply this distinction so as to deny the principial unity of Knowledge and Love on a higher level, and then go on to present Love as a poor "bourgeois" second to true spiritual Knowledge, is to turn the whole spiritual life over to the Devil. If there is anything that unmistakably characterizes the Counter-Initiation, it is the pursuit of a cold *technical* knowledge in the spiritual domain, a merely psychic knowledge devoid of Love and fundamentally inimical to it.

It's true that the disease of the *bhakta* is to believe that all sacred knowledge is only intellectual pride, but we mustn't forget that it is the disease of the *jñani* to act in such a way as to seem to prove the *bhakta* right; and in a post-Christian culture which apparently hates all expressions of sentiment and human tenderness, the plague of intellectual pride can develop relatively unchecked. The "spirit of modernity" (or rather post-modernity) is not only the denial of religious and metaphysical truth; it is also the vice of *cold-heartedness.*

No matter how well-defended we may be against that spirit on the doctrinal level, if the coldness of the latter days seeps into our bones without our knowing it, then we will find ourselves among the losers. Postmodern society tends to take a dim view of love, identifying it with sloppy sentimentalism—and if those called to walk the path of *jñana* follow society in this profane judgment, seeing love as merely sentimental and knowledge alone as possessing the virtue of detachment, spiritual impassivity, *apatheia*—thus, in effect, falsely identifying *apatheia* with emotional coldness—then they have made themselves vulnerable to co-optation by the Counter-Initiation. The Greek Fathers recognized and worked against this error when they taught that, without *apatheia*, true love cannot exist.

The "founder" of the Traditionalists, René Guénon, has been called "an eye without a body." This is certainly a good description of his writing style, but it will take a more thorough investigation of his writings to determine if a bias against love is really part of his doctrine. In his book *Symbols of Sacred Science* [Sophia Perennis, 2002], the chapter entitled "The Radiating Heart and the Flaming Heart," Guénon deals directly with the relationship between love and knowledge. He shows how the Heart as a universal symbol is related to the Sun, and speaks of iconographic representations of the Heart/Sun in which straight rays, standing for light, are combined with wavy rays or flames, symbolizing heat, as in the tarot card "The Sun" in the Ryder-Waite deck. Light is intelligence, heat is life, which is closely related to emotion. Guénon (without the use of footnotes) traces the supposed degeneration of the icon the Heart from earlier radiant forms with both straight and wavy rays or straight rays alone, to later forms where only wavy rays or flames appear. He says:

> [T]he radiation, even when the two aspects are there united, seems generally to suggest a preponderance of the luminous aspect. This interpretation is confirmed by the fact that the representations of the radiating heart, with or without the distinction of the two kinds of rays, are the most ancient, dating for the most part from periods when the intelligence was still traditionally related to the heart, whereas representations of

> the flaming heart became wide-spread especially with modern ideas and reducing the heart to correspondence with sentiment alone... the origin of this deviation is no doubt due to rationalism insofar as the latter claims to identify intelligence purely and simply with reason, for the heart is not related to this but to the transcendent intellect which is precisely what is ignored and even denied by rationalism. It is true, on the other hand, that once the heart is considered the center of the being, all modalities of the being can in a sense be related to it, at least indirectly, including sentiment or what psychologists call "affectivity"; but there is nonetheless every reason to observe the hierarchical relationships in all this and to uphold the true 'centrality' of the intellect, while all other modalities have only a more or less 'peripheral' character. However, intellectual intuition, which resides in the heart, being misunderstood, and reason, which resides in the brain, having usurped its 'illuminating' role, nothing remained for the heart but the possibility of being considered as the seat of affectivity.

Guénon informs us that Descartes viewed the heart as the seat of a "fire without light"—something undoubtedly true in Descartes' case—and sees in this a symbol of sentiment divorced from intellect, which "is why the ancients represented love as blind."

So it would seem that Guénon is saying here that knowledge is essentially higher and more central than love. But a few lines later he apparently takes a different tack, reminding us (and possibly himself) that

> [I]n man one can also find light without heat, this being the light of reason, which is only a reflected illumination, cold like the lunar light which is its symbol. In the order of principles, on the contrary, these two aspects, like all complementaries, again join together and are indissolubly united, for they are parts of one same essential nature; and so also it is for pure intelligence which properly belongs to the principial order, thus confirming yet again, as we have previously indicated, that the symbolic radiation under its double form can be integrally related to it. The fire at the center of the being is at one and the

> same time both light and heat; but if these two terms are to be translated respectively as intelligence and love, although fundamentally they are but two inseparable aspects of one and the same thing, it will be necessary . . . to add that the love in question then differs as greatly from the sentiment that is given the same name as does pure intelligence from reason.

In my humble opinion, we have here a strictly accurate treatment of the relationship between love and knowledge from the perspective of pure metaphysics, plus some profoundly illuminating insights into the historical degeneration of this doctrine, coupled with just the shadow of a whisper of a bias not fully justified by the doctrine as presented. If I read Guénon correctly, he's saying that the fact that the straight-rayed heart and the heart with both straight and wavy rays appear together in the same era means that intelligence (straight rays) can act as a valid synthesis of light and heat, intelligence and love, in a way that love (wavy or flaming rays) cannot, and thus that intelligence is the central faculty and love the peripheral one, which can only participate in the Center when subsumed *under* intelligence—though the fact that rationality, when separated from the higher spiritual faculties, moves to the brain, while emotion when so separated stays in the heart, might have led to the opposite conclusion. And that Guénon sees (and rightly so) the later icon of the flaming heart as representing a lower order of reality, where the heart is considered the site of sentiment alone, not the full synthesis of Intelligence/Love, but does not allow that the straight-rayed heart might sometimes represent rationality alone, is evidence of the same bias. But although I can accept Guénon's argument when it comes to his interpretation of the replacement of the straight-rayed heart by the flaming heart, I can't agree with him that this proves the hierarchical superiority of intellect over love. As I read it, the reason why a later and lower order of understanding generates the image of the flaming rather than the radiating heart is not because love when polarized with intellect is lower than intellect, but because, as Guénon says, the seat of intellect, reduced to mere rationality, is now the brain rather than the heart. The brain is cold light; the heart eclipsed (love reduced to sentiment) is dark heat. Thus the flaming heart is not love fallen from the station of Intellect, but one-half of the polarity of love (now sentiment) and intellect (now rationality) fallen, just like its counterpart, from the station of Love/Intellect, where the two exist in a higher synthesis.

I may seem to be splitting hairs here, but a hair badly split on the threshold of the Absolute casts a long shadow. On one level it is a question of tone, of feeling-values. Guénon is simply a little quicker to say that emotion is peripheral to intelligence, or that love is blind, than the reverse. Nonetheless the tone of our expressions is as important as their intellectual content, though not as easy to "present in court."

But is love really blind, according to the ancients? Certainly the Greek tragedies are enough to prove that much was known in antiquity about the damage blind passion can do. And yet to simply say "the ancients represented love as blind" is incorrect. It is true that Eros was sometimes shown as blindfolded, but this was in no way a universal symbol. Furthermore, the blindfold, as with the more familiar emblem of Justice, can also symbolize "not judging by appearances," but "seeing into the heart." Plato's *Symposium,* to take only one example, is based on the doctrine that Eros, defined as an attraction to Beauty, can be a road to the highest illumination. And in terms not of the ancient world but of the medieval one, Dante's love for Beatrice in the *Divine Comedy* is his way to the fullest intellectual realization, which is represented by Beatrice herself as a reflection of Holy Wisdom. Elsewhere in "The Radiating Heart and the Flaming Heart" Guénon makes it clear that love is not simply "exoteric" but finds its place in the esoteric dimension as well, and nothing that pertains to esoterism can be intrinsically blind.

And again, is emotion really peripheral vis-a-vis the intellect? In terms of the greater mysteries, where "intellect" denotes Spirit as a synthesis of Intellect/Love, clearly it is. But insofar as the lesser mysteries, the psychic or alchemical mysteries are concerned, without the successful completion of which the greater mysteries cannot be approached, emotion is a necessary element. Nor is emotion simply cut out of the greater mysteries, but rather fully integrated. Just as the alchemical use of rationality is to fix, pacify and clarify the turbulence of the affective soul, so that it develops the ability to mirror the Spirit, so the purpose of feeling is to dissolve the opacities and imbalanced coagulations of rationality, allowing it be crystallized by the Spirit on a higher level till it becomes transparent to the light of the Intellect. Excess of emotion makes the soul turbulent and heavy; excess of rationality makes it scattered and filled with fixed ideas. Only a balance and synthesis between the two powers can prepare the soul for a full encounter with Spirit as the seamless union of Intellect and Love.

As opposed to this synthetic notion of love and knowledge, Guénon speaks of them as in some sense mutually exclusive:

> It should also be noted . . . that when fire is polarized into these two complementary aspects of light and heat, they are so to speak the inverse of one another in their manifestation; and even from the simple point-of-view of physics, it is known that the less light a flame gives the hotter it is.

But is this really so? When a wood fire burns down to coals it can become darker and hotter, since flame is no longer carrying as much heat up the chimney by convection, and wood coals, and especially mineral coal (anthracite in particular), can radiate more heat into the room in the invisible infra-red spectrum; but to enunciate "the less light the more heat" as a general law of nature is incorrect. The blacksmith knows that as his iron becomes hotter it emits more light, changing from black to red to yellow to white. One of the hottest chemical fires we know, that of rapidly oxidizing magnesium, is also one of the brightest, burning with an incandescent, pure white flame. And in the case of stars, light and heat vary directly, not inversely: the more light, the more heat; the more heat, the more light. Guénon, however, sometimes seems to believe that while in the realm of the Principles love and knowledge may be one, in cosmic manifestation, including the human psyche, they are not merely polarized but actually in opposition. How far is this position, really, from that of D.H. Lawrence—the perfect example of an over-cerebral modern western man seeking the lost side of his humanity in the darkness of instinctive passion—when he said, in *Studies in Classic American Literature*, "KNOWING and BEING are opposite, antagonistic states. The more you know, exactly, the less you *are.*

The more you *are*, in being, the less you know."? And given that Guénon, in "The Radiating Heart and the Flaming Heart", identifies warmth with both love and life, isn't he in effect saying here that intelligence is both *loveless* and *lifeless*? This may indeed the common judgment by profane society upon the spiritual intellectual, but that it should cast its shadow upon the doctrines of the intellectual himself demonstrates a certain lack of detachment on his part.

Such opposition between love and knowledge is not the case, however, in manifestation *per se*, though it is present as a latent potential, but only comes into play, to use the Christian term, after the "fall." Although the difference in temperament between a person centered in affection and someone centered in thought is undeniably real, a universal opposition between love and knowledge in the realm of manifestation is not really "natural," something which is obvious enough if we remember that those who love their object of study really learn it, and those who really know anything worth knowing usually come to love it. And this is all the more true on the level of the Divine, since to know God, Who is the Sovereign Good, is necessarily to love Him, while to love Him, since love delights to dwell upon its object, is necessarily to know Him. As Maimonides said: "Love is the highest form of knowledge." Only in the fallen soul dominated by pride and concupiscence, or in a collective mentality ruled by these vices, could such an unnatural opposition exist, since to egotistically indulge in love as a self-involved emotion darkens the intellect, while to pridefully identify with one's indwelling intelligence violates love. Furthermore, the opposition between love and knowledge, since it is not in line with the essential nature of things, is inherently unstable. If we become comfortable with stupidity we will lose the ability to love, since we can't love what we don't want to know, while if we are comfortable with lovelessness we will become stupid, since we can't know what we can no longer relate to.

According to Guénon, "the way of love is more particularly appropriate for Kshatriyas, while the way of intelligence or of knowledge is naturally especially suitable for Brahmins." In terms of the general characters of these castes, this is true. But from another perspective, there is a type of love and a type of knowledge essential to each. There is such a thing as a "jñanic *bhakti*" which sees within love the principles, forms and secrets proper to love, and a "bhaktic *jñana*" by which love warms and germinates the seed of knowledge. The love of the Kshatriya is "emotive" in that it motivates him to combative, protective and self-sacrificial action, whereas the love of the Brahmin is contemplative rather than passionate; it is like the oil that feeds the steady flame of a lamp. Once again, the Christian mysteries are clearly under the sign of Love, and yet no one would assert that Christianity is essentially a Kshatriya rather than a Brahmanical revelation; Christian society has produced both saintly warriors and saintly contemplatives. The premier Christian *jñani*, Meister Eckhart, even spoke of love in these terms, beginning with a quotation from St. Augustine: "'What a man loves a man is.' If he loves a stone he is that stone, if he loves a man he is that man, if he loves God—nay, I durst not say more; were I to say, he is God, he might stone me. I do but teach you the scriptures." [Whitall Perry, *Treasury of Traditional Wisdom*, p. 617]

Emotion, which Guénon identifies with elemental vitality, is like a fuel which can be burned to empower either the will or the intellect. (I am referring here not to the Divine Intellect in itself, but to that part of the individual psyche capable of receiving a ray of this Intellect.) Will at odds with emotion cannot work reliably in accordance with the fertile potentials of the situation; it is without real strength, and so tends to express itself in terms of force, directed either outwards, against the situation, or inwards, against the self. Force is attachment to action without regard for the potentials inherent in the shape of the moment; it lacks staying-power and inevitably creates imbalances. Likewise emotion at odds with the will cannot vigorously act to realize potentials; all it can do is impotently wish; wishful thinking is attachment to unrealized potential based on an incapacity for action. Speaking strictly in terms of action rather than intellection, will can be defined as the actualization of affect, affect as the potency of the will. And insofar as the Spiritual Path requires human action—the other requirement being the Grace of God—we can say that will devoid of emotion cannot make good its intent to "pray without ceasing," and that emotion without will can produce nothing but sentimentality and spiritual fantasy.

On the other hand, there are times when the will *must* act in opposition to the emotions. If our feelings are essentially concupiscent, if they are dissipated and scattered, prone to attach themselves to wrong objects, then they must be vigorously combated—not *repressed*, which entails a darkening of the intellect, but rather *disciplined*, which requires placing them, via the agency of the will, under the rule of the intellect. In Muslim terms, this is the "greater *jihad*" which is "the war against the soul," specifically against what the Sufis call the *nafs al-ammara* or "the soul which incites to evil." This war is part of the "lesser mysteries," the psychic or alchemical mysteries, which purify and prepare the soul for its encounter with the Spirit of God. But even though the goal of these mysteries is to forge a soul where Intellect rules the will and will rules the affections, the war against the *nafs* cannot be seen simply as the struggle of rationality against affect. The Intellect which must rule the will is not the rational faculty but the Divine Spirit of Intellect/Love, operating within the soul; rationality is precisely the enlightening effect of the Intellect upon the will (or, from another point of view, the *apparently* limiting effect of the will upon the Intellect)—although, like any psychic faculty, it can sometimes develop an "ego" of its own and so upset the balance of the psyche. Touched by the Intellect, the will encounters a fixed, objective standpoint according to which it can now decide *what* to will, in terms either of thought (logic) or of action (strategy). In other words, it becomes *rational*; it no longer judges solely on the basis of emotion. Furthermore, since the will in rational mode has now become objective enough to foresee the consequences of impulsive action, it also acts to moderate the emotions.

But that's not the whole story. It is a one-sided view, precisely because the Spirit of Intellect/Love does not rule the affections only through the rational will, *but also touches the affections directly.* As the soul is purified, the feeling-nature begins to mirror that Spirit in the form of Beauty, according to Plato's doctrine that "Beauty is the splendor of the True." As the will in rational mode develops the power to harmonize the affections, the affections gain the complementary power to deepen, empower and move the will, to convert it from rational to *devotional* mode, to orient it toward the Spirit, to remind it of its Source.

So we can now conclude that, as Guénon admits, since love and knowledge are absolutely one in the Absolute, either can stand as a valid name for it; it is no more or less accurate to say "God is Truth" than to say "God is Love." Consequently the hierarchical relationship between love and knowledge can be drawn in two different ways. If it is valid to place Brahminical knowledge above Kshatriya love, it is equally valid from a different perspective to place love above knowledge, as Dionysius the Areopagite did when he situated the eye-studded Cherubim, symbols of Divine Knowledge, in the second-highest choir of angels, and the Seraphim, symbols of Divine Love (Love united with Knowledge), in the highest, or Dante, when at the apex of Paradise he came to the end of what could be known, and encountered "the love that moves the Sun and the other stars." Of course, as Guénon points out, "the love in question differs from the sentiment that is named love as much as pure intelligence differs from reason"; but true love on the plane of feeling is nonetheless an effect produced by this higher love. Divine Love manifests on the psychic plane as purity of affection, just as Divine Intellect manifests as clear rational thought. Certainly affection, if taken as an end in itself, veils Divine Love, just as rationality without an intuition of higher realities veils the Intellect. But affective love, when purified of egotism, is just as surely a sign of Divine Love in the soul as disinterested rational intelligence is a sign of Intelligence itself. To deny this is to fall into a "Manichean" dualism, divorcing Source from its manifestation and denying the immanence of God.

It was the mission of René Guénon to reintroduce, almost singlehandedly, integral metaphysics to the western world; his only real "contemporary" was Ananda Coomaraswamy. To accomplish this he had to set himself against, not only every dominant trend of modern thought and culture, but also against the European occultism of the first half of the 20th century. He was required, in other words, to deny himself even the solace of identification with a subculture of resistance to the modern world, since he eventually saw this subculture as already infiltrated by modernist assumptions, and thus, though seemingly open to many of his ideas, destructive to the very traditional doctrines he was attempting to restore. The moral and psychological stamina this stance must have required of him are daunting to contemplate. Guénon's mission occurred when the reign of bourgeois sentimentalism, begun in the 19th century, was still in force. The vulgar and sentimental veneration of St. Theresa of Lisieux, the "Little Flower" (who, as Thomas Merton reminds us, for all the bad taste of her popular cult was a real saint, and who Schuon himself accepted as a *jñani*), should give us some idea of the raw nerve he needed simply to state what he knew to be true, in terms both of metaphysical principles and the spiritual state of the world, without fervor, protected only by the thorn of an aloof and measured irony. In a time when sentimentalities and false enthusiasms threatened his enterprise from all sides, we can hardly blame him for failing to elaborate a complete doctrine of the affections. His pressing duty lay elsewhere.

Sentimentality, however, is no longer our problem. If there is any single sign of the transition from the twilight of the modern age to the dawn of post-modernism, it is the rage of popular culture to pull down all the idols of sentiment, idols which were still firmly entrenched in, say, 1965. If the "established" emotions of Victorianism were triumphalism and sentimentality, our post-modern status quo enforces vulgarity, sinister fascination, emotional numbness, terror, and despair. According to St. Paul in II Tim. 3:1–3, in the "last days" men shall be "without natural affection"; and in Matt. 24:12, Jesus numbers among the signs of the end that "because iniquity shall abound, the love of many shall wax cold." Consequently, in view of the general coldness of the times, Guénon's brand of *sang froid* is no longer the specific remedy for our ailment. Above all we need *warmth*, a warmth that is not at odds with intelligence, but rather deepens it.

Frithjof Schuon, *in Spiritual Perspectives and Human Facts* [Faber & Faber, 1954], asserts the following:

> For the spiritual man of emotional temperament to love is to be and to know is to think and the heart represents totality, the very basis of being, and the brain the fragment, the surface. For the spiritual man of intellectual temperament knowledge on the contrary is to be and love is to want or to feel and the heart represents universality or the Self and the brain individuality or the "I". Knowledge starts from the Universal, and love

from the individual; it is the absolute Knower who knows, whereas it is the human subject, the "creature," who is called upon to love [p.145].

This is in many ways a valid, and in fact a profound, perspective. But even for the spiritual man of intellectual temperament, is it really accurate to make the brain the seat of love, as Schuon seems to be doing here? I submit that this is only justified if we understand "brain" to define the parameters of the individual psyche, which includes among its faculties affective love as well as rational thought. But just as "brain" must, even for the spiritual intellectual, include rationality, so "heart" must include a Divine Love which transcends affective love, and which in essence is inseparable from Knowledge.

Four pages later, Schuon seems to contradict himself. After asserting that from the perspective of Knowledge God is the Knower and the human subject the lover, as we have seen, he now says: "The love of the affective man is that he loves God. The love of the intellectual man is that God loves him; that is to say, he realizes intellectually—but not simply in a theoretical way—that God is Love." [ibid., p.149] So here, even for the intellectual man, God loves, and is Love Itself. As Schuon says elsewhere in the same book, "[God] is Love, not because he loves, but he loves because he is Love." [p.107] So even when the acting, personal God, the "Lover," is subordinated the Divine Essence, Love remains a name for that Absolute Essence even from a perspective of Knowledge—in terms of the present passage, that of the Absolute Subject of the Vedanta. (As Ramana Maharshi said, "*Jñana* is love for God without form. Imperfect *jñana* and imperfect *bhakti* are different, perfect *jñana* and perfect *bhakti* are the same.") This apparent contradiction is resolved if we realize that Schuon is sometimes speaking of personal, affective love and sometimes of the Divine Love which is its archetype, without always making this distinction clear. His seeming lack of consistency may have been necessary to do justice to the particularity of the various perspectives he presents, in view of the fact that (as he says) "one reaches the truth to the extent that one accepts positions which are seemingly opposed, but which in reality are situated on the same circumference, invisible at first sight" [*Form and Substance in Religions*, p.52]. Yet if, as Emerson said, "consistency is the hobgoblin of little minds", it is equally true to say that "contradiction is the disease of minds that have not been able to view their material objectively enough to think things through." Not every seeming metaphysical paradox or shift in perspective is actually a contradiction, but some certainly are. In *The Roots of the Human Condition*, however, Schuon expresses a more complete doctrine: "The way of love—methodical *bhakti*—presupposes that through it we can go toward God; whereas love as such—intrinsic *bhakti*—accompanies the way of knowledge, *jñana*, and is based essentially on our sensitivity to the divine Beauty". And in *Survey of Metaphysics and Esoterism*: "Where there is Truth, there is also Love. Each Deva possesses its Shakti; in the human microcosm, the feeling soul is joined to the discerning intellect, as in the Divine Order Mercy is joined to Omniscience; and as, in the final analysis, Infinitude is consubstantial with the Absolute."

When someone says, "She may be smart, but she's not wise," or "He's affectionate enough, but he lacks wisdom," we can all understand what is being described. The synthesis of Love and Knowledge is, in fact, Wisdom, without which love must remain sentimental, knowledge theoretical, and both love and knowledge cut off from the actual situations of our lives, making us incapable of applying them, as *insight,* to interpersonal relations. As the figure of Holy Wisdom says, in the 8th chapter of Proverbs:

> I love them that love me, and those that seek me early shall find me.... Hearken unto me, O ye children: for blessed are they that keep my ways, hear instruction and be wise ... whoso findeth me findeth life ... but he that sinneth against me wrongeth his own soul: all that hate me love death.

Just as true Knowledge is essentially intellective, not simply rational, so true Love is *existential,* not merely sentimental; as someone wise in the ways of love once wrote, "There is no such thing as love—only *proofs* of love." The English word "wisdom", as well as many words from other languages that are usually translated by it, basically means "skill; know-how". Love alone has the ability to provide intellective realization with the existential substance it demands; as the Master Craftsman will certainly tell you, only Love possesses the power to transform Truth into Wisdom, Knowledge into Realization.

9

Drug-Induced Mysticism Revisited: Interview with Charles Upton

Samuel Bendeck Sotillos

CHARLES UPTON (b. 1948)[1] poet, author, activist, and veteran of the counter-culture has voyaged and experienced firsthand the many facets of the New Age *cul-de-sac* and its pitfalls which are all too often ignored. Psychedelics[2] or hallucinogens, now termed entheogens,[3] have played a pivotal role in the modern and post-

1. For more biographical information on Mr. Charles Upton see: *www.serious-seekers.com.*

2. British psychiatrist Humphry Fortescue Osmond (1917–2004) coined the term "psychedelic" or "mind-manifesting" via his correspondence with Aldous Huxley. In responding to a letter that Dr. Osmond received from Huxley written on 30 March, 1956 he wrote in poetic reflection: "To fathom Hell or soar angelic, / Just take a pinch of psychedelic", thus giving birth to the term "psychedelic", yet it was not known to the public at large or the scientific community until 1957 [Michael Horowitz and Cynthia Palmer (eds.), *Moksha: Aldous Huxley's Classic Writings on Psychedelics and the Visionary Experience* (Rochester, VT: Park Street Press, 1999), p.107]; see also Humphry Osmond, "A Review of the Clinical Effects of Psychotomimetic Agents", *Annals of the New York Academy of Sciences*, Vol. 66, No. 3 (1957), pp. 418–434. It is also relevant to point out that it was Dr. Osmond who in May of 1953 first introduced Huxley to a synthesized form of mescaline, the psychoactive compound in peyote (among other psychedelic cacti) which in turn produced his work *The Doors of Perception* in 1954, which according to some launched the psychedelic revolution.

3. "'Entheogen' means simply 'God generated within you!'" [Robert Forte, "A Conversation with R. Gordon Wasson" in *Entheogens and the Future of Religion*, ed. Robert Forte (San Francisco, CA: Council on Spiritual Practices, 1997), p.69]; see

modern seeker's quest to circumvent the trappings of the empirical ego and attain Self-Realization since the 1960s. After a hiatus of nearly thirty years, psychedelic research has now made a revival, which should provoke much inquiry as to what underlies this phenomenon. It is interesting to note that the New Age Movement, the Human Potential Movement, Humanistic Psychology and Transpersonal Psychology all emerged in a common setting; they do not only share many similarities but have also assisted in each other's development. For example, the English writer Aldous Huxley (1894–1963) could be said to be a single figure connecting of all of the above movements via his popularizing the perennial philosophy and his writings on psychedelics, both of which are acknowledged by the above movements and/or disciplines. Huxley not only helped shape each of the above but provided an integrative theory in which they could take root. That said, while he popularized the perennial philosophy he is not considered to be a traditionalist or perennialist.

Where Mr. Upton parts ways with his New Age and counter-culture comrades is that since his introduction to the works of the traditionalist or perennialist school—most significantly René Guénon (1886-1951), Frithjof Schuon (1907–1998) and Ananda Kentish Coomaraswamy (1887–1947)—he has affiliated himself with this orientation. Mr. Upton has written numerous books and articles on traditional metaphysics and the perennial philosophy, most noteworthy is: *The System of Antichrist: Truth and Falsehood in Postmodernism and the New Age* (2001). Although he has abandoned the practices of his early search in the New Age and counter-culture movements, he acquired an abundant knowledge and understanding of these pseudo-spiritualities and is in a commendable position to inform and also caution contemporary seekers. Mr. Upton is a committed Muslim and a practitioner of Sufism and simultaneously acknowledges the "transcendent unity of religions". The following interview offers a unique look at psychedelics in the light of

---

also Carl A.P. Ruck, Jeremy Bigwood, Danny Staples, Jonathan Ott, and R. Gordon Wasson, "Entheogens" in *The Road to Eleusis: Unveiling the Secret of the Mysteries*, Twentieth Anniversary Edition, eds. R. Gordon Wasson, Albert Hofmann and Carl A.P. Ruck (Los Angeles, CA: Hermes Press, 1998), pp. 137–139.

the perennial philosophy by way of perennialist theory and also personal accounts of the author. This interview was conducted by electronic correspondence during March, April and May of 2011.

Samuel Bendeck Sotillos: Perhaps we could begin with the central perennialist critique with regards to what has been termed "consciousness expansion", "altered states of consciousness" or "non-ordinary states of consciousness" which distinguishes the psychic from the spiritual (see *Endnote I*); it is this critique that many readers outside the perennialist or traditionalist circles will not be familiar with yet it is has created the greatest amount of confusion for contemporary seekers.[4] Would you mind elaborating on this fundamental distinction which has profound implications with regard to recognizing authentic spirituality versus pseudo-spirituality or New Age spirituality?

Charles Upton: The psychic or intermediary plane is the world of subjectivity; the Spiritual plane is objectivity itself. As the psychic world is higher than the material world and encompasses it, so the Spirit is higher than both psyche and matter, and encompasses them. The psychic world is made up of beliefs, perceptions, impressions, experiences; the Spiritual world is composed of certainties—of things that are true even if we are not certain of them. When Beat Generation poet Lew Welch said, "I seek union with what goes on whether I look at it or not", he was positing the level of Spirit. The psychic plane is *relatively* objective in that it is not enclosed within the individual psyche; as Jung demonstrated, it also has a collective aspect. This collectivity is not limited to a mass human subjectivity

4. Traditionalist or perennialist author Whitall N. Perry (1920–2005) illustrates why psychic phenomenon are so seductive and difficult to discern for most seekers: "The confusion is between the psychic and spiritual planes of reality, where the unfamiliar, the strange, and the bizarre are mistaken for the transcendent, simply by the fact that they lie outside the ordinary modes of consciousness." [Whitall N. Perry, "Drug-Induced Mysticism: The Mescalin Hypothesis" in *Challenges to a Secular Society* (Oakton, VA: The Foundation for Traditional Studies, 1996), p. 10]. Readers will notice that the title of this interview references Perry's pioneering article that was first published nearly sixty years ago and yet its thesis still holds strong and debunks many predominant errors. It is for this reason that we have chosen to mention it and we are grateful to the author for its appearance.

or "collective unconscious", however; it is host as well to many classes of non-human beings, including those the Greeks called the *daimones*, the Northern Europeans, the Fairies, and the Arabs, the Jinn. It carries nothing less than the impressions of the experiences of all sentient beings.

The psychic plane is the (relatively) objective environment of the human psyche, just as the earth is the (relatively) objective environment of the human body. Our apparently individual subjectivity is co-extensive with innumerable other subjectivities, both human and non-human; as Huston Smith said, "the brain breathes thoughts like the lungs breathe air." But it remains essentially subjective for all that; it is the realm of experiences, not realities. An experience is an *impression* of an objective reality, either material or Spiritual, as received by a limited subject, an impression that is edited by the inherent or acquired limitations of the subject experiencing it. It is *phenomenon*, not *noumenon*. Whatever relatively objective data can be accessed through psychic means (clairvoyance, precognition, etc.) always pertains to contingent entities immersed in one form or another of space and time, linear or multidimensional; eternal realities cannot be intuited by psychic means.

The Spiritual plane, on the other hand, is purely objective. It is not composed of our impressions, but of things we have impressions *of*—of *noumena* that transcend sense experience and do not depend for their existence upon our awareness of them, just as—on the level of sense experience—the mountain outside our window is really there, whether or not we happen to be looking at it. The Spiritual plane is the realm of the first intelligible manifestations or "names" of God—of metaphysical principles that are not simply abstract ideas, but living realities that have the power, under the proper conditions, to dominate, guide, purify and conform our psyches to them—to "save our souls".

So Spiritual realities transcend subjective experience. But if we never *experienced* them, they would not be effective to enlighten us and save us. Spiritual experiences, then—what the Sufis call the *ahwal* or spiritual states (which are necessary elements of the Spiritual Path) are psychic experiences grounded not in the psychic subjectivity of the one experiencing them but in objective realities that transcend the realm of sense—in the Names of God. To be subject to a Spiritual state is to have a direct intellective intuition of an objective Spiritual reality that transcends the state in question, one that the subjective state by which it is intuited will always both veil and reveal; and if Spiritual realities partially transcend our subjective experience of them, God transcends our experience of Him absolutely. To experience God is to be called to immediately transcend that necessarily limited experience of Him, and come into naked existential contact with Him as He is in Himself, beyond all experience; as the Sufis put it, "the human being does not know God in His Absolute Essence; it is God who knows Himself within the human form." The Sufi practice of contemplating God in this manner is known as *fikr*, which might be defined as "the ongoing sacrifice of every conception of the Absolute, generated by the Absolute, in the face of the Absolute."

So we can say that Spiritual realities are objective, and that God, the Source of all such realities, is the Absolute Object. But "object" here does not mean "whatever is perceived by a limited subject as other than itself"; taken in this sense, "object" is relative to that limited subject and so partakes of its subjectivity. God as Absolute Object is equally the indwelling Divine Subject, the Absolute Witness, what the Hindus name the *Atman*, what Frithjof Schuon calls "the absolute Subject of our contingent subjectivities." The Absolute Witness stands "behind" all psychic experience, impassively witnessing them, not identifying with them; here is the precise difference between the psyche and the Spirit.

We cannot reach God through the psyche, through experience; the essence of the Spiritual Path is to place ourselves in the presence of God, and let *Him* reach *us*. He may do this through experiences, through events, or through a secret action within the soul that we aren't even aware of. The function of spiritual experiences or states is not to "enrich the soul" with fascinating impressions of the Divine, but to *burn out* specific aspects of the ego, specific attachments and identifications; this is why the realized Sufi, the one who has transcended himself, died to himself, become objective to himself—or rather to the Absolute Witness within him—is beyond spiritual states entirely.

SBS: Following up with this point, what can you say about the assumption that the pursuit of expanding consciousness or achieving an altered state of consciousness is an end unto itself, as if it was a desirable human norm which contradicts perennial principles—"The goal is not altered states but altered traits."[5] This perilous approach often involves an *ad hoc* mixture of spiritual techniques rather than a persistent adherence to one orthodox spiritual form.[6] Could you please speak to this puzzling development?

CU: This is all a kind of council of desperation, as well as an indication that the breakdown of the traditional revealed religions, leading to a One-World Religion made up out of the resulting fragments—a development that will culminate in the regime of Antichrist—is proceeding right on schedule.[7]

5. Huston Smith, "Encountering God" in *The Way Things Are: Conversations with Huston Smith on the Spiritual Life*, ed. Phil Cousineau (Los Angeles, CA: University of California Press, 2003), p. 97; "Counterfeit spirituality, instead, will place emphasis on impressionistic experience, on the subjective pole of mystical endeavor, practically to the near-total or even total exclusion of the objective pole, and derives its motive force—and abusively personal justification—in heightened emotionalism or vagrant intuitionalism, or even in altered states of consciousness." [Mark Perry, "The Forbidden Door" in *Every Branch in Me: Essays on the Meaning of Man*, ed. Barry McDonald (Bloomington, IN: World Wisdom, 2002), p. 239]; see also René Guénon, "The Great Parody: or Spirituality Inverted" in *The Reign of Quantity and the Signs of the Times*, trans. Lord Northbourne (Ghent, NY: Sophia Perennis, 2001), pp. 267–274.

6. We recall the unequivocal words of Frithjof Schuon: "there is no possible spiritual way outside the great orthodox traditional ways. A meditation or concentration practiced at random and outside of tradition will be inoperative, and even dangerous in more than one respect; the illusion of progress in the absence of real criteria is certainly not the least of these dangers." [Quoted in Whitall N. Perry, "Drug-Induced Mysticism: The Mescalin Hypothesis" in *Challenges to a Secular Society* (Oakton, VA: The Foundation for Traditional Studies, 1996), pp. 15–16]; "To be precise: there is no spiritual path outside the following traditions or religions: Judaism, Christianity, Islam, Buddhism, Hinduism and Taoism; but Hinduism is closed for those who have not been born into a Hindu caste, and Taoism is inaccessible" [Titus Burckhardt, "A Letter on Spiritual Method" in *Mirror of the Intellect: Essays on Traditional Science and Sacred Art*, trans. and ed. William Stoddart (Albany, NY: SUNY Press, 1987), p. 251].

7. See Lee Penn, *False Dawn: The United Religions Initiative, Globalism, and the Quest for a One-World Religion* (Hillsdale, NY: Sophia Perennis, 2004).

As religion degenerates, the felt sense of the reality of God is progressively replaced by an obsession with morality for its own sake, and with religious fervor considered as an end in itself, both taken out of their own proper context. No longer is moral purity felt to be something we naturally owe to God in view of His love for us and of the fact that He created us, something that prevents us from falling into the ingratitude of worshipping the passions as idols in His place; now morality has become an idol in itself. By the same token, fervor has lost sight of the God Who supposedly inspires it; it has become a substitute for His felt presence rather than a response to it. In a lot of contemporary Protestant hymns, for example—or rather contemporary "Christian pop" songs—the singer sings primarily about his or her own feelings, not about God. Likewise various "consciousness studies" programs now available in academia tend to concentrate on subjective states of consciousness, as well as the belief-systems that support them and the techniques by which they can sometimes be produced, rather than understanding spiritual states as reflections of an objective metaphysical order, and thus as instances of *knowledge* rather than simply experience. According to Sufi doctrine, spiritual states are not acquisitions but gifts of God. He sends them in order to "burn out" specific passions, attachments and ego-knots; after the attachment in question is dissolved, that particular state does not return. For example, a habit of neurotic fear, burnt out by a state (*hal*) of ecstatic love, is transformed into a *station* (*maqam*) of courage and equanimity; a temporary "state" has resulted in an established "trait". And the fully-realized Sufi is said to be beyond both states and stations, since he no longer maintains any separative ego which could be the subject of them; he has attained objective metaphysical realization.

When traditional faith is strong, it is a source of security and certainty for the faithful; they feel that they are in the presence of sacred mysteries, mysteries that they can rely upon but need not pry into. But when traditional religions weakens, then certain people who would have otherwise been spiritually satisfied simply to live within a sacred tradition and ambience, and who would have saved their souls thereby, conceive the desire for a direct mystical relationship with God so as to make up for what has been lost—a relationship that may not in fact be proper to them. They imagine that such a relationship could only result from some extravagant spiritual tour-de-force—and psychedelic drugs immediately appear as a plausible way of taking that tour. But the psychedelics, as well as various spiritual techniques such as secularized non-traditional yoga, are often approached on the basis of the very false and limiting context that people are seeking them in order to free themselves from: of the spiritual life as an exercise in self-will (as in the case of compulsive morality), and of God conceived as an experience rather than a Reality (as in the case of self-referential fervor; the New Age movement for example, which deifies experience, can be described as a kind of "non-Christian Pentecostalism"). In the absence of a felt sense of the Grace of God based upon *faith*, which St. Paul calls "the presence of things hoped for, the evidence of things not seen", nothing is possible in the spiritual life outside of the Promethean attempt to take heaven by storm, and spiritual narcissism—two pathologies which are intimately related to each other and never appear apart. The will cut off from the spiritual Intellect (which is always virtually in force wherever Faith and Grace are present) produces Prometheanism; the alienation of the affections from the Intellect produces narcissism.

It is highly interesting that psychedelic drugs burst upon the scene at precisely the same moment that the Second Vatican Council was abolishing traditional Roman Catholicism and deconstructing the sacramental order. It's as if the grace of the Roman Catholic sacraments, while they were still intact, overflowed their specifically Catholic context and maintained a certain level of elevation in the "collective unconscious" of the western world, an elevation which was rapidly lost when that grace was cut off. Faced with a sudden unconscious or half-conscious sense of spiritual loss, and the stifling sensation that always results when the psyche is cut off from the plane of the Spirit, the western collectivity became susceptible to the temptation of psychedelics, which at the very least can provide (though not without extremely negative consequences) a horizontal *psychic* expansiveness which appears to compensate for, and sometimes actually counterfeits, the loss of a vertical spiritual elevation, while at the same time concealing the fact that such a loss ever occurred. Psychedelics, in other words, were a kind of Luciferian "booby prize" offered as compensation for the fall of western Christendom.

SBS: A compelling case that the psychedelic advocates and researchers make is that because psychoactive properties are naturally occurring in a number of plants (and even endogenous to the human body)[8] which have been used in sacred rituals throughout the world since time immemorial:[9] *Soma* hypothesized to be the Fly Agaric mushroom (*Amanita muscaria*), *Teonanácatl (Psilocybe mexicana)*—"God's flesh" or "flesh of the gods" in Náhuatl, the language of the Aztecs—Peyote cactus (*Lophophora williamsii*),[10] San Pedro cactus (*Trichocereus pachanoi*),[11] *Ololiuqui* (*Turbina corymbosa*) and *Tlililtzin* (*Ipomoea violacea*)—seeds of a Morning Glory—Ibogaine or Iboga (*Tabernanthe iboga*), *Ayauasca* or *Yajé* (*Banisteriopsis caapi*), *Kykeon* made with Ergot (*Claviceps paspali* and *Clavi-*

8. "In 1965 a research team from Germany published a paper in the flagship British science journal *Nature* announcing that they had isolated DMT from human blood. In 1972 Nobel-prize winning scientist Julius Axelrod of the U.S. National Institutes of Health reported finding it in human brain tissue. Additional research showed that DMT could also be found in the human urine and the cerebrospinal fluid bathing the brain. It was not long before scientists discovered the pathways, similar to those in lower animals, by which the human body made DMT. DMT thus became the first *endogenous* human psychedelic." [Rick Strassman, "What DMT Is" in *DMT: The Spirit Molecule* (Rochester, VT: Park Street Press, 2001), p. 48]; See also James Oroc, "5-MeO-DMT: Science, Discovery, and the History of Human Use" in *Tryptamine Palace: 5-MeO-DMT and the Sonoran Desert Toad* (Rochester, VT: Park Street Press, 2009), pp. 19–38.

9. The following provides a Traditionalist perspective regarding this point, "If drugs could change and transform consciousness, it is certain that this knowledge would have been incorporated into spiritual teachings from time immemorial. On the other hand, intoxicants and drugs have served universally as supports adjacent to ritual practices, even where the use is purely symbolic" [Whitall N. Perry, "Drug-Induced Mysticism: The Mescalin Hypothesis" in *Challenges to a Secular Society* (Oakton, VA: The Foundation for Traditional Studies, 1996), p. 15].

10. Barbara G. Myerhoff, *Peyote Hunt: The Sacred Journey of the Huichol Indians* (Ithaca, NY: Cornell University Press, 1983); Antonin Artaud, *The Peyote Dance*, trans. Helen Weaver (New York: Farrar, Straus and Giroux, 1976); Edward F. Anderson, *Peyote: The Divine Cactus* (Tucson, AZ: The University of Arizona Press, 1994)

11. Eduardo Calderón, Richard Cowan, Douglas Sharon and F. Kaye Sharon, *Eduardo el Curandero: The Words of a Peruvian Healer* (Richmond, CA: North Atlantic Books, 1982).

ceps purpurea), Henbane (*Hyoscyamus niger*), Belladonna (*Atropa belladonna*), *Mandrake* (*Mandragora officinarum*), *Datura*, *Brugmansia*, *Ska Pastora* (*Salvia divinorum*), *Pituri* (*Duboisia hopwoodii*), etc.—some advocates or researchers have explicitly or implicitly claimed that they have been the precursors to the foundation of religion itself.[12] These mind-altering plants have been suggested to be the central components of *Soma* of the Rig Veda or Hoama/Homa of the Avesta identified as none other than the mushroom *Amanita muscaria*[13] and the principal rite of the Eleusinian Mysteries (Plato,

12. "[Question:] *So your view is that hallucinogens were involved in the origin of some religious traditions but not necessarily all.*" "[Peter T. Furst:] No, I think that's also going too far. The use of the so-called 'hallucinogens' is a *function* of religion, not its origin." [Peter T. Furst, "Ancient Altered States" in Roger Walsh and Charles S. Grob (eds.) *Higher Wisdom: Eminent Elders Explore the Continuing Impact of Psychedelics* (Albany, NY: SUNY Press, 2005), p. 156]; see also Peter T. Furst (ed.), *Flesh of the Gods: The Ritual Use of Hallucinogens* (NY: Praeger Publishers, 1974); Peter T. Furst, *Hallucinogens and Culture* (San Francisco, CA: Chandler & Sharp Publishers, 1979); R. Gordon Wasson, Stella Kramrisch, Jonathan Ott, and Carl A. P. Ruck, *Persephone's Quest: Entheogens and the Origins of Religion* (New Haven, CT: Yale University Press, 1986); Richard Evans Schultes and Albert Hofmann, *Plants of the Gods: Their Sacred, Healing and Hallucinogenic Powers* (Rochester, VT: Healing Arts Press, 1992); Jonathan Ott, *Pharmacotheon: Entheogenic Drugs, Their Plant Sources and History* (Kennewick, WA: Natural Products, 1993); Peter Stafford, *Psychedelics Encyclopedia, Third Expanded Edition* (Berkeley, CA: Ronin Publishing, 1992); Marlene Dobkin de Rios, *Hallucinogens: Cross-Cultural Perspectives* (Prospect Heights, IL: Waveland Press, 1996); Aldous Huxley, "The History of Tension" in Michael Horowitz and Cynthia Palmer (eds.), *Moksha: Aldous Huxley's Classic Writings on Psychedelics and the Visionary Experience* (Rochester, VT: Park Street Press, 1999), pp. 117–128; Sidney Cohen, *The Beyond Within: The LSD Story* (New York: Atheneum, 1972); Jeremy Narby, *The Cosmic Serpent: DNA and the Origins of Knowledge* (NY: Jeremy P. Tarcher/Putnam, 1999); Andrew Weil, *The Natural Mind: An Investigation of Drugs and the Higher Consciousness* (Boston, MA: Houghton Mifflin, 1986); Andrew Weil, *The Marriage of the Sun and the Moon: A Quest for Unity in Consciousness* (Boston, MA: Houghton Mifflin, 1980); Daniel Pinchbeck, *Breaking Open the Head: A Psychedelic Journey Into the Heart of Contemporary Shamanism* (NY: Broadway Books, 2003).

13. R. Gordon Wasson, *Soma: Divine Mushroom of Immortality* (NY: Harcourt Brace Jovanovich, 1969). The Wasson hypothesis has been critiqued from within psychedelic circles: this from one of its most prominent voices, Terence McKenna: "The problem with this hypothesis is that *A. muscaria* is not a reliable visionary hallucinogen. It has proven difficult to obtain a consistently ecstatic intoxication

Aristotle and Epictetus were said to have been initiates) utilizing *Kykeon* purported to be the fungus ergot which contains psychoactive alkaloids such as LSD (lysergic acid diethylamide);[14] it has also been asserted that that *Manna* of the Hebrew Bible was a psychedelic,[15] the use of psychoactive mushrooms have also been ascribed to the cult of Mithras,[16] and said to be used in ancient Egypt,[17] even the origins of Christianity and Christ himself are hypothesized to be the mushroom *Amanita muscaria*.[18] What are your thoughts on this important discussion?

from *Amanita muscaria*. Wasson was on the right track, correctly recognizing the potential of *Amanita muscaria* to induce religious feeling and ecstasy, but he did not take into account the imagination and linguistic stimulation imparted by the input of African psilocybin-containing mushrooms into the evolution of Old World mycolatry." [Terence McKenna, "Mushrooms and Evolution" in *The Archaic Revival: Speculations on Psychedelic Mushrooms, the Amazon, Virtual Reality, UFOs, Evolution, Shamanism, the Rebirth of the Goddess, and the End of History* (New York: HarperCollins, 1991), p. 150]; See also Thomas J. Riedlinger (ed.), *The Sacred Mushroom Seeker: Tributes to R. Gordon Wasson* (Rochester, VT: Park Street Press, 1990); Peter Lamborn Wilson, *Ploughing the Clouds: The Search for Irish Soma* (San Francisco, CA: City Lights Books, 1999).

14. R. Gordon Wasson, Albert Hofmann, and Carl A.P. Ruck (eds.), *The Road to Eleusis: Unveiling the Secret of the Mysteries*, Twentieth Anniversary Edition (Los Angeles, CA: Hermes Press, 1998). Some researchers assert that both Kykeon and psychedelic mushrooms (*Amanita muscaria* and psilocybin) were used interchangeably in the rites of the Eleusinian Mysteries, see Carl A.P. Ruck, *Sacred Mushrooms of the Goddess: Secrets of Eleusis* (Oakland, CA: Ronin Publishing, 2006)

15. Dan Merkur, "Manna, the Showbread, and the Eucharist: Psychoactive Sacraments in the Bible" in *Psychoactive Sacramentals: Essays on Entheogens and Religion*, ed. Thomas B. Roberts (San Francisco, CA: Council on Spiritual Practices, 2001), pp. 139–144; See also Dan Merkur, *The Mystery of Manna: The Psychedelic Sacrament of the Bible* (Rochester, VT: Park Street Press, 2000).

16. Carl A.P. Ruck, Mark Alwin Hoffman, and José Alfredo González Celdrán, *Mushrooms, Myth and Mithras: The Drug Cult that Civilized Europe* (San Francisco, CA: City Lights Books, 2011).

17. Andrija Puharich, *The Sacred Mushroom: Key to the Door of Eternity* (Garden City, NY: Doubleday and Company, Inc., 1959).

18. John Marco Allegro, *The Sacred Mushroom and the Cross: A Study of the Nature and Origins of Christianity Within the Fertility Cults of the Ancient Near East*

CU: Since religions are founded by Divine action through prophets and avatars (Buddhism possibly excepted; yet Gautama Buddha is considered to be the ninth Avatar of Lord Vishnu within the Hindu tradition), to say that they have been initiated by psychedelics is to deny that God can act on His own initiative, and consequently to deny God. It is to make "religion" an entirely human affair, and thus to posit something that does not fit the definition of that word. No religious tradition claims to have been founded on the basis of psychedelic experience; such claims emanate from users of psychedelics who like to project their fantasies upon traditions they in no way intend to follow. Anyone who thinks that Moses met God on Sinai or Jesus became "Christ" after eating some mushroom, because how else could they have done it, has no sense of the sacred whatsoever. Within certain contexts and in certain *yugas* it *might* have been spiritually possible to open initiates to the graces of an already established spiritual Way through the use of psychedelics, but such things are certainly not possible to us in our own time, except at great cost—and with what coin could we pay that cost, poor as we are? In any case it is certain that the establishment of a legitimate spiritual Way through the use psychedelics has never been either possible or necessary.

SBS: While the perennial philosophy acknowledges the Shamanic traditions of the First Peoples, a central challenge to the notion that entheogens or psychedelics have been used since the beginning of time is that the "beginning of time" or "pre-history" which some

(New York: Bantam Books, 1971); See also Jan R. Irvin with Jack Herer, *The Holy Mushroom: Evidence of Mushrooms in Judeo-Christianity* (Riverside, CA: Gnostic Media, 2008); John A. Rush, *Failed God: Fractured Myth in a Fragile World* (Berkeley, CA: Frog Books, 2008); John A. Rush, *The Mushroom in Christian Art: The Identity of Jesus in the Development of Christianity* (Berkeley, CA: North Atlantic Books, 2011); Carl A. P. Ruck, Blaise Daniel Staples, and Clark Heinrich, *The Apples of Apollo: Pagan and Christian Mysteries of the Eucharist* (Durham, NC: Carolina Academic Press, 2001); Carl A. P. Ruck, Blaise Daniel Staples, José Alfredo González Celdrán, and Mark Alwin Hoffman, *The Hidden World: Survival of Pagan Shamanic Themes in European Fairytales* (Durham, NC: Carolina Academic Press, 2007).

suggest to be around 5000 BC,[19] when contextualized within cyclical time it is likely to be the *Kali-Yuga* or the Iron Age, the culmination of this temporal cycle or at best the *Dvapara Yuga* or Bronze Age, the phase preceding the final age.[20] Thus the use of sacred plants that have psychoactive properties occurred late in the cosmic cycle (*manvantara*) and not at its inception, the *Krita-Yuga* or *Satya-Yuga*, known as the Golden Age in Western cosmology which would support prominent historian of religion Mircea Eliade's (1907–1986) astute observation: "the use of intoxicants . . . is a recent innovation and points to a decadence in shamanic technique" (see *Endnote II*) Could you please elaborate on the perennialist perspective with regards to this point?

CU: I agree with Eliade's initial view of psychedelics; when a spiritual tradition degenerates there is no telling what people will try in order to regain what is felt to be lost. Perhaps, God willing, something can be partially regained through psychedelics under certain cosmic conditions—conditions we certainly do not enjoy today—but the very attempt to regain a former spiritual exaltation is evidence of a degeneration. The *Krita-yuga* was characterized by a "mass theophanic consciousness" in which psychedelics were not needed; in the words of Genesis, mankind "walked with God in the cool of the evening". In my view (and I am open to correction), Shamanism came in with the *Treta-yuga* or Silver Age, when the cosmic environment was subject to imbalances due to demonic incursions that the Shamans—as they themselves maintain, according to

19. Peter T. Furst, "Ancient Altered States" in Roger Walsh and Charles S. Grob (eds.) *Higher Wisdom: Eminent Elders Explore the Continuing Impact of Psychedelics* (Albany, NY: SUNY Press, 2005), p. 153. Some psychedelic researchers regard the rock art found in the mountain range of Tassili n'Ajjer southeast Algeria to be the most ancient verification of psychedelic use.

20. René Guénon, "Some Remarks on the Doctrine of Cosmic Cycles" in *Traditional Forms and Cosmic Cycles*, trans. Henry D. Fohr, ed. Samuel D. Fohr (Hillsdale, NY: Sophia Perennis, 2001), pp. 1–12; Charles Upton, *Legends of the End: Prophecies of the End Times, Antichrist, Apocalypse, and Messiah from Eight Religious Traditions* (Hillsdale, NY: Sophia Perennis, 2004); Charles Upton, "Comparative Eschatology" in *The System of Antichrist: Truth and Falsehood in Postmodernism and the New Age* (Ghent, NY: Sophia Perennis, 2001), pp. 424–479.

Eliade—were sent by God to correct. And as the Shamans of our own time have asserted, also according to Eliade, their ancestors were immensely more powerful than they, and didn't need psychedelics; so the use of the psychedelic "crutch" undoubtedly came in later than the Shamanic dispensation itself. Also of great interest is the fact that the Christian visionary and stigmatist Anne Catherine Emmerich [1774–1824], in her book *The Life of Christ and Biblical Revelations* [1979], based on her visions, mentions an early non-Biblical patriarch called *Hom*, who was either named after, or provided a name for, a particular plant he considered to be sacred. This plant, in my opinion, is the *Haoma* plant of the ancient Persians, equivalent to the Vedic *Soma*. According to Emmerich, the lineage that sprang from Hom, which included one Dsemschid (undoubtedly the legendary Persian king Jamshid), became polluted with Satanic fantasies, though she apparently did not recognize the plant in question as an intoxicant. It is highly unlikely that Emmerich, a nearly illiterate Westphalian peasant, would have known anything about Persian history or Zoroastrian lore, much less about the effects of exotic psychedelics. So it may well be true that the use of such plants, at least beyond the cosmic era that might have allowed their use under certain conditions, represents a truly ancient deviation in humanity's relationship with God. (It must not be forgotten, however, that according to René Guénon and Ananda K. Coomaraswamy, *Soma* and *Haoma*, in their higher symbolic sense, are not psychoactive plants but the source of the "Draught of Immortality" which effects the return of the Human Form to its *fitra*, its primordial Edenic state before the Fall. In other words, they symbolize a particular stage of spiritual realization.)

As for Eliade's later notion that psychedelic ecstasy is identical to ecstasy produced by other means, I speculate that he said this only because he experienced psychedelics himself and had nothing else to compare them to. He was an incomparable scholar of religion, but he had no religious faith; he characterized religions, myths and metaphysical beliefs as "artistic creations" referring to no objective reality; he placed them on the psychic plane, not the Spiritual.

SBS: There is the notion that the use of peyote (*Lophophora williamsii*) via the syncretistic Native American Church (NAC) is compatible with other traditional Shamanic rites which did not originally utilize this plant medicine. For example, there are some that suggest that the Sun Dance Religion is compatible with peyote use (some have even introduced *Ayauasca* or *Yajé* into this sacred ritual),[21] yet traditional spiritual authorities within these communities, such as medicine man and Sun Dance chief, Thomas Yellowtail (1903–1993) suggest quite the opposite, that they are not compatible and that such syncretism or mixing of foreign elements such as peyote are in fact dangerous and could be spiritually harmful,[22] not to mention that they do not do justice to either spir-

21. In this context we might also mention Prem Baba or Janderson Fernandes de Oliveira (b. 1965), a psychologist by training, also considered to be a spiritual master—combining the role of *guru* and shaman. Prem Baba is a disciple of Sri Hans Raj Maharajji, also known as Sri Sachcha Baba Maharajji (b. 1924) and teaches a method that he calls *O Caminho do Coração* or the "Path to the Heart" and refers to himself as follows: "I am an eclectic centre of universal light". Prem Baba asserts that he is an enlightened master and began his school Sachcha Mission Ashram located in São Paulo, Brazil. What interests us is that Prem Baba was not only a former member of the syncretic church Santo Daime but also a former disciple of the controversial figure Bhagwan Shree Rajneesh or Osho (1931–1990), known as the "sex guru", a prototypical representative of all that constitutes as "New Age" spirituality who amassed a syncretism *par excellence* of everything under the sun in his spiritual toolbox. It is seldom mentioned that Rajneesh was said to be addicted to a certain mind-altering substance known as "laughing gas" or nitrous oxide (N2O). He is reported to have dictated three books—*Glimpses of a Golden Childhood* (1985), *Notes of a Madman* (1985), and *Books I have Loved* (1985)—under the influence of his very own dentist's chair; however there is one title that has not yet seen the light of day for obvious reasons: *Bhagwan: The First Buddha in the Dental Chair.* That Prem Baba attempts to blend the use of *Ayauasca* or *Yajé* with Hindu *dharma*, as well as other techniques including a *mélange* of modern therapies, speaks loud and clear to the signs of the times. We cannot be too wary of such *ad hoc* approaches which are more and more the norm in this spiritually atrophied epoch. See also Robert Forte (ed.), *Entheogens and the Future of Religion* (San Francisco, CA: Council on Spiritual Practices, 1997); Allan Hunt Badiner and Alex Grey (eds.), *Zig Zag Zen: Buddhism and Psychedelics* (San Francisco, CA: Chronicle Books, 2002); Charles T. Tart, "Influences of Previous Psychedelic Drug Experiences on Students of Tibetan Buddhism: A Preliminary Exploration", *Journal of Transpersonal Psychology*, Vol. 23, No. 2 (1991), pp. 139–173; Myron J. Stolaroff, "Are Psychedelics Useful in the Practice of Buddhism?", *Journal of Humanistic Psychology*, Vol. 39, No. 1 (1999), pp. 60–80; see also the special issue "Buddhism and Psychedelics", *Tricycle: The Buddhist Review*, Vol. VI, No. 1 (Fall 1996).

itual way and end up watering each tradition down, ultimately leading to the demise of both. Do you have any thoughts on this?

CU: Yellowtail was right.

SBS: In conjunction with the amalgamation of Native American Church (NAC) there is also the phenomena of the psychoactive brew *Ayauasca* or *Yajé* from South America which has been widely exported throughout the world made extensively available through the syncretic churches of Santo Daime founded by Mestre Irineu or Raimundo Irineu Serra (1892–1971)[23] and União do Vegetal (Centro Espírita Beneficente União do Vegetal or UDV) founded by Mestre Gabriel or José Gabriel da Costa (1922–1971) combining Catholicism, Spiritism of Allan Kardec (1804–1869), African and South

22. Michael Oren Fitzgerald, "Rainbow" and "Notes" in *Yellowtail, Crow Medicine Man and Sun Dance Chief: An Autobiography* (Norman, OK: University of Oklahoma Press, 1994), pp. 56–57, 221; See also Fred W. Voget, *The Shoshoni-Crow Sun Dance* (Norman, OK: University of Oklahoma Press, 1984), p. 169. Frank Fools Crow (1890–1989), a Lakota (Sioux) spiritual leader, *yuwipi* medicine man, and the nephew of Black Elk or Hehaka Sapa (1863–1950) the Lakota Sioux sage, made the following declaration regarding the use of peyote: "I have not . . . used peyote like they do in the Native American Church. *Wakan-Tanka* can take me higher than any drug ever could" [Thomas E. Mails, "Little Hollow Bones" in *Fools Crow: Wisdom and Power* (San Francisco, CA: Council Oak Books, 2001), p. 40]; Lame Deer (1903–1976), Sioux medicine man underscores the incompatibility of peyote use with the sacred rites of the Oglala Sioux: "I have my hands full just clinging to our old Sioux ways—singing the ancient songs correctly, conducting a sweat-lodge ceremony as it should be, making our old beliefs as pure, as clear and true as I possibly can, making them stay alive, saving them from extinction. This is a big enough task for an old man. So I cannot be a *yuwipi*, a true Lakota medicine man, and take peyote at the same time." [John (Fire) Lame Deer and Richard Erdoes, "Don't Hurt the Trees" in *Lame Deer, Seeker of Visions* (NY: Simon & Schuster, 1994), p. 228].

23. In regard to Santo Daime, we need to mention another central figure, Sebastião Mota de Melo, better known as Padrinho Sebastião (1920–1990), one of the direct disciples of Mestre Irineu who founded The Eclectic Center of the Fluent Universal Light of Raimundo Irineu Serra (CEFLURIS) the two communities Colônia Cinco Mil (Colony Five Thousand) and Céu do Mapiá; the second is considered to be the church's headquarters, yet both are located in Brazil. See Alex Polari de Alverga, *Forest of Visions: Ayahuasca, Amazonian Spirituality, and the Santo Dime Tradition*, trans. Rosana Workman, ed. Stephen Larsen (Rochester, VT: Park Street Press, 1999); Alex Polari de Alverga, *The Religion of Ayahuasca: The Teachings of the Church of Santo Daime*, trans. Rosana Workman, ed. Stephen Larsen (Rochester, VT: Park Street Press, 2010).

American shamanism.[24] In conjunction with this, we need to also mention that the search for mystical experiences has also brought about the phenomenon of "spiritual tourism" (see *Endnote III*) to remote parts of the Amazon basin that has its damaging effects on the traditional societies living in these areas, extending itself to all sapiential traditions. Could you speak to these interesting phenomenon's which is unquestionably a hallmark of New Age thought?

CU: To syncretize different forms of the sacred, assuming that they were originally true Spiritual ways, not simply psychic "technologies", is to relativize and subjectivize them and thus drive everything down to the psychic level while sealing off access to the Spirit; and this is tantamount to demonic invocation. And even if the practices in question are fundamentally psychic to begin with, mixing them can only generate further chaos. Spiritual Unity is higher than psychic multiplicity and encompasses it, but once the Unity of the Spirit is veiled, the idea becomes: "You mean you only have *one* god? You are spiritually deprived! We have hundreds"—the "reign of quantity" with a vengeance! The problem with this approach is that no one of these many gods can be the Absolute Reality, or even a psychic symbol for it—given that, by definition, you can't have more than one Absolute. And the psychic chaos created by mixing African and South American shamanism with Catholicism and European spiritualism can only be compared to playing the music of Bach, the Moody Blues, Charlie Parker, and Inti Illimani all at the same time—a practice that could only destroy all presence of mind and unity of soul in the listener. Of course some people like that kind of thing; instead of transcending their individuality through Spiritual ascent, they simply want to shatter it, and consequently sink below it, into the infra-psychic. It's called "postmodernism".

And spiritual tourism in places like the Amazon damages not only the indigenous cultures but the tourists too. (I recently saw a

24. See Beatriz Caiuby Labate and Henrik Jungaberle (eds.), *The Internationalization of Ayahuasca* (Zürich: Lit Verlag, 2011); Beatriz Caiuby Labate, Isabel Santana de Rose and Rafael Guimaraes dos Santos, *Ayahuasca Religions: A Comprehensive Bibliography & Critical Essays*, trans. Matthew Meyer (Ben Lomond, CA: Multidisciplinary Association for Psychedelic Studies, 2008).

news item where one village prohibited such tourism; a villager characterized the North American strangers who'd visited them and immediately asked to be told all about the local sacred rituals and beliefs as, in effect, "creepy".) When well-heeled Norteamericanos and Europeans enter dirt poor villages in the Amazon and elsewhere looking to satisfy their spiritual hunger, a hunger based on their abandonment and betrayal of their own spiritual tradition (usually Christianity), they tempt the village elders to what traditional Catholics call the sin of *simony*: selling sacred things for money. Spiritual tourists are by and large not pilgrims but thieves, vampires. In most cases they aren't looking for a spiritual Path to dedicate their lives to, but simply picking up here and there whatever sacred art objects, or psychedelic experiences, or sacred rituals degraded to the level of mere spectacle, might suite their fancy—if, that is, they aren't actually sorcerers in search of "personal power". Very often their basic set is psychic rather than spiritual; like most tourists, they are looking for "experiences", not principles to live by. They leave behind them the destructive influences of their own profane postmodern attitudes, and return home polluted with the toxic psychic residues of the forms of the sacred they have plundered, so as to release them to do their damage within their own cultures.

SBS: Another important point to discuss is that while there are traditional Shamanic societies who today still utilize psychoactive plants in their sacred rites—i.e., the Huichol, Tarahumara, Cora, Mazatec, Bwiti, Kayapó, Fang, Mitsogo, Jivaro, Yanomami, Koryak, etc.—this does not necessarily mean that those outside these racial and ethnic groups will also have the same spiritual and beneficial response with the use of these plants.[25] It is as if the different indigenous peoples were given different plant medicines particular to their human makeup and ecological context. Could you please

25. "If the Indians can consume peyote without harmful results, the question of their own heritage—psychic and spiritual, and the concomitant ritual conditions are essential factors to be considered." [Whitall N. Perry, "Drug-Induced Mysticism: The Mescalin Hypothesis" in *Challenges to a Secular Society* (Oakton, VA: The Foundation for Traditional Studies, 1996), p. 15]. "One might counter that there are cultures, the Amazonian Indian tribes notably, in which ritualized drug use is a normal mode of communion with the divine. However, this fact calls for

speak to this sensitive theme as it is perhaps "politically incorrect"?

CU: This is undoubtedly true in many cases. If the invocation of the name Allah should not be expected to be spiritually fruitful for a Buddhist, then by the same token the use of certain psychoactive plants outside of their traditional cultural and ritual context is not likely to have the same effect as it would within those contexts, and will most likely have a much more negative one. Such psychic and cultural bleed-throughs may be accurately compared to the breakdown of discrete and self-contained ecosystems. Asian carp are fine in Asia; in the Great Lakes they are a disaster. And those who hope to benefit from the sacred worldviews of the Huichols, the Tarahumara, the Native American Church should be willing to live under the same conditions of deprivation and oppression and social marginalization as the Huichols and the Tarahumara and the Native American Church. If you want the spirituality of the Res, accept the suffering of the Res.

Shamanism, even relatively degenerate Shamanism,[26] has a certain practical justification under truly primitive conditions, since it represents a large portion of the *technological* heritage of the tribe. The Shaman heals disease, finds and attracts game, carries on criminal investigations, influences the weather, protects the tribe in war and guards it against psychological imbalances and/or demonic incursions. But under modern conditions, when at least some of these functions can be fulfilled by other means, Shamanism loses a certain amount of its *raison d'être.* French poet and cinematogra-

two comments that should apply to similar cultures. First, because of destiny, the psychic homogeneity of such peoples combined with the consistency of their shamanic cosmology, cannot be compared with the porous psychic heterogeneity of Westerners. Thus, if under the guidance of a shaman, an Amazonian Indian can enter into communion in a predictably consistent manner with a spirit animal which will act as a teacher and a guide, the same result cannot be necessarily expected for a Westerner intent on duplicating the experience. Secondly, the prevalence of such ritualized psychism…does not constitute a superiority per se." [Mark Perry, "The Forbidden Door" in *Every Branch in Me: Essays on the Meaning of Man*, ed. Barry McDonald (Bloomington, IN: World Wisdom, 2002), pp. 270–271].

26. René Guénon, "Shamanism and Sorcery" in *The Reign of Quantity and the Signs of the Times*, trans. Lord Northbourne (Ghent, NY: Sophia Perennis, 2001), pp. 177–184.

pher Jean Cocteau [1889–1963] recounts the story of an anthropologist who was studying native folkways in Haiti, where trees are (or were) used for long-distance communication; when a woman's husband was away at market, she might send a message to him by speaking to a tree, and receive his answer by the same means. When the anthropologist asked the natives why they spoke to trees, their answer was: "Because we are poor. If we were rich we should have the telephone".

In my opinion, those persons of the postmodern West whose psychophysical nature is not already fully integrated into the Spirit, or at least fully submissive to It—a condition extremely rare in our time—should never touch the Shamanism of the primal cultures, since westerners lack the protection provided by the basic spiritual set and character-formation of those cultures. The rare and exceptional case is that of the person who, by the grace of God, has found and been accepted not simply by a working traditional Shaman or medicine man, but a true holy man of one of the primal spiritual Ways—though how he or she could recognize such a holy man in the first place is hard to imagine.

SBS: You have undertaken an in-depth study of UFO phenomenon in light of traditional metaphysics in your book *Cracks in the Great Wall* (2005).[27] There are numerous writers and researchers within the psychedelic world who claim that there is a connection between the psychedelic experience and UFO's sightings and/or abductions, especially for those who use the substance DMT (dimethyltryptamine).[28] To many this might be the siren call or the advent of the New Age, but to the exponents of the perennial philosophy

27. Charles Upton, *Cracks in the Great Wall: The UFO Phenomenon and Traditional Metaphysics* (Hillsdale, NY: Sophia Perennis, 2005). See also Charles Upton, "UFOs and Traditional Metaphysics: A Postmodern Demonology" in *The System of Antichrist: Truth and Falsehood in Postmodernism and the New Age* (Ghent, NY: Sophia Perennis, 2001), pp. 325–386.

28. Terence McKenna, *The Archaic Revival: Speculations on Psychedelic Mushrooms, the Amazon, Virtual Reality, UFOs, Evolution, Shamanism, the Rebirth of the Goddess, and the End of History* (NY: HarperCollins, 1991); Rick Strassman, *DMT: The Spirit Molecule* (Rochester, VT: Park Street Press, 2001); Rick Strassman, Slawer Wojtowicz, Luis Eduardo Luna, and Ede Frecska, *Inner Paths to Outer Space: Journeys*

this has the characteristics of the *Kali-Yuga* written all over it. Could you please speak to this?

CU: As I see it, the UFO "aliens" are denizens of the intermediary or psychic plane, what Muslims call the Jinn. So it is not surprising that the use of psychedelics could make one more vulnerable to incursions from that world. René Guénon in *The Reign of Quantity and the Signs of the Times* [1953] spoke of "fissures" appearing in the "Great Wall" separating the material plane from the intermediary plane, fissures that open our world to "infra-psychic" forces; to me the UFO phenomenon is a perfect example of this process. These fissures appear due to cyclical degeneration and the approaching dissolution of our world, but they are further widened and exploited by human activity, sometimes unconscious, sometimes deliberate. I believe that such things as the spread of the electronic media, including the internet, the liberation of nuclear energy, the use of psychedelics and the general fascination with psychic powers and the paranormal continue to widen the cracks in the Great Wall, which, since it acts as the border between the material and the psychic worlds, can be affected by both material and psychic means; the very fact that such powerful psychic experiences can be produced by a material substance like LSD undoubtedly furthers this process. And it is interesting in this context that, according to Timothy Leary [1920–1996], LSD was not "activated" as a psychedelic until the first atomic bomb was detonated in New Mexico. (On the material side, this border apparently has something to do with the electromagnetic spectrum, which is why automobile engines will often die and electronic equipment malfunction in close proximity to a UFO.) Furthermore, those people Guénon called "agents of the Counter-Initiation"[29] are working to widen the cracks in the Great Wall consciously and deliberately.

The case of pioneer rocket scientist Jack Parsons [1914–1952]

to Alien Worlds through Psychedelics and Other Spiritual Technologies (Rochester, VT: Park Street Press, 2008); Stanislav Grof, "UFOs in the Amazon: Alien Encounter of the Third Kind" in *When the Impossible Happens: Adventures in Non-Ordinary Realities* (Boulder, CO: Sounds True, 2006), pp. 271–274.

29. See René Guénon, "Pseudo-Initiation" in *The Reign of Quantity and the Signs of the Times*, tr. Lord Northbourne (Ghent, NY: Sophia Perennis, 2001), pp. 241–251.

comes immediately to mind. Parsons was a follower of black magician Aleister Crowley [1875–1947] and an associate of L. Ron Hubbard [1911–1986], another follower of Crowley, who founded the Church of Scientology and who also (according to my correspondence with Beat Generation writer William Burroughs [1914–1997] in the late 1960s, when Burroughs was in the process of breaking with Scientology) had a background in Naval Intelligence, something confirmed by Peter Levenda in his trilogy *Sinister Forces: A Grimoire of American Political Witchcraft.* Parsons, according to UFOlogist Jacques Vallée [b. 1939] in his book *Messengers of Deception* [1979], claimed to have met a "Venusian" in the Mojave Desert; according to Levenda he performed Pagan rituals at his launchings. He went on to co-found both the Aerojet Corporation and the Jet Propulsion Laboratory; a crater was named after him on the dark side of the Moon. Parsons openly stated that he was working to open a "door" into another dimension; it was shortly after his Mojave Desert rituals that the first major post-WWII civilian sightings of UFOs occurred in North America, through of course there is no way of knowing if the two are related. (In the careers of Crowley, Parsons and Hubbard we can see clear indications of the action of the Counter-Initiation.)[30] So conscious or unconscious "invocations" of the Jinn appear to be a major factor in the breakdown of the energy-wall between the material and the intermediary plane; such invocations are undoubtedly inspired by the Jinn themselves, specifically the *kafir* or unbelieving Jinn (the demons, that is; the

30. On a side note, we might mention here that as Hubbard was a disciple of Crowley, and the fact that Hubbard influenced the field of transpersonal psychology, known in modern psychology as the "fourth force", this brings to light its unfortunate inclusion of New Age thought which has not been sufficiently explored. "The crystallization and consolidation of the originally isolated tendencies into a new movement, or Fourth Force, in psychology was primarily the work of two men—Anthony Sutich and Abraham Maslow—both of whom had earlier played an important role in the history of humanistic psychology. Although transpersonal psychology was not established as a distinct discipline until the late 1960s, transpersonal trends in psychology had preceded it by several decades. The most important representatives of this orientation have been Carl Gustav Jung,

Qur'an teaches that some of the Jinn are unbelievers and some are Muslims). In other words, the *kafir* Jinn are working to break down the Great Wall from their side as well. When the Wall finally crashes, our world will end.[31]

SBS: As you are a veteran of the counter-culture movement, I am wondering if you would not mind speaking about your own personal experiences with psychedelics. In doing so could you please describe the psychological and the environmental factors known in psychedelic circles as "set and setting", including what substance and quantity you ingested during any "positive" psychedelic experiences?

CU: My "set" was always: "I seek the Clear Light; I wish to open to higher consciousness; I hope to see God". And my setting was almost invariably a place of beauty in the natural world. Leaving aside my many more or less positive mescaline and peyote trips (though one was quite painful and rigorous—deliberately so), my two rather unpleasant experiences with psilocybin mushrooms, and my one extremely powerful trip on morning glory seeds (whose

Roberto Assagioli, and Abraham Maslow. Also the most interesting and controversial systems of Dianetics and Scientology developed by [L.] Ron Hubbard (1950) outside of the professional circles should be mentioned in this context." [Stanislav Grof, "Psychotherapies with Transpersonal Orientation," in *Beyond the Brain: Birth, Death, and Transcendence in Psychotherapy* (Albany, NY: SUNY Press, 1985), p. 187]; see also Stanislav Grof, *Psychology of the Future: Lessons from Modern Consciousness Research* (Albany, NY: SUNY Press, 2000), p. 130; Whitall N. Perry, "On Cults of Unreason" in *Challenges to a Secular Society* (Oakton, VA: The Foundation for Traditional Studies, 1996), pp. 59–60; Bent Corydon, "L. Ron and the Beast" in *L. Ron Hubbard: Messiah or Madman?* (Fort Lee: NJ: Barricade Books, 1992), pp. 50–61; Russell Miller, "Black Magic and Betty" in *Bare-Faced Messiah: The True Story of L. Ron Hubbard* (NY: Henry Holt and Company, 1988), pp. 112–130. It should also be noted that Timothy Leary too was an Aleister Crowley enthusiast and that Aldous Huxley is reported to have dined with Crowley in Berlin in the Fall of 1930. Some even suggest that it was Aleister Crowley rather than Humphry Osmond who introduced Huxley to mescaline.

31. For a further discussion of this topic see, "UFOs, Mass Mind-Control, and the *Awliya al-Shaytan*" available online at: *http://www.sophiaperennis.com/uncategorized/ufos-mass-mind-control-and-the-awliya-al-shaytan-by-charles-upton-anupdate-of-cracks-in-the-great-wall-ufos-and-traditional-metaphysics-sophiaperennis2005/*

active ingredient is "organic acid", lysergic acid amide), the settings for my three LSD trip were (1) the valley below Alpine Dam on Mt. Tamalpias, Marin County, California; (2) the Rocky Mountains of British Columbia; 3) Joshua Tree National Monument in the deserts of Southern California. As for dosage, we who bought our acid "on the street" never really knew. Various microgram numbers were given or not given by our sources; many times we were just told "this is one hit" or "5 hits", or someone who had already ingested some of the batch in question might suggest how much we should take. The first trip came out of a blue pill, the second out of a "window-pane" and the third out of a "blotter". A windowpane was a tiny square of clear solid gelatin of the kind used for gelatin capsules; a blotter was a square of blotter-paper. Acid was sold in the latter two forms to demonstrate that it was most likely not adulterated, since you never knew what might be in a pill or capsule besides acid, or instead of acid.

SBS: Could you please describe in detail what transpired both inwardly and outwardly during this psychedelic session?

CU: *Session One*: essentially a "Second Bardo" trip, "the Bardo of Experiencing Reality" (or rather, as I would now say, "existence") according to the system developed by Timothy Leary and based on the *Tibetan Book of the Dead*:[32] Time slowed down immensely and became "spatialized"; the landscape was transfigured into a scene of *unearthly* earthly beauty; matter was transformed into, or clearly recognized as, a coagulation of energy—if I squeezed a stone it would vibrate and sizzle in my hand; the Celestial Light of Heaven almost came down, or started to; wings almost sprouted on my shoulders; I looked at an acorn cap and thought I was seeing a newly-hatched baby snake still coiled up as he had been in his shell (later in Vancouver, British Columbia, after reading a poem based on that experience at a café, I was told by another of the performers, a traditional London "busker", that in that vision I had come upon a piece of Druid lore), etc. At one point a short, gnarled figure

32. See Timothy Leary, Ralph Metzner, and Richard Alpert, *The Psychedelic Experience: A Manual Based on the Tibetan Book of the Dead* (NY: Citadel Press, 1990).

appeared whom I thought of as a "pirate", he was disgruntled, irritated, as if to say "Hey you kids! Get off my property!" (I was tripping with a friend). Later I realized that he was in fact a gnome, a spirit of the Earth element in the system of Paracelsus; I further realized that by dropping acid in that forested canyon by that clear stream of water we had done the equivalent of breaking into his house uninvited or even walking through his wall; no wonder he was angry! Here's the poem I wrote about that trip:

The Lightning's Kiss

I

the storm is directly above us:
boiling fog,
surf crashing on the shoreline
of the hills—
mingling elements
flashing white, blue
moil in a turbulence—
luminous webs
vapours streaming
and blotting the Sun
and revealing him again
in his course—

our external destinies
rush to crazy oblivion
in the sky above—

here below,
the Quiet:

grey, green, dark & almost white,
the treetrunks boil up to Heaven!
silver-muscled branches
light up like bleeding arteries;
slender arms and sinews of branches,
sparkling hieroglyphs of leaves,

architectural script of rock,
the gnarled old face of the vegetable Druid
frowning thunderous from the roots,
his countenance beating
like a human heart—

and the creek is filled
with men's voices
the single-minded, the inexorable
in one motion through time—
rare fluencies of speech,
sparkling emerald syntax
in the masculine sunlight,
illuminating the brilliance
of contention and declamation—

sounds of crickets, secrets,
goblets of Egyptian sound,
moving downstream—

the linked syllables of Karma
talking forever
in the direction of the
listening Sea—

and behind me, over my shoulder
the Tyger growls—
chewing the bones of his prey to splinters
in a keening, crying Wind.

II

and the wind in the leaves
is the voices of women
wailing in love
or lamentation—
coiling whispers around the treetrunks—
drawing long shimmering cadences
through the five-fingered strings of branches,
and making an anguish of visible pleasure

that moves through the forest
like the cries of living violins
as the bow draws over the nipples
releasing a wind of singing
that shivers in the branches
and through the branches of my flesh
like ripples through a
shaft of smoke.

(exotic poisons:
vitalities coursing
through rock & wood:
the war outside
by bomb, or dollar,
is ground through
wheels of Nature—
or Nature herself,
moaning
like this,
makes war outside
this canyon:
(the question
should be: not
Which is Origin, Man
or what he sees,
but:
Where can I work—
in these cool and
harpstringed elements,
or in the gut
of the machine
made of human hands
these elements see
in their Mirror?

If anyone thinks it is a "good" poem, this simply demonstrates the great gulf that exists between the aesthetic dimension and the spiritual dimension, though spiritual truth can certainly express itself by way of aesthetic beauty. The Qur'an calls the Jinn-inspired poets of pre-Islamic Arabia those who *say that which they do not*, and Rumi, the greatest poet of Islam, had the following to say about his art:

> My disposition is such that I don't want anyone to suffer on my account. . . . I am loved by those who come to see me, and so I compose poetry to entertain them lest they grow weary. Otherwise, why on earth would I be spouting poetry? I am vexed by poetry. I don't think there is anything worse. It is like having to put one's hands into tripe to wash it for one's guests because they have an appetite for it. That is why I must do it.[33]

Session Two: a First Bardo trip, the Bardo of "the Clear Light of the Void", the "set" for which I had posited by reading the *Diamond Sutra* and the *Heart Sutra* right before ingestion: No hallucinations, no visual or auditory distortions, simply the obvious fact that experience could go along quite happily with no *experiencer* there at all; as the Beatles put it, "Life goes on within you and without you." And since "I" was empty of self-nature, essentially snuffed out, the world I saw—immense, beautiful, snow-capped mountains, viewed in pristine clarity—was equally empty. Nothing really there. This self-and-world annihilation only persisted, however, when I was alone; as soon as I approached another human being—a girl in this case—"I" began to come back into existence; from this I learned that relatedness, or polarity, is the principle of all manifestation—a truth that the Buddhists call "Indra's Net". As the *Heart Sutra* puts it: "Form is emptiness; emptiness is form". Precisely.

Session Three: probably a Third Bardo trip, "the Bardo of Seeking Rebirth", a condition in which ego-transcendence is blocked, and consequently the tripper (or the consciousness-principle after phys-

33. Jalal al-Din Rumi, *Signs of the Unseen: The Discourses of Jelaluddin Rumi*, trans. W. M. Thackston, Jr. (Putney, VT: Threshold Books, 1994), p. 77.

ical death) is experiencing the pain and suffering of chaos, leading him to attempt to escape from this chaos into some kind of stable form that isn't exploding in a million directions all the time. My "set" here may not have been as pure as that of Session Two, since I had already begun to read the books of "sorcerer" Carlos Castaneda [1925–1998],[34] whom I met on one occasion. I had a brief experience of the higher reaches of the Second Bardo when the world appeared as a "tree" whose fruit was a constellation of Buddha or Bodhisattva images as in a Tibetan *thanka* (sacred painting), but it didn't last; for the rest of the time I was just waiting to come down. When I closed my eyes the cactuses and thorny chaparral bushes of the desert around me were reproduced as writhing, thorn-studded whips or cables, like the ocotillo plant. I stared at my Toyota Land Cruiser and just couldn't make out *what it was*: it looked like an ever-shifting 17-dimensional arrangement of wheels, pulleys and intersecting planes, like an M.C. Escher print. In this trip, like my two psilocybin trips, I was mostly just "doing time".

SBS: From your own point of view why would you consider these psychedelic experiences—"good trips" or "bad trips"—and what criteria could be used to asses this?

CU: To answer this question I need to define what "good trip" and "bad trip" usually meant to the hippies: a good trip was one that felt good, a bad trip, one that felt bad. Moral or intellectual or spiritual criteria were rarely applied; the most common standard of judgment was hedonistic—though some trippers were capable of realizing that the pain of certain psychedelic experiences might teach one something or work as a psychic catharsis. From that point of view, my first trip was mostly "good", my second trip "good", and my third trip mostly "bad"—though nowhere near as bad as a *real* bad trip, filled with paranoia and panic.

34. See Charles Upton, "The Postmodern Traveler: Don Carlos Castaneda" in *The System of Antichrist: Truth and Falsehood in Postmodernism and the New Age* (Ghent, NY: Sophia Perennis, 2001), pp. 201–221; Richard de Mille, *Castaneda's Journey: The Power and the Allegory* (Santa Barbara, CA: Capra Press, 1976); Amy Wallace, *Sorcerer's Apprentice: My Life with Carlos Castaneda* (Berkeley, CA: Frog, 2003).

From the standpoint of spiritual insight, the second session was the only *real* "trip"—and it was the only one in which I wasn't going anywhere. It showed me the possibility and reality of ego-transcendence (though not how to attain it on any stable basis), and taught me, as I said above, that existence is fundamentally relational. The first session showed me the existence of another "world", specifically the "etheric plane", the layer of the intermediate or psychic plane where the elementals reside; that started me on a long series of excursions into the elf-world, probably because, without my knowing it, LSD had permanently breached the natural energy-barrier or "etheric wall" between my material and subtle (*not* Spiritual) levels of consciousness—the microcosmic analogue of the "Great Wall" René Guénon speaks of in *The Reign of Quantity and the Signs of the Times* [1953]. This left me with a lifelong over-sensitivity to psychic forces that has produced many experiences of great pain over the years, made it hard for me to meditate (too much psychic "static"), and caused me to be vulnerable to demonic attack. If any good came of this condition it was limited to an ability to "listen in", as it were, to the councils of the demons, and find out something about what they are up to on a collective level, so that I can avoid certain of their influences and warn others.

The third session was just sad; all I learned from that one was, "no more LSD".

SBS: Do you have any further reflections on these experiences in light of your present-day outlook on psychedelics? Did your use of psychedelics prompt you to enter a more sustaining spiritual path? And do you still use psychedelics in conjunction with your spiritual practice?

CU: Yes: the conclusion that, from the spiritual perspective, *no* trip is good—especially if one is actually able to access higher consciousness or "see God" by means of it (assuming, of course, that these experiences are not delusions, or so mixed with delusionary elements that the way to the valid experiences and insights they counterfeit is not in fact blocked forever). If you drop acid, see horrible hallucinations and experience excruciating feelings of loneliness, degradation and fear, you may actually be luckier than if you experience "ecstasy" and "profound insight" and "consciousness of

God", if not (momentary) "liberation from the wheel of becoming". If you break your way into the Inner Chamber on your own initiative, you have committed sacrilege—how can you ever become obedient to and annihilated in God's will if you think you have the right to break into His house any time the fancy suits you? I am not saying that the higher consciousness that can on certain occasions be experienced through psychedelics may not sometimes have a positive effect on one's life and outlook—but at what cost?

Dr. Javad Nurbakhsh [1926–2008], my first Sufi shaykh, strictly prohibited the use of all drugs, including psychedelics. My 20 years under his guidance were mostly spent laboriously recollecting and healing the psyche I had blown to the four winds through the use of psychedelics, and also undoubtedly through the abuse of kundalini-yoga practiced without benefit of a teacher and a tradition. If I had never entered the Sufi path, however, I might never have seen just how damaged I was; I might have tripped on from one psychic state to another and never realized that I was headed for destruction, if not in this world then certainly in the next. In the words of the Noble Qur'an, *God guides aright whom He will and leads astray whom He will.... God is the best of plotters.* And as for whether or not psychedelics in some way prompted me to enter the Sufi path, that is hard to answer. I entered that path because God called me. Whether He called me through certain valid insights or salutary warnings provided by psychedelics is by and large irrelevant. If you find God after being disappointed in love or wounded in war, does this mean you can recommend such experiences to other people as a way of finding God? All these trappings of personal destiny are at best irrelevant, and at worst a case of idolatry. If you worship the occasion you will never find the Essence; if you worship the means you will never reach the End. It may be that psychedelics were part of the occasion for my entry into the Spiritual Path, but the occasion is not the cause. And I haven't used any psychedelic substance, including marijuana, for over 20 years.

SBS: In response to your comments about the implicit dangers of having a "good" trip versus a "bad" trip due to the nature of the experience, could not such an experience be a "door opener" to an authentic spiritual path, if not grasped on to—"When you get the message, hang up the phone."?[35] Especially in light of the many seekers that have had psychedelic experiences and have nonetheless formally affiliated themselves within a revealed tradition. Most notably Huston Smith (b. 1919) comes to mind, would you mind elaborating?

CU: It could be; clearly it has been for some people. But its function as a door-opener is often overshadowed by the fact that psychedelic experience is so intense that all later spiritual experience and practice tend to pale by comparison; you keep judging them, consciously or unconsciously, as to whether they "measure up" to LSD. Huston Smith once complained to me that even after years of spiritual practice in a variety of traditions, notably Sufism, he was never able to "regain" the level of opening and insight provided by acid. That's the problem in a nutshell: to attempt to bring back the former glory of one's psychedelic days is to reject, often in total unconsciousness, what God is offering you *now*. God's will for you is always in the present, whereas, in the words of William Blake [1757–1827], "Memory is Eternal Death". In the Sufi view, the Spiritual Path is not the quest for higher consciousness but the purification of the soul from anything that would block the influx of higher consciousness. In light of this conception, experiences of rigor and abasement and contraction (*qabd*) are as important as experiences of spiritual expansion (*bast*); Ibn Ata'allah [d. 1309] even says that there is much more danger of violating spiritual courtesy (*adab*) with God in a state of *bast* than in a state of *qabd*—and to beg or demand that God bring back a past state as you remember it is certainly the height of discourtesy, besides being impossible. Furthermore, after LSD, it is very hard to overcome the illusion that God is an *experience*.

SBS: The socio-historical context in which psychedelics first emerged onto the public domain is very interesting and there are probably many who even partook in the psychedelic experience without knowing the nefarious context in which their mass dissemination to the American public took place. Many individuals might

35. Alan Watts, *The Joyous Cosmology: Adventures in the Chemistry of Consciousness* (NY: Vintage, 1965), p. 26. (Please note that this quote is not found in the original 1962 edition).

be alarmed to know that the National Survey on Drug Use and Health (NSDUH) reported in 2007 that approximately 34.2 million Americans aged 12 and older (or 13.8% of the population) reported trying hallucinogens at least one time and some might argue that these numbers are quite low and underestimate the mass and widespread use.

CU: And we also need, not just to remember, but to grasp the full import of, the fact that LSD was first distributed in the United States by the CIA, partly in the context of the infamous MK-ULTRA mind-control program, which included experiments practiced upon unsuspecting American citizens that were worthy to stand beside those conducted in the Nazi death-camps (see the research of David McGowan, Henry Makow and Peter Levenda; also see *Endnote IV*). Timothy Leary was assigned to feed acid to the intelligentsia, Ken Kesey [1935–2001] to everybody else; the idea was to compare how it acted under "controlled conditions" with its effects in a totally free-wheeling, "party" atmosphere. And the hippies actually knew about this! They said, "SURE we were a CIA experiment, man—an experiment that GOT OUT OF CONTROL!" (See *Endnote V*). But the fact is that LSD initiated a sort of "bardo" or revelatory decay of American culture; all the latent tendencies, good and bad, the dominant belief-systems, conscious or otherwise, were called up in a very short time, laid out for all to see—and much of the social and cultural potential of America and the Western World rapidly exhausted in the process. The family was largely destroyed (not by LSD alone of course); Christian morality (including the concept of human dignity) was undermined; political responsibility was seriously eroded. And the social engineers simply sat back and took notes. They noted the main trends, the major "cultural archetypes" operating in the "collective unconscious" of society, and devised various ways to appropriate, pervert and control every one of them; in so doing they initiated the world we live in today. The hippies naively equated social control with a simplistic authoritarian repression; they rarely awoke to the fact that REAL control is based on co-optation, on the covert implantation of engineered beliefs and attitudes in the mass mind. The powers that be do not want heroes who courageously oppose them and die as martyrs;

they would much rather find, or create, dupes who will obey their every command in the firm belief that they are following their own desires, their own creative expressions and "spiritual" intuitions, all in perfect freedom.

One other deleterious effect of psychedelics, which has clearly operated on the mass level (though not in every individual case), is that they broke down people's protection against the surrounding psychic environment; first you "open up" too much, and then compensate by "closing down" so as to protect yourself from the painful influences emanating from your surroundings, including other people. Excess empathy ends in paranoia; the artificial breaking down of what psychologist Wilhelm Reich [1897–1957] called "character armor" often results in a worse case of such armor later on. (Perennialist Titus Burckhardt [1908–1984], in his book *Alchemy: Science of the Cosmos, Science of the Soul* [1986], speaks of the close relationship between psycho-physical dissolution and psycho-physical petrification.) As Jesus put it, the demon we have exorcized wanders in waterless places until, returning to the soul from which he has been expelled and finding it swept and adorned, he brings with him seven demons more evil than himself. We probably could never have produced a society where millions spend hours a day alone before computer screens—while imagining that, via Twitter or whatever, they actually have thousands of "friends"!—if LSD hadn't softened us up first; the isolation and excess introversion produced in part by psychedelics has effectively broken down the kind of social solidarity we need if we are to maintain our political freedoms and human rights; we are all too happy in our cubicles, or at least afraid to leave them. A friend of mine once said to me, back in the 60s: "Acid would be great if you could have all that incredible imagery without those *feelings*". Bill Gates must have heard his plea; cyberspace reproduces in many ways the hallucinatory content of psychedelics without the accompanying insights.

And now government-sponsored psychedelic research is making a comeback. Anyone tempted to become involved with it should first do some in-depth research on exactly which individuals and institutions are sponsoring, publicizing and funding such a move, as well as their background and connections (what is the Internet for, after all?). Looking back over the cultural and spiritual "scorched earth" of the psychedelic revolution in the years since the 60's, I shudder to think what they may have in store for us now. We should never forget that the CIA likely sponsored the *mass* dissemination of LSD as part of their MK-ULTRA mind control program. According to Peter Levenda, William Mellon Hitchcock, who was associated with CIA front organizations Castle Bank and Trust and Resorts International, as well as being Timothy Leary's landlord for his "psychedelic manor house" at Millbrook, paid a chemist by the name of Nicholas Sand [b. 1941] to produce *millions* of doses of acid.[36] Another figure from the psychedelic underground that should be mentioned along with Sand is his collaborator chemist Robert "Tim" Scully [b. 1944]; together they produced enormous quantities of LSD known in these circles as "Orange Sunshine."

SBS: While you have elaborated on the psychic and spiritual dangers of using psychedelics,[37] there are many individuals and researchers that affirm the healing potential of such substances. After a three decade hiatus there is now renewed interest in psychedelic research and they are increasingly being studied as possible

36. Peter Levenda, *Sinister Forces—A Grimoire of American Political Witchcraft: A Warm Gun* (Waterville, OR: TrineDay, 2006), p. 317). See also Art Kleps, *Millbrook: The True Story of the Early Years of the Psychedelic Revolution* (Oakland, CA: Bench Press, 1977); Martin A. Lee and Bruce Shlain, "Preaching LSD" in *Acid Dreams: The Complete Social History of LSD: The CIA, the Sixties, and Beyond* (NY: Grove Press, 1992), pp. 97–100; Stanley Krippner, "Music to Eat Mushrooms By" in *Song of the Siren: A Parapsychological Odyssey* (NY: Harper & Row, 1977), pp. 19–45.

37. For some examples see John C. Lilly, *The Scientist: A Novel Autobiography* (NY: J. B. Lippincott, 1978); Aleister Crowley, *Diary of a Drug Fiend* (York Beach, ME: Samuel Weiser, 1997); Tom Wolfe, *The Electric Kool-Aid Acid Test* (NY: Farrar, Straus and Giroux, 1968); Wade Davis, "The Red Hotel" in *One River: Explorations and Discoveries in the Amazon Rain Forest* (NY: Touchstone, 1997), pp. 151–152; Terence McKenna, *True Hallucinations: Being an Account of the Author's Extraordinary Adventures in the Devil's Paradise* (NY: HarperCollins, 1994); Terence McKenna and Dennis McKenna, "Psychological Reflections on La Chorrera" in *The Invisible Landscape: Mind, Hallucinogens, and the I Ching* (NY: HarperCollins, 1994), pp. 109–117; Laurent Weichberger (ed.), *A Mirage Will Never Quench Your Thirst: A Source of Wisdom About Drugs* (North Myrtle Beach, SC: Sheriar Foundation, 2003); Charles Hayes (ed.), *Tripping: An Anthology of True-Life Psychedelic Adventures* (NY: Penguin Books, 2000).

adjuncts to psychotherapy for various psycho-physical ailments: treatment-resistant anxiety disorders, post-traumatic stress disorder (PTSD), pain associated with terminal and end-stage cancer, cluster headaches, obsessive-compulsive disorder (OCD), alcohol,[38] cocaine and heroin dependency to name a few (See *Endnote VI*). Could you please comment on this matter?

CU: The use of toxic pharmaceuticals and traumatic interventions is common and sometimes necessary in the practice of medicine, but these things have little or nothing to do with the Spiritual Path per se. Psychedelics—whose toxicity is by and large psychic, not physical—may have a therapeutic effect in cases of alcoholism, heroin addiction etc., but this doesn't mean that they create no problems of their own; it's a question of the lesser of two evils. And what may be a lesser evil in psychophysical terms may or may not be a lesser one in Spiritual terms. Our post-Christian secular society obviously does not have the final end and eternal good of the human soul on its radar screen, nor does it hold a very clear idea of human dignity or the intrinsic value of the person; abortion, for example, is not even seen by many people as the taking of human life. Our society has no concept of suffering as spiritual purgation (by which I certainly don't mean to imply that all suffering is purifying simply because it hurts); its highest good seems to be *production*, consequently it tends to define healing in terms of making us "productive members of society". There are even muted but increasingly audible suggestions that non-productive citizens ought to be euthanized; Bill Gates recently stated that a certain degree of medi-

38. William Griffith Wilson, more commonly known as Bill Wilson (1895–1971), the co-founder of Alcoholics Anonymous (A.A.) was convinced of the therapeutic potential of psychedelics, especially LSD with alcoholism. It is reported that Gerald Heard (1889–1971), close friend and colleague of Aldous Huxley, in 1956 guided Bill Wilson on an LSD session which had profound and lasting impact on his life. Interesting to note that like Huxley it was Dr. Osmond who first drew Wilson's attention to psychedelics. See also *'Pass It On': The Story of Bill Wilson and How the A.A. Message Reached the World* (NY: Alcoholics Anonymous World Services, 1984); Betty Eisner, "The Birth and Death of Psychedelic Therapy" in Roger Walsh and Charles S. Grob (eds.), *Higher Wisdom: Eminent Elders Explore the Continuing Impact of Psychedelics* (Albany, NY: SUNY Press, 2005), pp. 93–94.

cal care ought to be denied the elderly and diverted to the maintenance of productive workers. And now, under the "war on terror", torture has become acceptable to us for the first time since the passage of the Bill of Rights. How can a society capable of such barbaric actions and sentiments be relied upon to accurately evaluate the effects of psychedelic drugs in either moral or spiritual terms?

Afterword

CU: Some time after granting this interview, I talked with a physician acquaintance of mine who had participated in the second round of psilocybin experiments within academia in the 1990's; I hadn't realized they had started up again that early. He investigated the source of the funding for the experiment he'd been part of at the University of New Mexico, and discovered that the money for the DMT research that led up to the experiments he had been involved in had been provided by the Scottish Rite Foundation for Schizophrenia Research—the Freemasons! (See *Endnote VII.*) In view of the fact that many traditional Catholics see the Second Vatican Council as a kind of Masonic coup within the Catholic Church, the apparent "coincidence" that psychedelic drugs became available to the masses at exactly the same time that traditional Roman Catholicism was being destroyed may in fact be much more than that; as René Guénon pointed out, though cyclical conditions may make the growth of the Counter-Initiation possible, the concrete manifestations of this counterfeit, Luciferian spirituality can only be brought about by actual human groups. Dr. Rama P. Coomaraswamy [1929–2006] in his essay "The Problem of Obedience", unpublished in hardcopy but available on the web, recounts the following:

> [A] leading Freemason, Yves Marsoudon (State Master, Supreme Council of France, Scottish Rite) tells us: "The sense of universalism that is rampant in Rome these days is very close to our purpose of existence.... With all our hearts we support the 'Revolution of John XXIII'...." Not satisfied with this, Yves Marsoudon dedicated his book *Ecumenism as Seen by a*

> *Traditionalist Freemason* to the Pope in the following words: "To the Memory of Angelo Roncalli, Priest, Archbishop of Messembria, Apostolic Nuncio in Paris, Cardinal of the Roman Church, Patriarch of Venice, POPE under the name of John XXIII, WHO HAS DEIGNED TO GIVE US HIS BENEDICTION, HIS UNDERSTANDING AND HIS PROTECTION."[39]

And then, shortly after that conversation, I had a dream—a dream filled with flaming apocalyptic imagery which represented *the glory of God*. When I woke up, I realized that I was in fact being purified of the psychic residues of LSD, which I last ingested over 35 years ago. In light of this dream I began to understand in a much different light the tendency of all other spiritual states or practices to pale in comparison with the LSD experience. We may sincerely say, and believe, something on the order of: "I took LSD several times; later I practiced a Sufi *dhikr* for several years. Looking back on these experiences, I can now truthfully report that the LSD provided a more intense spiritual state and a greater depth of insight than did the *dhikr*." In making this judgment we assume of course that we are objectively comparing two experiences from a standpoint of detachment, that the scales we are using to weigh these experiences against each other are fundamentally sound. What almost never occurs to us is that LSD may have *imprinted* or *conditioned* a deeply-buried layer of our psyche such that all subsequent experiences of any psychic or spiritual depth are *filtered* through this conditioning, resulting in a biased evaluation. If it is possible to have LSD "flashbacks" years after the original experience, who is to say that a subtle "hangover", physically undetectable, or perhaps indicated by a potentially measurable "re-programming" of the brain due to the extreme intensity of psychedelic experience, may also remain in the deep psyche?

The fact that Richard Alpert, aka Ram Dass [b. 1931], was told by his Hindu yoga instructors, "You have a *kundalini*-blockage in your *vishuddha-chakra* [throat center] due to your past use of psychedel-

39. See Rama Coomaraswamy, "Catholic Writings" at the following website: *www.the-pope.com/coomcawr.html*

ics", supports this hypothesis. It's as if LSD can act to breach the natural barrier between *Nous/Intellectus*, associated with the *ajña-chakra* or "third eye", and *dianoia/ratio*, associated with the *vishuddha-chakra*, thus flooding the lower rational mind with material from the higher Intellectual mind; the lower mind becomes overloaded with this higher material, now expressed on a lower level, and ends by counterfeiting the quality of the *Nous/Intellectus* and thus blocking access to it. Consequently, if spiritual methods practiced and spiritual states experienced after LSD seem in some sense to lie in the shadow of acid, this may simply mean that acid is still there, casting that shadow. The import of my dream was that the *glory of God* had arrived in order to burn out the residual psychic *glamour* left behind by psychedelics, and purify my soul of their ongoing influence; I attribute this event to the spiritual effect of my entry into my second Sufi order. It may in fact be the case that the use of LSD has the power to subtly damage the highest reflections of *Nous/Intellectus*, the "eye of the heart" [*'ayn al-qalb*], in the individual psyche, just as the physical eye may be damaged by staring into the sun; the reason we almost never become aware of this damage is that it lies at a psycho-spiritual depth so great that we are rarely able to consciously return to it *without once more ingesting LSD*, thus compounding the damage. The use of powerful psychedelics may also produce in us a taste, or need, for deep spiritual experiences that we otherwise would never have sought out, and that may not really be proper to us, while at the same time preventing such experiences from translating us to the final station, where (in Sufi terminology) *fana*—spiritual annihilation—gives way to *baqa*—subsistence in God. Like Moses, we may be left standing on the mountain, looking down to where the Children of Israel are crossing over into the Promised Land, but eternally denied entrance into that land ourselves as punishment for the sin, while searching for water, of striking the rock twice instead of only once as our Lord commanded—in terms of spiritual realization, the sin of trying to force the hand of God. Furthermore, those who are brought so near to the *mysterium tremendum* while being denied the final consummation may be subject to Luciferian temptations that the rest of us will probably never encounter, chief among them being the temptation to embrace a Luciferian consummation in a counterfeit Absolute designed in the infernal regions. Anyone who succumbs to such a temptation (which will most likely be presented to him or her in the deep unconscious regions of the soul), or is even confronted with it—assuming that the victim is not able to allow God to heal the psycho-spiritual damage that makes him or her susceptible to it—may effectively be denied Union with Absolute Reality for the remainder of this life, and possibly also the next.

Endnotes

ENDNOTE I (page 209): For an interesting discussion on the distinctions between the subtle and nondual states of consciousness see the following two part video with Ken Wilber (b. 1949), a pioneer within transpersonal psychology, speaking about the uses of *Ayahuasca* or *Yajé* and psychedelics in general highlighting the obstacles and dangers of their use to authentic spiritual growth: *http://www.youtube.com/watch?v=*. After viewing the two video clips by Wilber, Charles Upon stated the following: "People do take psychedelics hoping for spiritual transformation, and a simple 'just say no to drugs' will not influence many of them; in view of this, Wilber did a good job of putting psychedelics in an insightful context when he said that their best use is to teach you that the most impressive visionary states and realized insights are not Absolute Reality since they all pass away; only the Atman, the Witness that witnesses them, is Absolute. This is something like the Sufi doctrine that spiritual states happen in relation to specific ego-attachments in order to burn out those attachments, after which the states in question do not return; the realized Sufi is beyond states. One difference between states based on drugs and states sent by God, however, is that drug-induced states can be psychologically habit-forming—largely because it is possible to pop the 'same' pill again and again, imagining you can repeat an earlier state—but it is not possible to induce God to send the same state again, seeing that *Every day doth some new work employ Him* (Qur'an 55:29). A massive expansion of psychic experience is in no way an unmitigated good, since it can either wear away one's attachment to experience in favor of the Witness or veil the Witness by inflaming one's desire for more and more experience." With this said, Wilber should not be considered a "friend" of the perennial philosophy or the spiritual traditions themselves, nor a representative of the traditionalist or perennialist school for he has methodically undermined and attacked the integral metaphysics of the perennial philosophy, first as an insider by aligning himself with this universal orientation and then by attempting to usurp the traditions within the fold of his ever inclusive evolutionary and syncretic AQAL Model—all quadrants, all levels, all lines, all states and all types. If Wilber has his way in superimposing his hegemonic integralism upon the spiritual traditions of the world, Hinduism will no longer be Hinduism but Integral Hinduism, Buddhism will no longer be Buddhism but Integral Buddhism, Christianity will no longer be Christianity but Integral Christianity, Islam will no longer be Islam but Integral Islam and so on—which is nothing less than the insurgence of Wilberianism on a totalitarian scale. Will an integral New Age spirituality also be put on the table, as some have suggested, by the absurd notion of integral theosophy which would wed Helena Petrovna Blavatsky (1831–1891) and Ken Wilber? This could not be anything other than pseudo-spirituality at its height. Despite the fact that Carl Gustav Jung (1875–1961) appeared to be a "friend" of spirituality, he in reality and to the surprise of many psychologized these traditions; Wilber in a similar fashion not only supersedes but champions his forerunner, going above and beyond by Absolutizing his integralism. The fact that Wilber and his comrades of the Integral Institute cannot perceive the integral nature of each sapiential tradition *in divinis* calls into question their very understanding of the world's spiritualities, yet from another perspective this speaks to the very postmodern narcissism that they have painstakingly discussed *ad nauseam*, a symptom that he and many of his con-temporaries, strangely enough given the circumstances, have not been able to evade. That the postmodern mentality has become emaciated and is unable to perceive the inner dimension or esoterism of the "transcendent unity of religions" in no way signifies that these divinely revealed traditions need to be updated to appeal to this atrophied outlook; to do so would be a *reductio ad absurdum*. See José Segura, "On Ken Wilber's Integration of Science and Religion", *Sacred Web: A Journal of Tradition and Modernity*, Vol. 5 (Summer 2005), pp. 71–83; Samuel Bendeck Sotillos, "Book Review: Frithjof Schuon and the Perennial Philosophy", *International Journal of Transpersonal Studies*, Vol. 29, No. 1 (2010), pp. 138–142; Samuel Bendeck Sotillos, "Book Review: The Return of the Perennial Philosophy", *Sacred Web: A Journal of Tradition and Modernity*, Vol. 25 (Summer 2010), pp. 175–184.

In looking at the "four forces" of modern psychology, some might ask where does Ken Wilber's "integral psychology", which some are calling a "fifth force", fit into this critique? In response, we would like to repeat that while Wilber at one time strongly identified with the integral metaphysics of the perennial philosophy he has incrementally distanced himself from this perspective and, as we have seen, has become fundamentally hostile to the perennial philosophy and even attempts to absorb it within the fold of his "integralism". While we cannot expand here upon Ken Wilber's relationship with the traditionalists or the perennial philosophy, we need to emphasize that when we refer to "integral psychology" it is inextricably linked to the perennial philosophy and has nothing to do with Wilber's usage of the term. Furthermore, while some might attribute Wilber's "Integral Movement" to Jean Gebser (1905–1973) or Sri Aurobindo (1872–

1950), who have both heavily influenced Wilber's work, it needs to be said that both René Guénon and Frithjof Schuon used the epithet "integral" throughout their work long before Wilber made it his singular trademark. In reviewing the opus of Guénon and Schuon, we find references to integral metaphysics, integral anthropology, integral knowledge, integral development, integral realization, integral individuality and even integral spirituality which are not based on individualistic speculation but on universal principles that are common to all sapiential traditions, according to the principle known as the "transcendent unity of religions". This is relevant when recalling the fundamental influence that the traditionalists, especially Schuon, have had upon Wilber's decisive work, *The Spectrum of Consciousness* (1977). While we do not wish to claim a monopoly on the usage of "integral", we do need to mention these other potential influences upon Wilber's work, especially since the perennial philosophy once permeated his theoretical vision. Although Wilber's so-called integral psychology ambitiously attempts to synthesize the best of the premodern, modern and postmodern conceptions, it remains true to none of them; it is not really "integral" in the traditional or perennialist sense but is merely a case of Wilber cloaking himself in the garb of the saints and sages of all times and places while attempting to give them a face-lift. Let us conclude by affirming that nothing could be more precarious than to assume that the spiritual traditions of the world need to be updated or that they need Wilber to do so.

ENDNOTE II (p. 219): Mircea Eliade, *Shamanism: Archaic Techniques of Ecstasy*, trans. Willard R. Trask (Princeton, NJ: Princeton University Press, 1974), p. 401. While it has been indicated that Eliade shifted his position with regards to psychedelics at the end of his life as noted by anthropologist Peter Furst: "[entheogens] forced him to change his mind on this issue, and ... to accept that there was no essential difference between ecstasy achieved by plant hallucinogens and that obtained by other archaic techniques." [Paul Devereux, *The Long Trip: A Prehistory of Psychedelia* (NY: Penguin Books, 1997), p. 108]. We would still argue that his initial assessment makes an important point in light of cyclical time which all traditional societies throughout the world adhered to and still to this day recognize; Karl Kerényi (1897–1973) noted Hungarian mythologist and professor of classics and the history of religion agrees with Eliade's initial position: "For a time, an artificially induced experience of transcendence in nature was able to replace the original experience. In the history of religions, periods of 'strong medicine' [entheogens] usually occur when the simpler methods no longer suffice. This development may be observed among the North American Indians. Originally mere fasting sufficed to induce visions. It was only in the decadent period of [North American] Indian culture that recourse was taken to peyotl, or mescalin. Earlier it was unnecessary. This powerful drug had not always been an element in the style of [North American] Indian life, but it helped to maintain this style." [Karl Kerényi, *Dionysos: Archetypal Image of Indestructible Life*, trans. Ralph Manheim (New Jersey, NJ: Princeton University Press, 1996), p. 26]; "In fact, there is reason to believe that much, not all, but much of this [psychedelic using] culture constitutes more of a degeneracy when compared with the possibility of what one will call golden age spirituality where a man was his own priest and carried Heaven's Law directly and naturally within himself and had access, through his intellect, to divine and earthly wisdom. Immanence of divine wisdom is the human norm." [Mark Perry, "The Forbidden Door" in *Every Branch in Me: Essays on the Meaning of Man*, ed. Barry McDonald (Bloomington, IN: World Wisdom, 2002), p. 271]; See also Peter T. Furst, "Introduction: An Overview of Shamanism" in *Ancient Traditions: Shamanism in Central Asia and the Americas*, eds. Gary Seaman and Jane S. Day (Niwot, CO: University Press of Colorado, 1994), pp. 1–28.

ENDNOTE III (p. 223): Marlene Dobkin de Rios, "Drug Tourism in the Amazon", *Anthropology of Consciousness*, Vol. 5, No. 1 (1994), pp. 16–19; One can perceive the tumultuous effects of this quest for altered states of consciousness in the lamenting words of María Sabina (1894–1985), the contemporary Mexican shaman from Huautla de Jiménez of Oaxaca: "Before Wasson, I felt that the *saint children* elevated me. I don't feel like that anymore. The force has diminished. If Cayetano hadn't brought the foreigners . . . the saint children would have kept their power. . . . From the moment the foreigners arrived, the *saint children* lost their purity. They lost their force; the foreigners spoiled them. From now on they won't be any good. There's no remedy for it." [R. Gordon Wasson, "A Retrospective Essay" in Álvaro Estrada, *María Sabina: Her Life and Chants*, trans. Henry Munn (Santa Barbara, CA: Ross-Erikson, 1981), p. 20]; Michael Winkelman, "Drug Tourism or Spiritual Healing? Ayahuasca Seekers in Amazonia", *Journal of Psychoactive Drugs*, Vol. 37, No. 2 (2005), pp. 209–218; Marlene Dobkin de Rios and Róger Rumrrill, "Drug Tourism" in *A Hallucinogenic Tea, Laced with Controversy: Ayahuasca in the Amazon and the United States* (Westport, CT: Praeger, 2008), pp. 69–86; Kenneth W. Tupper, "Ayahuasca Healing Beyond the Amazon: The Globalization of a Traditional Indigenous Entheogenic Practice", *Global Networks: A Journal of Transnational Affairs*, Vol. 9, No. 1 (2009), pp. 117–136; Marlene Dobkin de

Rios "Psychedelics and Drug Tourism" in *The Psychedelic Journey of Marlene Dobkin de Rios: 45 Years with Shamans, Ayahuasqueros, and Ethnobotanists* (Rochester, VT: Park Street Press, 2009), pp. 166–169. See also R. Gordon Wasson, "Seeking the Magic Mushroom", *Life*, May 13, 1957, pp. 101–120; William S. Burroughs and Allen Ginsberg, *The Yage Letters* (San Francisco, CA: City Lights Books, 1975); Terence McKenna, *True Hallucinations: Being an Account of the Author's Extraordinary Adventures in the Devil's Paradise* (NY: HarperCollins, 1994); Susana Valadez, "Guided Tour Spirituality: Cosmic Way or Cosmic Rip-off?" *Shaman's Drum*, No. 6 (1986), pp. 4–6; We might add on a final note that even though New Age representatives such as Deepak Chopra (b. 1946), who reports that he had his first "spiritual experience" when he was seventeen years old through ingesting LSD, warns against recreational uses of psychedelics he nonetheless indiscriminately advises seekers eliciting such experiences to find an authentic traditional shaman in South America who will provide guidance on the use of these sacred plants. However, he says nothing about how this is to be accomplished nor does he warn against the many obstacles in finding such a traditional guide; furthermore he says nothing about the potential psychological dangers even if such an individual was to be found. See the following video clip: *http://www.youtube.com/watch?v=C*; Chopra is a former disciple of the controversial figure Maharishi Mahesh Yogi (1914-2000), founder of the secular technique of Transcendental Meditation; see also Charles Upton, "Having It vs. Eating It: The Entrepreneurial Hinduism of Deepak Chopra" in *The System of Antichrist: Truth and Falsehood in Postmodernism and the New Age* (Ghent, NY: Sophia Perennis, 2001), pp. 267–284; Rama P. Coomaraswamy, "The Desacralization of Hinduism for Western Consumption", *Sophia: The Journal of Traditional Studies*, Vol. 4, No. 2 (Winter 1998), pp. 194–219.

ENDNOTE IV (p. 239): Interestingly enough, James Fadiman (b. 1939), a pioneer within both humanistic and transpersonal psychology and cofounder of the Institute of Transpersonal Psychology (ITP), worked at the VA hospital in Palo Alto, California in a program that was administering psychedelics and researching their behavioral effects on veterans. In 1965 Fadiman completed his doctoral dissertation at Stanford University on this research, which was entitled: "Behavioral Change Following (LSD) Psychedelic Therapy." "In the shadows, the CIA had tried to use these [psychedelics] substances to confuse and terrify people. Through front organizations, the CIA also sponsored small conferences and publications where therapists and researchers shared their findings." [James Fadiman, "Therapeutic Effectiveness of Single Guided Sessions" in *The Psychedelic Explorer's*

Guide: Safe, Therapeutic, and Sacred Journeys (Rochester, VT: Park Street Press, 2011), p. 104]. In response to the above citation, Charles Upton notes: "The idea that the CIA wanted to use psychedelics to 'confuse and terrify' people is true as far as it goes, but they also apparently hoped that these substances could help their own agents gain magic powers: telepathy, remote viewing, etc. And they were entirely willing to confuse and delight people if that would serve their ends. The hippy myth that the CIA were a bunch of uptight straight people who 'couldn't hold their acid' and saw it only as a crazy-making pill needs to be permanently debunked. The Bohemian/magician/secret agent is a well-known type; both occultist John Dee [1527–1608/1609] (the original 007) and Satanist Aleister Crowley worked for British Intelligence. The ultimate goal of the powers-that-be in terms of psychedelic research may be to create a type of 'spirituality' where even mystical experiences that are valid on a certain level will serve to establish their control. They want to own everything—even mysticism, even spiritual aspiration, even God." See also Jay Stevens, Storming Heaven: LSD and the American Dream (NY: Grove Press, 1987); Martin A. Lee and Bruce Shlain, Acid Dreams: *The Complete Social History of LSD: The CIA, the Sixties, and Beyond* (NY: Grove Press, 1992); Richard B. Spence, *Secret Agent 666: Aleister Crowley, British Intelligence and the Occult* (Port Townsend, WA: Feral House, 2008).

ENDNOTE V (p. 239): It is useful to recall that Adi Da or Franklin Albert Jones (1939–2008), who Ken Wilber regarded as the "the greatest living Realizer", this being only one of a host of other extraordinary endorsements offered by Wilber in his praise, and who considered himself the first and last seventh stage Adept above all other saints and sages of the perennial philosophy, was, interestingly enough, a scientologist before becoming the first American Avatar. It is widely known that Adi Da has had a tremendous influence upon Wilber's work and that of quite a few others within the general humanistic and transpersonal orientation, many of whom prefer to be anonymous disciples from afar in order to escape the numerous controversies and criticism surrounding Adi Da. In light of this, it would be interesting to inquire into how many ideas Wilber has contributed to both humanistic and transpersonal psychology which are borrowed from Adi Da; one might even wonder if Wilber's Integral Movement itself is more or less a product of Adi Da's teaching. The following excerpt, taken from Adi Da's spiritual biography which has subsequently gone through numerous revisions, provides much food for thought on the government's role in engineering not only the counter-culture at large but New Age spirituality as well: "I voluntarily submitted to drug trials at the

Veterans Administration hospital in Palo Alto, California.... At the VA hospital, I was given a dose of drugs one day per week.... I was told that I would be given mescalin, LSD, or psilocybin at three separate sessions, and, during a fourth session, some combination of these.... There were also various bizarre experiences and periods of anxiety.... I suffered mild anxiety attacks and occasional nervousness for perhaps a year beyond the actual tests.... I had become conscious of the formal structure of the living human being, associated with ... the 'chakra body'. The Kundalini Shakti was spontaneously Aroused in me...." [Adi Da Samraj, *The Knee of Listening: The Divine Ordeal of the Avataric Incarnation of Conscious Light* (Middletown, CA: The Dawn Horse Press, 2004), pp. 81–83]. While we do not want to overstep our inquiry by making any hasty assumptions or enter into polemics, it would be worth mentioning that Adi Da considers Adidam to be a new revelation or religion as can been seen in the title of the following work: *Adidam: The True World-Religion Given by the Promised God-Man, Adi Da Samraj* (Middletown, CA: The Dawn Horse Press, 2003). However, we are reminded of the traditional position regarding this possibility in the current phase of the *Kali-Yuga*: "After a certain period, whatever is put forward as a new religion is inevitably false; the Middle Ages mark grosso modo the final limit." [Frithjof Schuon, "The Quran" in *Understanding Islam*, trans. D.M. Matheson (Bloomington, IN: World Wisdom, 1998), p. 47], including: "The cyclic moment for the manifestation of the great perspectives (*darshanas*) is past; readaptations—in the sense of a legitimate and therefore adequate and efficacious synthesis—are always possible, but not the manifestations of perspectives that are fundamental and 'new' as to their form." [Frithjof Schuon, "Orthodoxy and Intellectuality" in *Stations of Wisdom* (Bloomington, IN: World Wisdom Books, 1995), p. 5]. The following is a declaration of Ken Wilber's enthusiastic endorsement for Adi Da: "My opinion is that we have, in the person of Da Free John [Adi Da], a Spiritual Master and religious genius of the ultimate degree.... Da Free John's [Adi Da's] teaching is, I believe, unsurpassed by that of any other spiritual Hero, of any period, of any place, of any time, of any persuasion." [Ken Wilber, "Forward: 'On Heroes and Cults'" to Da Free John, *Scientific Proof of the Existence of God Will Soon Be Announced by the White House!* (Middletown, CA: The Dawn Horse Press, 1980), p. 6]; see also Franklin Jones, "The Problem of the Mind, and the Year of Waiting for Grace" in *The Knee of Listening: The Early Life and Radical Spiritual Teachings of Franklin Jones* (Los Angeles, CA: The Dawn Horse Press, 1973), pp. 83-87; Bubba Free John, *Garbage and the Goddess: The Last Miracles and Final Spiritual Instructions of Bubba Free John*, eds. Sandy Bonder and Terry Patten (Lower Lake, CA: Dawn Horse Press,

1974); Ken Wilber, "The One Who Was To Come Is Always Already Here: A Short Appreciation of the Teaching of Bubba Free John", *Vision Mound Magazine*, Vol. 2, No. 9 (May 1979), pp. 28–29; Ken Wilber, "The Case of Adi Da" (October 11, 1996), available on the Shambhala website: *http://wilber.shambhala.com/html/misc/adida.cfm*; Ken Wilber, "An Update on the Case of Adi Da" (August 28, 1998), available on the Shambhala website: *http://wilber.shambhala.com/html/misc/adida_update.cfm/*; Georg Feuerstein, "The Many Faces of Da Love-Ananda (Da Free John)" in *Holy Madness: The Shock Tactics and Radical Teachings of Crazy-Wise Adepts, Holy Fools, and Rascal Gurus* (NY: Paragon House, 1991), pp. 80–100; Harry Oldmeadow, "Eastern Teachings, Western Teachers, 1950–2000" in *Journeys East: 20th Century Western Encounters with Eastern Traditions* (Bloomington, IN: World Wisdom, 2004), pp. 276–277.

ENDNOTE VI (p. 242): Harris Friedman, "The Renewal of Psychedelic Research: Implications for Humanistic and Transpersonal Psychology", *The Humanistic Psychologist*, Vol. 34, No. 1 (2006), pp. 39–58; W.V. Caldwell, *LSD Psychotherapy: An Exploration of Psychedelic and Psycholytic Therapy* (NY: Grove Press, 1968); Lester Grinspoon and James B. Bakalar, *Psychedelic Drugs Reconsidered* (NY: Basic Books, 1979); Lester Grinspoon and James B. Bakalar, "Can Drugs Be Used to Enhance the Psychotherapeutic Process?", *American Journal of Psychotherapy*, Vol. 40, No. 3 (1986), pp. 393–404; Rick Strassman, "Hallucinogenic Drugs in Psychiatric Research and Treatment: Perspectives and Prospects", *Journal of Nervous and Mental Disease*, Vol. 183, No. 3 (1995), pp. 175–186; Gary Bravo and Charles Grob, "Psychedelic Therapy" in *Textbook of Transpersonal Psychiatry and Psychology*, eds. Bruce W. Scotton, Allan B. Chinen, and John R. Battista (NY: BasicBooks, 1996), pp. 335–343; Myron J. Stolaroff, *The Secret Chief: Conversations with a Pioneer of the Underground Psychedelic Therapy Movement* (Charlotte, NC: Multidisciplinary Association for Psychedelic Studies, 1997); Rick Doblin, "A Clinical Plan for MDMA (Ecstasy) in the Treatment of Post-Traumatic Stress Disorder (PTSD): Partnering with the FDA", *Journal of Psychoactive Drugs*, Vol. 34 (2002), pp. 185–194; Marilyn Howell, *Honor Thy Daughter* (Santa Cruz, CA: Multidisciplinary Association for Psychedelic Studies, 2011); J.B. Hittner and S.B. Quello, "Combating Substance Abuse with Ibogaine: Pre- and Posttreatment Recommendations and An Example of Successive Model Fitting Analysis", *Journal of Psychoactive Drugs*, Vol. 36, No. 2 (2004), pp. 191–199; Jeffrey J. Kripal, "Mind Manifest: Psychedelia at Early Esalen and Beyond" in *Esalen: America and the Religion of No Religion* (Chicago, IL: The University of Chicago Press, 2007), pp. 112–134; Francisco A. Moreno, Christopher B. Wiegand, E.

Keolani Taitano, and Pedro L. Delgado, "Safety, Tolerability, and Efficacy of Psilocybin in 9 Patients With Obsessive-Compulsive Disorder", *Journal of Clinical Psychiatry*, Vol. 67, No. 11 (2006), pp. 1735–1740; A.C. Parrott, "The Psychotherapeutic Potential of MDMA (3,4-methylenedioxy methamphetamine): An Evidence-Based Review", *Psychopharmacology*, Vol. 191 (2007), pp. 181–193; Michael J. Winkelman and Thomas B. Roberts (eds.), *Psychedelic Medicine: New Evidence for Hallucinogenic Substances as Treatments, Vol.* 1 (Westport, CT: Praeger, 2007); Michael J. Winkelman and Thomas B. Roberts (eds.), *Psychedelic Medicine: New Evidence for Hallucinogenic Substances as Treatments, Vol.* 2 (Westport, CT: Praeger, 2007); M.W. Johnson, W.A. Richards, and R.R Griffiths, "Human Hallucinogen Research: Guidelines for Safety", *Journal of Psychopharmacology*, Vol. 22, No. 6 (2008), pp. 603–620; P.Ø. Johansen and T.S. Krebs, "How Could MDMA (Ecstasy) Help Anxiety Disorders? A Neurobiological Rationale", *Journal of Psychopharmacology*, Vol. 23, No. 4 (2009), pp. 389–391; Michael C. Mithoefer, Mark T. Wagner, Ann T. Mithoefer, Lisa Jerome, and Rick Doblin, "The Safety and Efficacy of ±3,4-Methylenediox-ymethamphetamine-Assisted Psychotherapy in Subjects with Chronic, Treatment-Resistant Posttraumatic Stress Disorder: The First Randomized Controlled Pilot Study", *Journal of Psychopharmacology*, Vol. 25, No. 4 (2011), pp. 439–452.

ENDNOTE VII (p. 243): "A grant from a branch of the Masons, the Scottish Rite Foundation for Schizophrenia Research, helped establish the merit of my study a year before I actually began it. Why the Masons had an interest in schizophrenia in general, and DMT in particular, I do not know, but I believe that garnering such support enhanced the esteem of my study in the eyes of the relevant regulatory and funding agencies." [Rick Strassman, "DMT: The Brain's Own Psychedelic" in Rick Strassman, Slawer Wojtowicz, Luis Eduardo Luna and Ede Frecska, *Inner Paths to Outer Space: Journeys to Alien Worlds through Psychedelics and Other Spiritual Technologies* (Rochester, VT: Park Street Press, 2008), p. 48]; "Curiously, another MK-ULTRA faction consisted of representatives of the Scottish Rite of Masonry, which had sponsored research into eugenics, psychiatry, and mind control since at least the 1930s. MKULTRA doctor Robert Hanna Felix [1904–1990] was director of psychiatric research for the Scottish Rite of Freemasonry, and the director of the National Institute of Mental Health. Felix was the immediate senior of Dr. Harris Isbell, already noted in relation to MKULTRA. Another prominent Freemason involved in MKULTRA was Dr. Paul Hoch [1902–1964], financed by the Army Chemical Center." [Jim Keith, "The CIA and Control" in Mass Control: Engineering Human Consciousness (Kempton, IL: Adventures Unlimited Press, 2003), p. 65]. Another interesting figure to be mentioned in this discussion is Andrija Puharich, also known as Henry K. Puharich (1918–1995), who was well-known for his work in parapsychology and affiliated with many influential members of the counter-culture and was also intimately involved with "The Council of Nine" or "The Nine", a New Age channeling cult. "After the demise of Puharich's Round Table [Foundation, located in Glen Cove, Maine] he spent time with social engineer Aldous Huxley in Tecate, Mexico, again studying the effects of electronics on the human organism. Puharich was also employed at the Army's Chemical and Biological Warfare Center at Fort Detrick, Maryland, researching the effects of LSD for the CIA in 1954. He delved into the effects of digatoid drugs at the Permanente Research Foundation, with funding from the Sandoz Chemical Works." [Jim Keith, "Electronic Mind Control" in *Mass Control: Engineering Human Consciousness* (Kempton, IL: Adventures Unlimited Press, 2003), p. 176]; See also H. P. Albarelli, Jr., "Notes" in *A Terrible Mistake: The Murder of Frank Olson and the CIA's Secret Cold War Experiments* (Walterville, OR: Trine Day, 2009), p. 792. For an interesting book on "The Council of Nine" see Lynn Picknett and Clive Prince, *The Stargate Conspiracy: The Truth about Extraterrestrial life and the Mysteries of Ancient Egypt* (NY: Berkley Books, 2001).

10

Corruptio Optimi Pessima: The Templars, The Freemasons, and The Counter-Initiation

THE TRADITIONALISTS/PERENNIALISTS teach that in the golden age all of humanity spoke a single spiritual "language" (for which read "held a common spiritual worldview") known as the Primordial Tradition. Later on in the present cycle of manifestation (of which all we know of as "history" forms only a very small part), this common vision of God and the metaphysical order was lost—perhaps due to the spiritual degeneration presented in Genesis, which God answered by sending the Flood. The Tower of Babel would then represent an attempt by a later society and regime to reconstitute this original vision *by power alone*, to found an oppressive political empire based on an *enforced syncretism* of all religions. Such syncretism earned God's wrath, however, and the Tower fell, because it was and is His Will that there be a plurality of religions in our times rather than some One World Religion, precisely to prevent the resurrection of the kind of evil world empire that Babylon represents. The Freemasons and Theosophists also speak of a Primordial Tradition; they depart from the Traditionalists, however, in that they conceive of this Tradition as something that can and should be *restored* in the utopian spiritual society of the future they are working to build—as opposed to the Traditionalists/Perennialists who, in line with the traditional eschatologies of the orthodox faiths, see the New Heaven and the New Earth as representing not a condition that can be built or worked for or evolved to by the present humanity, but as the Golden Age of another cycle-of-manifestation entirely, beyond the fires of Apocalypse.

The Knights Templars also created an institution, similar in some ways to a transnational corporation, wielding financial and ultimately political power, one that shows signs of having possibly been based on a covert syncretism, or something higher that later degenerated into syncretism. According to René Guénon, the Templars represented an esoteric influence emanating from the Primordial Tradition, which had withdrawn from public view but was still active; this would explain certain indications that they had "esoteric" dealings with Muslims in the Holy Land, even as they fought them on the battlefield. Their occupation of the Temple Mount—which Guénon suggests they considered to be a "center" of the Primordial Tradition, since to this day it is sacred to three religions, Judaism, Christianity and Islam—can be seen in this light. The Templars did in fact allow Muslims to pray in an oratory within the precincts of the Mount [see Edward Burman, *Templars, Knights of God*, p.76].

The Templars certainly seem to have begun as purely Christian knights with an unmitigated hatred for all Muslims, but they could well have developed a greater respect for their adversaries during their occupation of the Holy Land, especially since the Muslims were led by the great and chivalrous Saladin. And whatever contact they might have had with the Primordial Tradition in Jerusalem did not prevent them from transforming themselves from the "Poor Fellow-Soldiers of Christ and of the Temple of Solomon"[1] motivated by the Christian monastic ideal into an international power elite with a great deal of independence, beholden only to the Pope but not totally under even his control, and one of the founding forces of the international banking system. Furthermore, it is claimed by some they brought back with them from the Holy Land members of guild of stonemasons, whom Sufi writer Idries Shah (not all of whose assertions are to be trusted, however; some have called him more a Freemason than a Sufi) identifies as a Sufi order known as *al-Banna*, "The Builders", founded by the famous Sufi

1. The Seal of the Templars, depicting two knights riding the same horse, was explained as representing poverty. In esoteric terms, however, the horse symbolizes the body or the will, and the two knights the soul or rational mind and the Spirit, the psychic personality and the *atman* or indwelling divine Witness.

Dhu'l Nun Misri, who is reputed to have introduced ancient Egyptian lore into the Sufi tradition. It was this order who, according to Shah, might well have been the direct ancestor of Freemasonry. Today's Freemasonic rituals (as I understand them) have little resemblance to normative Sufi initiations or practices, but the three fundamental degrees of initiation of the Craft—Entered Apprentice, Fellowcraft and Master Mason—do bear a resemblance to those of the Islamic *futuwwah* or "chivalric" brotherhoods [see "An introduction to the History of Freemasonry in Iran", below] and also to the three grades common to most of the craft guilds of medieval Christendom: Apprentice, Journeyman and Master. The *futuwah* brotherhoods strongly influenced Sufism and were also undoubtedly influenced by it.

Craft guilds tended to take on some of the characteristics of esoteric secret societies in both Islam and Christianity, as they indeed did in classical antiquity. They were considered to have been founded by a certain saint or prophet with a legendary association with the craft in question,[2] and they possessed "trade secrets" that were often given a symbolic/esoteric interpretation; outside of masonry, the craft where such tendencies are most clearly evident is that of alchemy. And it is often asserted that some Templars, after the suppression of the Order, took refuge with the Freemasons. (After the dissolution of the Knights Templars, much of their function and property was turned over to the Knights Hospitalers, who were the ancestors of today's Knights of St. John of Jerusalem—also sometimes known, in certain branches, as the Knights of Malta—so beloved of conspiracy theorists.) It stands to reason that the Dome of the Rock and the al-Aqsa Masjid on the Temple Mount would have been repaired and maintained by such a guild of masons, seeing that the maintenance of a holy site, the third holiest in Islam, was unlikely to have been simply "outsourced" to the lowest bidder.

2. I once received the gift of a tortoise-shell comb made by a guild of Muslim comb-makers in North Africa who took as their patron the prophet Seth. Later I consulted the chapter on Seth in Ibn al-'Arabi's *Fusus al-Hikam*, and found that this particular prophet represents the first ordering of manifest existence after the profusion unleashed by the Divine creative act—just as the chaos of the hair is drawn into lines of order and beauty by the use of a comb.

The gothic arch, which appeared in France in the 12th century, could well have been based upon the pointed arch used in Islamic architecture, the first appearance of which was as part of the al-Aqsa Masjid; the Knights Templars also constructed octagonal churches reminiscent of the Dome of the Rock. And given that the Templars occupied al-Aqsa, they certainly could have had dealings with a guild of sacred masons charged with the maintenance of the site (presuming these survived the conquest of Jerusalem and the ensuing massacres), whose techniques would most likely have been interpreted symbolically, and thus quasi-esoterically; they did in fact make renovations to this building, as well as enlisting local craftsmen to build siege engines. Such a guild might have made overtures to the Templars as one group of "spirituals" to another who shared with them a veneration for the same sacred site, and have been eminently capable of fascinating them with tales of the history and symbolism of the Dome of the Rock and the Temple Mount, possibly in hopes of mitigating their hatred of Islam and moderating their depredations in the Holy Land. The Templars in turn could have established and maintained an alliance with such an order of esoteric stonemasons, some of whom might have accompanied them to the west. As I see it, this is a more likely vector for Islamic influence on the Order of the Temple than the Ismaili Hashishim often mentioned in this regard. The Templars, who built castles in Palestine and churches in Europe, employed many stonemasons; and since they apparently incorporated certain design features that were taken from Islamic architecture, the construction techniques if not the technicians themselves would have entered the west through their patronage. Such techniques would likely have been given symbolic interpretations by the Muslim craft guilds who used them, and this lore could certainly have passed to the Templars. As Peter Levenda points out, "if the architectural innovations came from the Middle East, then it stands to reason that someone had to train the local European craftsmen in these techniques and designs. These would have been men who served in some capacity in the Crusades, either as masons and carpenters hired by the military orders to build fortifications or as members of the orders themselves" [*The Secret Temple*, p. 66]. And who would the Templars have been more likely to hire to repair the al-Aqsa Masjid than the local craftsmen charged with maintaining it?

The Templars did, however, enter into a military alliance with the Hashishim at one point—who, as Shi'a, were also opposed to Saladin, a Sunni. The Hashisim, like the Templars, were a brotherhood of "sacred warriors" with grades of initiation, but it is difficult to imagine that a temporary alliance dictated by the shifting fortunes of war would have led to an exchange of esoteric doctrine, though this is not impossible. Some have also speculated that the Templars came into contact with "Johannite" doctrines in the Holy Land, though whether this refers to the beliefs of the Gnostic sect known as the Mandaeans, possibly descended from the Essenes, who claimed to have been founded by John the Baptist, or to the doctrinal school of John the Evangelist is uncertain; today's Freemasons in fact celebrate the feast days of both Johns. Peter Levenda speculates that the head of "Baphomet" supposedly venerated by the Templars could have represented the severed head of John the Baptist. However, since the Mandaeans hated Jesus, never forgiving him for revealing their esoteric doctrines to the public, it is unlikely that the Knights Templar, the flower of Christian chivalry, had secret Mandaean connections—though this, too, is not impossible. Any Johannite influences would more likely have come from those Christian believers who followed the doctrines of John the Evangelist, especially since the description of the Heavenly Jerusalem from the Book of Apocalypse, attributed to John, could certainly have be seen as transmitting secret lore relating to the Jewish Temple, particularly in view of the "Kabbalistic" flavor of the book as a whole. The vision of the *imaginal* Temple, as recounted in Ezekiel as well as Revelations, was an aspect of esoteric spiritual practice for Jewish mystics (and possibly also for their Christian successors), as for example in the *merkavah* or "chariot" mysticism that some see as the ancestor of the Kabbalah. Furthermore, since the Heavenly Jerusalem is described as equal in length, breadth and height—as a cube, in other words—Muslims would have understood it as indicating the Kaaba in Mecca. Jerusalem, specifically the Temple Mount, was the first *qibla* or direction-of-prayer in Islam before the *qibla* was transferred to the Kaaba; this fact could have led Muslims to read the Apocalypse as predicting the later pre-eminence of Islam, and esoteric Muslims to see the Kaaba itself as a kind of three-dimensional hermeneutic of Temple lore in terms of sacred geometry [see Henry Corbin, *Temple and Contemplation*]. And the Templars might well have been open to this kind of esoteric/symbolic lore—more so than to the Christ-hating Gnosticism of the Mandaeans—particularly since Muslims venerate Jesus as one of the greatest of the prophets. Medieval Christians generally saw Muslims either as Pagans or as a heretical Jewish sect; their high regard for Jesus could have come to the Templars as an intriguing shock, and led them to enquire further.

There is also the strange parallel between the history of the Templars and that of a similar order within Islam. The first "chartered" Muslim order of chivalry—*futuwwah*, the Arabic synonym for the Persian *javanmardi*—founded in 1182 by the caliph al-Nasir ad-Din Allah (reigned 1180-1225) and composed of mounted knights, was given its rule by the Sufi saint Abu Hafs Umar Suhrawardi (1144–1234), just as the rule of the Templars was composed by St. Bernard of Clairvaux (d. 1153); and after this "courtly" *futuwwah* went into decline, some of its rituals and part of its role were picked up by the "popular" *futuwwah* brotherhoods who were for the most part connected with artisans' guilds, just as certain Templar influences, after the suppression of the Order, later turned up in Freemasonry—though whether this represents an unbroken chain of clandestine transmission or merely a late "literary" revival in the 17th and 18th centuries of a fantasy-version of Templarism remains open to question. Nonetheless it is highly interesting that, according to Hamid Algar in "An introduction to the History of Freemasonry in Iran" [*Middle Eastern Studies*, Vol. 6. No. 3], the *futuwwah* brotherhoods, who exercised a powerful influence on Sufism, were quite similar in form to Freemasonry; their points of similarity included "a hierarchy of degrees bearing the same names in both traditions" as well as "the binding on of an apron or piece of cloth" as part of the initiation ceremony. This leads us to ask whether the *courtly* Islamic *futuwwah* patronized by Nasir al-Din Allah, with its armed horsemen, might have grown in part out of a Templar/proto-Freemasonic influence that passed east from the Holy Land during the Crusades, just as a similar influence, flowing west, possibly influenced western Freemasonry. (*Futuwwah* itself, however, significantly predates the Crusades.) In order to posit a relationship between the Templars and the Freemasons dating from the Middle Ages as being the origin of the Freemasonic Templarism of today, we need not base this conjecture on the legend that fugitive Templars took refuge with Scottish Freemasons after the suppression of the Order, though this certainly could have happened. It is more likely that legends of a past relationship between the Templars and certain Masons who had a symbolic and quasi-esoteric understanding of their craft survived within the Masonic world, providing a foundation for the various fantastic and ill-considered attempts in the 18th century to revive Templar lore and practice within a Freemasonic context.

As for Idries Shah, his assertion that the Freemasons are descended from al-Banna is plausible, though the only "corroborating evidence" for this that I have been able to uncover seems traceable back to Shah alone. Shah may well have been right in this conjecture, which appears in his book *The Sufis*—and yet the context in which he places it is highly problematical; as William Blake put it in his "Auguries of Innocence", "A truth that's told with bad intent/ Beats all the lies you can invent." One obvious intent of that book is to uncover Sufi influences in many western groups, movements and manifestations—in Freemasonry, in courtly love, even in witchcraft—so as to establish the power and legitimacy of *tasawwuf*. Some of the evidence he presents is clearly valid, though other assertions (the one having to do with witchcraft in particular) are quite suspect. One is led to ask, however, if his real intent, rather than (or in addition to) demonstrating the Sufic roots of Freemasonry, might not have been to posit the "Freemasonic" roots of Sufism, portraying it not as an esoteric manifestation intrinsic to Islam, but as an ancient religious universalism—such as Freemasonry itself pretends to be—whose relation to the Islamic revelation is only accidental. Certainly Sufism is universal in the sense that, in addition to the Noble Qur'an and the prophetic hadith, as well as the direct oral teachings of the Prophet Muhammad to 'Ali and Abu Bakr, peace and blessings be upon them, it is also based upon the immediate intellectual intuition of God and the metaphysical order, universal realities that cannot be limited to any single tradition. But to use this truth as an excuse to portray Sufism in Freemasonic mode as an explicit and as it were *exoteric* (though partly clandestine) universalism that has always superseded the revealed religions and has only concealed itself within them for purposes of self-protection and survival, adopting their language, doctrines and rituals as a sort of ruse to fool the externalists, is the precise misrepresentation applied by the Counter-Initiation to *all* traditional esoterisms. The ancestors of the Freemasons may or may not have been al-Banna, and it is certain that Freemasonry entered, or re-entered, dar al-Islam via European political and economic influence in the 18th century, and may have exercised a certain influence on the Sufi orders—but to extrapolate from these facts and conjectures the independence of Sufism from the Islamic revelation is both unwarranted and subversive. Furthermore, Shah's connections with both the western occult underworld (Gerald Gardner) and the globalist elites (the Club of Rome), as well as his thinly-veiled suggestion that he was in fact the elected "king of the Sufis", and thus represented Islamic esoterism as a whole—a completely spurious claim based on a falsification of the Sufi doctrine of the *qutb* or "Pole [of the Age]", whose paramount station in the spiritual hierarchy has nothing whatever to do with the voting process—should at the very least teach us to be highly cautious when approaching him.

Shah's predecessor in his apparent attempt to demonstrate that Sufism stems from Freemasonry was the Iranian Mason Adib ul-Mamalik Farahani (1860–1917) who, in his poem "*A'in-i Framasun va Faramushkhana*", published in 1899), claimed that Freemasonry began with Zoroaster, then passed by way of Salman al-Farsi to the Prophet Muhammad. Besides positing Freemasonry as the actual *progenitor of Islam*, it also suggests many Freemasonic influences on Sufism [see Algar, "An Introduction to the History of Freemasonry in Iran"]. "*A'in-i Framasun va Faramushkhana*" also exhibits certain Manichaean affinities. Manichaeism grew out of Iranian Zoroastrianism, but it went further in positing a sort of pan-prophetism whereby the same Message and the same prophetic Soul appear at different points throughout history. The *Pseudo-Clementine Homilies*, for example, speak of a "true Messenger who from the beginning of the world, altering his forms with his names, courses through the Aeon. . . ."

Here we encounter one of the central half-truths upon which the Counter-Initiation is based. It is true that Tradition, in Guénon's sense, passes through the ages—"from the Stone Age till now" as Ananda Coomaraswamy put it—altering its names and forms but retaining its essence. This truth of horizontal transmission, however, must never be used to deny the reality of vertical Revelation. Each true and revealed religion descends directly from God. Islam, for example, did not stem from Old Testament prophetology or rabbinical lore or the Christian apocrypha or docetic Gnosticism or Zoroastrian/Mazdean doctrine or any mixture of these; it descended from Allah, via the angel Gabriel, to the Prophet Muhammad, peace and blessings be upon him, first appearing at one specific time and place: when Muhammad was in retreat in his cave on Mt. Hira. This is how and when the Islamic revelation was established. *After* this vertical and revelatory descent, it magnetized to itself whatever material it needed from other religions and historical periods, as every Revelation must; but this mass of lore and doctrine and myth and symbolism and historical legend was not *stitched together* to create Islam. Rather, it was completely Islamicized by the new revelation given to Muhammad, a revelation that accepted whatever outside elements were intrinsically compatible with it and rejected all that were not. The material taken from other times and places and religions was the guest at that table, but Islam was the host—and it is the host who provides the nourishment. Consequently we can say as a general rule that whenever a religion begins to see itself—often under the influence of secular scholarship—more as a product of historical antecedents than as the manifestation of an timeless archetype sent by God and eternally at rest in God, then it has opened itself to corruption by the Counter-Initiation.

Within Islam, the Builders, or whatever guild of artisans had likely been charged with maintaining the al-Aqsa Masjid and the Dome of the Rock, might well have been a legitimate Sufi order serving God and his Prophet. But as soon as they were taken out of their proper spiritual matrix and artificially grafted onto the body of Christendom, they became subversive—after which they could spread their influence back to dar al-Islam and corrupt it as well. Such are the dangers of religious syncretism. (Rosicrucianism also shows signs of being a deviated Sufi order. Its mythic founder, Christian Rosenkreutz, is reputed to have traveled in the Near East in search of wisdom, and the rose is a common symbol of Divine Love in Sufi poetry; the founder of the Qadiri Order, Abdul Qadir Jilani, was known as "The Rose of Baghdad." *Rose-Cross* may simply be a visual/linguistic symbol translatable as "Christian Sufism".)[3] Sufism within Islam is the sacred, inner core of the religion; "Sufism" within Christianity could only be a barren hybrid and thus a spiritually subversive force. And it is also possible that exiled Templars, out of their sense of betrayal at the suppression of their order and the martyrdom of their brothers with the collusion of the Church they had so long defended, were moved to re-interpret their own deposit of ritual, lore and symbolism—which would have been essentially Christian, though possibly incorporating certain Islamic influences—so as to subvert Roman Catholicism rather than defend it; this could have been the original anti-Papist tendency around which modern anti-clerical Freemasonry developed.

At the very least, Freemasonry has given aid and comfort to those dedicated to creating a One World Religion, or a universalist federation of the faiths, by acting as an "exteriorized esoterism" open to members of all religions and supposedly springing from an ancient source.

This development took a huge step forward at the Second Vatican Council that deconstructed the Catholic tradition, a Council in which many have discerned Freemasonic influences and agendas. According to Brother Michael Dimond O.S.B. in *Has Rome Become the Seat of the Antichrist?*, following Vatican II the Grand Orient

3. However, the union of Cross and Rose could with equal validity represent the union of Jesus and Mary, which appears architecturally in those medieval cathedrals that exhibit both the Crucifix and the Rose Window. One of the forms of the "Jesus Prayer" in the Eastern Orthodox Hesychast tradition is *Jesu-Mariam*, which, like the alchemical emblem of "the Sun in the Moon-cradle", invokes the indwelling of the Divinity within the matrix of the sanctified soul; the same general meaning is expressed in the Vajrayana mantram *Om Mani Padme Hum*, "*Om*, Jewel-in-Lotus, *Hum*", where the jewel is analogous to *Jesu* and the lotus to *Mariam*.

Lodge of Freemasonry in France reported a "gigantic revolution in the Church", calling it "a prelude to victory". And Rama P. Coomaraswamy, in *The Problems with the Other Sacraments* [Sophia Perennis, 2010, p.46, n.57] presents evidence for the Freemasonic connections of Pope John XXIII.[4] It is conceivable that the whole Freemasonic deviation stems from a false "exteriorization" and "literalization" (albeit largely clandestine), by the Templars or their affiliates, of the perennial doctrine of the Transcendent Unity of Religions, which harked back to an earlier phase of exteriorization and Counter-Initiatory syncretism in Babylon.

According to an anonymous poem that appeared in England in 1721, as recounted by Whitall Perry in his monumental *Treasury of Traditional Wisdom*,

> If history be no ancient Fable,
> Free Masons came from the Tower of Babel.[5]

Nimrod, the builder of that Tower, is described in Genesis as a "great hunter". Guénon, in *Symbols of the Sacred Science* [Sophia Perennis, 2004] sees in him the story of an ancient revolt of the *kshatriyas* against the *brahmins*, the warrior-caste against the priestly caste. The traditional exaltation of the *brahmins* over the *kshatriyas* is, however, the outer image of an inner spiritual truth, an *eternal* truth, occupying the plane of esoteric anthropology: the precedence of the Intellect over the will in the human soul. The direct perception of spiritual Truth, not the will, is the crown and center of humanity. If the will serves the Intellect, it will order the life of the

4. The web provides us with two interesting images which apparently show both Tony Blair and Shaykh Nizam Haqqani exchanging a Masonic handshake with Benedict XVI of the type known as the "pass grip of a fellow-craft". Such photographs are relatively easy to fake, but I believe they are worth investigating. In any case it has been definitely established that Cardinal Annibale Bugnini, architect of the Novus Ordo mass, was a Mason; a letter was found in his briefcase from the Grand Master of Italian Freemasonry, addressing him as a brother [see Rev. Anthony Cekada, *Work of Human Hands: A Theological Critique of the Mass of Paul VI*, p. 76].

5. I do not mean to suggest that today's Freemasons are descended from the builders of the Tower of Babel by an unbroken, clandestine chain of human transmission, only that both developments were inspired by the same *spirit*.

soul—and insofar as is possible, the outer life of the man—so as to protect the Intellectual center, both from disturbing social influences and the possibility of rebelliousness on the part of the will itself. In such a condition the human form is correctly hierarchialized or *edified* ("built up", in the sense that the human soul is the *edifice* or *temple* of the Spirit); the several faculties of the soul all occupy their proper places, consequently such an individual may be described as an "upright man" (in Hebrew, a *tzaddik*). But if the will rebels against the Intellect and attempts to occupy its place, the result is a luciferian fall, a loss of the full stature of the human form, and consequently the degeneration of the entire cosmic environment, of which the human being, esoterically speaking, is the seed and the center; in the words of the Holy Qur'an (33:72), *We offered the Trust to the heavens and the earth and the hills, but they shrank from bearing it and were afraid of it. And man assumed it. Lo! He hath proved a tyrant and a fool.* Power can only act meaningfully in service to knowledge; if it attempts to serve itself, it loses its entire use and rationale, and becomes a "mad dog." [NOTE: The edified human form considered as temple of the Holy Spirit is the *esoteric* doctrine that the more progressive/revolutionary Freemasons exteriorized by wrongly identifying this temple with a utopian society of the future, with human individuals as no more the stones out of which this global collective will be built. This misapplication of the lore of inner spiritual development to the notion of the progress of the collective or the spiritual evolution of the macrocosm is an unfailing sign of the Counter-Initiation; we can see this tendency in Hegel, Rudolf Steiner, Teilhard de Chardin, Sri Aurobindo, and Ken Wilber.]

The Tower of Babel, as we have already pointed out, is not so much a symbol of the Primordial Tradition in its original purity, when all men spoke the same spiritual "language", as it is of a moment when an attempt was made to re-establish this Tradition after its time had passed—not through the "mass theophanic consciousness" available in the Golden Age, but through naked power. The story of Nimrod undoubtedly represents the memory of a campaign of "religious imperialism" carried on not by wandering sages but by warriors; his plan was to "hunt and take" the gods of the various tribes and nations of the Near East so as to establish Babylon as a spiritual as well as a political empire; Rome did much the same thing when it abducted the gods of its conquered peoples and set them up in the Roman Pantheon, obviously more for political than for spiritual purposes. And certain globalist institutions are apparently attempting something similar today in their plan to crown their one-world financial hegemony with a One-World Religion, or at least a federation of religions under a non-traditional authority [see *False Dawn*]. Nimrod, then, was a direct precursor to the Antichrist; he, not the "Hiram Abiff" who according to Masonic legend built Solomon's Temple and is claimed by them as a founder, is the first ancestor—speaking in spiritual, not strictly historical terms—of today's Masons. Freemasonry, whether or not we accept the existence of the Counter-Traditional cabal which some call the Illuminati, is in so many ways the "traditional" religion of the globalists, having provided much of the ideological background for the notion of world unification, whether or not it is still at the "cutting edge" of the globalization process. Groups such as the Freemasons and the Theosophists may lose popularity and decrease in membership while still remaining of use to the global elites, no longer as mass movements but as well-established networks through which various influences can be spread. The New Age as well, in certain cases, has now moved from an expansive populist phase to a more centralizing elitist phase, as evidenced for example by the Disclosure and Exopolitics movements in the UFO world. And just as popular movements may be co-opted by the elites, so the elites will sometimes seed popular movements for purposes of social research and control, first broadcasting their ideas to society at large during the expansive phase, and then culling and drawing in those they see as useful to them during the contractive phase.

King Solomon, Hiram the King of Tyre, and Hiram Abiff are considered to be the three mythic founders of Freemasonry. According to First Book of Kings, King Hiram was the patron behind the building of Solomon's Temple; another Hiram was the bronze-worker who cast the pillars of the Temple and the great "sea" or vessel in the outer court. Adoniram, not Hiram the bronze-worker, is presented as the master-builder, though "Adoniram" might simply mean "Lord Hiram". And I will hazard a pure conjecture that

"Abiff" may be a corruption of "Abu Afif", Arabic for "father of the chaste one". Jesus was a "chaste one" who compared Himself to the (Second) Temple at Jerusalem: "Destroy this temple (i.e., My Body), and in three days I will raise it up" [John 2:19]. "Hiram Abu Afif" would then be a symbol of God as the Great Architect of the Universe, who died and came back to life again—just as Hiram Abiff did in Masonic legend—in the person of His Son. If this solution is correct, then we have a figure with an Old Testament first name and an Arabic surname enacting a version of the Christian story, pointing to a synthesis of the three Abrahamic religions. Likewise Boccaccio—reputed to be an initiate of the Fedeli d'Amore ("the Faithful to Love") or Fede Santa, a supposed secret initiatory order sometimes characterized as a "third (lay) order" of the Templars—maintained in his *Decamerone* that no one really knows whether Judaism, Christianity or Islam is the true religion. Such a synthetic vision, as long as it remained entirely clandestine, might have legitimately operated to prevent the religions from becoming totally sealed against any mutual understanding, which, to the degree that they were in contact with each other, could have also compromised their access to their own esoteric depths by reducing the One God they all worshipped to a triplicity of mutually-inimical tribal deities. But as we have made clear above, the open revelation of such a vision, if the religious collectives of the time had been receptive to it (which clearly they weren't), could only have resulted in a premature advent of Antichrist. Unfortunately—and also, as I must declare in fear and trembling, providentially—such a revelation has become necessary in our day, and will consequently play a central role in the eschatological drama of the End Times.

Guénon associates the triplicity of King Solomon, the King of Tyre and Hiram Abiff with the fact that any "regular" Masonic lodge must be founded by no fewer than three Master Masons, and with the notion that the "Lost Word" was composed of three syllables, each of which was guarded by a different Master. This lore is undoubtedly related to the Hermetic concept that the initiate, having attained the station of Hermes, is (like him) *trismegistus*, "thrice greatest", as well as to the three fundamental Masonic grades of Apprentice, Fellowcraft, and Master. In the esoteric dimension this may refer to the complete hierarchical integration of Will, Affection and Thought within the soul of the one who has completed the "lesser mysteries", as well as to a comprehensive knowledge that embraces the *hylic* dimension (nature, society and the human body), the *psychic* dimension (the human psyche and the Intermediary Plane), and the *pneumatic* dimension (the Spirit). Islamic Sufism possesses three analogous "grades", though these are not expressed in terms of formal, ritualistic initiations. These are *islam*, *iman*, and *ihsan*: submission, faith and excellence, which relate respectively to Will, Affection, and Knowledge or Gnosis. And these stations also partially correspond to the grades of craft initiation. The Apprentice must simply practice what he is told before he fully understands it, learning by imitation. The Fellow loves his craft in the sense that he has become intimate with it and begun to gain insight into its secrets. The Master has attained full knowledge of the craft to the point where he has become *essentially* identified with it, and so can act as a "philosopher's stone" capable of "transmuting the substance" of the initiates in his charge. He can impart technique to his pupils without ultimately binding them to it because he himself is beyond technique. When transposed to the purely gnostic order, these grades correspond in a certain way to the *ilm al-yaqin*, *ayn al-yaqin* and *haqq al-yaqin* of Islamic esoterism: the Knowledge of Certainty, the Eye of Certainty and the Truth of Certainty—the realms of Lore, Vision and Realization. It would appear, however, that the esoteric triplicity of Will, Affection and Knowledge was exteriorized at one point in the history of Templarism and/or Freemasonry by being identified with the three Abrahamic religions of Judaism, Christianity and Islam, an exteriorization that also appears in Frithjof Schuon's characterization of Judaism as an expression of Power (i.e., Will), Christianity of Love (Affection), and Islam of Knowledge, though Schuon certainly had no direct connection with Freemasonry. Schuon's schema is useful in a general way, as long as we realize—as he points out—that all three elements must exist in all three revelations. But if this attribution is taken too far (which Schuon did not), the three Abrahamic religions then appear as concretizations of three necessary elements of the "true" religion, which can presumably only be "reconstituted" by *syncretizing* them. (This pan-Abrahamic syncretism has in fact been promoted in our time by such Pseudo-Initiatory or Counter-Initiatory organizations as the Temple of Love, whose proposal, authored by one Karen Fish, that Judaism, Christianity and Islam be united appeared at one point on the website of the "A Common Word between You and Us" initiative.) Here we have a clear illustration of the etiology of the Counter-Initiation, or one aspect of it: a true, intrinsic unity is exteriorized; its elements become dissociated; finally a hopeless and destructive attempt is made to reunite these elements by means of an imposed syncretistic unification. The truth is, however, that once the "hermetic egg" of esoterism is cracked open, all the king's horses and all the king's men can never put it together again.

In addition to the myth of Hiram Abiff, the Freemasons also repeat a legend that Noah concealed the secrets of the universe inside a pillar, or two of them. This myth may derive from the Islamic legend that the Ark bore the corpse of Adam, who was the Pole or *Qutb* of his time, as Noah was the Pole of his own; the word *qutb* also means "pillar". The *Qutb* of the Age can certainly be seen as containing the secrets of the universe, given that the human form is the universe in microcosm, and the Pole is *al-insan al-kamil*, "the Perfected Man". [6]The idea of a pair of pillars could refer to Adam and Noah, or simply be the assimilation of the Sufi notion of the Pole to the two pillars, Jachin and Boaz, of Solomon's temple. The depiction of the Pole Star on the north wall of Masonic temples may be part of this same symbolism, which appears in Ezekiel's vision of the (future) Second Temple. [Ezekiel 8:3] as "inner gate [of the Temple] that looketh toward the north, where was the seat of the image of jealousy, which provoketh to jealousy". The Polar North symbolizes the rigor of Transcendence: the Transcendent God is a "jealous God" who "will have no strange gods before Him." The Pole Star is the door to the Hyperborean Paradise; in Dante's *Purgatorio* the constellations of the Bears which surround that Star appear above the Mountain of Purgatory, indicating that purgation is the

6. Guénon's "King of the World" in Central Asia appears to be something like a Vajrayana version of the Qutb.

only path back to the Garden of Eden, the Terrestrial Paradise at the Mountain's peak. And the Masonic "All-Seeing Eye", set at the apex of a pyramid, is undoubtedly another rendition of the Pole Star.

[NOTE: For a more detailed explication of Hyperborean symbolism, see the section "Atlantis and Hyperborea" in *Who is the Earth? How to See God in the Natural World*, Charles Upton, Sophia Perennis, 2005.]

The story of the Fall of Hyperborea is told in the Hans Christian Andersen fairy tale "The Garden of Eden." A prince is transported to the Garden on the back of the North Wind. When he arrives he wishes to remain there forever, and so vows not to sin like Adam and Eve did. But of course he does sin, at which point he falls from Paradise and finds himself lying on the rocky earth in the rain; as he fell, the Garden of Paradise rose above him to become the single star he now sees in the sky—Polaris. The North is considered to be the point of rigor if not demonic evil in many traditions, which indicates that the direct path back to Hyperborea via the Primordial Tradition is now barred, and that to attempt this ascent under present cosmic conditions, outside the grace of a particular revelation—to "take heaven by storm"—is to enact a titanic rebellion and fall. The North can now only be approached in response to the *descent* of divine revelation from God, whose point (especially in Christian terms) is the East, which is why traditional Christian churches are "oriented" toward that point. And so the Hyperborean symbolism found in Freemasonry is definitely problematic. An "initiate" (like Dante) who remains faithful to and passes through the Eastern Mysteries of revelation may still enter the field of the Northern Mysteries, but to attempt to access this field *outside* revelation, as is indicated by certain Freemasonic symbols coupled with the Masonic intent to function independently of the revealed religions (while still "accepting" them), constitutes a Promethean rebellion against God. This rebellion is symbolized in Tolkien's *Lord of the Rings* by the Dark Tower of Sauron in Mordor, which is precisely the Towel of Babel surmounted by the Masonic All-Seeing Eye.

Whenever I pass by the George Washington Masonic Memorial in the Washington D.C. area—a building I like to call "The Ziggurat of Alexandria"—I am reminded of the Tower of Babel. And I fear that a deviation similar to the one represented by that Tower now threatens to arise from a false exteriorization of the Transcendent Unity of Religions as taught by René Guénon and Frithjof Schuon, in the context of today's interfaith movement, which is so heavily sponsored and funded by the global elites, including Ted Turner and Maurice Strong and George Soros, a number of globalist foundations and think-tanks, and the U.S. State Department [see *False Dawn*]. It is unfortunate but true that Guénon himself spent much of his life vainly trying to return Freemasonry to its "esoteric roots", not realizing how perfectly *his idealized version of it* fit his own definition of the Counter-Initiation. Nonetheless, he rightly understood much Masonic symbolism as relating to traditional esoterism and metaphysics; the Compass, for example, represents Heaven, which is often symbolized by both the trinity and the circle, while the Square indicates Earth; the same symbolism appears in the *I Ching*. From another perspective, the Compass symbolizes the vertical dimension of Grace, expressed in terms of the three theological virtues, and the Square the horizontal dimension of Works as defined by the four cardinal virtues. The theological and cardinal virtues together correspond to the Seven Liberal Arts; the emblem of their synthesis is the pyramid.

The Liberal Arts, composed of the *trivium* and the *quadrivium*, the "three roads" and the "four roads", were traditionally viewed as preliminaries to the understanding and practice of philosophy and theology. The trivium—Grammar, Logic and Rhetoric—corresponds to the three Theological Virtues of Faith, Hope and Love. Grammar may stand in for the entirety of language as it comes down to us, and consequently for the entirety of what exists within the Divine Nature before the act of creation, the *logoi* or eternal designs of all things; as such it corresponds to the virtue of Faith, "the presence of things hoped for, the evidence of things not seen". Logic is the discernment of the particulars within the Divine Nature, both as intrinsic axioms and as the necessary relationships between them, the act of contemplating God as Necessary Being. And given that logic is dialectical, since it operates in order to reach an end, it corresponds to the virtue of Hope. Rhetoric, as the full expression of what Faith knows and what Hope discovers, corresponds to Love. When

Jesus said "none has seen the Father at any time", He was positing the Father as "the evidence of things not seen", knowable only by Faith. When He said, "who has seen Me has seen the Father", he revealed Himself as the Hope of the World. And when the Apostles on Pentecost proclaimed the One Truth in all languages by the power of the Holy Spirit, through an inspired Rhetoric that swayed every heart—thereby redressing the Confusion of Tongues that followed the abandonment of the Tower of Babel—that was Love unveiled. Jesus Christ, in positing "one fold and one Shepherd", again unveiled the vision of Intrinsic Unity that had been veiled by the false Promethean unification represented by the Tower. So the trivium is also the reflection within the human intellect of the Persons of the Holy Trinity, another of Whose symbols is the circle described by the Compass, where the central point corresponds to the Father, the circumference to the Son, and the radii to the Holy Spirit.

The quadrivium on the other hand—Mathematics, Geometry, Astronomy and Music—is related to the four Cardinal Virtues: Prudence, Justice, Fortitude and Temperance. The theological virtues are the roof; the cardinal virtues are the foundation. Mathematics, whose central expression is the equation, the equalizing of two terms, relates to temperance, or equanimity; as an expression of Necessary Being, it is a form of detachment from the world, of *apatheia*, through the contemplation of abstract principles. Geometry is related to Justice. Through the art of Geometry we overcome the chaotic aspects of the created world by establishing form; thus William Blake spoke of "the hard and wiry dividing-line of rectitude", the virtue by which we "rectify" things, which means to *square* them. (Los, the Eternal Prophet and blacksmith who builds Golgonooza the City of Art, is what Blake made of his Freemasonic influences, after declaring his independence from the Craft in "A Song of Liberty" in *The Marriage of Heaven and Hell*. In his Prophetic Books the adversary of Los is Urizen, who, in the famous engraving where he is shown as creating the world with a compass whose branches are rays extending from his fingers, is pictured precisely as the Great Architect of the Universe.)

Astronomy relates to Prudence. The science of horary astrology, based on Astronomy, lets us know when it is *prudent* to enact or refrain from this or that; it helps us act with due *consideration*, a word that means "with the stars". And Music is related to Fortitude, since it is a science by which the soul's affections and vital energies are strengthened, moved and healed; anyone who has marched into battle to the skirl of bagpipes has proved this correspondence in life and death terms, in the very act. Mathematics and Astronomy are the archetypes of Geometry and Music, as Geometry and Music are the earthly expressions of Mathematics and Astronomy. Geometry is Mathematics made visible; Music is Astronomy, the silent Music of the Spheres, made audible. And Astronomy and Music are also applications of Mathematics, which is the most transcendental of the four roads. Geometry is the expression of Mathematics in terms of space, as in architecture; Music is its expression in terms of time and rhythm; Astronomy is its expression in terms of the celestial order, in which space and time unite. This is one of several ways in which Freemasonic symbolism can be understood in more-or-less Catholic terms, or at least in according to a Christian Hermeticism that is not necessarily heterodox; René Guénon, in *Studies in Freemasonry and the Compagnonnage* [Sophia Perennis, 2004], spoke of the close affinities between Masonic and Hermetic symbolism. However, when Guénon saw such symbolism as indicating an *esoteric Catholicism*, actually or potentially, he missed the mark. Such symbolism may be understood as an exegesis of the Catholic Mysteries, or a mnemonic device that allows us to contemplate them imaginatively, but it is not the Mysteries themselves, which—as Frithjof Schuon correctly understood—are the seven Sacraments. To place Masonic symbolism on a higher level than the Sacraments is like giving the scriptural exegesis produced by the Fathers of the Church precedence over scripture itself.

Guénon was right in his contention that Freemasonry embraces an ancient and valid esoteric symbology that in certain renditions might be compatible with Catholic doctrine. But he forgot two of the necessary elements that define any valid esoteric organization: *apostolic succession*, an unbroken line of initiated teachers stretching back to the founding of the tradition in question—which Masonry almost certainly lacks—and *dispensation*, the "charter" granted to the organization by a valid Divine revelation that is still in force, of which it will constitute the inner essence, allowing it in turn to act as a doorway to esoterism per se. If Freemasonry claims to accept or embrace all religions, this simply means that it has received the blessing of none of them, lacking which it can only be a "loose cannon".[7] Sufism outside Islam, Kabbalah outside Judaism, Hesychasm outside Christianity cannot in any sense be called *esoteric*, nor can the Primordial Tradition outwardly express itself as a discrete tradition with its own particular forms, especially in our time. And the more profound and esoteric a spiritual perspective is, the more Satanic its deviation must be, which is why the regime of Antichrist will necessarily represent the Satanic counterfeit of the Primordial Tradition itself.

Leo Schaya, writing primarily from the standpoint of Jewish esoterism, sees the eschatological mission of Elias as a re-establishment of the "unanimous tradition" in preparation for the advent of the Messiah. Before the confusion of tongues which followed the abandonment of the Tower, humanity shared a single spiritual vision—which, incidentally, demonstrates how any attempt to impose unity by force inevitably results in greater fragmentation. After that time, however, God's Self-revelation to Man took the form of discrete religious traditions, each one self-enclosed and self-sufficient. The Tree of Life, which had been a single trunk, now divided into several branches. According to Schaya, however, the primordial unanimity is destined to be re-established before the end of the cycle:

> According to Jewish tradition, the entire Torah of Moses amounts to no more than a single line of the *Sepher ha-Yasher* [the "Book of Justice" which Elias must bring with him], which means that this Book, by virtue of not being "scriptural"

7. The "Book of the Sacred Law" that is displayed in Masonic temples, which will be the Bible in Christian nations, the Qur'an in Islamic nations etc., may simply represent the Qur'anic doctrine that all "peoples of the Book"—Jews, Christians, Muslims, Sabaeans (and by later extension, Hindus, according to some)—possess valid revelations. But to make the Masonic temple the context for all these revelations—constant (it is implied) where they are mutable—is to claim that the Primordial Tradition supersedes the particular revealed faiths on the plane of form; and this is the Counter-Initiation precisely.

but "operative" in nature, will be the veritable final accomplishment of Scripture, the "realization" which by definition goes immeasurably beyond the "letter". At the same time, Judaism tacitly places the remaining "lines" of this "Book" at the disposal of all the Divine revelations, whatever they may be, each one formulating or announcing in its fashion the same Eternal Truth and the same Destiny of man and the world. The "Book" of Elias is the integral Wisdom of the unanimous Tradition and the eschatological Manifestation of the one and only Principle. For the Jews, Elias represents the transition from traditional exclusiveness to the universality which they too possess, since they affirm that the Tishbite will raise his voice so loud to announce the spiritual peace that it will be heard from one end of the earth to the other; and the Doctors of the Law teach that "the righteous of all nations have a portion in the life to come" or, again, that "all men who are not idolaters can be considered Israelites".... Elias must re-establish all things in the name of, and for the sake of, that spiritual "peace" which the Messiah will bring once and for all: it will be crystallized forever in the New Jerusalem "founded by—or for—peace", according to the etymology of *Yerushalem* or *Yerushalaim*. Elias came down, and has come down for centuries, to the world below to prepare, with the concurrence of those he inspires, this final state of humanity. He reveals, little by little and more intensively and generally toward the end, the spiritual and universal essence, the transcendent unity of all authentic religions. It is as if the radiant city were being patiently built by putting one luminous stone after another into place. The motivating power of this task can be called the "Eliatic flow", at least in the orbit of the Judeo-Christian tradition, whereas other traditions will each use their own terms to describe this same universal flow. According to the terminology of Jewish esoterism, this flow belongs to the "river of highest Eden", the "river of Yobel" or "great Jubilee" which is final Deliverance. Revelations calls it "the river of the water of life, clear as crystal" Rev. 22:1); it will be crystallized in the "precious stones", the unquenchable lights of the New Jerusalem

["The Mission of Elias", *Studies in Comparative Religion*, Vol. 14, Numbers 3 & 4, pp. 165–166].

It is possible that the Templars were in touch at one point, on a profoundly esoteric level, with this Unanimous or Primordial Tradition through the "Eliatic function" of which Schaya speaks. (The immortal Prophet of the Sufis, *al-Khidr* or "the Green Man", has been identified both with Elias and, by some Eastern Orthodox Christians, with St. George. The Sufis are in some ways "esoteric ecumenists", though in no way syncretists; classical Sufism has always insisted on a strict Islamic orthodoxy.) It is also possible that certain esoteric influences operating through the Templars continued, perhaps later taking the form of the Fedeli d'Amore, with which Dante Aligheri, Guido Cavalcanti, Cino da Pistoia, Moroello Malaspina, Pedro de Pisa, Boccaccio, Petrarch, Andreas Cappelanus, Cardinal Francesco Barberino, Dino Compagni, and Brunetto Latini were reputed to have been associated. And though this group might have been no more than an informal association of like-minded artists and philosophers, a number of researchers have presented it as a true initiatory order. René Guénon, Julius Evola, Dante Gabriel Rosetti, Luigi Valli, Eugene Aroux, Alfonso Ricolfi, Arthur Schult, Henry Corbin, William Anderson, and others have published researches on the Fedeli d'Amore; some maintain that Dante's *La Vita Nuova* refers specifically to this order and their grades of initiation. And certainly Templar lore of an apparently esoteric nature appears in both the *Divine Comedy* and in the *Parzival* of Wolfram von Eschenbach. The works of Dante and Wolfram are of such profound spiritual import that whatever actual Templar influences might have passed to them could only have derived the highest source.

The Templars were given their rule by the Cistercian monk St. Bernard of Clairvaux, and the Order of the Temple maintained ongoing ties with the Cistercian Order; expelled Templar knights were required to take refuge in monasteries of that Order. Furthermore, in the 11th century Arthurian romance *The Quest of the Holy Grail*, largely of Cistercian inspiration, the *miles Christi* (soldiers of Christ) appear, who some believe are simply the Templars under a different name. The ultimate goal of the questing knights in this romance is the holy city of Sarras, near Jerusalem, where the service of the Holy Grail is performed, and which was believed in the Middle Ages to be the original home of the Saracens. In one of the episodes of the *Quest*, Sir Galahad vanquishes seven evil knights, thereby liberating the Castle of Maidens where abducted women were held captive, and ends by causing all the knights of the district to swear fealty to the Lady of the castle. This motif from the Courtly Love tradition reminds us that St. Bernard wrote extensively on the Song of Solomon, whose erotic mysticism undoubtedly made Solomon's Temple the central shrine of spiritual romance in many people's minds, especially in view of the legend of Solomon and the Queen of Sheba. Madame Myrrha Lot-Borodine believes that the *Quest* most directly expresses the doctrines of the Cistercian Guillaume de St. Thierry, friend of St. Bernard, who taught that *amor ipse intellectus est*, "love itself is the Intellect". Here we can discern a constellation of ideas, organizations and influences—the Templars, the Cistercians, the Saracen capital as a holy city, a sublimated version of chivalry and courtly love, and the concept of Intellective Love as the goal of the spiritual Path (which is also central to the *Divine Comedy* in which St. Bernard plays a prominent role)—that when taken together provide a context in which the idea of the Fedeli d'Amore as an esoteric initiatory order, incorporating certain Sufic influences and devoted to Courtly Love as a spiritual Path, does not appear quite so far-fetched. In any case, *The Quest of the Holy Grail*, *The Divine Comedy*, and Wolfram's *Parzival* prove that the notion (if not the reality) of the Templars as a focus of a more-or-less esoteric knightly-romantic spirituality differing from, though not necessarily opposed to, the standard spirituality of the visible Church, was not simply an the invention of 18th century fantasts. Nothing does more to debunk the "ancient mysteries" in the minds of serious scholars than spurious revivals by irresponsible literary occultists. Such revivals, in the case of Freemasonry and Templarism, given that claims to an unbroken transmission of lore and authority from the Middle Ages or the ancient world are almost certainly false, undoubtedly served to obscure and falsify the very legends they were based upon, legends that could well have contained more than a grain of truth.

So I believe Guénon was right in his assertion that Order of the Temple functioned at one point as the guardians of the Primordial Tradition. But as soon as this esoteric Templar universalism became literalized and exteriorized via their ambition to act as a trans-national power elite, superseding not only the nation-state but even Christian orthodoxy and papal authority, their connection with that Tradition—outside of a possible hidden remnant who could have retained their original purity and function—would have been perverted, and consequently turned over to Satan; it would have become part of the history of the Counter-Initiation, which will culminate in Antichrist. As we have seen, when the Primordial Tradition is profaned and exteriorized like this, it gives aid and comfort to those who, like some of today's globalists, want to solidify their power partly through establishing a One-World Religion, or at least a federation of the religions under a secular or universalist authority, as Nimrod attempted when he built his Tower.

The central, Promethean error of Freemasonry is that, by separating itself from the revealed religions, it severs the work of *edification*, the building up of the human form to make it a fit temple of the Holy Spirit, from the Grace and Guidance of that very Spirit; as we have already seen, there is no reliable access to Grace without dispensation and apostolic succession—*silsilah*. [NOTE: Anyone interested in the deeper significance of "edification" might consult "The Tripartite Human Psyche in Fall and Restoration" in *The Science of the Greater Jihad: Essays in Principial Psychology*, Charles Upton, Sophia Perennis, 2011.] Thus what the Hebrew prophets might well have said when they first discerned the dark, Counter-Initiatory side of the building of the First Temple, which certainly could have appeared to them as a kind of shocking restoration of Egyptian hieratic gigantism within the House of Israel, can certainly be directed to the Masons—if not as a judgment, then at least as a challenge: "If the Lord build not the house, they labor in vain who build it." [Psalms 127:1]. And to the degree that the Templars became infected by the same Promethean spirit, they deserve, every bit as much as those modern Freemasons who have acted to undermine the authority of the divine revelations, to be classed in their later degeneracy as agents of the Counter-Initiation. In their original and esoteric purity (original not necessarily in time, but surely in essence, as recognized by Dante, Wolfram von Eschenbach and René Guénon), the Templars are the sons of the Temple; in their exteriorized, profane and perverted form, they are the Sons of the Tower.

As for Freemasonry, it is most likely not a unified conspiratorial organization, ruling the world from behind the scenes, itself under the command of the higher-degree initiates or "secret chiefs". But it has done three things that warrant our vigilance: (1) It has spread through society the notion that there is, has been or might be an esoteric teaching superseding the Revelations that allows its initiates to accept all religions because this "secret doctrine" transcends them and relativizes them—a notion that paints the revealed religions as relatively shallow and exterior, and further conceals their esoteric depths by promoting various counterfeit esoterisms (as it did for Guénon in the case of Catholicism); this conception has made Freemasonry a seed bed for both syncretism and the *idea* of a Counter-Traditional spiritual elite; (2) It has provided, through its structure of interlocking networks protected by secrecy, a venue for other forces—revolutionary movements, intelligence services, criminal organizations, networks of the rich and powerful—allowing them to gather information, make contacts, collect and launder funds, and spread their influence, forces that from time to time have turned specific Freemasonic lodges or jurisdictions into conspiratorial cadres; 3) It has provided a model of secrecy, modes of recognition, degrees of initiation and methods of commanding allegiance that have been of great use to other organizations attempting to seize or wield power, whether revolutionary, elitist, or a combination of the two (as an intelligence service might work to create a "controlled opposition" which believes itself opposed to the powers that be while actually serving their interests). The Bavarian Illuminati founded by Adam Weishaupt are an example of a revolutionary secret society designed partly on the Freemasonic model; Propaganda Due (P2), the Italian Freemasonic lodge involved in the Vatican banking scandal, was (and perhaps still is) a secret society founded by and for the power elite. Nonetheless, there *is* a unanimous, Primordial Tradition—one that has branched into the several great world religions as the Divine Revelations have defined and unfolded those branches; but it is only through these Revelations, not outside them, that it can be reliably accessed.[8]

One wonders if the modernizing tendency visible in the originally Iranian Nimatullahi Sufi Order in the west is not due in part to the indirect influence of the "freethinking" Masonry that entered Iran via western economic and political influence in the 18th century. (I hasten to add that no Sufi order of which I am aware is actually *affiliated* with the Freemasons. Apparently the heterodox order known as the Bektashis had dealings with them in the 19th century, but the tale told by the founders of the Shriner movement that some of their North African branches were composed of Bektashi dervishes seems entirely unfounded; like the Theosophical Society's fantastic accounts of Tibetan lamas, discarnate or otherwise, it's the kind of story that could only gain currency when actual Sufis, or actual lamas, were virtually unknown in the West.) In "An Introduction to the History of Freemasonry in Iran", Hamid Algar demonstrates how Freemasonry was used by both the French and the British as a way of exerting influence on Iranian society through a pro-western elite—an influence which, however, did not always have the desired effect. He says: "The claim of masonry to have established a 'religion of humanity' and passed beyond the divisive claims of established religions may have formed one element of its appeal to some Iranians of Muslim background. It is interesting to find certain European travelers of the early and mid-nineteenth century regarding as 'freethinkers' many of those whom they encountered and who styled themselves Sufis, and comparing their religious attitudes to those inculcated by freemasonry. To such individuals the masonic lodge may have appeared to be an ideal form of

8. The "Unknown Superiors" or "Secret Chiefs" of Freemasonry (which Guénon apparently believed in at one point), though they might actually exist as a Counter-Initiatory "steering committee", also likely represent an imperfect memory of the (largely) hidden hierarchy of the Sufis, which includes the Pole, the Arbiters, the Supports, the Substitutes, the Hidden Ones, the Strangers, the Noble, the Chieftains, the Pillars etc. These are not the clandestine officers of some secret society but rather Sufis who have attained various spiritual stations, and whose levels of development may or not be known to others, or even to themselves. They are in some ways the Sufi equivalent of the Communion of the Saints.

organization, offering the possibility of a nominal profession of Islam and of an amorphous 'religion of humanity'. Similarly, if the legend of the transmission of the masonic light from Zoroaster to the Prophet Muhammad, as expounded by Adib ul-Mamalik Farahani, was commonly or widely accepted by Iranian masons, the lodge was probably conceived of too as a means for the nurturing of nascent Iranian nationalism, with its generally muted implication of hostility to the Arabs and Islam."

"Freethinking" entails both the abandonment of tradition and the stirring up of revolutionary ferment, which in western terms are aspects of the same tendency. In the context of an eastern society subjected to westernizing pressures, however, "freedom of thought" can polarize into the desire to abandon tradition by embracing western modernization on the one hand, and a call to foment revolution with a view to throwing off western influences on the other. And as Algar demonstrates, these freethinking sentiments, in the case of Iran, included a spurious "traditionalism" of their own: the nostalgia for Zoroastrianism, considered not primarily as a religion, a way to God, but as a badge of national or ethnic identity. (In terms of both Islam and Hinduism, a similar tendency can be discerned in colonial and post-colonial India up to the present day.) In this context, I see the fact that I am related through my mother's family to Howard Conklin Baskerville, the "American Lafayette in Iran" who fought with the constitutionalist forces for Iranian independence against Muhammad Ali Shah, a "traditional" ruler who was backed by the Russian imperialists, as a mixed blessing: I am proud that my illustrious ancestor gave his life for Iranian freedom and independence, but sad that there was no way he could do so except by supporting a cause that further Westernized Iran and weakened its ancient traditions— especially that of Sufism, where a *true* marriage was made, in a strictly Islamic context, between Islam and what remained of the Zoroastrian spirit by masters such as Shahab al-Din Suhrawardi, not a spurious one such as was posited by al-Farhani in the context of Freemasonry.

The figure of Jamal al-Din al-Afghani (1838–1897), a Persian with cosmopolitan connections, illustrates the ambiguity of various Anti-Traditional or Counter-Traditional influences on Islam. Afghani was at one point a Freemason, a colleague of Theosophist Madam Blavatsky, closely associated with the Baha'i, and is also described as having Sufi sympathies. He was largely European in lifestyle and did not follow many basic Muslim practices; on the other hand, he supported the Sudanese "Mahdi", the Sufi rebel against British imperialism. His disciple Muhammad 'Abduh, grand Mufti of Egypt, made accommodations with the British and is described in the *Encyclopedia of Religion* as "the architect of Islamic modernism", but according to Karen Armstrong in *Holy War: The Crusades and their Impact on Today's World*, both Afghani and 'Abduh "tended to look back in many ways to the principles of the eighteenth century Wahhabi revolution". Suffice it to say that the simplistic notion of "tolerant Muslims and/or Sufis open to modern and universalist ideas" vs. "terroristic reactionary Islamic fundamentalists" is a red herring. The modernizing tendency in Islam has not been free of Wahhabi/Salafi influences; western modernism has influenced both anti-western pan-Islamism and the "Neo-Sufi" tendency to accommodate to the west and de-emphasize Islam; Sufism itself, while a-political in essence, has a history both of resistance to western influences and of manipulation by pro-western interests; and in our own time western and/or globalist forces have sought to co-opt both pro-western Sufism and Islamist militancy which, as we have conjectured in the case of some branches of the Naqshbandi Order, may in certain instances be the same thing. Suffice it to say that those westerners who are seeking the essence of traditional Islam should take neither liberal modernization nor anti-western "fundamentalism" as a sign of that essence; both are signs of nothing but *al-Dunya*, "the Darkness of This World". God is known only by God; only those seekers who desire God above all else will succeed in finding the true Islam.

In a more inner sense, in terms of the spiritual Path, Masonry is an imitation or parody of a true esoteric way. In the Freemasonic world the meaning of the rituals is not fully understood; the initiate is invited to investigate further on his own; the true Word is lost, but may be found again. As Guénon points out in *Studies in Freemasonry and the Compagnnonage*, the universal legend of a lost Word or Grail or Treasure symbolizes the loss of the Primordial State our first parents enjoyed in Eden—but in the case of Freemasonry, what seems in many cases to have been lost is the very understanding of what a "Lost Word" might represent. In any legitimate initiatory form the symbolism of the rituals is thoroughly understood by those administering them, and the progress of the initiate is not defined simply by his or her ability to understand this symbolism, or to endlessly add to his or her collection of arcane lore, but rather to assimilate the spiritual influence he or she has come into contact with on levels that leave symbolic exegesis far behind—though a deepening understanding of symbols may still be useful in the preliminary stages of the path, or at specific stations of it. The true Word is not literally lost; it is known and always has been, though certainly not by everyone. Progress is defined in terms of one's capacity to let that Word alchemize the soul; this is one all-important difference between true Initiation and Pseudo-Initiation. Some Masons may indeed understand their symbolism in this sense, but symbolism devoid of the Grace of a Divine Revelation must remain—to invert the Freemasonic terminology—merely "speculative"; it can never become truly "operative". Furthermore, the symbolism of Freemasonry, while undoubtedly valid when certain fragments are considered in isolation, is fundamentally heterogeneous, and a heterogeneous hodge-podge of valid symbols does not constitute a valid symbology; as Jay Kinney puts it [*The Masonic Myth*, pp. 126–127], "the traditions and symbols of Rosicrucianism, alchemy, Kabbalah, and every other esoteric and mystical system under the sun were plundered in an effort to give the 'higher' degrees some secrets worth finding." A promiscuous collection of doctrines and influences like this cannot unify the soul. Its very heterogeneity—which is *not* the same thing as synthetic complexity—cuts it off from the Unity of the Spirit and consequently from the Grace of God, limiting its influence to the psychic plane. At best it might represent a relatively positive system of moral or psychological conditioning rather than, as in the case of the true spiritual Path, a way of deconstructing *all* conditioning. But the fact that a psychic influence takes the place proper to a spiritual Grace at best muddies the waters and at worst erects a serious barrier to the soul's receptivity to true Grace, simultaneously attracting the attention of demonic (or deluded) Principalities and Powers and tempting them to set themselves up as counterfeit Spiritual principles. This replacement of the Spiritual by the psychic is not limited to Freemasonry, of course, but is equally characteristic of the New Age, of various forms of "occultism" practiced outside the bounds of a Divine revelation, and of the realm of magic and sorcery, traditional Shamanism possibly excepted. In the realm of the Spirit no concept or disposition-of-soul can be merely "neutral". If a doctrine or ritual does not lead toward spiritual Truth along a path established by that Truth, or embody a real aspect of It, then it is destructive to that Truth's manifestation; this is one of the things that Jesus meant when He said, "he who is not with Me is against Me."

As for the spiritual influence of the Knights Templars, the best of it—which might be described as a true Initiatory kernel freed from its Counter-Initiatory shell—seems to have passed, as we have seen, to Dante Aligheri. Dante, as a White Guelph, harked back to the defeated Ghibelines in his opposition to the growth of the papacy as a temporal power under Boniface XIII; in so doing he opposed the Black Guelphs who, according to John Coleman, became the Black Nobility of Genoa and Venice, whose power was based more on finance than feudal authority. That Dante might have been heir, via the Fedeli d'Amore, to a spiritual stream of esoteric Templar lore is all the more interesting in that he seems to have set himself against certain elements of the Italian banking interests who had in some ways inherited the darker side of the Templar influence, including the practice of charging interest on loans; in Canto XVII of the *Inferno* he puts the Black Guelph Gianfigliazzi among the Usurers. Dante seems to have been placed at the precise point where the light and dark sides of the Templar influence forked.[9] Usury was prohibited in medieval Christendom, as it is in present-day Islam (ideally at least) under the name of *rida*, but the Templars got around this stricture on a technicality. It's as if the Knights Templars in their role as international bankers had interpreted Matthew 25:29, "For unto

9. Ezra Pound, in *Canto XLV*, carried on Dante's attack against usury; but though he wrote on the subject of Romance, he was not a true initiate on that path. He inherited Dante's social and cultural understanding but not his spiritual insight; he was not of the Fedeli d'Amore.

every one that hath shall be given, and he shall have abundance: but from him that hath not shall be taken away even that which he hath" in a cynical, ironic, Counter-Initiatory sense, as allowing them to *rent money* in a way that neither generates nor represents any real value at all, and thereby make much of Christendom their debtor. In the esoteric sense, this scriptural passage means that those who have realized the Presence of God are able to see the Divine Generosity in circumstances, and receive from it, whereas those who haven't attained this realization necessarily occupy *al-Dunya*, the Darkness of This World, where every experience robs the experiencer of some of his substance, driving him ever deeper into debt to that World. And on the highest level, Matthew 25:29 means, speaking in Sufis terms, that those who have realized the Black Paradise of the Essence of God will be given as well the Green Paradise of the Names and Attributes of God [see Frithjof Schuon, "The Two Paradises" in *Form and Substance in Religion*]. And it is precisely usury, the principle behind the kind the sovereign debt that Pope Clement V and King Philip the Fair of France cancelled when they suppressed the Templar Order, that is presently destroying the world economy and dissolving the sovereignty of nations.

The following scenario is plausible as of this writing: The loss of national sovereignty to the banks will initiate a call for the banks to be nationalized—but with national sovereignty already seriously compromised and the banks international in scope, only a One World Government would have the power to "nationalize"—or rather *internationalize*—the global financial interests who have bought title to that sovereignty. And if something like this were to take place, one would be hard pressed to say whether the World Authority had "globalized" the banks or the banks *bought* the World Authority; perhaps these are simply two different descriptions of the same thing. Furthermore, if the nations were to default on their debts rather than attempting to nationalize the banks, thus causing the banks to fold, this would simply allow them to be snapped up by the megabanks; such a scenario might in fact be behind the Vatican's recent call for a unified international monetary and banking system [see Chapter One]. In any case, the central economic trend of our time is the concentration of capital in fewer and fewer hands—an inherently unstable situation in *capitalistic* terms, which might be why billionaire Warren Buffett begged the Federal government to tax the rich so as to redistribute the wealth—but one that might make sense if the goal were a kind of global re-feudalization so as to produce a "sustainable" economy no longer based, like capitalism, on endless growth. This use of financial interests to destroy national sovereignty, after which those interests are themselves appropriated by a *global* sovereignty, is predicted in Revelations 17:16–17, where international finance—or the phase in which the free flow of capital enriches a large percentage of the population, resulting in a hedonistic society—is symbolized by the Whore of Babylon, and One-World Government—or the megabanks who ultimately facilitate the global concentration of capital in the hands of a tiny elite who constitute that Government—by the Beast:

> And the ten horns [who are ten kings, representing either ten nations or the small handful of megabanks] which thou sawest upon the beast, these shall hate the whore, and shall make her desolate and naked, and shall eat of her flesh, and burn her with fire [austerity!]. For God hath put it into their hearts to fulfill his will, and to agree, and give their kingdoms unto the beast, until the words of God shall be fulfilled.

Those like Guénon who lament the suppression of the Templars as the last visible outpost in the western world of the Primordial Tradition do not seem to grasp that the Order, outside of a small, faithful remnant whose influence passed to Dante and a few others, had likely been infiltrated by the Counter-Initiation well before that suppression took place. And insofar as the Templars are associated with Jerusalem, the prediction repeated by many (including Dennis Engleman in his book *Ultimate Things*, speaking for the Eastern Orthodox tradition) that the Antichrist will rule the world from a rebuilt Jewish Temple in Jerusalem, such as actually being planned by ultraconservative Jews, gains added resonance. We should also note in the above verses that the rise of the Beast, who is Antichrist, takes place according to God's will; if we will not obey Him we will be forced to openly deny Him, and suffer the consequences.

Sad to say, René Guénon hoped to find or create a Freemasonry that would both function as a "Catholic esoterism" and turn the Catholic Church, on some level, into a syncretistic universalism. He spoke of "realizing Catholicism in the true sense of the word . . . this Catholicism would have a fully effective existence only when it had succeeded in integrating the traditions contained in the sacred books of all peoples" [*Studies in Freemasonry and the Compagnonnage*, p. 129]. In proposing this he was attempting to falsely import into Christianity the Qur'anic doctrine of "the peoples of the Book". And in our own time we can see how the apostate Novus Ordo Catholic Church is well on its way to realizing this "ideal" in the most externalized, most bastardized, most Counter-Initiatory manner imaginable. Guénon understood that a unity of religions based on universal metaphysical principles would have to "celebrate diversity" on the exoteric level and that it could make no common cause with political "internationalism". And he knew that such unity could only be realized in strictly "intellectual" terms, though he hoped that this intellectual realization would serve to reorder Western Civilization on all levels. But he did not, in my opinion, clearly realize just how *esoteric*, in terms of both the necessity of relative secrecy, and of insights that could in no way be put into human words, such a realization would have to be; rather, he conceived of it as something capable of being expressed in terms of organized, institutional Freemasonry, however reconstituted and purified the Masonic lodges would first have to become in order to host it. He failed to understand that "internationalism"—what we now call "globalism"—was lying in wait, like the Dragon of the Apocalypse, for the spiritual/intellectual renewal he hoped for, ready to devour it as soon as it was born. And it *was* born, up to a point, in the guise of the Traditionalist School and certain parallel manifestations; it is now in the process of being devoured—by the Novus Ordo, by the Interfaith Movement, by the Globalists—except insofar as the Woman Crowned with Twelve Stars gives birth to a Son who, to hide him from the Dragon, is immediately caught up to God and His Throne [Apocalypse 12]. The Woman of the Apocalypse symbolizes, on one level, the constellation or zodiac of the world's religions—remembering that, according to the Sufi Ruzbehan Baqli, the Virgin Mary, with whom the Woman is often identified, is "The

Mother of the Prophets". It is a constellation whose issue can find no resting place in This World, till He comes again in glory to judge the living and the dead. The Esoteric Essence, as with al-Hallaj, is revealed in a brief flash, after which it must rapidly conceal itself again, or go to feed the Dragon; if this concealment had not taken place through Hallaj's martyrdom, however much we may lament it, Hallaj would have become Baha'ullah. This is the "brief reinstatement before the coming of the Hour" predicted by Guénon in *The Reign of Quantity and the Signs of the Times.*

The only Unity worth pursuing is *intrinsic* Unity, which is attained by realizing it, not by constructing it. Every constructed, and especially every *imposed* unity, after it passes a certain point, inevitably generates fragmentation and chaos. As Frithjof Schuon indicated, such a unity of religions can only be *transcendent*; ultimately the paths meet only in God, in the single Source that first sent them down into this world. And in more human terms, such unity can be expressed—without heterodoxy and corruption—only by a Communion of Saints not visible to outer eyes, or in terms of providential meetings arranged by God between a few saints or sages who, by His grace, know how to understand each other and salute each other. It is not and cannot be expressed through steering committees, ecclesiastical bureaucracies or voluntary associations of any kind without losing its true nature, and thus going to serve the Powers of Darkness.

11

The Fall of Lucifer—A Synthesis of Emanationist and Volitional Theodicy

IN *Survey of Metaphysics and Esoterism* [World Wisdom Books, 1986, p.18], Frithjof Schuon says:

> [It] is in the nature of the Good to wish to communicate itself: to say Good is to say radiation, projection, unfolding, gift of self. But at the same time, to say radiation is to say distance, hence alienation or impoverishment; the solar rays dim and become lost in the night of space. From this arises, at the end of the trajectory, the paradoxical phenomenon of evil, which nonetheless has the positive function of highlighting the good *a contrario*, and of contributing in its fashion to the equilibrium of the phenomenal order.

In Schuon's metaphysics and cosmology (at least as I understand them), the Formless Absolute (*Nirguna Brahman*; Godhead; Beyond Being; *al-Dhat*) "emanates" the Personal God (*Saguna Brahman*; Pure Being; the Creator; *Allah*), Who in turn brings into outward manifestation the possibilities latent in All-Possibility or *maya-in-divinis*, and thereby creates the spiritual, psychic and material universes. God does not positively will evil, and He possesses the power to abolish any particular evil; however, in the nature of things, He could not negate the existence of evil as such without annihilating creation itself, which only exists by virtue of the ontological level it occupies, where evil is an inescapable possibility, woven as it were into the fabric of things. If the universe did not contain the possibility of evil, it would not be the universe, but God Himself.

So universal Emanation necessarily contains within it, as a subset, the possibility of particular Creation, which in turn introduces the possibility of a Fall. Neither Emanation nor Creation, however, *are* the Fall. Creation introduces the possibility of a Fall, but does not actualize it; only rebellious free will can do that. One might argue that it is inevitable—in more or less "actuarial" terms—that some among an indefinite multitude of beings endowed with free will would choose rebellion, but this does not negate the reality of freedom in each individual case, nor the justice of the grim consequences earned by those who misuse it.

According to Schuon, The Real, the Sovereign Good, must communicate itself to (and as) celestial and cosmic manifestation, by virtue of the fact that what is Absolute is also necessarily Infinite, and no bound can be set to the Infinite. And it is certainly true that celestial and cosmic manifestation arise from the necessary and Infinite overflow of the superabundant Reality of the Absolute. But insofar as this manifestation is also a veil, the possibility of Satanic subversion is latent within it. For God to communicate Himself to cosmic existence is only good, but it is a limited good, not the unlimited reality of the Sovereign Good; the Supraformal necessarily manifests Itself in terms of form, and every form is a limitation. But insofar as existence is good in itself, such limitations are neither evil nor subversive. And yet they harbor the possibility of evil and subversion, by the very fact that limited forms are always paired with imperfect knowers, sentient beings who are limited in perspective just as the forms they perceive are limited in scope. And as soon as limited forms as perceived by limited knowers make their appearance, the possibility of idolatry arises, which I will define here as the tendency to "willfully mistake" a limited form for the reality of the Absolute which has manifested it, and which subsists within it as its essential Reality. There can be no evil in the Divine realm; the seeds of evil do exist in the celestial realm, but they remain latent since they have no context for deployment; it is only in the psychic realm that evil actually constellates as a subversive force. Schuon is right that evil only makes its appearance at the end of the trajectory of cosmic manifestation—not at the ultimate end, however, which is matter, but rather on the psychic plane, where "worlds" constructed with the ego not God as their proximate cause first become possible. Nonetheless, the existence of Lucifer testifies to the fact that the subversive privation which is, or will become, evil, has its beginnings at the apex of the celestial order; otherwise he could not have fallen "from heaven".

Lucifer represents not the descent from Principle into manifestation, but the potential, on every level of the ontological hierarchy, for delusion, privation, and subversion—the concrete manifestation of which, however, is only made possible by that very descent. As the "light bearer" he is symbolic, in his unfallen mode, of the *Nous*, the First Intellect, the first eternal motion of God's knowledge of Himself as "other". In his fallen mode, he symbolizes the possibility of spiritual subversion and metaphysical error on the highest possible level—in terms of the human microcosm, the subversion the *Nous* (which appears, in the Qur'an, as the refusal of Eblis to bow down to Adam.) The *Nous*, the Uncreated Intellect within man, cannot be subverted in its essence, but it most certainly can be counterfeited and veiled.

According to Schuon, for the "volitional and affective" man, the ego is "I" and God is "He", while for the "intellective" man, God is "I" and the ego is "he." Applying this distinction to Lucifer, we can imagine his fall as made possible by a descent from the intellective or *jñanic* station to the volitional/affective one, coupled with *a refusal to accept the necessity* of this creative descent—the later consequences of which God, in Genesis, looked upon and called good. If he had accepted the necessity of the descending radiation of the Absolute in the direction of manifestation, Lucifer would have been able—in his own case—to redress its potential deficiencies. Instead, he opposed it. In holding on to a "higher" conception of God as the Formless Absolute, he failed to understand that God's celestial and cosmic manifestation is in no way a departure from His Essence, but rather a veiling of that Essence for the very purpose of revealing It. In other words—like the sectarian Gnostics—he looked upon God's creative act not as a positive Self-manifestation, but strictly as a Fall. And by this very rejection of cosmic existence, which was both an intellectual error and a willful rebellion, he *transformed* it into a Fall; this is the "primordial irony". Lucifer failed to understand that "If I ascend up to heaven, Thou art there; if I make my bed in hell, behold, Thou art there." The ambiguity of existence, which is the ambiguity of *maya*, is: that while manifestation must depart from the Essence, the Essence can never depart from Itself—and what is manifestation, on every level, but the revelation of that very Essence?

Lucifer looked within himself and saw the image of the *atman*, the Absolute Divine Witness, but he saw it as an object of *his* knowledge, not himself as an object of Its knowledge. This primal *limitation* placed upon Intellection—or rather, this primal appearance of Intellection apart from the Absolute One, an Intellection capable for the first time of knowing the One as an object—can still be defined as a stage of the descent of the Absolute into manifestation, not as a subversion of that manifestation, not as a Fall. Lucifer's intellectual *error*—which, in terms of his free will, was also an act of rebellion—was *to identify his now limited selfhood with the Absolute Reality he saw within him*, rather than submitting to It and worshipping It, which was now required of him given the present stage-of-descent of Divine manifestation. As soon as manifestation descends from the purely intellective station to the volitional/affective one—in other words, as soon as free will is born—then the will is required to submit, and the affections, to love. This act of immediate submission to the new and more limited condition—*not* the will to reject it by holding on to the *memory* of the former and higher one—is the only way back to that higher one.

If Lucifer had retained the higher level of consciousness represented by the *atman*, he would have remained rooted in the Absolute Witness which witnesses only Itself, and would consequently have been able to witness the cosmic unfolding, by virtue of the Eye of God within him, as a positive Divine manifestation, not a Fall. As soon as he saw that Reality as an "object", however, no longer as the Witness by which he witnessed, and which also witnessed him, then the Fall became possible. This was the primal intellectual *limitation*—a limitation which, because it posited God as an object, equally posited Lucifer as an independent entity. As an apparently independent entity, he found himself possessed of an independent will, which could either submit to and adore this newly-arisen objective God, or else deny Him and worship itself instead. Unwilling to redress the consequences of his intellectual limitation through submission and adoration, which would have immediately unveiled the *atman* once more, and effected—for him—the reintegration of the Personal God into the Formless Absolute, God into Godhead, Lucifer held on to the memory of that higher state in which himself as subject, and God as object, had not yet polarized—a state which, at this stage of the cosmic unfolding, *he could now identify only with himself*, not with God. He saw the objective Personal God as a veil covering the Essence (which It is) but not as a theophany of that very Essence (which It certainly also is). Thus, in the name of the "preservation" of the level of consciousness of the *atman*, he barred the only effective road of return to that *atman*, rejected God, entered into a state of self-worship, and fell: and the etiology of the fall of Lucifer is, precisely, the etiology of the ego. We can understand by this that the possibility of self-idolatry, of the egoistic denial of God, was present from the first moment of the unfolding of universal manifestation. But it was present only as one possibility within the embrace of All-Possibility ("the possibility of impossibility" as Schuon has called it), not as a necessity on the level of free will (since if it were present as such a necessity, then the will would not be free). As soon as form is born, both potential obedience, resulting in a vision of the metaphysical transparency of all forms, and potential rebellion, based upon the idolatry of these forms, are born along with it.

Universal manifestation can also be viewed in terms of the Hindu doctrine of *Maya*, which is substantially identical with Schuon's "emanationism" (and, in many ways, with Neo-Platonic emanationism as well), with the notion that Reality must, by Its nature, communicate Itself in an descending order of celestial and cosmic manifestations, each lower ontological plane being both more attenuated and more opaque and solidified than its higher predecessors. But this truth does not license us to ignore the ontological level upon which, and subsequent to which, evil must progressively be defined in terms of the abuse of free will by angelic, animic and human entities. When the Noble Qur'an says *I seek refuge in the Lord of Daybreak from the evil of that which He created*, it is not saying that God deliberately created evil, or (as Carl Jung maintained in *Answer to Job*) is somehow half evil Himself; if this were true, there would be no refuge in Him. As Schuon repeatedly points out in his writings, God is the Sovereign Good, and as such He cannot positively will evil, seeing that evil is not a positive reality on any level, but precisely a privation.

As Schuon teaches, in *Gnosis: Divine Wisdom* and elsewhere, *Maya*, as the "magical" manifestation of the Absolute, presents us with a universe that is neither real nor unreal, a world that is not strictly non-existent, but nonetheless not what it seems. Insofar as it manifests a cosmos apparently composed of limited forms arranged in various relations to one another, and subject to natural law, it is *avidya-maya*, or "ignorance-appearance"; insofar as it presents us with forms which by their very existence testify to the Real, and which, by their essential qualities, exist as reflections of the Names or Qualities of God, it is *vidya-maya* or "wisdom-appearance." Thus *Maya* cannot be strictly identified with the evil Demiurge of the sectarian Gnostics, who recognized cosmic manifestation in its aspect of *avidya-maya*, but not in its aspect of *vidya-maya*; to them, the crystalline spheres of the circling heavens were an ingeniously-contrived prison ruled by oppressive spiritual powers; in no way could they "declare the glory of God," nor could "the earth show forth His handiwork."

The Devil is not evil because, like the Gnostic Demiurge, he *creates* this cosmos of heaviness and material limitation, but rather because he subverts it. The goal of all cosmic manifestation, the "lowest" point where God can be reflected as integral Being, is the human form. And as every religious revelation tradition teaches, either openly or "esoterically", the centrality of the human form, despite the heaviness and opacity of its material manifestation (whether or not this be considered as the product of a "Fall"), gives it a potential spiritual precedence over even the highest angels, since it is the direct, though distant, reflection of God in the material cosmos, while the angels are the higher, but relatively peripheral, reflections of the various Names or Qualities of God. Man alone exists as a synthesis of all the Names—a "stewardship" or "Trust" that he is free to either realize or betray.

(Man at the limit of cosmic manifestation, imprisoned in a material existence transformed from a theophany into a veil, in relation to which he has lost the power to see material forms in their metaphysical transparency, is well symbolized by Prometheus bound to the rock, his liver being eaten by the eagle of Zeus. The liver—related to the *manipura-chakra* of the Hindu Tantra—when alienated from man's higher faculties becomes the seat of a "Promethean" self-will, a reckless willfulness that steals the fire of Zeus—the Intellect, the *Nous*—and transforms it into blind impulse. Man in the state of self-will represents the lowest point of cosmic manifestation—matter itself being incapable of rebellion, and thus fundamentally innocent—at which point cosmic existence must either begin its return to God, via the sacrifice of self-will, or else fall into an infernal or *titanic* state, which is no longer a veiling of God with a view toward His outward manifestation, but a plunge into chaos and non-entity. And the sole path of this return is the path of *Intellection*, either actual or virtual: the eagle of Zeus is a symbol of the *Nous* in the process of devouring the fallen self-will, thus transforming it back into Intellection again. The "punishment" of Prometheus, being precisely purgatorial, is the beginning of his salvation.)

So the Absolute, by virtue of Its Infinity, radiates Itself through the descending eschelons of celestial and cosmic manifestation until it reaches the human form—which, by virtue of the possibility of spiritual realization and Liberation, is the point where the return of universal manifestation to its Origin begins. (This entire cycle of radiation and return is encapsulated in the *Basmallah* that begins every *surah* but one of the Noble Qur'an: *Bismillah al-Rahman al-Rahim*; "In the Name of God, the merciful, the Compassionate." *Al-Rahman* is the "universal Mercy" that allows all beings to come into separate existence, the Mercy of Creation; *al-Rahim* is the "particular Mercy" that provides the criteria and established the spiritual Path by which each being, insofar as it *chooses* to avail itself of them, may return to Allah.) But, due to the freedom of the human will, without which God's own freedom could not be mirrored in humanity, the expansion and attenuation of the Absolute's cosmic manifestation does not end at the human level, but may also sink below it. In Hindu terms this "sinking" may be seen as the result of the action of the *guna* named *tamas* (the *gunas* being the three modes of Universal Substance or *Prakriti*) which, in terms of its positive function, materially stabilizes the cosmic environment in which earthly, incarnate man must exist, but which also, in terms of its negative or subversive function, veils the face of God, thus introducing "materialism" in all the senses of that word.

That man has a body is not evil, though that body is subject to many evils. That he lives in a material world is not evil, though matter and material concerns are a heavy veil. The nature and activity of the Devil must not be sought in these mere facts of earthly man's existence, but in the satanic subversion of the true significance of them. In one sense they are the product of a fall, of the loss of Eden which made it necessary for humanity to don these "garments of skin" [Genesis 3:21]; in another, this very fall was a *felix culpa*, destined not to confirm and solidify Satan's kingdom, but to overturn it definitively. In light of this we can understand our present physical forms not as a punishment for Adam's sin, but as a product of God's mercy, who willed a partial redress of the effects of that sin on a lower level of being, thus opening man to the possibility of Redemption.

When cosmic manifestation, in its expansion and attenuation, falls below the human form, because the human being has failed to recognize God in the totality of that manifestation—and thus, by that act, to return cosmic manifestation to its Origin—it enters the realm of what René Guénon calls the "infra-psychic", which is, precisely, the kingdom of Satan. Ontologically lower, but also subtler, than gross matter, the infra-psychic possesses all the darkness and opacity of matter without its nobility and stability, as well as the all swiftness, penetration and ingeniousness of pure Intellection without its orientation to Divine Truth: the "possibility of impossibility" with a vengeance! (We might term the tendency toward heaviness and opacity as "Satanic", and the quality of ingeniousness and lightning-swiftness as "Luciferian".) It is here, not in the bare facts of material existence, that the nature and "function" of the Devil are to be found.

Though evil is certainly a *privatio boni*—a depletion of, or limited access to, the Good, on a particular level of being—it is not a "mere" insufficiency. Certainly evil is a privation and nothing else, a privation of both Divine Reality (in ontological terms) and the Sovereign Good (in "moral" ones)—as well as, in terms of both the possibility of spiritual intuition and an understanding of the doctrines derived from revelation, a privation of the Truth, a veil over pure Intellection. But what is often poorly understood by many who espouse a more-or-less emanationist view of Divine manifestation is that evil, privative though it be, does not manifest simply as a kind of weakness or lack, but also as *attack*, *subversion*, and *counterfeit*. Where sound doctrine is wise, evil (as error) is not simply stupid, but also infernally ingenious; where love is strong, evil (as hatred) is not only weak, but demonically cruel; where universal manifestation constitutes a Cosmos, an Order composed of a descending hierarchy of orders within orders, the kingdom of Satan also has its infernal modes of organization, its "lowerarchies" (to use the humorous term coined by C.S. Lewis), its dark *agendas*. Hell is not a neutral chaos, but an inverted order; not a loveless indifference, but an active attack upon Love; not a stupid impermeability to metaphysical Truth, but a swift, ingenious and infernally "intelligent" war upon that Truth. As a parasite on order, evil forms its own counterfeit order, chaotic in essence but nonetheless marshaled into a semblance of order through naked power. As a parasite on love, it tempts us to give our love to that which is in the process of destroying us, as the drunkard loves his bottle or the addict his drug; as a parasite on Truth, it forms its own inverted metaphysics, and inverted morality as well; it forges its own Counter-Tradition and Counter-Initiation with scraps and fragments of doctrines stolen from the Primordial Tradition, and from the various Divine Revelations that are its branches. It prepares, is presently preparing, and is at this moment acting, to subvert, attack, destroy, counterfeit and supplant whatever remains of this Tradition—whether doctrine, institution, moral standard, faithful believer or metaphysical sage—in this earthly world. Only when it has succeeded in destroying the last vestiges of the Primordial Tradition, thus bringing this cycle of manifestation to a close, will it itself die, and die by starvation, since it has no principle of life within itself, but can exist only as a parasite on the Real.

And so evil is not a "mere" privation, any more than starvation is a "mere" lack of food. It is all too easy, however, for those who hold to the true doctrine that evil is a privation, not a positive force, to see it as a "mere nothing" that can be safely ignored—particularly those who in their spiritual life overly concentrate on the intellective pole, the realm of metaphysics, to the detriment of the existential pole, the realm of sanctity. Such people may foolishly believe that it is relatively easy, at least for those with a degree of metaphysical discernment, to "rise above" evil, that there is really no such thing as "spiritual wickedness in high places". Such complacency is not derived from true metaphysical insight, however—which includes the gift known as "discernment of spirits"—but from that state of spiritual delusion which the Buddhists name *deva-loka*, in reference to the *samsaric* world of the long-lived gods, where the realities of impermanence and karmic rigor are hidden under a veil of aesthetic refinement and false spiritual elevation—until it is too late.

In order to understand the doctrine of evil-as-privation in any effective way, and avoid its potential pitfalls, we need to hold to a metaphysic—as well as to the intrinsic moral standards which exist as reflections of it—that both grants evil its true place in the universal order, so as to free God from the twin slanders that He is either good but too weak to prevent evil, or all-powerful but too evil, or too nihilistically indifferent, to will the good, and that also grants evil its full gravity, while providing access to the complete panoply of traditional powers and skills by which it may be combated—doctrinally, ascetically, and theurgically. To settle for anything less is to reduce metaphysics to an abstract, academic exercise, a parlor game for people who want to entertain themselves with religion instead of saving their souls by means of it.

This world, filled with suffering though it may be, is a creation of Divine mercy, not a product of infernal subversion. In human terms, the possibility of the subversion of a merciful creation—at least in the present *Kali-yuga*—arises first from our mis-perception of that creation as material only, opaque to the light of God, and secondarily from the many ill-conceived actions that flow from this primal error. Subversion is based in *possibility* on the necessary "departure" of creation from God via emanation, so that it may exist in its own right—but it is only realized *in act* by the misuse of free will, which—again in human terms, and ignoring the angelic rebellion which preceded us and still affects us—begins when we succumb to the *temptation* of ignorance, and ends when we express this ignorance concretely through transgression and sin, further reinforcing it by means of them.

Jesus encapsulates in a single line [Luke 17:1], both the necessity of the *possibility* of evil in terms of emanation, and the *actualization* of evil in terms of the misuse of free will: "It is impossible but that offenses shall come, but woe to him through whom they come!" A truly plenary esoterism, in view of the metaphysical truth that limitation is necessary for divine manifestation, does not ignore perspectives more limited than itself, but rather embraces them as providential, and grants them their precise position and function in the universal order.

12

Luciferian Transhumanism and the War against Religion

[*An email dialogue between the author and Prof. Rodney Blackhirst, LaTrobe University, Bendigo, Australia, January, 2012*]

Dear Charles,

The Traditionalists of my acquaintance are only rehearsing and rehashing the old critiques, but the world is moving on to deeper and darker dangers very rapidly. From where I stand there is now a "War on Religion" in general. That is the danger I see. There are all manner of forces converging to create a "post-religion" world—not a world with one religion, but a world with none. Possibly things look different in America, which is still a much more religious society than Australia. In Australian public life religion is now not only marginalized but is under attack from every direction. And yet the Traditionalists are not keeping up with these developments. For instance, the old critiques of Freud and Jung are pretty much irrelevant now. Both Freud and Jung have been expelled from the psychological sciences. It is now all Physicalism, brain chemistry, etc. So why are Traditionalists ... continuing to rage against Freud and Jung, one wonders? As you say, it is all about 50 years out of date.

In my job at present, distinctions between orthodox and heterodox religions seem far less urgent than they once did. I have religious people of all persuasions coming to me because they are under attack. Their right to practice any sort of religion, their right to raise their kids in a religion, are being stripped away at an alarming rate, under the banner of "Social Inclusion" (whatever that is!) The war on religion is in full force here. As I say, my course has now been swallowed up by "Environment and Planning" (imagine that! Religion & Spirituality Studies—which is what it is called now—is now a discipline in "Environment & Planning"—what utter nonsense!) but that is what I am dealing with. The violent hatred of religion—all things spiritual—among these environmentalists is chilling and has really opened my eyes. Once again, though, I feel I am living in a microcosm of the wider world. Everything I teach is under attack. I think that reflects what is going on more generally. Syncretism is only a minor part of it. We are witnessing the complete victory of the Physicalist/Mechanist paradigm. All talk of the spirit will be forbidden.

With Regards
RB

Dear Rodney,

I ask myself how the triumph of Physicalism in your world—which is also advancing in America, though not quite so fast—relates to Guénon's prophesy in *The Reign of Quantity* that Anti-Tradition, which I identify with materialism and scientism, will prepare the way for and be succeeded by Counter-Tradition, false inverted religion. Certainly the syncretism sponsored by government-imposed "interfaith" initiatives weakens religion, but what happens when materialism and atheism wipe it out entirely? The fact is, though, that they can't really eradicate it. Ultimately the human being cannot live in a totally materialistic environment any more than a fish can live out of water. Whatever we believe or don't believe, we are still theomorphic beings. Eastern Orthodox Christianity survived Soviet Russia; in some ways it was even strengthened by the oppression it faced. (It was also unconsciously infected, however, by Communist ideology, which is why the Eastern Orthodox in America now sometimes teach the twin heresies that the soul is not created immortal but is only immortal by grace, which means that Hell is both unnecessary and impossible, and that it is saved only in community—forget all the early Christian hermit-saints of Egypt and Syria!—which is like a Communist saying that the notion of the "individual" is a bourgeois superstition, that it is only the destiny of the *class* that matters: the individual is mortal and the collective eternal because only history is real.) China destroyed traditional Tibet, but now Vajrayana Buddhism is experiencing a vogue in China, though whether this is just a flirtation on the part of the professional classes influenced by the West or something deeper remains to be seen. To the degree that religion is openly oppressed, catacombs develop—the blood of the martyrs is the seed of the Church—but if it is simply debunked and satirized until it becomes insufferably unhip, at the same time being subjected to "soft" oppression minus the secret police and the gulags, while the cultural memory of the religious traditions, at least in their legitimate forms, is progressively wiped out over decades and generations, then something worse can happen. The human spiritual impulse cannot be totally wiped out, but if it finds nothing valid and traditional in the surrounding society to answer it, it emerges again in the most negative and inverted form. I don't know what it's like in Australia, but here in America there is an unbelievable amount of Satanism in popular culture, especially among the young (usually fairly soft Satanism, as represented for example by the popularity of the "Twilight" novels and movies with their vampire theme, or by the heavy metal bands, but almost certainly sprinkled here and there with much more sinister and criminal elements). When the dominant culture enforced Judeo-Christian moralistic religion, the counterculture responded with an interest in mysticism, in "direct experience", simultaneously jettisoning many elements of bourgeois morality, especially in the areas of sexual promiscuity and drug use. What kind of counterculture might we expect a culture of official atheism, which is already in its incipient stage in this country, to invoke? Some of it might take the form of catacomb Christianity (we can already see the beginnings of this in the Traditional Catholic movement) if not catacomb Islam, like that of the Naqshbandi Sufis under Soviet and Chinese oppression, but it is also possible that an imposed materialism and scientism will generate (or already have) an underground with overt Satanic elements. From this vantage point in time we can see that the 60's counterculture was in certain respects a social engineering experiment carried on by the CIA and other clandestine agents of the elites—and the elites, as it turns out, were just as dedicated to destroying bourgeois culture as the hippies were; the global liquidation of the middle classes, such as is taking place before our eyes today in Europe and America, is necessary for the concentration of power. CIA agents fanned out across the world, seeking psychedelic substances and shamanic advisors well before the Beats and the hippies followed in their wake. The hippies, of course, could never believe that the CIA might be *hipper* than they were; they looked at the Firm as a bunch of uptight Christian anti-Communists (which was partly true), but could never imagine that it might also include the type known as the "Bohemian/Magician/Spy"—a common enough character, by the way, to appear in Kipling's novel *Kim*. But the fact is that the occultist John Dee, the original "007", was a member of British Intelligence, as was Aliester Crowley. The CIA, via its MK-ULTRA mind-control program, produced *millions* of doses of LSD; they obviously didn't mean to limit its use to "controlled conditions" but intended to distribute it broadcast throughout U.S. society. Why? Well, if their intent was to destroy bourgeois/Christian "straight" civilization, they succeeded brilliantly. When the elites take charge of the forces of revolution, they very often adopt the methods of the Fabian Socialists and the Tavistock Institute of Human Relations: the slow, insidious, incremental destruction of the dominant constituting forms of a given society, one of which is traditional religion, so a new ideology and worldview can be imposed with little resistance. Couple this with the evidence now emerging that certain sectors of the global elites hold an overt Luciferian ideology (see the researches of Henry Makow, Alan Watt, David McGowan, Peter Levenda, and Fr. Malachi Martin) and you begin to wonder: If members of the elites and the intelligence community who were experimenting with LSD—sometimes on themselves—sponsored the psychedelic counter-culture (which is not to say they created it out of nothing or that it had no positive spiritual content), exploiting the rising reaction against stifling Christian morality—stifling because the intellectual and mystical elements of the religion had already been lost or suppressed—might they now be equally prepared to exploit the inevitable reaction against an imposed regime of atheistic scientism by covertly sponsoring a Luciferian counterculture? Because the elites, unfortunately, are masters of dialectics; they are experts at playing both sides against the middle—at supporting, co-opting and utilizing both wings of major social "contradictions" from a vantage point beyond them. If the west and its allies could patronize "peaceful, tolerant" Sufism, as Ali Eteraz pointed out in his article "State-Sponsored Sufism" [*http://www.foreignpolicy.com/articles/2009/06/09/state_sponsored_sufism*], and at the same time support elements of al-Qaeda, which was founded in part by the CIA as an anti-Soviet insurgency in Afghanistan and was also active in the so-called "Arab Spring" aided by the CIA and supported by NATO air-strikes, who is to say that the popular Satanism that is now so common among the young is not being seeded up to a point by Luciferian elements among the elites? If the inevitable reaction against official atheism, which they are smart enough to anticipate, is diverted in a Luciferian direction—Lucifer being both the Great Rebel and (ironically) also the Great Spiritual Materialist—then whatever is left of *any* religion outside the Luciferian one will be caught in a formidable pincers movement. When Guénon said that Anti-Tradition would give way to Counter-Tradition, and Counter-Tradition to the regime of *al-Dajjal*, he knew exactly what he was talking about, and he meant what he said.

In light of this possibility, I wouldn't downplay the distinction between orthodox and heterodox religion too far in the name of a united front against the enemies of religion. The very imposition of official atheistic materialism will cause the religions to band together for mutual protection, allowing the powers that be to point that movement in a syncretistic, "interfaith" direction, further compromising the orthodox faiths. And those faiths, no matter how bad a state they may be in, were sent by God himself, not invented by human cleverness (if not infernal inspiration) like the Theosophical Society and modern Wicca, which are vectors of the Counter-Initiation in themselves. The question is, *is a united front among the orthodox religions against their common enemies a real possibility today?* I understand your desire to support even heterodox believers against atheism and scientism, out of simple compassion, but the fact remains that heterodox ways do not lead the soul to God, unless God wills to save a particular soul not because of them but in spite of them. And the heterodox religions will have at least one foot in the materialist camp whether they know it or not, whether or like it or not; only the orthodox traditions, the ones that fully understand the transcendence and immanence of God, provide real ways OUT of our self-created, collective hell.

In times like these, the one way remaining may be to follow your own Path as deeply—as mystically, as esoterically, call it what you will—as is humanly (or rather Divinely) possible. Whatever we may be able to do in terms of the world, or to help our fellow human beings, will grow out of that.

Sincerely,
Charles

Dear Charles,

I am less convinced than you that the spiritual cannot be removed from the human domain. Overlapping with the environmental/Physicalists is "transhumanism". It is true that "human beings" as we have known them throughout history are inherently spiritual beings, but a whole range of factors are now conspiring to effectively replace "human beings" with a new type of creature/machine, and the spiritual dimension is not part of the plan. I am finding that even among so-called "spiritual" people in the Eco/Physicalist world, the "spirituality" they have in mind is simulated and machine-generated, e.g. "Persinger's God Helmet". Or the "enlightenment pill". And so on. It has a long history, of course, going back to "biofeedback" machines, Hubbard's "dianetics" and Leary's LSD spirituality. This type of stuff now seems increasingly mainstream. The technology/spirituality interface, as they like to call it.

But this amounts to a radical denaturing of man, and I am not confident that the supposedly innate need for "spirituality" will survive this denaturing. It may be irrepressible in human beings as we have known them, but the very category "human being" is now under unprecedented attack. Most of the Green types around here are also "transhumanists" —nothing "back-to-nature" about them. When I was young and owned an organic farm the Green movement was full of back-to-nature types. Not any more. Now it is full of ultra-science types. I am seeing this contrast as Vitalist vs. Physicalists now, and I'd say the Physicalists have won, comprehensively. And part of the grand plan is to re-engineer human beings from the gene up. So, while I do take some comfort in your analogy to the Russian Church under the Soviets, finally I fear that the analogy is inaccurate because "transhumanism" goes much, much further than Sovietism even dreamed. Make no mistake—the push is on to eliminate the entire spiritual dimension of human beings. Not just by social enforcement. As you say, that won't work because the spirit is irrepressible. But, beyond social engineering, we are facing biological eradication—reconstructing the very definition of the human creature.

I see these forces as the face of contemporary evil. In fact, I think the threat of one world government and one world religion as dated now. I don't think either is likely. I think one world religion has as little chance as all the world speaking Esperanto. But a world of soulless man/machines. That is a real prospect, I think. And the God-haters in the contemporary Green Left are all for it. They don't want one world religion. They want to reconstruct human beings inside and out to eradicate the religious urge altogether. That, at least, is what I am running into. I used to hear people talking about one world religion, a meta-religion, but it now seems like empty talk like the pipe dreams of Esperantists wanting one world language. Their rhetoric was much the same. Esperantists [saw] language is a barrier to peace, therefore we need one universal language. Similarly, religion is a barrier to peace and therefore we need one universal religion. I don't think either idea has much chance or is part of the new design. I think we are moving on from that universalist utopianism. The new utopianism is all about "transhumans"—and "transhumans" have no need for any religion, universal or otherwise.

Cheers,
RB

Dear Rodney,

I fully agree with you that the goal is to deconstruct the human form, and the transition from "back to nature" environmentalism to techno-environmentalism appears quite clearly in the movie

Avatar, for example. And once we (or rather *they*) are no longer human, religion—orthodox or otherwise—will no longer apply. But as long as human beings exist religion will continue, because the human form is the bearer of the Trust, and whatever subhuman robots may or may not be able to do or think or feel can have no effect upon this simple truth. If the human form is indeed the supporting pillar of the earth, which Muslims and Christians both assert in their differing ways, then the earth will not survive man. The prospect of a "transhuman" earth is horrible, but once we have destroyed our humanity, even if we do so in the name of physical immortality, we will no longer *want* to survive—and in view of the fact that we continue to multiply the means of total destruction so that we are now capable of terminating all life on earth, or at least all human life, in an increasing number of unique and innovative ways, once we are no longer human one or more of these ways will supervene; it will simply be drawn into the spiritual vacuum left by our abdication of the Trust, and that will be the end of us—human, trans(sub)human, the whole works.

Guénon clearly predicted the advent of "transhumanist" man in *The Reign of Quantity and the Signs of the Times*:

> The reign of the "counter-tradition" is in fact precisely what is known as the "reign of Antichrist".... This being, even if he appears in the form of a particular single human being, will really be less an individual than a symbol, and he will be as it were the synthesis of all the symbolism that has been inverted for the purpose of the "counter-initiation".... In order to express the false carried to its extreme he will have to be so to speak "falsified" from every point of view, and to be like an incarnation of falsity itself... the Antichrist is represented as deformed in all the more or less symbolical descriptions that have been given of him.... These descriptions indeed particularly emphasize the bodily asymmetries, and this implies precisely that they are the visible signs of the actual nature of the being to whom they are attributed....The Antichrist must evidently be as near as it is possible to be to "disintegration", so that one could say that his individuality, while it is developed

> in a monstrous fashion, is nevertheless at the same time almost annihilated, thus realizing the inverse of the effacement of the "ego" before the "Self", or in other words, realizing confusion in "chaos" as against fusion in principial Unity....
>
> Besides this, the false is necessarily also the "artificial", and in this respect the "counter-tradition" cannot fail, despite its other characteristics, to retain the "mechanical" character appertaining to all the productions of the modern world, of which it will itself will be the last; still more exactly, there will be something in it comparable to the automatism of the "psychic corpses" spoken of earlier, and like them it will be constituted of "residues" animated artificially and momentarily, and this again explains why it can contain nothing durable; a heap of "residues", galvanized, so to speak, by an "infernal" will: surely nothing could give a clearer idea of what it is to have reached the very edge of dissolution.

The physical "asymmetry" of *al-Dajjal* will undoubtedly only be "visible" through the use of a microscope, on the molecular level: a distortion of the genes. The transhumanists also believe that human consciousness can be uploaded into sophisticated computers; they are capable of this absurdity because they define consciousness as *memory*, plus whatever algorithms may be necessary to manipulate it—and as Blake succinctly put it, "Memory is Eternal Death". These computerized "memories", galvanized by an infernal will, ("galvanized" means "animated by electricity") are precisely the "psychic residues" Guénon speaks of.

Transhumanism, and whatever other developments may rival it in evil and absurdity, is not simply the negation of religion; it is precisely the final expression of that *Luciferian religion of the elites* I mentioned earlier. It will not replace the push for One-World Government and One-World Religion, but will be the ultimate expression of these trends. Do you think transhuman man will live in small, autonomous, anarchistic communities? Of course not; he, or it, will be globally interlinked. And transhumanism will be much easier to develop once the human population is radically reduced. Furthermore, it will only be possible to temporarily allay the anxiety and horror of living as a human robot by some system for pharmacologically or electronically stimulating what the transhumanists consider to be the "God-circuits" of the human brain, or whatever replaces the human brain, a remedy that will have to be universally applied; they are already claiming that machines could be capable of "spiritual" experiences. And something doesn't have to be *thought* of as a religion by its devotees to be one, if we define "religion" as a view of reality to which a person gives all his allegiance and in which he places all his hopes, including the hope for immortal life. Luciferianism doesn't require hooded robes or spooky organ music or flickering candles or crumbling gothic arches; what it does require is a total capitulation to chaos in the name of order and to absurdity in the name of truth, a profound longing for unreality masquerading *as* reality, the erection of lifelessness incarnate as a merciless idol in the place of Life, one that demands for its worship precisely *human sacrifice*: the genetic and cybernetic deconstruction of the human form. Scientistic Luciferianism, no matter how much it may hate such mythopoetic terminology, is nonetheless a sort of religion—or the shadow of it or the corpse of it—because its obvious if not openly stated aim is to destroy religion, and replace it with itself. It is based on the deification of matter, which represents the final phase in the worship of those "idols of wood and stone made by human hands." And the thing we often don't realize about this development, the thing it most wants to hide from both us and itself, is that the total technologization of man and nature is the most unstable condition imaginable. It presents itself as the ultimate, unassailable and merciless ordering of earthly existence, but all it really is the absolutization of chaos. It is a kingdom divided against itself. It will not stand. Look at what's already happening to our technological society; it's falling apart. And the more ruthlessly we apply the disease as if it were actually the remedy, the faster it will crumble. Fr. Malachi Martin said something like, "Yes, global evil will triumph. The Antichrist will have his day—and that's how long his kingdom will last: one day." We can't exist in any stable form as computer programs or human robots because we are not strictly material beings; we are earthly incarnations or projections of a celestial archetype—and whatever form departs from its archetype will inevitably perish. This fact must be denied and suppressed at all costs, however, since the main vector for the development of transhumanism is the fear of death. The denial of God and the celestial order inevitably exacerbates this fear, since it presents the loss of earthly existence as the destruction of all there is, and the transhumanist temptation of virtual immortality in cybernetic or genetically-engineered form is there to profit from that fear, which it itself has partly created. The transhumanists must do all they can to blot out the truth that they are asking us to worship, in the name of the triumph over death, what is actually killing us.

So "destruction is naked before us, and hell hath no covering". Good. I've seen the Devil face to face and I'm still alive, because my life rests in God. Rodney, I'm so glad that you named the evil beyond which there can be no more evil; I couldn't quite get it said, but you came right out and said it. Thank you.

So what now? Now things are simple: only God remains to us. HE is the Guarantor of our eternal humanity, in this life and the next. If the world is headed in the direction of the ultimate darkness, then we can let it go, let it slip from our grasp, with no regrets. Do you think I am saying that there will be no trials and sufferings? If so, let me disabuse you: what else can we logically expect? But all our trials and sufferings, in these days of the Tribulation, the *fitan*, are drowned in Mercy, if we simply turn to God. *Simply*, not easily—but, nonetheless, simply. The naked evil of the world has made it simple, as simple as opening a door. And once that difficult yet simple act is complete, then it *is* easy to let go of the world, as easy as not believing in something that has definitively exposed itself as a lie. *Truth has come and falsehood has vanished away; certainly falsehood is ever bound to vanish.*

Excuse for me for preaching and waxing poetic; it's one of the few things I really know how to do. Words are weak—but, *insha'allah*, the meaning and the power that stands behind them is not weak, if the words are true. As I see it, the only thing you and I can do in the face of this horror, this heart of darkness, is to stand in the presence of God. If we take one step toward Him He takes ten toward us; if we go to Him walking he comes to us running. If we can do that, then those desperate people who are now turning to you for help will receive a Mercy beyond conception. Because what can *we* do? Less than nothing—less, I say, because if we believe that we can accomplish something against this atrocity on our own slim strength and authority, we will only muddy the waters, tangle the natural lines of things, do further damage. The only thing is to really KNOW that the Good is Real, and that evil, though it truly does exist, is unreality incarnate. So let the transhumanists go screw themselves, which they seem hell bent on doing in any case; that's something they can certainly take care of with no help from us. "Resist not evil".

The last *surah* of the Holy Qur'an—*an-Naas*, or "Mankind" was given by Allah to the Prophet Muhammad, peace and blessings be upon him, precisely for these times, the times of the End of the Book:

In the name of Allah, the Beneficent, the Merciful,
Say: I seek refuge in the Lord of Mankind,
The King of Mankind,
The God of Mankind,
From the evil of the sneaking whisperer,
Who whispereth in the hearts of mankind,
Of the jinn, and of Mankind.

The Lord, the King, the God of Mankind is the human archetype *in divinis*, al-Insan al-Kamil. He is the face that Allah turns to humanity alone, not to the angels, not to the animals, not to the jinn. He is the Guarantor of our integral humanity, in this world and the next. And the "sneaking whisperer" is the temptation to betray the Trust, to jettison the human form. I seek refuge in the God of Mankind from that temptation, which is simply the temptation to believe, and thereby grant my allegiance to, what unreality calls real and what evil calls good—or if not good, then at least inevitable, a pre-ordained choice that has swallowed up all the alternatives. Beware of worshipping the "inevitable"!

Marty Glass wrote, in *Yuga: An Anatomy of our Fate* [Sophia Perennis, 2005]: "We're still human, but we lead inhuman lives"; he gives as the five hallmarks of the Kali-yuga "The Reign of Quantity, the Fall into Time, the Mutation into Machinery, the End of Nature and the Prison of Unreality". The progression is irreversible, but ephemeral. It is the vanishing away of falsehood to reveal the Truth, which is what "apocalypse" means. What, if anything, will be left of life on earth, and human life, after this process completes itself we can't know. It has to be enough for us to know that the Truth will indeed come; the practice of orthodox religion and metaphysical discernment is the one thing capable of ensuring that it *will* be enough.

Sincerely,
Charles

Appendix I

Review of *False Dawn*
Rama P. Coomaraswamy, MD

False Dawn: The United Religious Initiative, Globalism, and the Quest for a One-World Religion by Lee Penn, Sophia Perennis, 2005

FOR MANY YEARS Malachi Martin tried to convince us that the three major forces abroad in the world today were the creation of a global economy (to a great extent achieved), the creation of a One World government (though there seems to be some dispute about who should be at the top of the heap), and the creation of a One World religion (which is behind much of the ideation of Vatican II and its aftermath). If these goals are fully achieved, it is believed by many that we will have a period of peace and prosperity—this despite the obvious fact that such is condemned by all the Scriptures of the world as but a prelude to the reign of Antichrist.

Part of the impetus for creating a One-World religion is that the major religions seem to preach similar truths. It is forgotten that St. Thomas Aquinas, quoting St. Ambrose, taught that all truth, no matter where it is found, has the Holy Ghost for its author. For some reason this leads many people to become indifferent to these truths rather than to accept them as the common inheritance of mankind. There is nothing in such recognition that should induce people to abandon their own religion and their God-given sources of truth. But there is a vast difference between recognizing common truths and creating a new religion, a kind of smorgasbord based on picking and choosing the lowest common denominator of commonality and including in such selections the various false cults of the New Age pseudo-spirituality. Yet such is the goal of the United Religions Initiative. Many will dismiss the efforts of individuals like Bishop William Swing (the former Episcopal Bishop of California, founder of the URI) as of no significance. However, Lee Penn has done a remarkable piece of well-documented research showing how powerful and effective this aspect of the New World Order really is, how closely it is tied to such deviations as Theosophy, Masonry and Spiritism, and how intrinsically it is not only anti-Christian, but also, for lack of a better term, anti-traditional. It is, to use René Guénon's telling phrase, part of the "counter-tradition".

Lee Penn, while writing from a Christian prospective, clearly sees the broader implications of this movement as is demonstrated by his familiarity with the writings of Guénon, and his editorial assistant who is Muslim—Charles Upton, author of a somewhat parallel book entitled *The System of Antichrist* [Sophia Perennis, 2001]. He not only exposes the strong anti-Christian bias of the movement, but also reveals its Satanic connections, and how it aims at creating, not some kind of syncretism, but much more at creating an entirely new religion with a new code of ethics that includes euthanasia, abortion, population control etc. The author provides an excellent section on the role of Mikhail Gorbachev; he also shows the tie-in with ecological movements aimed at fostering "nature worship", the Shamanistic religions and Wicca—an integral part of the overall plan. Now all this is not being fostered by a group of "crazies" but rather is extremely well funded by some of the most powerful economic forces in the world, with inter-governmental ties and deep connections to the United Nations. The list of interlocking organizations is truly extraordinary and the documentary proof of such is clearly provided. It is important that we be aware of these connections insofar as we can be misled into supporting groups which present us with seemingly traditional values.

Such ideas are, of course, not new. One interesting quote which the author provides, which among many other things goes to show the depth of his research, is taken from Stevenson's *The Four Reformers*, published in 1888:

> Four reformers met under a bramble bush. They were all agreed the world must be changed. "We must abolish property," said one. "We must abolish marriage," said the second. "We must abolish God" said the third." "I wish we could abol-

> ish work," said the forth. "Do not let us get beyond practical politics", said the first, "the first thing is reduce men to a common level." "The first thing," said the second, "is to give freedom to the sexes." "The first thing," said the third, "is to find out how to do it." "The first step," said the first, "is to abolish the Bible." "The first thing," said the second, "is to abolish the laws." "The first thing," said the third, "is to abolish mankind."

This book can be easily categorized as but further evidence of the times we live, as part of the literature of indictment. It has, however, two advantages over similar texts: 1) It sees things on a global level and not from a purely Christian point of view, and 2) It provides the reader with an encyclopedic source of information, and as such functions as a protection against this powerful deviation which has succeeded in infiltrating into the core of even traditional religion. It is highly recommended.

Appendix II

The December 21, 2012
"Mayan Apocalypse" as a Social Engineering Event

THE IDEA of a "paradigm shift" based on the end of one version of the Mayan calendar, supposedly to take place on December 21, 2012, was either discovered or originated by visionary artist and author Jose Arguëlles (1939–2011), the man who also brought us the first (and probably last) international "folk" event known as Harmonic Convergence, August 16 & 17, 1987, which he presented as a way for the human race to prepare itself spiritually for the 2012 shift. In his last book, *Manifesto for the Noösphere: The Next Stage in the Evolution of Human Consciousness* (2011), Arguëlles drew upon the theories of one Oliver L. Reiser (1885–1974) as laid out in Reiser's *Cosmic Humanism* (1966). Reiser was a scientist who developed an early version of superstring theory, was praised by Albert Einstein, and proposed the actual creation of Teilhard de Chardin's "noösphere" by technological means, as well as a project for human eugenics through manipulating the radiation of the ionosphere; he apparently believed that mass radiation poisoning, such as was experienced at Hiroshima and Nagasaki, might ultimately have a eugenic effect upon the human race. According to Drew Hemple [*http://www.nonduality.com*],

> Reiser's book *Cosmic Humanism* was held in the highest esteem by a think tank called the Institute for Integrative Education. This think tank was set up by Forest Products magnate Julius Stulman and its office was then located at the UN Plaza. Its board of directors included the family that directed the non-dualist Theosophist [Theosophical?] Society [which branch we are not told] and it also included scientists from Harvard and Yale. The goal of this Institute, as spelled out in

> their flagship academic journal *Main Currents in Modern Thought* (1940–1975) was to review all prominent academic journals and integrate all knowledge to the goals of nondualist theosophy. With this in mind the journal had a very advanced interest in eastern philosophy, paranormal research, eugenics, higher dimensional physics and social engineering.

It would appear that "non-dualist theosophy" has little or nothing to do with the true Advaita Vedanta, but is rather a kind of code-phrase for an attempt to force global unification by means of arcane technology, where "unity" is not the Absolute Unity of God but merely the quasi-unity of higher-dimensional spaces and energetic fields. Hemple also alleges, without supporting documentation, that Jose Arguëlles had links to the CIA.

Be that as it may, in *Cosmic Humanism and World Unity* (1975), Reiser names as among his main collaborators Dr. Andrija Puharich, who as we have already seen was involved in the channeling of a consortium of entities known as "The Nine", and whose connections with the military and the intelligence communities are much better documented than those of Arguëlles. These tenuous though suggestive affinities appear a bit more significant in light of the fact that in the 2009 TV documentary *2012: The Mayan Prophesy and the Shift of the Ages*, Geoff Stray identifies the Nine Underworld Gods or *Bolontiku* of the Mayans, who are predicted to return on December 21, 2012, with "The Nine" channeled by Puharich and his friends, and also claims that CIA-trained "remote viewers", while peering ahead through the mists of time, ran up against an almost impenetrable barrier when they reached the date in question, and also saw that the human population had been radically reduced.

Whether or not a major "paradigm shift", or the end of the world, takes place in December of 2012, that date certainly provides an ideal opportunity for various social engineers or *agents provocateurs* to launch this or that mass deception or "self-fulfilling prophesy"; we've certainly been well primed for any such occurrences. And if the reader is starting to wonder why I have decided to address the Mayan Apocalypse theme in this book, the answer is that I myself happened to have been the leader of a ceremonial circle on Mt.

Tamalpais, in Marin County, California, on Harmonic Convergence. It was my first and last appearance as a "New Age teacher", and I now feel called to redress any wrongs I may have been guilty of on that occasion. A little before the Convergence I had met and talked with Jose Arguëlles, and the event itself seemed to go off well, without any obvious catastrophes, either physical or psychic. Within a year of the Convergence, however, I realized that I had gone too far in too many unknown directions, into a world without guides or signposts, but not without powerful psychic influences pushing their own agendas. At that point I turned 180 degrees, and made for the world of traditional esoteric spirituality with all deliberate speed—specifically, the province of Islamic Sufism. And now, a quarter of a century later, I wonder if I had actually been an unwitting participant in a mass social engineering experiment of global proportions; imagine directing the worldly and spiritual aspirations of millions of people toward a pre-determined goal over a period of 25 years! In any case, spiritual disasters (as is well-known) can often produce half-way decent poetry; the following verses, written in the late 80's or early 90's, are dedicated to Jose Arguëlles:

After the Convergence

Granted, we all have to pass again
Through whatever it was that killed us,
Transposed through the looking glass right to left,
Enfolded in a wall of shimmering quicksilver,
To emerge where the Anti-Self lies in wait for us,
Extending a sly, left-handed handshake on the
Opposite shore of Death—

But, remember, Jose Arguëlles,
There are two kinds of mirrors:
The dark smoking mirror of Tezcatlipoca
Where the soul is twisted till it becomes the mask,
And the crystal mask of Quetzalcoatl,
Holding not the face who is seen
But that other face—the one who watches.

The mirror masks and it unmasks,
It unveils and it disguises.
Wishing to hold himself something other
Than the face in the volcanic glass,
Quetzalcoatl on his raft of serpents was exiled
To the Western Paradise—

While the fool who thought he *was* the mask
Curled up like a snail shell
Fossilized in limestone
To become the hell inside the mirror.

There are also indications that the social engineers are now associating the Mayan Apocalypse belief-system with the UFO/exopolitics/disclosure mythology (see Chapter Six) in order to produce a "synergistic" effect. (Google "Mayan Apocalypse/UFO" for evidence supporting this contention.) And if anyone happens be reading this section *after* Dec. 21, 2012, I would suggest that he or she look back on that date and try to remember any happenings that seemed particularly odd to them, odder than could be explained simply by the festivals and initiatives of the Mayan Apocalypse believers themselves, as well as any elements of these events and activities, or the media productions surrounding them, that seemed designed to influence mass belief in an oblique or semi-covert manner. A thorough study of that day and the days leading up to it might provide us with greater insight into the social engineering forces we are all subject to in these times.

It only remains to be pointed out that Harmonic Convergence and the Mayan Apocalypse represent one more case of the theft and bastardization of Native American religion by white people—not in naïve and misinformed appreciation like the hippies did it, but apparently for much more cynical purposes. The *real* Mayan Apocalypse took place in Guatemala in 1981–1983 when the Guatemalan army massacred the Quiché Maya. They destroyed 626 villages. Over 200,000 people were killed or disappeared, 1.5 million were displaced by the violence, and more than 150,000 were driven to seek refuge in Mexico. Will these tragedies be remembered and mourned on December 21, 2012? It is not likely, since they do not fit into the concocted mythology that Jose Arguëlles, "ethnobotanist" Terrence McKenna, Geoff Stray and others have presented us with (McKenna, like Timothy Leary, apparently having been first given LSD and DMT by the CIA), and to which many of us are increasingly vulnerable now that we have been robbed of our own spiritual traditions, largely traditional Christianity, and so must raid the traditions of others to fill the gap. The poet T.S. Eliot said, "The tribe without a history is not redeemed from time", and it could be said with equal accuracy that "the tribe without traditions is vulnerable to total control". Mass social engineering requires that the traditional worldview, particularly the religious worldview, of the target population be deconstructed; this is the function of "postmodernism", the assignment that the academic institutions who purvey this deadly, nihilistic dogma have been carrying out. And once the cultural slate is wiped clean of religious doctrine, historical memory and even literary and artistic culture, replacing these with mere technical expertise totally devoid of any informing context, the indoctrination of the victims with spurious mythologies designed solely for purposes of social control becomes relatively easy. We may not be able to prevent or reverse this agenda, but it is our duty, before the tribunal of our own humanity, not to do anything to further it.

Appendix III

"Revelation of the Method",
A Letter to Henry Makow in Response to
"Why the Illuminati Expose the Conspiracy"

Dear Henry,

One danger of your line of work (and mine) is the development of "infinite paranoia". If we don't have a firm belief in God or some form of Absolute Reality, in a solid criterion against which illusion and deception can be measured and judged, then our intent to gaze into the darkness of the mind-controllers and the Illuminati will finally make us believe more in darkness than in Light. We may hate and fear that darkness, but if we start to think it's the only game in town, then we will end up worshipping it in spite of ourselves; like Nietzsche said, "while you are gazing into the Abyss, the Abyss is also gazing into you."

Michael Hoffman identifies a mind-control technique he calls "revelation of the method". In the midst of a mass of deceptions, the mind-controllers will sometimes come right out and tell us what they've been up to. I believe they do this (1) to overawe us, to imply that "if we don't even have to hide our actions any more it's too late for you to do anything", and (2) to weaken our sense of reality by making the truth seem like just one more shapeless blob in an endless series of deceptions, thereby making us vulnerable to domination by unreality. And of course if "revelation of the method" is a ploy of the Illuminati, then anyone who tries to expose the Illuminati is by definition working for them—and so, (3) the very revelation that there is such a thing as "revelation of the method" becomes a part of that method.

Robert C. Tucker, who wrote *An Age for Lucifer*, started out as a cult investigator operating from a more-or-less secular humanist position, but by the time he'd finished his investigation of the

Luciferians, who were a lot more horrendous and *convincing* than he'd expected, he ended up saying, "maybe the Luciferians are right after all; maybe the universe IS a predatory system ruled by the Devil." If you're going to investigate darkness you need a strong enough sense of Light and Truth to avoid that fate. Evil is certainly not non-existent, but it IS unreal; it's "unreality incarnate". The Intellectual/Spiritual Light that makes it possible for us to expose darkness finally dispels that darkness entirely, leaving nothing to expose; Good only finally triumphs over evil when Truth triumphs over illusion. That's why I've tried to expose the "Rulers of the Darkness of This World" from the standpoint of that greater Light. Unless you have a solid faith in an Absolute Reality that is always there, always available and always ready to help, you will probably not be able to withstand the vision of the tremendous evil of our times without finally caving in to it. Maybe we should start sharing the ways in which we personally have learned how to protect ourselves from getting eaten up by the darkness we're trying to expose.

And of course you're right that the ultimate reason for "revelation of the method" is to produce *complicity*: the Devil wants *souls*, and the juiciest souls of all are those who worship him knowingly, even after they've seen what he's up to. The Devil's finest creation (he tells himself) is the kind of *willing despair* that leads his servants to consciously worship the thing that's destroying them. God, on the other hand, asks to be worshipped "in Spirit and in Truth"; He offers his servants not blind compulsive belief, but willing *faith*: "the presence of things hoped for, the evidence of things not seen". Faith is virtual intellection; when its light is perfected in us, darkness is denied its final foothold.

Sincerely,
Charles Upton

Appendix IV

Renouncing the World

THIS WORLD is not simply to be dismissed, it is to be renounced—and you can't renounce something unless you know what it is and what it's up to. This World, *al-Dunya*, is not the earth or the material universe or other people. This World is the collective ego. My ego, when projected, becomes the Darkness of This World; This World, now introjected, possessing my soul, becomes my ego. This World is all that my ego can see of the Real World beyond me; consequently the only way to renounce This World is to renounce my ego. But since This World is the *content* of my ego, there is no way to renounce my ego without renouncing This World.

The idea of renouncing the world is, however, subject to degeneration. "Renounce the world" becomes "rise above the world, look down upon it, assert your superiority to it", which in turn becomes "studiously ignore this world as beneath your contempt; make sure you are ignorant of its methods, motives and agendas; identify with the Spirit alone". This egotistical attempt at renunciation can produce complacency, the sort of complacency that transforms true Spiritual knowledge into a dream, a fantasy—and this dreamy lack of vigilance is precisely what opens the false renunciate to co-optation by the very world he claims to have courageously renounced, but has in fact only arrogantly dismissed.

John Coleman, in *The Conspirators' Hierarchy: The Committee of 300*, his analysis of the global "shadow-government", speaks of the technique pioneered by the Tavistock Institute of Human Relations of deconstructing societies by subjecting their populations to repeated shocks—the Jonestown Massacre perhaps being one example—thus inducing them to despair of any collective solutions to their problems, after which the idea of "self-actualization" is progressively introduced as the major goal of human life, which gradually replaces all communal goals and values. Thus a "culture of narcissism" is created (Christopher Lasch's term), amenable to social engineering and covert control; this is precisely the ego's idea of detachment, the Satanic inversion and counterfeit of the contemplative renunciation of the world. Coleman's specific assertion may not be provable, but there is no question that similar methods of social control have been utilized in many nations and historical periods, including the Roman use of "bread and circuses" to appease and distract the masses, the conversion of conquered provinces to matriarchies by both the Romans and the Han Chinese, the methods of governance recommended in the *Arthashastra* of Chanakya and *The Prince* by Nicolo Machiavelli, Lenin's practice of creating a "controlled opposition", the Nazis' burning of the Reichstag and then blaming it on the Jews, and Hitler's restructuring of all aspects of German society, including its "spiritual' life.

To pre-civilized humanity, "This World" was little more than the *maya*-power inherent in sense experience, its tendency to present itself as the whole of reality, plus the rather rudimentary human attachments to security, pleasure and power. All this changed when the archaic hieratic civilizations developed, universal symbol-systems by which metaphysical and cosmological principles were mediated by an environment of words and images, liturgies, rituals and sacred architecture conceived and managed by a caste of priests. When such civilizations enjoyed God's favor, they were sacred in the true sense of that word. But as the Spirit of God slowly withdrew from these civilizations due to the degeneration of the collectives who maintained them and for whose benefit they were established, these sacred symbol-systems—systems that once mediated between the metaphysical, natural and social orders, between Heaven, Earth, and Man—progressively degenerated into mere social control systems, still managed by ancient priesthoods who, like the collectives they represented, had degenerated over time. (The brief "Gnostic" masterpiece that most completely expresses this state of affairs is the story "The Lottery in Babylon" by Jorge Luis Borges.) "New World Order" researchers such as Henry Makow and Alan Watt have a fairly accurate understanding of these control-systems in their degeneracy, but little grasp of the sacred symbol-systems of which they were the degenerate expressions.

These archaic and corrupt hieratic civilizations, appearing in the Bible and the Qur'an as "Egypt" and "Babylon", are the ancestors of the socially-engineered control-societies of today. Our own control-societies, however, differ in that the control they exercise is sometimes hidden under the illusion of "freedom"; in that their control is applied through various technological methods unavailable to the ancients as well as through the traditional psycho-social methods; and in that they have nearly destroyed humanity's primordial experience of the natural world: before even beginning to confront and see through the *maya* of sense experience, post-modern humanity must break out of the secondary, superimposed *maya* of technological society.

So This World, *al-Dunya*, is now something different—except in its deepest essence—than the World renounced by the Christian Desert Fathers or the early Muslim Sufis or the Hindu Sannyasins or the Taoist Sages. The Desert Fathers and the Taoist Sages and the Sannyasins—and the early Sufis as well in some cases—were able to renounce the *maya* of society by physically leaving it, which made the task of seeing through the *maya* of sense experience immeasurably easier. (In Islam however, which is the last revelation, the spiritual norm is to be "in the world but not of it", monasticism being disallowed; physical removal from society for spiritual purposes is the exception, even among Sufis.) But in our own time, this option is closed to almost everyone. Whether we like it or not, our place—except for a tiny, scattered minority—is within the context of society. Consequently a necessary step for most of us in the work of renouncing This World is *to become aware of it as an engineered control system.* Thus the act of investigating the structure and exposing the agendas of the New World Order, for those dedicated to the spiritual path and also called to this work, can be of direct service to the contemplative life.

Some in our time have hoped to be able to renounce This World, or at least protect themselves from its attacks, by taking up residence in the inner world of the psyche, as if the "collective unconscious" were a spiritual universe into which worldliness could never come, whereas a great part of it is simply made up of everything we collectively don't want to be conscious of, of what Carl Jung called (speaking in individual terms) the Shadow. This Shadow is not only that part of the psyche we haven't gotten around to yet; it also harbors all those things that we refuse to face, that we *can't* face.

This World is now in a state of terror—politically, financially, culturally, technologically, and ecologically. If we don't face this fact, not just in general but in as much detail as is called for by the duties of our station in life, then it all falls into the Shadow, where it operates unconsciously according to the precise parameters of that archetype. Our refuge from the rigor of events is not the psyche, the inner subjectivity, individual or collective; our only refuge is the objectivity of the Spirit. That alone is a "Kingdom Not of This World." And one necessary step toward this Spirit is the difficult but crucial task of facing the shadow that This World has cast upon our souls. If we can witness the darkness of This World with *apatheia*, with detachment and equanimity, then we will have accomplished the greater part of the work of "shadow-integration"; we will be led, God willing, to the point of supreme nausea where we can vomit the World, along with the Ego, its master and slave, out of our souls forever.

Often a person of "tender-minded" character, interested in art or metaphysics, will believe that anyone who wants to know what This World is up to, who investigates the plans and agendas of the New World Order, is probably some sort of political fanatic, or at the very least a worldly person closed to the spiritual life. To believe this, however, is to be neutralized, blinded by fear. And This World has no greater weapon in its arsenal, to control us and violate our humanity, than fear—especially *unconscious* fear. The work, then, is to see precisely how we have allowed ourselves to be terrorized, to become conscious of our fear, and thereby break its power.

To simply know what is going on in the world of politics and society and technology in no way implies that the one knowing this has any sort of political agenda. The Desert Fathers and the Taoist Sages and the Sannyasins and the early Sufis knew quite well what was going on in the respective societies of their times; that's why they elected to leave those societies behind, either internally, through detachment and *apatheia*, or externally as well, by heading for the hills. Their *raison d'être*, like that of every true renunciate, is succinctly expressed in the following lines from the *Ramayana*:

In the first age of the world
men crossed the ocean of existence
by their spirit alone.
In the second age sacrifice and ritual began,
and then Rama lived,
and by giving their every act to him
men lived well their ways.
Now in our age what is there to do
but worship Rama's feet?
But, my friend, the last age
of this world shall be best,
for then no act has any worth, all is useless. . . .
except only to say *Rama*.
The future will read this. Therefore I tell them:
When all is in ruin around you, just say *Rama*.
We have gone from the spiritual to the passionate.
Next will come Ignorance. Universal war.
Say *Rama* and win! Your time cannot touch you.

The "first age" in the Hindu conception is the age of *sattwa*, of Knowledge; its appropriate spiritual Way is *jñana-yoga*. The "second age" is the age of *rajas*, of Passion; its appropriate spiritual Way is *karma-yoga*. The last age is the age of *tamas*, of Ignorance; its appropriate spiritual Way is *bhakti-yoga*. All three of these *margas* or sacred paths are possible in every age, as Ramana Maharshi, the great modern *jñani*, demonstrated. But our times are darker than his were. The one called to walk the path of *jñana* in these final days of the Kali-yuga may also be called, as we have said above, to understand This World, *al-Dunya*, as an engineered control system, especially if he or she—like almost everyone—has become involved with it; the ones who are born and remain innocent of worldliness are few and far between. In these times, to become conscious of how we are being controlled and terrorized is, precisely, to deconstruct the ego, or the greater part of it. It is to vomit out the World, to undergo the *catharsis* posited by the Greek tragedians, to "die before you die". As in the highest metaphysics, so in our investigations of the most abysmal human evil, "the Truth shall make you free". Seeing through the darkness of This World is certainly not sufficient for the realization of God, but it is becoming increasingly necessary, day by day. And it serves this realization in two ways: first, because the Light by which we see through the darkness is invoked by that very effort of seeing; secondly, because only facing that darkness can prevent us—or some of us—from turning God into a self-serving fantasy. And the power to see through the world-illusion is God's doing, not ours; only He has the power to drive the *Dunya* from our souls. To become obsessed with darkness is to turn away from Him, but to fear to look at it indicates a lack of faith in Him. And the ultimate goal of seeing God everywhere cannot be attained if we are willing to see Him in His beauty and mercy but not in His majesty and justice, which is precisely what the Darkness of This World is to the eye of spiritual vision; to unconsciously harbor the notion of a place where God "is not" is to grant that shadow more power than it deserves, turning it into a second God, a dark rival to the Light. But God's majesty and justice are also beautiful; they are beautiful because they are necessary. This is why This World must end, and is always ending, and (in one sense) has already ended. To renounce an object we unconsciously take to be a solid reality is next to impossible, but to renounce something we consciously understand as empty and ephemeral is easy. In the words of the Noble Qur'an, *Truth has come and falsehood vanished away; surely falsehood is always bound to vanish.*

And, sometimes, the world just leaves you; this indicates that God, who is a jealous God, wants you for Himself.

Appendix V

Two Poems, and an Afterword

Voice of the Antichrist

Inside my own body, my will is law: I leave nothing to
  chance.
Neither priest's black book nor pale human morality
  hold the power
To bend the fixed rod of my course.
I purchase and put on the fiery image that gives me
  power over the stars;
I admire myself, when day is done, in the frozen mirror of
  cocaine.
Circumstances fall to me, and jobs, and sales, and deals;
I reap my profits, invest them in global empire,
Because man is made to conquer the future, to cut his
  way, by pure self-will
To the galaxies of his ultimate form.
The findings of impartial research reveal my word to
  have been inevitable from the beginning;
The future is assured to my flesh;
No other lives in my image. I cut out the impostors
With knives, with military interventions,
With judiciously placed rumors, with massive transfers of
  capital;
I grip the wheel of the stock exchange, aiming for target
  center with the
Weapon of mobile assets; the pirates of my right and
  my left hands
Come from all the finest mafias and universities. . . .
I am without rival. The sentimentalized face of God the
  Father

I have limited to residual pockets of sub-colonial
  darkness in rural backwaters;
The Virgin, too, is abducted by my warriors and bound to
  my desire;
Night and Silence have no power over my
Hard, undying light.

The Teacher

He reached down, picked up a handful of sand, and said:

"In each one of these grains of sand is all the pain of all the worlds.

In this one grain is Famine, War, Pestilence and the Fear of Death.

and this"—

he poured out his handful of sand against the Wind—

"is Joy."

The Wind is the *nafas al-Rahman*, the Breath of the Merciful. When the Counter-Initiation is near, it is a sign that God is also near. In His Presence, the darkness of the deepest Pit surges up and spreads across the whole earth—and then the Wind carries it away.

We name evil, which is relative non-existence, so that it will not tempt us through deception. We name it so that, if we have already swallowed it, it will not be falsely sweet on the stomach, but will show its true nature by turning bitter, making it easier for us to spew it out.

And we name God so that evil and illusion will have no place to hide or exist in the face of the One Truth, the Sovereign Good, the Absolute Reality.

The Counter-Initiation is herald of the Remnant, architect of the catacombs of the final days. If they want evil, then let them have it. Let them scrape my soul clean of it. Let darkness return to darkness and light to light, before light fills the entire gulf where darkness had been, and shows it never to have been at all. As the Qur'an says,

Truth has come and falsehood has vanished away; certainly falsehood is ever bound to vanish.

So what, precisely, is the use of investigating the strategies and agendas of the Darkness of This World? The activist will answer, "so we can counter the actions of evil men." The man interested in shielding himself and his family will answer, "so I can foresee dangers and protect myself and my loved ones against them." I myself have already answered, "so false spiritualities won't tempt us and lead us astray." I now add, "so we can finally give up on This World, leave it to its darkness, and fix our hearts on God." There is always more to discover about the evils of the End Times, which are really nothing other than the passion and ignorance of *all* places and times brought together into a single mass; and because there is always more, the war against these adversaries is endless—unless we have succeeded in finding the ultimate source of their power, so that—in the words of John the Baptist—we can "lay the axe to the root."

And the root of that whole mass of passion and ignorance and evil and suffering is nothing other than the ego. *My* ego. Not somebody else's, not *everyone's* ego—just mine. The World, in the last analysis, is nothing but the projection of that ego—and involvement with the World, either as a naïve believer in it or as an angry rebel against it, is the only thing that prevents us from seeing this. Certainly there are evil men, destructive forces, demonic entities; but as soon as the ego is done with, these adversaries find no point of attack, and rapidly exhaust their powers. When Siddhartha Gautama was meditating under the Bodhi Tree in his quest for Enlightenment, he was attacked by Mara the Tempter, who is the entire store of passion and ignorance that constitutes the *samsara*, the illusory world. Mara marshaled demonic warriors, brought out seductive maidens, hurled fiery mountains; then he prepared to attack the Buddha-to-be person-to-person and face-to-face. But Gautama, instead of summoning the mountain of merit he had collected (so to speak) through his great austerities and years of spiritual practice so as to battle the fiend, simply disappeared. There was the lotus seat, but there was no Buddha sitting on it. Here we can understand the Zen directive "if you see the Buddha, kill him!" as another way of saying that passion and ignorance, though they strive to kill Enlightenment, cannot see it, and consequently that whatever passion and ignorance mistake for Enlightenment must be something else entirely, something to be ruthlessly swept aside. So in that moment, Mara became the Buddha's ally whether he liked it or not. When the Tempter himself enters the battle, when the whole ego finally appears *as* ego, then Liberation, Enlightenment, Union with the Absolute, is no longer identified with form—and with no form to attack and oppose, the whole mass of evil and passion and ignorance, the mass of karma, simply burns itself away in the Void, as if it had never been. If there were endless youth . . . if there were endless time . . . but there is NO time. There never was. As Romans 8:22 informs us: "The whole creation groaneth and travaileth in pain together—until *now*."

When the character of Dante, in Dante's *Divine Comedy*, emerges from Hell and reaches the summit of the Mountain of Purgatory where the Terrestrial Paradise blooms, he must first drink the water of the River Lethe, which brings forgetfulness of sin and evil and suffering; only then can he drink of the River Eunoë, which means "good mind"—the River of Divine Knowledge. May the taste of this book make This World hateful to all who read it; and by the power of that intelligent hate—which is hatred of no living thing, only of dead things pretending to be alive—may it invoke the taste of a Beauty that is totally beyond This World's conception: the taste of the Unknown God.

Bismillah ar-Rahman ar-Rahim,
In the Name of God, the Merciful, the Compassionate

48: question of conscious/uncon agents of Satan

153: possession

168: Mormons mentioned

8/21/12: impressions:

- occult elites members still unnamed - also methods undescribed

CPSIA information can be obtained at www.ICGtesting.com
Printed in the USA
BVOW030403260712

296205BV00001B/155/P